THE AA GUIDE TO
Ireland

About the author

Jane Egginton is a travel writer and author of numerous travel books, including many for the AA. Jane has walked almost every inch of the maze of the medina in Marrakech and has driven off-road to hilltribes around the Golden Triangle in Thailand.

Jane was an in-house researcher and editor for Reader's Digest books department for several years. Now a freelancer, she has fallen in love with Ireland and its people all over again, and says it is one of the most spiritual places she has visited. As an Irish woman said to her on the plane: 'The Irish value other people; family and friends are everything. We make life so complicated, but really it is so simple.'

Jane's beloved grandmother, Ellen, was Irish and she is proud to be a quarter Irish. She has fond memories of trips to Cork, where her family came from, with Ellen. This book is dedicated to Ellen, Ireland and its people.

Published by AA Publishing (a trading name of AA Media Limited, whose registered office is Fanum House, Basing View, Basingstoke, Hampshire RG21 4EA; registered number 06112600)

© AA Media Limited 2016

Maps contain data from openstreetmap.org
© OpenStreetMap contributors
Ordnance Survey data © Crown copyright and database right 2015

A CIP catalogue record for this book is available from the British Library.

ISBN: 978-0-7495-7757-5

Cartography provided by the Mapping Services Department of AA Publishing.

Printed and bound in Italy by Printer Trento Srl.

A05342

Every effort has been made to trace the copyright holders, and we apologise in advance for any accidental errors. We would be happy to apply the corrections in the following edition of this publication.

The contents of this book are believed correct at the time of printing. Nevertheless, the publishers cannot be held responsible for any errors or omissions or for changes in the details given in this book or for the consequences of any reliance on the information it provides. This does not affect your statutory rights. We have tried to ensure accuracy in this book, but things do change and we would be grateful if readers would advise us of any inaccuracies they may encounter by emailing us at travelguides@theaa.com.

Visit AA Publishing at theAA.com/shop

THE AA GUIDE TO

Ireland

YOUR TRUSTED GUIDE

CONTENTS

USING THIS GUIDE

Introduction – has plenty of fascinating background reading, including articles on the landscape and local mythology.

Top attractions – pick out the very best places to visit in the area. You'll spot these later in the A–Z by the flashes of yellow.

Before you go – tells you the things to read, watch, know and pack to get the most from your trip.

Campsites – recommends a number of caravan sites and campsites, which carry the AA's Pennant rating, with the very best receiving the coveted gold Pennant award. Visit theAA. com/self-catering-and-campsites and theAA.com/bed-and-breakfast-and-hotel for more places to stay.

A–Z – lists the best of Ireland, with recommended attractions, activities and places to eat or drink. Places Nearby lists more to see and do.

Eat and drink – contains restaurants that carry an AA Rosette rating, which acknowledges the very best in cooking. Pubs have been selected for their great atmosphere and good food. Visit theAA.com/restaurant-and-pub for more food and drink suggestions.

Index – gives you the option to search by theme, grouping the same type of place together, or alphabetically.

Atlas – will help you find your way around, as every main location has a map reference, as will the town plans throughout the book.

Malin Head

Rathlin
Island

Tory Island
Toraigh

Portrush

Ballycastle

DERRY
LONDONDERRY

Larne

Arranmore
Árainn Mhór

Letterkenny

A6

Ballymena

A36

BANGOR

NORTH
ATLANTIC
OCEAN

Donegal

Omagh

N13

N14

N15

NORTHERN
IRELAND

A5

Lough
Neagh

BELFAST

M1

Downpatrick

Donegal Bay

N15

A46

Enniskillen

A4

N2

Armagh

A7

MTS OF
MOURNE

IRISH
SEA

Ballina

Sligo

N16

Monaghan

Dundalk

N2

OX
MTS

N25

Boyle

N4

Carrick-on-
Shannon

A509

Cavan

N3

Clare Island

Inishturk

Inishbofin

Westport

N5

Castlerea

Navan

Drogheda

M1

REPUBLIC

N2

M2

Clifden

N17

Athlone

OF

Mullingar

N4

M3

M6

M4

DUBLIN

GALWAY

M6

IRELAND

Dún
Laoghaire

M50

Galway Bay

Loughrea

Aran Islands
Oileáin Árann

Roscrea

SLIEVE
BLOOM
MTS

Portlaoise

M11

Wicklow

M18

Ennis

M7

Carlow

M9

WICKLOW
MTS

Tullow

Arklow

LIMERICK

Thurles

M8

Kilkenny

N11

Kilrush

Adare

M20

N24

Wexford

Loop Head

N21

N20

GALTEE MTS

Clonmel

N25

Tralee

Cahir

Dingle
An Daingean

Mallow

KNOCKMEALDOWN
MTS

WATERFORD

N25

Dingle Bay

BOGGERAGH
MTS

Dungarvan

Killarney

N22

N25

Youghal

CORK

Celtic Sea

Bantry

Kinsale

Bantry Bay

Clonakilty

Mizen Head

Cape Clear Island
Oileán Chléire

0	20	40 miles
0	20	40	60 kilometres

INTRODUCTION

There is something magical, even mystical, about Ireland, which in many ways is like one big village. This green island in the Atlantic captures imaginations, and when the sun shines on the many shades of the Emerald Isle it is one of the most beautiful places on earth. Despite Ireland's troubles, which have included famine and ongoing political strife, the craic – the indefinable good spirit of enjoying the company of others – is a thread that is woven into the very fabric of life here. It is particularly at home in the traditional pubs, where music, stories and humour flow as freely as the Guinness.

Four green fields
Ireland's four provinces reflect the island's ancient kingdoms: Leinster in the east, Connacht in the west, Ulster in the north and Munster in the south. They may hold no official significance today but they are still important historically and culturally. The provinces feature strongly in Ireland's rich body of literature and are often referred to longingly in poetry and song as 'the four green fields'.

Divided island

This island has always been more complicated than it might first appear and is still undeniably divided. Ireland measures 32,924 square miles and is part of the British Isles. The independent Republic of Ireland comprises 26 counties. Six northeastern counties make up Northern Ireland and are part of the United Kingdom, but 20th- and 21st-century political divisions cannot erase Ireland's strong ties to its united past.

Celtic heritage

Ireland's rich history stretches back to prehistoric times. Megalithic tombs, cairns, stone circles, ring forts and crannógs (artificial islands built on lakes) throughout the countryside are testimony to an ancient and mysterious race. Early Irish craftsmen were making weapons and exquisite gold jewellery as far back as the Bronze Age. These skills were enhanced by the Celtic people, who came to Ireland from Europe in the sixth century BC. Celtic art featured interlaced geometric patterns, and its motifs are still used in Irish arts and crafts.

Light in the Dark Ages

The early Christian era gave Ireland some of its most striking architecture. The slender round towers, unique to the island, and tall, elaborately carved high crosses are key features of monastic sites around Ireland, such as Glendalough and Clonmacnoise. From the seventh to the ninth centuries, while the rest of Europe was in the Dark Ages, art and learning flourished in Ireland's monasteries. Celtic arts reached their zenith in magnificent illustrated manuscripts such as the *Book of Kells*.

Peace and politics

The violent clashes known as 'the Troubles' came largely to an end with the Good Friday Agreement of 1998, but peace is still a political issue on the island. The problems of Northern Ireland are often simplified as a religious conflict between Catholics and Protestants but the reality involves more complex economic, social and political issues. Both Unionists (who want to remain part of the United Kingdom) and Nationalists (who wish for Irish unity) have long historical ties to their positions. Since 2007, the devolved Assembly (the legislature of Northern Ireland) has operated effectively by balancing the political interests of both communities.

The Irish

Despite the boom of the 'Celtic Tiger' of the 1990s, which transformed the economy of the Republic of Ireland, there is an undeniably slower pace of life here – a conversation with a stranger over a pint of the black stuff (Guinness) can easily last for hours. Yes, there are castles and high crosses, monuments, myths and monasteries, but what lives on in your memory long after you have left Ireland are the Irish themselves.

◄ Previous page: Glenariff
▶ Temple Bar, Dublin

TOP ATTRACTIONS

▲ Giant's Causeway

Follow in the footsteps of Finn McCool (Fionn MacCumhaill) and explore the amazing hexagonal basalt pillars that make up the Giant's Causeway (see page 123). There are around 40,000 of them, caused by cooling lava, 60 million years ago. Alternatively, of course, the Irish giant tore off chunks of coastline to form the causeway while threatening a Scottish rival – Finn Gall.

◀ Trinity College & The Book of Kells

The college is home to one of Europe's most beautiful books and a stunning example of the illuminator's craft. The *Book of Kells* (see page 268) was produced *c* AD 800 but stolen in the 11th century and thrown in a ditch, its precious stone-encrusted cover lost forever. But it's not just about the Book – don't miss the magnificent Long Room in the Library.

◄ The Skelligs
Some eight miles off the Kerry coast lie Little Skellig and its larger sibling, Skellig Michael (see page 342). This tiny, steep and rocky island is a UNESCO World Heritage Site, home to the incredible beehive huts of a 6th-century monastic community, perched 600 feet above the sea.

▶ Clonmacnoise
An early monastic site and centre of learning, Clonmacnoise (see page 211) dates in parts from the 6th century, with the ruins of two round towers and seven churches, as well as Western Europe's largest collection of Early Christian graveslabs. Many of the High Kings of Tara and Connacht were buried here.

◄ Titanic Belfast
A monument to Belfast's maritime heritage, this is the former Harland & Wolff shipyard, where the RMS *Titanic* was built (see page 89). Learn about the ill-fated liner and her sister ships the RMS *Olympic* and HMHS *Britannic*, as well as the importance of shipbuilding, and the docks, in the history of the city.

◀ Kinsale

Known as the seafood capital of Ireland, Kinsale (see page 327) is a delightfully picturesque and charming little town. As well as stuffing yourself with oysters, you can go yachting, angling and dolphin- and whale-watching. There's plenty of history, too, with a pair of fine 17th-century fortresses guarding the harbour.

▶ Newgrange

Ireland is full of amazing neolithic sites but none is more dramatic and impressive than Newgrange (see page 191). This immense passage tomb is more than 5,000 years old – older than the pyramids or Stonehenge. Follow the stone passageway to the central chamber and marvel at the richly carved kerbstones outside.

◀ Glendalough and the Wicklow Mountains

The Wicklow Mountains and the monastic settlement at Glendalough (see page 297) offer splendid upland scenery on Dublin's doorstep. Wooded valleys, deep lakes, winding mountain roads and fast-flowing streams characterise the area and there's a real sense of wilderness and freedom, despite the proximity to the city.

▲ Blarney Castle

Hang upside down and kiss the Blarney Stone and you'll never be short of something to say. People have been visiting the romantic ruins of this castle (see page 182) for more than 200 years and many of them have hoped to pick up the gift of the gab, ideal for distracting Elizabeth I.

▼ Hill of Tara

Hugely significant in Irish folklore, the Hill of Tara (see page 304) is traditionally the seat of the High Kings of Ireland. Most famous of the ancient monuments on the site are the Mound of the Hostages, a passage tomb, and a standing stone said to be the Stone of Destiny (Lia Fáil), where the kings were crowned.

◄ Derry Walls

Derry's city walls (see page 112) are some of the best-preserved in Europe, built as defences for English and Irish settlers. The early 17th-century wall walk is a unique way to see the layout of the original town. Check out the collection of cannon, including Roaring Meg, used during the siege of 1689.

► Kilmainham Gaol

One of the largest unoccupied gaols in Europe and an essential visit for those wishing to understand Ireland's emergence as an independent nation, Kilmainham Gaol (see page 258) has a history that is inextricably linked with the story of Irish nationalism. Every significant nationalist leader except Collins and O'Connell was imprisoned here.

◄ Killarney National Park

Fabulous views, beautiful lakes, rugged scenery and ancient native oak forest can all be found in Killarney National Park (see page 323). The climate is mild, encouraging the profusion of trees and shrubs, and you'd be hard pushed to find a more scenic place. Highlights include the 19th-century mansion Muckross House.

▲ Mount Stewart

Home of the Marquesses of Londonderry, who played a leading role in the political and social life of Britain and Ireland, Mount Stewart (see page 69) re-opened in 2015 after extensive restoration. The beautiful 18th-century house has fascinating contents. The mild climate explains the splendidly lush gardens.

▼ Rock of Cashel

The Rock of Cashel (see page 339), said to be where St Patrick converted the King of Munster in the 5th century, is a dramatic limestone outcrop. Topped with a spectacular group of medieval ruins – castle, cathedral, chapel and round tower – it has one of the most remarkable collections of Celtic art in Europe.

AROUND IRELAND

This book has been divided into Northern Ireland
(see page 58) and the Republic of Ireland (see page 152)
and features destinations in alphabetical order within
each section.

Northern Ireland

Belfast (see page 84) is Northern Ireland's capital, with its
attractive city buildings. The coast of County Antrim has some of
Ireland's most remarkable scenery, including the Giant's Causeway
(see page 123) with its dramatic cliffs and volcanic rocks, as well
as quaint fishing villages and Carrickfergus Castle (see page 105).

The Mountains of Mourne (see page 142) rise along the coast in
the southeast corner of County Down, which has several sites
linked to St Patrick around Downpatrick. The historic city of
Armagh (see page 74) is in nearby County Armagh, as is the huge
Lough Neagh (see page 139).

To the west is County Tyrone, with the Ulster American Folk
Park (see page 150). Enniskillen (see page 119) is the main city of
County Fermanagh, a lakeland county with many attractions set
around Lough Erne (see page 135). The city of Derry (see page 110)
is in County Londonderry, which has a fine stretch of coast.

◀ View over Belfast and Belfast Lough from Cavehill

Dublin

Dublin (see page 248) is the Republic's capital and its coolest city. Boutique hotels, fine dining and chic bars are all here, among a wealth of historical and cultural sights. The city of Dublin itself is wonderfully compact, inviting wandering along the banks of the lovely Liffey, with the city outskirts leading to further delights such as the fishing village of Howth (see page 308), which offers coastal walks and sea views.

The East

Bordering the waters of the Irish Sea, the eastern counties contain some of the country's most visited attractions. North of Dublin, the ancient sites of the Boyne Valley lie in County Meath (see page 187), while County Louth has outstanding monastic ruins (see page 247). Inland along the border with Northern Ireland, Monaghan (see page 334) and Cavan (see page 205) are quiet lakeland counties. West of Dublin, Ireland's famous racehorses are bred in the rolling pastures of County Kildare, home of the National Stud (see page 310). South of the capital are the Wicklow Mountains (see page 300), along with Powerscourt Gardens (see page 337) and the monastic site of Glendalough (see page 297), leading south to Wexford and its wildfowl reserve (see page 369). Inland are counties Carlow (see page 201) and Kilkenny, with a fine castle and medieval sites (see page 314).

The South

The bustling city of Waterford (see page 359), along the south coast, is famous for its crystal, while the surrounding county has pretty harbours, fishing villages and market towns. Inland, bordering the Midlands and the East, County Tipperary is ringed by low mountains that form the backdrop to attractive river valleys, historic towns such as Clonmel (see page 216) and Cahir (see page 200), and the famous Rock of Cashel (see page 339).

Bordering the West is County Limerick, whose northern boundary is defined by Ireland's longest river, the Shannon. Limerick (see page 329), Ireland's fourth-largest city and western international gateway, has a historic hub with fine churches, museums and galleries.

Many castles, both ruined and restored, dot the rolling landscape that leads to lovely beaches on the coast. Inland are picturesque villages such as Adare (see page 158), and the Stone Age settlement of Lough Gur (see page 331).

The dramatic scenery of counties Cork and Kerry in the island's southwestern corner makes them among the most visited regions of Ireland. Killarney (see page 320) and Kenmare (see page 175) make good bases for driving the famous Ring of Kerry (see page 241), round one of several wild, rocky peninsulas. To the north, the Dingle Peninsula (see page 238) lies west from Tralee, with rugged mountains, stunning seascapes, ancient forts and beehive huts.

Cork (see page 229) is Ireland's second-largest city, known for its art and music scene. Nearby is the famous Blarney Castle (see page 182) and the pretty coastal town of Kinsale (see page 327).

The West

Bordered by the Atlantic Ocean, the South and the Midlands, the western counties have some of the most fascinating scenery in Ireland. North of the River Shannon, County Clare is home to the stark limestone plateau called The Burren (see page 194) and the towering Cliffs of Moher (see page 208). Ennis (see page 193) is its largest town. County Galway's capital is lively Galway city (see page 291), set on Galway Bay. Offshore are the largely Irish-speaking Aran Islands (see page 160). Between here and Clifden (see page 222) stretches beautiful Connemara (see page 221), with its craggy Atlantic sea coasts, rugged mountains and expansive heathlands. Westport is the main town in County Mayo, home to Croagh Patrick (see page 236), standing sentinel over Clew Bay, and the miraculous shrine of Knock (see page 210). It is a large county of vast boglands, lonely headlands and dramatic sea cliffs.

▼ The Cliffs of Moher

From Sligo town, visit County Sligo's picturesque coastline, mountains, lakes and forests that inspired the poet W B Yeats. There are also many prehistoric sites.

Carrick-on-Shannon (see page 202) is the capital of nearby County Leitrim. Its location on the River Shannon means it's a great place to hire a boat and explore by water.

County Donegal in the northwestern corner borders Northern Ireland. Donegal town (see page 244) and Letterkenny (see page 303) are the biggest towns in this large but sparsely populated region. Its spectacular Atlantic coastline is studded with rocky inlets, towering cliffs and deserted beaches.

The Midlands
The defining features of the landlocked Midlands are the loughs (lakes) that dot the landscape and the vast stretches of bogland in counties Offaly and Laois. Clonmacnoise (see page 211), on a bend of the River Shannon, is one of Ireland's finest ecclesiastical sites. The Georgian town of Birr (see page 180) has delightful castle gardens. County Westmeath boasts the region's largest town, Athlone (see page 164), and the country's largest castle, Tullynally (see page 291).

County Westmeath adjoins counties Longford and Roscommon; in the latter is Georgian mansion Strokestown Park and the Famine Museum (see page 350).

▼ Lough Gur

HISTORY OF IRELAND

Steeped in the stories of saints and sinners, bloody battles and political conflicts, Ireland has a rich and turbulent history. This is visible not just in the island's museums, churches and castles but also in its landscape, which features neolithic monuments, early stone crosses, the roadside graves of those who died in the famines and, most of all, in its people.

Early Ireland

There is evidence of people living in Ireland as long ago as 6000 BC. The neolithic passage tomb in the northeast of Ireland's Boyne Valley (see page 187) is said to predate Stonehenge and the pyramids of Egypt. You can hardly pass through the countryside without stumbling upon a historic cairn, burial mound or ancient well. In particular, Carrowmore and Creevykeel in County Sligo (see page 347), and Loughcrew Cairns in County Meath (see page 333), offer a rich and fascinating landscape of passage tombs, court tombs, wedge tombs and portal tombs.

Before the fifth century AD, Ireland was a collection of ancient kingdoms and a place of myths and legends telling of kings warring between themselves and invading nearby shores such as England and Wales. The seat of the kings of Munster, the Rock of Cashel, can be visited in County Tipperary (see page 339). The ruins of a fourth-century fortress, it still has a chapel and a tower, although some of the buildings are thought to have been added in the 11th century.

Saints, snakes and manuscripts

Although it is accepted that Christianity existed in Ireland before St Patrick, the famous patron saint of Ireland is credited with bringing Christianity to its shores in AD 432. He is usually depicted carrying a staff to drive out snakes, which do not live in Ireland today. St Patrick's tomb can be seen at Down Cathedral but, as with many Irish saints, he is surrounded by mystery. It appears that he wasn't Irish at all but born in Scotland and brought to Ireland by pirates. Nevertheless, his feast day is celebrated on 17 March, the date of his death, and parades and parties take place not just in Ireland but all over the world.

The early Middle Ages were a golden era of learning in Ireland, a time which saw beautiful illuminated manuscripts such as The *Book of Kells* (which can be seen in the Museum of Dublin, see page 268) being produced by monks and the building of elegant monasteries like Clonmacnoise on the banks of the River Shannon, one of the most famous monastic sites in the country (see page 211). The monks also made the symbolic carved stone crosses which are dotted all around the island.

Vikings, Normans and Tudors

Following Viking invaders, the 12th century brought the Normans from England and so began the island's long-standing relationship with Britain. During these times, the economy was predominantly based on farming oats and potatoes. The Normans built edifices such as Reginald's Tower in Waterford (see page 360), the city's main fortification, which is still intact today. Other distinctive Norman towers and forts are common sights around Ireland, whereas the Vikings left their mark in place names, such as the Skellig Islands and Wicklow.

One of the most influential figures in English history, Henry VIII, also tried to make his mark on Ireland. He wanted to bring Ireland under British rule and separate it from the papacy, as he had done in England, but Henry only succeeded in intensifying Irish dislike for the English. The Reformation failed in Ireland and sectarian conflict became part of Irish life.

Henry's daughter, Queen Elizabeth I, suppressed a revolt in Ulster and used the opportunity to bring over English people to settle in the province, in what became known as an English

'plantation'. Such plantations changed the face of Ireland by creating large communities with a British, Protestant identity. Elizabeth also founded the first university in Ireland, Trinity College Dublin. However, during the reign of her successor, James I, relationships between Catholic and Protestant, Irish and English, worsened significantly.

On 15 August 1649, Oliver Cromwell, the next leader of England, Scotland and Wales, landed at Ringsend, near Dublin, with an army of 3,000. In Ireland the Roman Catholics had been in revolt since 1641 and held much of the island. From Dublin, Cromwell marched to Drogheda, which was defended by an English Catholic and royalist, stormed the city and ordered the death of every man in the garrison. Cromwell then turned to Wexford, slaughtering more townspeople and garrisons. Within two years, Catholic resistance was at an end. Many Irish soldiers were allowed to seek their fortunes in Europe, while Catholic landowners were largely dispossessed and 'The curse of Cromwell on you' became an Irish oath.

The Battle of the Boyne in 1690 saw the Protestant William of Orange's victory over Catholic James II. Some 60,000 men took to the field, and with William seizing control, it was considered to be a turning point in Irish history. The actual battle site can be visited in Drogheda (see page 246).

▲ Famine Memorial, Dublin

Emigration and famine

Large-scale emigration from Ireland began many years ago, a trend that continued for centuries as Irish people fled their homeland for happier shores, at first through disillusionment but increasingly by necessity. Some claim that today the Irish diaspora – those around the world with Irish ancestry – numbers 80 million.

In the 1600s, about 25,000 Irish Catholics left – some voluntarily, others by force – for the Caribbean and the American state of Virginia. Others sailed to other parts of North America and many to Newfoundland.

Between 1845 and 1852, approximately one million Irish people died of starvation and disease and another 1.2 million fled in search of a better life. The famine of 1848 was caused by a blight of the important potato crop, which was the staple diet for many. As a result, roughly one in two people born in Ireland in the 19th century emigrated, many to the USA and Canada, with the poorest fleeing to Liverpool, Glasgow and South Wales.

A number of related memorials can be seen around Ireland, including the Broken Heart in Limerick, a sculpture in memory of the forced emigration of those who left from the nearby Steamboat Quay. Other moving monuments to this grim period include Strokestown Park Famine Museum (see page 350) and the painfully thin sculptural figures at Customs House Quays in Dublin.

Home rule, independence and the Troubles

In 1842, an organisation called Young Ireland was formed to campaign for independence. Following the famine, Catholic Ireland slowly increased in prosperity and demand for self-rule grew. After a number of skirmishes and uprisings, the British Prime Minister, William Gladstone, attempted to introduce the Home Rule Bill in 1886, but it was defeated. Later bills saw resignations and riots, and were also unsuccessful and, in 1914, legislation was passed to delay home rule until the end of World War I.

The Ulster Unionist Party was formed in 1886 and Sinn Féin (which means 'we ourselves') was formed in 1905.

The Easter Rising of 1916 is one of the main events that dominate modern Irish history. On Easter Monday, a group of Irish nationalists staged a rebellion against the British government in Ireland, seizing buildings and clashing with troops. Many of the leaders of the rebellion were executed and were later seen as martyrs. Following the revolt, thousands of people suspected of supporting the uprising were imprisoned in England.

The Irish Republican Army (IRA) was formed in 1917, initially by those Irish volunteers who refused to enlist in the British army during the war.

In 1921, a treaty was signed to establish the Irish Free State, which eventually became the Republic of Ireland. Northern Ireland immediately left the Irish Free State and rejoined the United Kingdom. In 1937, southern Ireland drafted a new constitution, creating the state of Éire (Gaelic for Ireland) and Eamon de Valera, the leader of Sinn Féin, was elected as president. Eventually, in 1949, the Republic of Ireland was born and links with the Commonwealth were severed.

The period from 1969 to 1998 was one of conflict and violence, referred to as the Troubles in both Northern Ireland and the Republic of Ireland. Ireland joined the European Union in 1972 and in the same year the Northern Irish State was dissolved and the six counties put under direct rule from London. In 1972, a civil rights march in the city of Derry was interrupted when British soldiers opened fire on the crowd, killing 14 people. The army believed the IRA had fired first but the effects of Bloody Sunday, as it came to be known, were felt for years afterwards.

Finally, the Good Friday agreement of 1998 set out the framework for progress and peace. In 2002, the Euro replaced the Irish punt as the official Irish national currency, and in 2011, Queen Elizabeth II visited Ireland, the first official visit of a British monarch since Ireland's independence.

▶ The Peace Bridge, Derry

BACK TO NATURE

The Emerald Isle isn't all green. There are lunar landscapes of limestone pavements, huge swathes of dense farmland, as well as great expanses of mudflats and islands. The Ice Age sculpted this ancient land millennia ago when great sheaths of ice retreated and glaciers melted to form a wild, rocky landscape. Today, the island is a patchwork of heather-strewn mountains, vast gorges, dense forests, golden hills and glassy lakes.

40 shades of green

Ireland's incredibly and beautifully varied landscape has, over the centuries, inspired painters, poets and songwriters and continues to do so. Johnny Cash wrote the song 'Forty shades of green' when he was on a trip to Ireland in 1959. Iconic peat bogs covering significant patches of the land's interior, mostly in the northwest and centre, give way to a large section of limestone plain in the heart of the country. Despite increasing industrialisation, and the sad disappearance of many of its ancient oak forests, Ireland is still the agricultural country that looms so large in our imaginations, with far-reaching, attractive swathes of green, from lush, flat pasture land to gently rolling hills.

▲ From left: Ballinafad Lough; kayaking in Donegal

Waterways

Much of Ireland's wriggling, often fog-shrouded coastline is lined
with mountains and dramatic sea cliffs that plunge hundreds of
feet into the Atlantic Ocean. These towering masses fringe a riot
of colourful seascapes, from gold and grey to turquoise and jade.
Ultimately exiting at the ocean are the clear waters of hundreds
of rivers filled with salmon and sea trout that crisscross the island.
Ireland's longest river is the 235-mile slowly snaking Shannon; its
biggest body of water, Lough Neagh (see page 139), is just one of
many loughs or lakes around the country. Visitors can enjoy the
vast network of scenic waterways on boat trips, whether from
small vessels or luxury cruisers. Fishing, kayaking, sailing and,
increasingly, surfing are just some of the activities on offer.

Rock star rocks

When London's Geological Society listed the world's top 100
geological sites in 2014, no less than five sites in Northern Ireland
made it onto the rock star list. Predictably, one of the five was the
region's most famous geological landmark, Giant's Causeway (see
page 123), which UNESCO has described as a spectacular area of
global geological importance. Also named were the Marble Arch
Caves (see page 122), an intricate network of underground caves
that is now a geopark for visitors as well as a centre of research.

The rocky shore of Portrush (see page 126) was listed too; it's a place of pilgrimage for holidaymakers and geologists alike. The Ring of Gullion, a breathtaking circle of hills, is a designated Area of Outstanding Natural Beauty, to which visitors flock to hike in the acclaimed Slieve Gullion Forest Park (see page 149). The fifth site to warrant inclusion was Loughareema, which means 'vanishing lake'. Close to the seaside town of Ballycastle (see page 78), this apparently magical body of water can go from full to empty in the course of a day.

The Wild West

The very first British coins featuring Ireland had pictures of the country's wildlife and it is no surprise that more than 80 per cent

▼ The Giant's Causeway

of overseas visitors come to Ireland for the scenery. Both the North and the Republic are home to some of the most scenic road trips in the world. These include the waymarked Wild Atlantic Way, which traces the untamed west coast to form the longest island driving route in the world.

Walking trails, nature and scenic tours abound, with a variety of camping options (see page 56). Areas of Outstanding Natural Beauty, country parks and World Heritage Sites form a variety of green playgrounds. One such example is the 27,000 acres of the Nephin Beg Range in Ballycroy National Park (see page 336). It has been designated Ireland's – and also Europe's – first wilderness area, signalling a positive future for this island's wild landscapes.

LORE OF THE LAND

Ireland is the land of the 'little people': the fairies or
faery people who make their homes outside residents'
back doors, close to the surface of the ground, and who
must never be offended, for fear of retribution. These
spirits, which may have originated from the neolithic
firbolgs, who once inhabited holes in the ground, are
most active on Halloween and May Day Eve. Brides and
babies are especially vulnerable to their spells.

Fairies are renowned for creating a faery wind or *sidhe-goath*,
which can blow offending sailors disastrously off course or assist
the escape of those they favour. One tale tells of Ireland's famous
giant killer Conn, a cook's son who was brought up by royal parents
alongside their own son Dara. When Conn was finally dismissed by
the queen, he was swept away by the faery wind.

Most dangerous of all is to cut down a fairy thorn or *skeogh*,
a bush revered because it was not planted by human hand. In a
traditional telling of the tale, a farmer who took an axe to a fairy
thorn found the blade turned on himself before the bush started
to bleed. When he awoke next morning, all his hair was gone and
never grew back.

◀ The Fairy Thorn Tree, Killary Harbour

More malign than the fairies are Ireland's banshees, or faerie women. These raucous Celtic messengers foretell a death, and may stalk their victims while emitting ear-splitting screams. Said to be the spirits of women who had been brutally killed, banshees confuse their victims by appearing as dirty old hags dressed in black or as beautiful, pale women dressed in white or silver.

Folk hero

Legends abound of Fionn MacCumhaill or Finn McCool. He is said to have built the majestic Giant's Causeway on County Antrim's coast as stepping stones to Scotland, the home of his arch-enemy Finn Gall (in some versions, the giant Benandonner). His work accomplished, McCool fell asleep, giving Finn Gall the chance to attack. McCool was saved only because his wife Oona persuaded Gall that the huge man she had dressed in baby clothes was her infant son.

McCool's feats include a number of other significant victories. At Moorestown in Kerry he vanquished the huge-eyed angry prince MacCuain, son of the sea, while at Tara he gained an entire army, the Fianna, by killing the fire-breathing Aillen with a magical red-hot spear. At Slieve Gullion in County Armagh visitors are still warned against touching the cold, dark waters of Cailleach Beara's Lough, for it was here that McCool met Miluchra, a sorceress disguised as a beautiful woman who had lost a golden ring. He retrieved it for her – only to discover that she had turned into a ghastly hag and that he had become a feeble old man.

Feats of the saints

That Ireland has no snakes is due, according to legend, to revered St Patrick, the country's patron saint, who bravely killed its last fearsome winged serpent on Saints' Island in Lough Derg, Donegal, turning the waters red. The remains of the devil's beast were put into a cave, symbolising the state of purgatory. At Hawk's Well in County Sligo, the imprints of the saint's hand and back, and the hoof print of the horse from which he fell, mark the place where St Patrick created the holy well.

Nearby, St Patrick drove the demon Fire-Spitter into the Atlantic. The subsequent swell of water filled the well first with salt water and then with fresh water with healing properties. In another encounter, the fairies were given a message by St Patrick's servant Domhnaill that their days were numbered. On receiving this gloomy verdict, they sent life-threatening storms after him, but the servant took the saint's advice by digging a grave and covering it with a cross formed by a spade and a shovel. He hid in the grave for two days before emerging unscathed. In commemoration of his salvation it has since been customary to place a crossed spade and shovel over a newly dug grave.

Other saints are no less influential. On his way from Ireland to Iona, St Columba asked some fishermen in Mulroy Bay, Donegal, who had already caught two fish, if they had any salmon. The fishermen lied, claiming that they had not. That no salmon has been caught there since is said to result from the fishermen's fibs.

At Ardmore in Waterford, St Colman's sacred tree grew after he planted a dry stick into the ground. Anyone harming the tree risks punishment – like the man who stole some twigs from it for fuel and saw his house burn to the ground.

Legendary waters

Hundreds of holy wells can be found in Ireland, many credited with the power to cure many medical conditions. Among the most extraordinary are Wart Well in Derry, and Tobar na nGealt, The Well of the Insane, in the valley of Gleann-na-nGealt, West Kerry, where it is said that Gall, King of Ulster, was cured by eating the watercress growing there. Trees near holy wells are traditionally hung with rags or handkerchiefs; red is a favoured colour as it is believed to deter evil spirits.

▼ Janus figure, Boa Island

The River Shannon has its source at the Shannon Pot in County Cavan where, so legend has it, Sinnann, daughter of Lodan and granddaughter of Lear, the sea king, arrived searching for the Salmon of Wisdom. As she approached, the fish spotted her and became so angry that the pool bubbled up fiercely enough to flow in ribbons over the entire country.

Loughs also have stories to tell. Lough Neagh is said to be the work of the mermaid Liban, who neglected to warn people to build boats and escape from imminent floods. An alternative version attributes it to Finn McCool who, striding across the land, threw clods of earth at a giant, creating a vast hole that filled with water. Glenade Lough in Sligo is renowned as the home of Dabharchú, a monster who devoured a bride who was washing her clothes at the water's edge. Dabharchú was eventually killed by the woman's vengeful husband.

Stories in the stones

Ireland's rocks and stones have strong associations with myth and legend. At the Priest's Leap on the border of Kerry and Cork, the rocks are said to have melted to assist the escape of a priest pursued by English soldiers. The location is marked by a simple iron cross. In Donegal the copper-rich Flagstone of Loneliness is said to cure homesickness, especially if copper coins are placed there. When it rains heavily the stone 'weeps' lonesome tears of rusty red.

On Boa Island in Lough Erne stands the remarkable stone two-faced Janus figure. At 29 inches high, it is thought to represent one or more Celtic deities, possibly the war goddess Badhbh after whom the island is named, and one of her two sisters. The structure's chief significance is the belief that the head – often taken as a war trophy – retains the spirit of a person after their death. Tourists place good luck tokens in the deep indentation between the two faces. Even older is the Lustymore Idol on the eponymous island south of Boa, thought to represent the fertility idol Sheela-na-gig.

For those wishing to gain the gift of eloquence, it has been the custom for more than 200 years to kiss the Blarney Stone. Set in the outside of the wall beneath the battlements of Blarney Castle in Cork (see page 182), the stone must be kissed while being suspended head down from the ankles. According to one story it was Jacob's Pillow, brought by the prophet Jeremiah, and used as a throne by Irish kings. In another it is St Columba's deathbed; in yet another the goddess Clíodha advised the castle's builder, Cormac Laidir McCarthy, to kiss it before appearing in court to answer a lawsuit – his newfound eloquence was rewarded with a successful outcome.

LITERARY IRELAND

This small island has contributed an extraordinary amount to world literature, producing no less than four Nobel Prize-winning writers. Ireland's relationship with the written word is embedded so deep in its history and landscape that it is almost palpable, with a literary heritage that is not confined to ivory towers or libraries. Visitors can experience this important part of Ireland's identity through a calendar of literary festivals, on dedicated tours and even on its city streets.

Literary giants
James Joyce, W B Yeats, Oscar Wilde and Samuel Beckett are Ireland's key literary figures. These four masters created innovative and poetic work that continues to inspire writers and readers today. They form part of Ireland's living literary legacy, which includes more contemporary wordsmiths such as Seamus Heaney, Colm Tóibín, Roddy Doyle and Edna O'Brien.

City of Literature
Ireland's pubs are still at the heart of its literary traditions and it is possible to follow in the footsteps of its writers on pub crawls

◄ Oscar Wilde statue, Merrion Square, Dublin

around the land. In Dublin, a UNESCO City of Literature, you can embark on a Dublin literary pub crawl (dublinpubcrawl.com). Begin at The Duke, which dates back to 1822, haunt of Patrick Kavanagh, and move on to O'Neill's, Brendan Behan's local. Sip on a Guinness in WB Yeats' favourite bar and visit the city haunts of *Dracula* author Bram Stoker. James Joyce famously used Davy Byrnes pub in *Ulysses*, where its main protagonist, Leopold Bloom, tucks into a gorgonzola sandwich washed down with a glass of burgundy.

Joyce is celebrated in the Dublin Writers Museum (see page 265) as well as in the James Joyce Centre (see page 265). Dublin's streets are packed with literary associations and the city is rightly proud of its heroes of the written word, with statues honouring them on many street corners. Come face to face with Oscar Wilde, who is remembered in a statue reclining on a rock in Merrion Square. Wander across the River Liffey over the Samuel Beckett Bridge or, for a taste of the city's current lively literary scene, visit the Dublin Writers Festival in May.

Northern literary lights

Take a walking tour of Belfast from the Linen Hall Library to Writers' Square for a fascinating and sometimes dark snapshot of the literary heritage of Northern Ireland's capital. Belfast's prominent literary figures include the great C S Lewis, who was born here. His family home, Little Lea on Circular Road, is thought to be the inspiration for Professor Kirke's home in the children's eternal classic, *The Lion, the Witch and the Wardrobe*.

Born in County Londonderry, the renowned poet Seamus Heaney was inspired by the rich rolling farmland in the Magherafelt area of Northern Ireland; Bellaghy Bawn, a fortified house in Bellaghy, is now a museum that is partly dedicated to the area's famous son and includes the interesting Seamus Heaney Library.

▶ W B Yeats statue, Sligo

Marvel at manuscripts

The *Book of Kells* (see page 268) may well be one of the world's most beautiful books, but Ireland also boasts the *Book of Durrow*, which predates it by over a century and is the most complete illuminated gospel in the world. They are just two examples of the illuminated manuscripts that were painstakingly created by monks around the land between the seventh and ninth centuries. Trinity College Dublin tells the interesting and often amusing story of how they were made, while its Long Room is one of the world's most inspiring libraries. It can be a moving experience to wander among the towering tiers of over 200,000 rare books, watched by the white marble busts of writers such as Swift and Socrates.

Literary landscapes

Sligo's beautiful lakes and mountains moved Yeats to write some of his best-loved poems, such as 'The Lake Isle of Innisfree'. Yeats' fans can make a pilgrimage to the brooding mountain of Ben Bulben, which shadows the churchyard of Drumcliff, where the poet is buried.

For further literary inspiration, take a trip to the Mourne Mountains (see page 142), the inspiration for C S Lewis' magical land of Narnia, and visit dramatic Cave Hill, which locals fondly call Napoleon's Nose and which Jonathan Swift used as the inspiration for the sleeping giant in *Gulliver's Travels*.

Living celebrations

Literature in Ireland is very much alive and is certainly not confined to the page. Visitors can enjoy a vibrant and full calendar of literary festivals throughout Northern Ireland and the Republic. The Belfast Book Festival (see page 54) celebrates the city's passion for books, writers and readers. During the unique and rather bizarre Bloomsday event in Dublin (see page 54), Joyce fans become a character in the world of *Ulysses*, following the protagonist, Leopold Bloom, and his thoughts around Dublin.

Happy Days in Enniskillen commemorates its own famous son with a multi-arts approach called Wilde Weekend, a celebration of Oscar Wilde, and some literary celebrity guest speakers. The Cape Clear Island International Storytelling Festival in the county of Cork hosts an exciting programme of storytellers not just from Ireland, but from around the world.

▸ Inishmaan Aran Islands

IRELAND ON SCREEN

Today may well be a golden age for Irish film and television, with the industry worth several hundred million pounds, but there was a time when many programmes, such as those depicting the Troubles, were filmed overseas. Now, however, the Republic, and even more so Northern Ireland, are basking in the glory of a string of cinematic and television successes that have been filmed on Irish shores.

Past Troubles

Historically, the island's perceived remote location, lack of infrastructure and political situation conspired to prevent the Irish film industry from flourishing. Films like *Hennessy* (1975) and *The Long Good Friday* (1979) about the IRA were not only minor failures in the box office but also courted controversy because of their subject matter and were not even filmed in Ireland. Things seemed to shift in the 1980s and, thanks to a string of incentives introduced in the 1990s, regional TV and film production began to gather pace, recognising Ireland's incredible natural beauty and its extraordinary local talent. The decade saw the release of other movies featuring the IRA and filmed, at least partially, in Ireland:

Titanic Town (1994) and *Divorcing Jack* (1998) being notable. A more light-hearted film, *Mad about Mambo* (2000), was filmed in Dublin but set in Belfast.

Game changer

The filming of the blockbuster TV series *Game of Thrones* has propelled Northern Ireland onto the TV world stage. The programme's success is such that a new breed of visitors, nicknamed 'Throners', is flooding into Northern Ireland to visit the filming locations. Themed *Game of Thrones* tours have sprung up in County Antrim and the Causeway Coast area of Northern Ireland, locations for dozens of memorable scenes in the cult TV show.

In the Republic, *Braveheart* (1995) may have told the story of Scotland's greatest hero, William Wallace, but it was filmed in County Wicklow, Meath and County Dublin. By contrast, the locations for historical TV drama *Vikings* can pretty much be visited on a day's walk along the Wicklow Way, which takes in loughs Tay and Dan. The production also had a base at the increasingly popular Ashford Studios outside Dublin.

Most of the filming for the fictitious location of Craggy Island in cult sitcom *Father Ted* took place in County Clare. The real version of the now-legendary Parochial House is a popular place of pilgrimage for *Father Ted* fans. Other scenes were shot on the Aran Islands, which now host one of the world's most ridiculous festivals, Tedfest.

▼ Dunluce Castle – the House of Greyjoy in *Game of Thrones*

The Giant's Causeway, the wild expanse of Divis Mountain and the Italian Garden of Mount Stewart were just a few of the Irish locations for the 2014 film *Dracula Untold*.

An animated industry
In the 1980s, the success of animated films by director Don Bluth, including *All Dogs Go to Heaven* (1989), was such that they were said by some to rival Disney's cartoons. After an extended hiatus for successful Irish animations, *The Secret of Kells* (2009), based on a fictitious account of the creation of the *Book of Kells*, was nominated for an Academy Award in 2010. It was the work of Kilkenny-based animation studio Cartoon Saloon, which went on to be nominated for an Oscar for its film *Song of the Sea* (2014), based on the ancient Celtic myth of the selkie.

Open doors
Ireland's extraordinary variety of landscapes, sustained investment and significant tax breaks have all conspired to ensure the continued success of its TV and film industries. Two new studios are planned for the Titanic Quarter in Belfast, making Belfast one of the largest film production centres in Europe. In 2014, Northern Ireland Screen, the agency for the film, television and digital content industries, announced its four-year 'Opening Doors' strategy to support the local TV and film industry. The name is an allusion to C S Lewis, who was inspired by the Irish countryside to write about the magical land of Narnia and pay homage to Ireland.

▼ The Dark Hedges, Ballymoney – the King's Road in *Game of Thrones*

IRISH SPORT

The Irish love their sport, whether it's cheering on the Irish national rugby team in the annual Six Nations tournament on TV or encouraging schoolchildren in a game of Gaelic football on the village green. Sport in Ireland is always highly competitive but still convivial, with as much emphasis on celebrating or commiserating afterwards as on the game itself.

Rugby: up and under

Ireland is represented on the rugby world stage by a team which covers both Northern Ireland and the Republic. They have won the Six Nations Championship 12 times and regularly qualify to play in the Rugby World Cup. Famous Irish players include the retired Brian O'Driscoll, Ireland's all-time leader of tries scored. Ireland play at the Aviva Stadium in Dublin, formerly Lansdowne Road.

Horseracing: first past the post

Ireland has a long-standing association with horseracing and breeding race horses. Trading in bloodstock and tote betting plays a large part in the economy, and some of the sport's most famous

▲ Aviva Stadium, Dublin   ▲ Racing at the Curragh

jockeys are Irish, such as Pat Eddery, winner of three Derbys, and Northern Ireland's A P McCoy. Racing takes place at 26 courses in Ireland. Top racecourses are the Curragh, the home of flat racing, and Punchestown and Fairyhouse for national hunt racing. Leopardstown in south Dublin hosts the Christmas Festival and Galway is the setting for a week of summer race meetings.

Hurling: fast and furious
Thought to be the fastest field sport in the world, hurling is native to Ireland and, while not familiar to many visitors, its energetic pace and skill make it a great sport to watch. The game is thought to be over 3,000 years old. Two teams of 15 players aim to get the *sliothar* (ball) into their opponent's goalpost. Games are played most weekends throughout the country, with the strongest teams coming from Kilkenny, Tipperary, Wexford, Cork, Clare and Galway. Every year the counties compete in the All Ireland Championship, with the final held in September in Croke Park, Dublin.

Gaelic football: amateur magic
Gaelic football is quite distinct from soccer and is more popular in some parts of Ireland. The goalposts are the same shape as those on a rugby pitch and the round ball is smaller than a football.

Played by teams of 15, the game's object is to score by kicking or striking the ball with the hand to get it through the goals. Expect to see it played all over Ireland. Like camogie, a field game like hurling that is played by women, and handball (another Irish sport which is like squash without the rackets), Gaelic football is one of the Gaelic games played only at amateur level and is thriving in local communities.

Golf: tee time

With miles of emerald green grassland, the Irish landscape was made for golf. Famous Irish players such as Rory McIlroy and Pádraig Harrington, now Ireland's Golf Ambassador, have added to golfing glamour here. Some of Ireland's golf courses are ranked among the best in the world, including Royal County Down, Dunluce and Ballybunion. The Irish Close Championship is just one of many amateur golf tournaments where spectators can see potential stars in the making. Golf's Open Championship will be held at Royal Portrush in 2019, the first time the event has returned to the venue for 68 years.

Surf, scuba and sail: water world

With its spectacular rugged coastline, conditions in Ireland are ideal for surfing, which has given rise to a lively surf scene. The surf season starts in September, when warm weather and swells come in from both north and south and surfers head here from all over the world. Some of the top surf spots are found in counties Clare, Sligo, Donegal, Kerry and West Cork. The fun continues after sundown in the many cosy, friendly pubs nearby.

Diving is also popular, as Ireland has some of the best wreck sites in Europe. These include the largest number of sunken German World War II U-boats in the world and also the largest number of sunken ocean liners (off Malin Head, County Donegal). Off the northern coast, divers can find the remains of HMS *Justica*, a liner built by the same company that built the ill-fated *Titanic*.

Above the water, the sea around Ireland is a magnet to some of the country's top sailors. Races and regattas include the Volvo Dún Laoghaire Regatta, Ireland's biggest sailing event, which takes place in July every other (odd) year. During the four days of racing across Dublin Bay, there is a festival atmosphere along the waterfront, with pipe bands and family entertainment.

Football

Northern Ireland fans finally have something to cheer about as they have qualified for the Euro 2016 finals – the first time they have made it to a major tournament for 30 years. The Republic join them after winning a play-off against Bosnia-Herzegovina.

LOCAL SPECIALITIES

Ireland's food and drink scene has really come into its own in the last few years. Traditional local ingredients from the island's fishermen and farmers are being cooked up by world-class chefs and recreated by a new breed of artisan producers. Microbreweries and new gin producers have exploded onto the drinking scene, and slow food festivals, wild food workshops, food trails and farmers markets abound.

FOOD

Oysters

Oysters are synonymous with Ireland, and its west coast in particular, gracing the tables of some of the finest restaurants in the world. The Galway International Oyster and Seafood Festival that takes place every September is the biggest of its kind on the planet. The festival includes the Guinness World Oyster Opening Championship that annually finds the fastest shucker.

Plain potato

Yes, the humble potato is still king of the Irish food scene, and you can enjoy it in any number of ways. Why not try colcannon (potato with cabbage), champ (potato with spring onion), fadge (potato bread) or traditional boxty (potato pancake)?

Ulster fry

A full Irish breakfast was recently voted as Northern Ireland's favourite national dish and must be tried when visiting the area. Like the English and Scottish versions, it includes bacon, sausages, eggs and tomatoes but has the very important additions of soda farls (split and fried soda bread) and potato bread. This cholesterol-laden meal can be served for breakfast, lunch or dinner and is very popular as a hangover cure.

Fish and seafood

The clear waters of Ireland's sea, rivers and lakes are home to crab, lobster, cockles and mussels. Take note: eels are a speciality traditionally eaten at Halloween and the Dublin Bay prawn is in fact an oyster. Salmon is an integral part of both Celtic mythology and Irish cuisine. Look out for smokehouses on the island that specialise in smoking salmon with oak, beech and turf.

Say cheese

It wasn't long ago that Irish cheese was mostly mass-produced and rather looked down upon by food lovers. In the 1970s, that all changed when artisan producers began to revive the lost art of handmade cheese. These cheeses are now known the world over for their distinctive flavour and innovation. Look out for the likes of Cashel Blue, perhaps Ireland's most famous cheese, along with Gouda-style Coolea and Ardrahan, in both plain and smoked varieties, all with a unique flavour and provenance.

Superfood seaweed

Michelin-starred chefs have picked up this nutrient-packed Irish staple to take the food scene by storm. Atlantic seaweed, purple kale and sea spaghetti are just some of the delicious and healthy varieties of this Irish superfood. Carrageen (also known as Irish

◀ Guinness and oysters

Moss), a classic Irish seaweed, is used in both sweet and savoury dishes, from ice cream to salad.

DRINK
Whiskey with an E
Irish whiskey is special. It's spelt with an 'e', triple-distilled and enjoying a renaissance, with both artisan and heritage brands creating a stir. Visitors can take in traditional distilleries (many of which offer tours), visit dedicated whiskey pubs and embark on a whiskey trail (irelandwhiskeytrail.com) taking in distilleries, bars, pubs and shops.

The dark stuff
Yes, there's Guinness, but there's Beamish and Murphy's stout too, as well as a few new kids on the block. None of the big three are actually Irish-owned but many young craft breweries now abound, providing a plethora of choice. Knock back a Belfast Blonde or order a Galway Hooker from the booming craft beer scene, and look out for tastings and an increasing number of dedicated tours.

Spirit of Ireland
Ireland has a new local spirit: gin, which boutique newcomers are making with local botanicals. The latest and most impressive addition to the scene is Bertha's Revenge, made with 18 local botanicals, giving it a unique flavour and an undeniably peppery kick.

Alternatively, Dingle Original is infused with heather and bog myrtle from the Kerry landscape, while Shortcross has the subtle flavours of Irish apples and wild clover.

PARTY IRISH STYLE
Craic
Pronounced 'crack', craic is a Gaelic word that has no literal translation but basically means 'party' or 'fun'. The youth of Ireland, as well as the not-so-young, may often cry on a Saturday night, 'Let's go and get some craic'. Alcohol is usually involved, along with conversation and music, possibly dancing and even romance. While owners of Irish pubs around the world have cashed in on this uniquely Irish phenomenon, academics have identified 'the craic' as an element of Irish society and culture that differentiates it from other cultures and believe that conversation and enjoyment is regarded as a key part of the Irish quality of life.

Ceilidhs
Ceilidhs (pronounced 'kay-lees') are traditional Gaelic social gatherings. Typically involving folk music, dancing and often storytelling, the word ceilidh can be used to describe any kind of party.

BEFORE YOU GO

THINGS TO READ

A Secret Map of Ireland
Rosita Boland
Boland, an award-winning *Irish Times* journalist, takes her readers on a personalised tour of Ireland, describing its 32 counties in a series of separate essays. Full of fascinating facts and quirky observations, this is a heartfelt guide that is informative yet easy to read.

The Height of Nonsense
Paul Clements
On a romp through Ireland's great mountain roads, Clements visits little-known corners of the island, telling tales of witches and druids, of history and humanity.

Silver Linings: Travels Around Northern Ireland
Martin Fletcher
This engaging book with a positive spin tells of a region that has emerged from its war-torn history. The author meets its people and tells the history of Northern Ireland with an unflinching gaze but also with warmth and humour.

Round Ireland with a Fridge
Tony Hawks
This best-selling book is a fun and funny read about a drunken bet that led the author to travel around Ireland with a fridge. Stories of his trip offer an insight into Ireland, as well as laughs.

The Modernisation of Irish Society, 1848–1918
Joseph Lee
Despite the heavy-sounding title, this is an accessible book that will appeal to anyone interested in the key period between the great famine and Sinn Féin's triumph in the general election of 1918.

McCarthy's Bar: A Journey of Discovery in Ireland
Pete McCarthy
Another funny book about an Irish road trip, in which half-Irish McCarthy follows the rule of never passing a pub that has his name on it. As a result, he visits McCarthy's bars all over Ireland, encountering fascinating characters along the way.

Angela's Ashes: A Memoir
Frank McCourt
The 1996 memoir of McCourt became an international best-seller. It focuses on his childhood and growing up in poverty-stricken, rural Ireland.

The Back of Beyond: A Search for the Soul of Ireland
James Charles Roy
Roy, a well-respected authority on Irish history, manages to be informative, humorous and adventurous in this book. This is an ambitious title that looks at how the Celtic Tiger changed Ireland into an economic powerhouse, but Roy approaches his subject matter with an engaging, light and compelling touch.

THINGS TO WATCH
Big Screen
Finian's Rainbow (1968)
It may have put a Hollywood gloss on Ireland, but the story of a loveable rogue, a pot of gold and leprechauns will put anyone in the mood for a bit of Irish whimsy.

The Commitments (1991)
Roddy Doyle's novel sprung to life under Alan Parker's direction with this heart-warming tale of a group of working-class Dubliners who form a soul group.

The Crying Game (1992)
The difficult issues of nationality, gender and sexuality were all confronted in this ground-breaking film, which is set against the backdrop of the Troubles.

Michael Collins (1992)
One of the most expensive films to be made in Ireland, this told the story of Irish patriot and revolutionary Michael Collins and covered the historical events from 1916 to 1921.

In the Name of the Father (1993)
This Irish-British-American courtroom drama, starring Daniel Day Lewis, is based on the true story of the Guildford Four, who were falsely convicted of the 1974 IRA's Guildford pub bombings.

Good Vibrations (2012)
This film charts the life of Terri Hooley, who opened a record shop during the Troubles and became key in developing Belfast's punk-rock scene.

Philomena (2013)
The moving search of a mother looking for her son, who had been taken away from her years before, is surprisingly uplifting. It's based on the book of the same name by Martin Sixsmith.

Small Screen
Ballykissangel
Screened between 1996 and 2001, this BBC drama about a fictitious community in Ireland was filmed in County Wicklow.

Father Ted
This comedy series was first screened in 1995 and the tales of Father Ted Crilly and his life

on Craggy Island soon became a cult classic. It was filmed in County Clare and in other locations around Ireland.

Game of Thrones

A cult American fantasy drama series adapted from George R R Martin's best-selling book series *A Song of Ice and Fire*, filmed partly in Belfast and Northern Ireland. First aired in 2011.

Mrs Brown's Boys

A TV sitcom created by and starring Irish writer and performer Brendan O'Carroll but produced in the UK. The titular character Agnes Brown is played by O'Carroll himself. The show has become a ratings success in Ireland, where it is set, as well as in the UK.

Terry Wogan's Ireland

In this 2015 BBC show, the veteran presenter revisited the Ireland of his youth.

THINGS TO KNOW

Day of the Dead

Halloween, although now big in the United States, is actually Irish in origin and derived from an ancient, pre-Christian festival called Samhain, which was not unlike the Mexican Day of the Dead. The first day of November marked the beginning of the Celtic year and was its most significant holiday, when the souls of the deceased mingled with the living, and were honoured with bonfires and animal sacrifices. In the Catholic church, 1 November is also All Saints' Day and the 2 November is All Souls' Day.

Patron Patrick

St Patrick, Ireland's patron saint, was not actually Irish. He was born in Scotland to Roman parents, kidnapped by pirates and taken as a slave to Ireland. St Patrick's Day is observed on 17 March, which is said to be the date of his death.

▼ St Patrick's Day celebrations

Local language

Gaelic is the official language of the Republic of Ireland but English is very much the working language. The Official Languages Act in 2003 gave new rights to Gaelic speakers; children are encouraged to learn it and the Irish-language TV channel TG4 is rising in popularity. In 2007, Gaelic Irish became the 21st official language of the EU.

The Titanic

The 'unsinkable ship' was made in Ireland; built at the Harland & Wolff shipyards of Belfast. At the time she was the world's biggest and most luxurious boat and set sail, after a brief stop at Cork, to much fanfare from Cobh. 'It was fine when it left us,' the Irish love to joke.

Irish Olympics

Ireland had its very own Olympics in the Bronze Age. Called the Tailteann Games, they were originally introduced to commemorate the death of the much-loved Queen Tailte. The games were reinstated between 1924 to 1932 to demonstrate the new state's independence and to consolidate national identity.

Singing success

The Republic of Ireland has won the Eurovision Song Contest no less than seven times and it holds the record for winning the contest three times in a row.

Irish overseas

Around 80 million people of Irish descent live abroad, which is about 15 times the population of the Republic of Ireland. The Irish diaspora is mostly in English-speaking countries such as the United Kingdom, the United States, Canada and Australia, with around 35 million Americans and some 12 million Australians claiming Irish ancestry.

▼ RMS *Titanic* under construction in Belfast

THINGS TO PACK

Ireland is full of surprises, and these can include the weather – they say you can experience all four seasons in one day here. Weather patterns throughout the regions are fairly consistent, but the southwest area of Ireland receives the most rain, while the southeast is the driest. Cork and Galway have similar summer temperatures to Dublin, but with slightly warmer winter days and months.

Wet weather gear: Pack lightweight, rainproof and waterproof trousers. It can be very windy near the coast so umbrellas may be more of a hindrance than a help.

Cold weather gear: Winter is cold, so warm sweaters, sturdy shoes, thick socks and a warm hat are necessary. It can also get cold in the summer, so it is best to be prepared.

Warm weather gear: Ireland can have really sunny days so remember your sun block and sunglasses. If you are heading to the coast, or to one of Ireland's many lakes, bring your swimming costume.

Comfortable shoes: Whether you are walking the streets of Ireland's cities, visiting its museums and historic sites, or trekking through some of its beautiful scenery, be sure to pack walking shoes and perhaps even walking boots for comfort. If you are out in the country or walking along the coast, bear in mind that many rural attractions, such as the Wild Atlantic Way, may involve walking over rough ground.

Casual clothes: Even the smartest hotels have a fairly casual dress code, so you won't need smart outfits unless you are attending a function.

Torch: This will be useful if you are staying in rural places or have to walk back from the pub along dark, unlit lanes.

Map: If you're travelling by car, the *AA Road Atlas Ireland* will be invaluable in getting you from A to B.

Dictionary: If you are planning to chat with the locals in remote villages, pack Collins *Easy Learning Irish Dictionary*, or, for a more irreverent take on the language, *The Feckin' Book of Irish Sayings*.

Suitcase space: Leave room for some souvenirs, especially a bottle or two of Irish whiskey.

Friendliness: The Irish are a friendly, talkative lot, so don't be surprised to find yourself in a spontaneous chat when you least expect it.

Musical instrument: If you play, then you may find yourself invited to join in an impromptu musical session held in pubs all over Ireland.

FESTIVALS & EVENTS

The island is host to a calendar of events that range from the cultural to the comical. The beautifully written book *A Year of Festivals: One Man's Journey Through Ireland's Festival Culture*, by Mark Graham, takes a closer look at Ireland's hundreds of festivals.

▶ MARCH

St Patrick's Festival, Dublin
stpatricksfestival.ie
St Patrick's Day on 17 March is a national holiday, and the festival in Dublin, with its parade, music, dancing and entertainment, is the best place to experience it.

▶ APRIL

Cathedral Quarter Arts Festival, Belfast
cqaf.com
This arts festival, at small venues around St Anne's Cathedral to the north of Belfast city centre, offers drama, readings, live music, visual arts, comedy and children's events.

▶ MAY

Deep RiverRock Belfast City Marathon
belfastcitymarathon.com
Belfast's marathon takes competitors on an undulating course through the city. It attracts thousands of serious athletes and fun-runners.

Fleadh Nua, Clare
fleadhnua.com
The county town of Clare plays host to the very best in Irish traditional music, song, concerts and dance.

Corona Fastnet Short Film Festival, Schull, County Cork
fastnetshortfilmfestival.com
Held in the picturesque fishing village of Schull, this festival screens short films from all over the world, and industry professionals are invited to share their knowledge with visiting film-makers.

International Literature Festival Dublin
ilfdublin.com
Some of the world's best writers gather here to debate, discuss and inspire.

Sky Cat Laughs Comedy Festival, Kilkenny

thecatlaughs.com

Considered by many to be one of the best comedy festivals in the world, Cat Laughs features five days of stand-up, movies and improvisation, with a superb line-up of talent.

▸ JUNE

Bloomsday Dublin

jamesjoyce.ie/bloomsday

James Joyce set his masterpiece *Ulysses* on 16 June 1904, the day he met Nora Barnacle, his wife and muse. Every year on 16 June, Joyce enthusiasts and academics celebrate the man and his works with tours, readings and seminars at the James Joyce Centre, at 35 North Great George's Street in Dublin.

Belfast Book Festival

belfastbookfestival.com

This week-long festival is a celebration of the city's love of books, with both national and international writers.

Westport International Sea Angling Festival

westportseaanglingfestival.eu

One of the best of its kind in Ireland, the festival takes place around the sheltered and well-stocked waters of Clew Bay.

▸ JULY

Galway International Arts Festival

giaf.ie

Music, plays, films, exhibitions, street parades and theatre are all part of this two-week festival.

Volvo Cork Week, Crosshaven, County Cork

corkweek.ie

One of the largest sailing events in Europe, this prestigious regatta takes place every two years. Events focus on the famous Yacht Club at Crosshaven.

Galway Races, Ballybrit Racecourse

galwayraces.com

Over seven consecutive days, this is the longest of all race meets in Ireland, with 51 races throughout the festival. They've been racing at Ballybrit for more than 100 years.

▸ AUGUST

Kilkenny Arts Festival

kilkennyarts.ie

A celebration of classical music, theatre, dance, literature, visual art and crafts. Many events take place in the historic venues of the lovely medieval city, including Kilkenny Castle.

Puck Fair, Killorglin

puckfair.ie

The Puck Fair is one of Ireland's oldest and most unusual street festivals, where a wild mountain goat is crowned King and reigns over the town for three days and nights. There's free concerts, music and dancing and much to entertain the kids.

Ukulele Hooley by the Sea, Dún Laoghaire

ukulelehooley.com

The world-renowned Ukulele Hooley in the seaside town of Dún Laoghaire is now one of Europe's most popular ukulele festivals.

Rose of Tralee International Festival

roseoftralee.ie

People are fond of this festival in Ireland, and it is more than just a beauty pageant. Vast numbers gather for one big party and the crowning of The Rose. The event began in 1959 and now has entries from around the world.

Lisdoonvarna Matchmaking Festival

matchmakerireland.com

This matchmaking festival is steeped in history, having been a tradition since 1887, when people flocked to the area during holiday seasons, and bachelor farmers would go in search of a wife. Over a century later, the annual festival has evolved into Europe's largest singles event. With the world's first LGBT matchmaking festival, The Outing, also taking place at Lisdoonvarna in October, there are opportunities for everyone to find their very own perfect match.

Dalkey Lobster Fest

Dalkey's annual lobster festival tickles taste buds with delectable local lobster and seafood, and soothes ears with silky smooth jazz music.

▶ SEPTEMBER

Bushmills Salmon and Whiskey Festival

The annual Bushmills Salmon and Whiskey Festival celebrates local culture, heritage and produce. Artisan stalls, street performers and, of course, whiskey and salmon tastings take place at various sites in the area.

Culture Night Belfast

culturenightbelfast.com

More than 200 artists, organisations and performers take to the city streets for a night in one of Belfast's biggest cultural festivals.

International Clown Festival, Downpatrick

Ireland's International Clown Festival rolls up in Downpatrick at the end of September. Entertainment for all ages is included in the line-up, so you'll see acrobats, stilt walkers, pantomimes and clown shows all performing over this fun four-day festival.

Aspects Irish Literature Festival, Bangor

aspectsfestival.com

Showcasing a wide range of Irish literary talent with readings, workshops, discussions and much more.

Galway International Oyster & Seafood Festival

galwayoysterfestival.com

Home to the World Oyster-Opening Championship, as well as much partying, music and the consumption of oysters and Guinness. It's held at the end of September to coincide with the oyster harvest.

▶ OCTOBER

Kinsale Gourmet Festival

kinsale.ie

This annual event is one of the oldest food festivals in Ireland. You can expect a range of food experiences and there's lots of emphasis on seafood.

Bram Stoker Festival, Dublin

bramstokerfestival.com

Dublin celebrates the life, work and legacy of horror novelist Bram Stoker and his Gothic novel *Dracula*, with film screenings, live music and even vampire make-up tutorials.

Guinness Cork Jazz Festival

guinnessjazzfestival.com

One of the best jazz festivals in Europe, attracting top musicians from all over the world.

Wexford Festival Opera

wexfordopera.com

Known for breathing new life into less well-known operas, the festival has been running for 60 years.

CAMPSITES

For more information on these and other campsites, visit theaa.com/self-catering-and-campsites

NORTHERN IRELAND

Ballyness Caravan Park ▷▷▷▷▷
ballynesscaravanpark.com
40 Castlecatt Road, Bushmills,
County Antrim, BT57 8TN
028 2073 2393 | Open 17 Mar–Oct
A quality park on farmland beside St Columb's Rill, the stream that supplies the nearby Bushmills Distillery. The friendly owners created this park with the discerning camper in mind and continue to invest year on year to enhance the customer experience. There is a pleasant walk around several ponds, and the park is peacefully located close to the beautiful north Antrim coast.

Castle Archdale Caravan Park & Camping Site ▶▶▶▶
castlearchdale.com
Lisnarick, Irvinestown, County Fermanagh, BT94 1PP | 028 6862 1333 | Open Apr–Oct
This park is located within the grounds of Castle Archdale Country Park on the shores of Lough Erne with stunning scenery and forest walks.

Causeway Coast Holiday Park
HOLIDAY CENTRE
hagansleisure.co.uk
21 Clare Road, Ballycastle, County Antrim, BT54 5DB | 028 2076 2550
Open Mar–Oct
This bustling holiday park is a great base for this unspoilt coastline, including the Giant's Causeway just 15 minutes away.

Dungannon Park ▶▶▶▶
midulstercouncil.org
Moy Road, Dungannon, County Tyrone, BT71 6DY | 028 8772 8690
Open Mar–Oct
A modern caravan park in a quiet area of a stunning public park with excellent facilities, especially for disabled visitors.

Lisnaskea Caravan Park ▶▶▶
Lisnaskea, County Fermanagh, BT92 0NZ | 028 6772 1040
Open Mar–Sep
A pretty riverside site set in peaceful countryside, with well-kept facilities and friendly owners. It's an ideal location for touring the lakes of Fermanagh. Fishing is available on the river.

REPUBLIC OF IRELAND

Boyle's Caravan Park ►►

Portnoo, County Donegal
074 9545131 | Open Mar–Oct
This open park sits among the sand dunes overlooking Narin Beach and close to a huge selection of water activities on a magnificent stretch of the Atlantic. There is an 18-hole golf links, and a cafe and shop at the entrance to the site. The park is very well maintained by the Boyle family.

Camac Valley Tourist Caravan & Camping Park ►►►►

camacvalley.com
Naas Road, Clondalkin, Dublin 22
01 4640644
A pleasant, lightly wooded park with good facilities, security and layout, within an hour's drive, or a bus ride, from the centre of Dublin.

Eagle Point Caravan and Camping Park ►►►►

eaglepointcamping.com
Ballylickey, Bantry | 027 50630
Open Apr–Sep
An immaculate park set in an idyllic position overlooking the rugged Bantry Bay and the mountains of West Cork. There are boat launching facilities, small and safe pebble beaches, a football field, tennis court, a small playground and TV rooms for children.

Garrettstown House Holiday Park ►►►►

garrettstownhouse.com
Ballinspittle, Kinsale, County Cork
021 4778156 | Open May–Sep
This elevated holiday park with tiered camping areas has superb panoramic views. There are plenty of on-site amenities, and it's close to the beach and forest park.

Knock Caravan and Camping Park ►►►►

knock-shrine.ie/accommodation
Claremorris Road, Knock, County Mayo | 094 9388100
Open Apr–Oct
A pleasant, very well maintained camping park within the grounds of Knock Shrine, offering spacious terraced pitches, excellent facilities and friendly staff.

Lough Key Caravan & Camping Park ►►►

loughkey.ie
Lough Key Forest Park, Boyle, County Roscommon | 071 9662212
Open Apr–Sep
A peaceful and very secluded site within the extensive grounds of a beautiful forest park. Lough Key offers boat trips and waterside walks, and there is a viewing tower.

Lough Lannagh Caravan Park ►►►►

loughlannagh.ie
Old Westport Road, Castlebar, County Mayo | 094 9027111
Open Mar–Aug
This park is part of the Lough Lannagh Village which is situated in a wooded area a short walk from Castlebar. Leisure facilities include tennis courts, boules, a children's play area and cafe.

A–Z of
Northern Ireland

VISIT THE MUSEUMS | GET OUTDOORS | EXPLORE BY BIKE | GO BACK IN TIME | TAKE A TRAIN RIDE | MEET THE WILDLIFE
TAKE IN SOME HISTORY | HIT THE BEACH | EAT AND DRINK | GET INDUSTRIAL | VISIT THE GALLERIES | GO CANOEING
TRY HORSE-RIDING | PLACES NEARBY | CATCH A PERFORMANCE | GO ROUND THE GARDENS | TAKE A BOAT TRIP

▶ Antrim Coast MAP REF 383 E1

Backed by the lovely, deeply wooded Glens of Antrim (see page 130), which run east and north to meet the Irish Sea, the coastline of County Antrim is one of the most beautiful and geologically diverse in the whole of Britain.

The coast is characterised by alternating sandy bays, rocky shores, high cliffs and forbidding rocky headlands, which combine to produce the dramatic scenery. Inland, the beautiful wooded glens rise to meet dizzying moorland heights.

Gorgeous geology

The complex geology of the Antrim Coast is a virtual textbook of the geology of the whole of the United Kingdom. In its astonishing variety, it is as comprehensive as anywhere in Britain, ranging from relatively recent volcanic activity several millenia ago – represented by the massive basalt moorland plateau – to the silvery schists in the northwest, which are about 250 million years older. It includes rocks laid down more than 500 million years ago on an ancient ocean floor, pudding-stone that was later a desert floor, a belt of coal formed out of a swampy delta, salt trapped in the stone 200 million years ago, and mudstones and limestones from the time of the dinosaurs.

In between are rich red sandstones, grey clays and unexpectedly dazzling cliffs of white chalk. This fascinating mixture is best seen at Fair Head and Murlough Bay (see page 64), where, in startling contrast, the chalk cliffs overlie the older red Triassic sandstones.

The Antrim Coast and Glens were designated an Area of Outstanding Natural Beauty (AONB) in 1988, and form the second-largest AONB in Northern Ireland, covering 280 square

▲ Waterfoot, Glenariff

miles. The Antrim Coast was shaped by Ice Age glaciers and the subsequent fluctuating level of the sea, which is marked by raised beaches like those at Southbay, near Glencloy. Other features – sea stacks like the White Lady, north of Garron Point, and the now high-and-dry caves in the red sandstone cliffs at Red Bay – were sculpted by the pounding of the waves.

Among the many features of geological interest along the coast are the cliffs of basalt overlying limestone from Larne to Red Bay; the great volcanic sill in the chalk of Fair Head; the similarly volcanic North Star Dyke at Ballycastle; the rich red sandstones around Cushendall; and the caves in the conglomerate rocks at Cushendun.

Seabird colonies

The shoreline is also a rich environment for marine plant, animal and bird life. Low-lying Rathlin Island (see page 79), separated from the Antrim Coast by Rathlin Sound, is famous for its seabird colonies. Hundreds of thousands of guillemots, razorbills and puffins breed on its low chalk cliffs and sea stacks, while fulmars soar off the cliffs near Glenarm.

With good visibility, the views from the coast extend east to the Mull of Kintyre and Ailsa Craig off the Scottish coast, while northwards the islands of Arran, Islay and Jura can be seen. At the narrowest point of the North Channel at Torr Head, you are just a dozen miles from the Scottish mainland.

Fragile habitat

Inland, the plateau rises to summits including Trostan, the highest point at 1,804 feet (551m), Slieveanorra (1,667 feet/ 508m) and the Carncormick range at 1,431 feet (436m). Rocky

Slemish (1,434 feet/438m) rises above the enclosed farmlands of the Braid Valley in the south.

Generally, the plateau forms a series of rugged hills, shallow valleys and internationally rare blanket peat bogs. It is an exposed and desolate area, appreciated by those seeking solitude and tranquillity. Heathers and grasses tolerant of the harsh conditions cover the hilltops, along with a uniquely specialised group of plants and animals. In some places, insectivorous plants, such as butterwort and sundew, supplement the soil's poor nutrients by trapping and absorbing flies, and, in the wettest boggy hollows, peat-forming sphagnum mosses dominate dark pools.

The peat, or turf, was used locally as a source of fuel, and it is still hand-cut in the traditional way in many of the glens, where the scars of peat banks are evident. However, the mechanised cutting that is increasingly used today is damaging this fragile habitat.

Some of these areas have been protected as National Nature Reserves (NNRs) or Forest Nature Reserves (FNRs), for example at Slieveanorra (see page 64) and Beaghs. But much of the upland area is still extensively grazed by sheep, and large tracts have been planted with coniferous forest, as at Slieveanorra, Breen, Glenariff (see page 131), Ballycastle, Ballypatrick and Ballyboley.

▼ Murlough Bay

Monuments and castles

The larger stone monuments, such as Ossian's Grave in Glenaan and Glenmakeeran in Ballypatrick Forest, date from the neolithic period, while later structures, such as raths (defended farmsteads), cashels (stone-built forts), crannogs (man-made islands) and souterrains (underground chambers), survive from early Christian times (*c* AD 400). Medieval ruins include the friary at Bonamargy, near Ballycastle; Red Bay Castle at Cushendall; Castle Carra at Cushendun; and Bruce's Castle on Rathlin Island (see page 79). The 17th-century castle at Glenarm remains the private residence of the Earls of Antrim, while Ballygally Castle is now a hotel.

Centres of conservation

The five major settlements of the Antrim Coast – Cushendall, Ballycastle, Glenarm, Cushendun and Carnlough – are conservation areas full of architectural interest and history.

Sometimes referred to as the Capital of the Glens, Cushendall is one of the prettiest villages on the coast, its distinctive architecture associated with Clough Williams-Ellis, who designed Portmeirion in North Wales. Cushendall is watched over by the medieval Curfew Tower. Famous for its Lammas fair, characterful Ballycastle includes many fine shopfronts along Ann Street, Castle Street and The Diamond.

▼ Ossian's Grave

TAKE IN SOME HISTORY
Bonamargy Friary
see page 78

Castle Carra
Torr Road, Cushendun, County
Antrim | Open daily 24 hours
This 13th- or 14th-century
tower house, built over a
mesolithic flint working site,
became an infants' cemetery at
the end of the medieval period.
Close by lie a number of early
Bronze Age standing stones.

Red Bay Castle
Cushendall
Ballymena, Moyle, County Antrim
BT44 0SH
Perched on a headland jutting
into the sea north of Glenariff,
the ruins date from the
mid-1600s when the castle was
destroyed by Oliver Cromwell.
Below the castle is a cave,
thought to have been used
as an escape route.

GET OUTDOORS
**Slieveanorra National Nature
Reserve**
8 miles southwest of Cushenden
High on the slopes of
Slieveanorra Mountain, four
plots of peat bog in various
stages of the development,
formation and erosion process
are the main feature of this
nature reserve, where peat-
loving flora and fauna thrives.
The peat bed is very fragile and
it's a dangerous place to visit
due to the deep swallow holes.

GO BACK IN TIME
Ossian's Grave
see page 131

▶ **PLACES NEARBY**
The Glens of Antrim (see page
130) are just inland, and you can
visit Glenariff Forest Park (see
page 131). Carnfunnock
Country Park (see page 106) is
further south, overlooking the
Irish Sea. Head north for the
lovely Murlough Bay, then west
for Ballycastle (see page 78).

Murlough Bay
You have to walk a section of
the Ulster Way cliff path to
reach Murlough Bay, so it's
rarely crowded. The curved bay
is book-ended by Torr Head and
Fair Head, with a mostly rocky
shore beneath green slopes and
woods. Sheltered by cliffs, it
has rich plant life, from orchids
to sea thrift, and birds such as
peregrines and buzzards. There
are the remnants of old lime
kilns and of Drumnakill Church,
where Independence activist
Sir Roger Casement, executed
in 1916 for his part in the Easter
Rising (see page 26), had asked
to be buried (though he is
actually buried in Dublin).

◀ Bonamargy Friary

▶ Ards Peninsula and Strangford Lough MAP REF 383 F3

Filled with small farms and fishing villages, the Ards Peninsula has always been a place apart from the mainstream, and Strangford Lough shares its feeling of isolation. The scatter of islands in the lough, some accessible by causeways known only to locals, made ideal defensive positions for early settlers, and the pioneer Christians also found them safe havens. The Ards was a busy place – Donaghadee served as Ulster's main entry port from Britain – but now the area is a very peaceful place.

The peninsula hangs off the shoulder of County Down like a long, outward-crooked arm and stretches south for some 25 miles, edged with a fine sweep of coastline. From the pretty seaside resort of Bangor (see page 80) you follow the A2 to Donaghadee, Ulster's chief passenger port from the 16th to the 19th centuries. Boats ran from Portpatrick in Scotland, and the big harbour, with its lighthouse and Georgian houses, speaks of its past importance. Eventually, the Stranraer–Larne ferry route overtook the Portpatrick–Donaghadee service, and it stopped in 1849.

Easy access east and west
Strangford Lough and the Ards Peninsula are located just to the east of Belfast and are easily reached by road from the city.

▼ Strangford Lough

The A2 road runs east from Belfast through Bangor before turning south along the outer Ards coast through a string of east-facing seaside villages, and down to Portaferry at the southern tip. Here it meets the A20, which has come from Belfast through Newtownards, and then goes south along the inner, or Strangford Lough, shore of the Ards Peninsula by way of Mount Stewart (see page 69) and Grey Abbey (see page 71).

The A22 Downpatrick to Belfast road follows the landward or western shore of Strangford Lough. The A25 from Downpatrick links to the A2/A20 at the southern tip of the Ards Peninsula by way of the Portaferry–Strangford ferry.

Beaches and fishing villages

The switchback coast road runs beside a shoreline of sandy beaches, passing through Ballywalter, Ballyhalbert and the fishing village of Portavogie. Stop here to sample some fresh Portavogie prawns before continuing to Cloughey, where you turn off to Kearney, a former fishing village that has been carefully restored to an unlikely but beautiful neatness by the National Trust.

Strangford Lough

The huge 72-square-mile Strangford Lough is a virtually landlocked area of the Irish Sea, stretching north from Strangford to Newtownards. It is a fine example of a ria (drowned estuary), caused by rising sea levels at the end of the Ice Age, and it is dotted with some 70 small islands, actually the highest points of drowned drumlins (small rounded hills) that were formed of material left behind by those Ice Age glaciers. Many of the lough's islands, such as Chapel Island, South Island and Mahee Island, are now owned and managed by the National Trust.

Designated in 1972, the Area of Outstanding Natural Beauty is centred here, separated from the Irish Sea by a 500-yard-wide gap, known as the Narrows, the straits between Portaferry and Strangford. A flush of tides pours through this tiny gap twice a day.

Strangford Lough is internationally important for the large flocks of wintering wildfowl that congregate on the extensive mudflats surrounding its shores. About 9 square miles of the lough are a designated reserve for this reason. There are other reserves at Dorn, on the eastern shore of the lough, and Ballyquintin Point, the shingle promontory that creates the southern tip of the Portavogie peninsula.

▶ Scrabo Tower, Newtownards

◀ Arctic tern

Birds and wildlife
These rich feeding grounds support a wide variety of wildfowl, including pale-bellied Brent geese, with two-thirds of the species' European population overwintering here. Also present are mute and whooper swans, wigeon, shelduck and shoveler, as well as waders, including knot, dunlin, curlew, bar-tailed godwit, oystercatcher and redshank. In addition, some of the lough's 16 major islands are breeding sites for sandwich, roseate, common and arctic terns. Other aquatic residents include seals and porpoises. This abundance of wildlife makes the AONB an important site for biodiversity; both Strangford Lough and Dundrum Bay are protected European conservation sites.

One good tern...
The four species of tern – the sandwich, roseate, common and arctic – which raise their young during the summer on the islands of Strangford Lough are among the avian world's greatest travellers.

The arctic tern, for example, travels around 10,000 miles north from the Antarctic pack ice as far as the Arctic Circle (Ireland marks the southern edge of its breeding range), virtually circumnavigating the globe and enjoying eight to nine months of perpetual daylight each year. Named after the Kent seaside town, the sandwich tern is the largest and heaviest of the British terns and has a huge oceanic range, stretching from western Canada to India. The roseate tern, so-called because of the rosy flush on the breasts of adults in spring, spends its winters in West Africa. The common tern, also known as the sea swallow, is a bird of the temperate regions, and is widely distributed over Europe, Asia and North America.

Hills and farmland
The shores of Strangford Lough form a pleasantly rolling landscape of well-tended farmland. At the northern end of the lough, the 394-foot-high Scrabo Hill is a prominent feature of the landscape. Perched on top is a tower (see page 71) built in honour of the third Marquess of Londonderry, with extensive views over the water. Mount Stewart House (see opposite), seat of the Marquess of Londonderry, and now in the care of the National Trust, overlooks the eastern shores of the lough.

▶ Mount Stewart MAP REF 383 F3

nationaltrust.org.uk

Newtownards, County Down, BT22 2AD

028 4278 8387 | See website for opening times

Mount Stewart, on the eastern shore of Strangford Lough, is the ancestral home of the Stewart family, marquesses of Londonderry. The Stewarts were major players in British and Irish politics, and the atmosphere in their fine 18th-century mansion is a mixture of the grand and the homely.

A tour of the house starts in the pink-and-white galleried central hall. Look for the tail of the racehorse Hermit, which hangs beside his portrait here. Hermit won the Derby in 1867, causing the Marquis of Hastings, an enemy of Hermit's owner Henry Chaplin, to lose £120,000 on a wager. From here, you move through the

▼ Mount Stewart House and its gardens

richly appointed dining room, the study, the drawing room with its Aubusson carpets and huge pier glasses, the Rome Bedroom looking out over the terrace and Italian garden, a room full of copper pans and knife machines, the library with its signed volumes by Sean O'Casey, the sitting room lit by a ship-shaped crystal chandelier, and a wonderful music room whose floor inlay is mirrored by the pattern of the plaster ceiling. Between the sitting room and music room you'll find a charming detail of domestic life – the door jamb against which the growing Stewart children measured their respective heights in the 1920s. You can see their progress, neatly ruled in pencil.

Mount Stewart has been in the hands of the Stewart family (later Vane-Tempest-Stewart) since 1744, when Alexander Stewart (1699–1781) bought the estate, then known as Mount Pleasant, apparently with money acquired through sales of linen. His son, Robert Stewart, became the first Marquess of Londonderry and, after his death in 1821, the house was left to his son, also Robert, Viscount Castlereagh, a prominent Tory politician.

The next owner of the house was his half-brother, Charles, third Marquess of Londonderry (1778–1854), who married the heiress Lady Frances-Anne Vane-Tempest and spent a considerable £150,000 on the refurbishment and enlargement of the newly named Mount Stewart. Charles was also largely responsible for the elegant, 11-bay and porticoed Georgian house we see today.

The estate is especially known for its gardens, where rare and beautiful plants thrive on all sides. The gardens were laid out between the 1920s and the 1950s with verve, imagination and more than a dash of eccentricity by Edith, Lady Londonderry. An early 20th-century Tory hostess, she had a coiled snake daringly tattooed on her leg and a circle of friends both great and raffish.

The formal gardens, which include the Shamrock Garden, the Sunken Garden, the Spanish Garden and the Italian Garden, have a strong Mediterranean feel about them, while the wooded areas support plants from all over the world.

In a pond in Lady Mairi's Garden there's a 'Mary, Mary, Quite Contrary' statue, surrounded, as in the nursery rhyme, by silver bells and cockle shells.

The Dodo Terrace is decorated with freakish animal sculptures such as dodos and griffins, and the Red Hand of Ulster is planted in red daisies and begonias. Water gardens, formal gardens, woods and dells lead on to the Land of the Fairies, and also to the Temple of the Winds, a Georgian banqueting hall on a hillock looking out over Strangford Lough.

Growing in the grounds of Mount Stewart is the Fitzroya tree (Fitzroya cupressoides), one of the oldest living trees in the world and a native of Chile.

TAKE IN SOME HISTORY
Grey Abbey
Church Street, Greyabbey, County
Down, BT22 2NQ | 028 9181 1491
Open daily 24 hours

Grey Abbey was founded in 1193
by Affreca, wife of the Norman
Lord of Ards, Sir John de
Courcy. Then, only 20 years
after the Norman invasion,
Irish-born monks were thought
to be too sympathetic to local
warlords so Grey Abbey's first
monks were brought from
Cumbria in northwest England.
The ruins by the shore include
a recreated herb garden.

Mount Stewart
see highlight panel on page 69

CLIMB A TOWER
Scrabo Tower
doeni.gov.uk/niea203A
Scrabo Road, Newtownards,
County Down, BT23 4SJ

If you want the chance to see a
memorable view, climb the 122
steps to the top of Scrabo Tower
at the summit of Scrabo Hill.
The tower, visible from miles
away, was erected in 1857 by
the tenants of Charles Stewart,
third Marquis of Londonderry,
to commemorate his attempts
to alleviate suffering during the
Great Famine. The tower was
restored and stabilised in 2015
and now, from the viewing
platform some 135 feet up, you
can enjoy a fabulous view over
the Ards Peninsula and the
waters of Strangford Lough,
south to the Mountains of
Mourne and east across the
sea to the Scottish hills.

PAMPER YOURSELF
Pure Day Spa
puredayspa.com
48a Ballybunden Road, Killinchy,
County Down, BT23 6RF | 028 9754
3000 | Open Mon–Thu 9–8, Fri–Sat
9–6, Sun by appointment

Pure is a rural day retreat that
offers a comprehensive range
of relaxing treatments. The
service is highly personalised.

▼ Grey Abbey

▲ Castle Espie Wetland Centre

PLAY A ROUND
Clandeboye Golf Club
cgc-ni.com
Newtownards, County Down, BT23
3PN | 028 9127 1767
Here there is a parkland and
heathland course. The Dufferin
is the championship course
and offers a tough challenge
demanding extreme accuracy,
with gorse, bracken and
strategically placed trees
that flank every hole. The
Ava complements the Dufferin
perfectly; accuracy is the key
on this course, with small
targets and demanding tee
shots. There are outstanding
panoramic views.

EAT AND DRINK
Balloo House
balloohouse.com
1 Comber Road, Killinchy,
Newtownards, County Down,
BT23 5NE | 028 9754 1210
This is a lively bistro and serene
dining room in a venerable old
house. The man in charge
here is Danny Millar and he's
something of a TV star these
days, with stints on the BBC's

Saturday Kitchen and *The Great
British Menu*. But you'll usually
find him behind the stoves at
this former farmhouse close
to Strangford Lough.

▸ **PLACES NEARBY**
Nearby visitor attractions
include country parks; one of
Europe's largest aquariums
and seal sanctuaries; a birder's
paradise, the Strangford Lough
Wildlife Centre at Castle Ward
(see page 107); and the Quoile
Pondage Countryside Centre.

Castle Espie Wetland Centre
wwt.org.uk
78 Ballydrain Road, County Down,
BT23 6EA | 028 9187 4146
Open daily Jul–Aug 10.30–5.30,
Feb–Jun, Sep–Oct 10.30–5, Nov–Jan
10.30–4.30
Here is the largest number of
native and exotic waterbirds in
Ireland. Spot bats and migrant
birds and don't miss the spring
duckery tour.

Delamont Country Park
discovernorthernireland.com
Clanmaghery Road, Downpatrick,

County Down, BT30 7DE | 028 4482 8333 | Park: open daily 9–dusk; Railway: Jul, Aug daily 12–5, Mar–Jun, Sep, Oct Sat, Sun 12–5

As well as fine views across the lough to the Mourne Mountains, this park has a campsite and plenty going on for families, including a miniature railway.

Exploris

exploris.org.uk

The Ropewalk, Portaferry, County Down, BT22 1NZ | 028 4272 8062 Open Apr–Aug Mon–Fri 10–6, Sat 11–6, Sun 12–6, Sep–Mar Mon–Fri 10–5, Sat 11–5, Sun 1–5

This aquarium is popular with families. Expert guides tell of the enormous marine riches of Strangford Lough in an easy-to-understand way.

Quoile Pondage Countryside Centre

ni-environment.gov.uk

5 Quay Road, Downpatrick, County Down, BT30 7JB | 028 4461 5520 The bird hide overlooking the freshwater lake offers great birdwatching opportunities. A variety of birds visit according to the season: summer sees breeding wildfowl and geese, while in the other months bird life such as ducks and widgeon are prevalent.

Scrabo Country Park

discovernorthernireland.com

203A Scrabo Road, Newtownards, County Down, BT23 4SJ | 028 3885 3955 | Open daily dawn–dusk Free entry to walk the many paths and enjoy the views.

▼ View from Scrabo Tower

▶ Armagh MAP REF 383 D4

Handsome Georgian buildings and two splendid cathedrals greet visitors to Armagh. One of the oldest cities in Ireland, this little grey-roofed city was the capital of Ulster, and the seat of both Catholic and Anglican Bishops of Ireland.

The two great cathedrals are the most eye-catching and significant buildings in town but the city has several other enjoyable attractions. On English Street near the neat Georgian Mall, St Patrick's Trian has displays on Armagh's links with the saint, the story of the city itself, and *Gulliver's Travels* (the book's author, Jonathan Swift, spent a lot of time in Armagh). The Planetarium on College Hill is a popular tourist attraction.

TAKE IN SOME HISTORY

The Anglican Cathedral of St Patrick

stpatricks-cathedral.org
Cathedral Close, Armagh, County Armagh BT61 7EE | Open daily Apr–Oct 10–5, Nov–Mar 10–4

This is the smaller and older of the two cathedrals. Its largely 19th-century exterior of pink sandstone conceals parts of a mid-13th-century cathedral, which was preceded by other churches going back to AD 444 when St Patrick himself built the first church on this site. Highlights include the various gargoyles and stone-carved grotesques on the walls both inside and out. The Chapter House contains the Iron Age effigy called the Tandragee Man. Brian Boru, the High King of Ireland, killed in 1014 at the Battle of Clontarf, lies buried beneath the north transept.

Roman Catholic Cathedral of St Patrick

armagharchdiocese.org
Cathedral Road, Armagh, County Arnagh, BT61 7QY | 028 3752 2045
Open Mon–Sat 10–5

Across the valley, on Cathedral Road, are the two huge rocket-like towers of this Cathedral. The interior is an unrestrained Gothic burst of mosaic, marble and golden angels on the wing. Construction of the building, funded chiefly through public subscription, bazaars and raffles, started in 1838 but was halted during the Great Famine of the 1840s. It was finally completed and dedicated in August 1873. The long-case clock in the cathedral was first prize in one of the raffles held to raise money for construction, and is still waiting to be claimed by the person who won it – in 1865.

Navan Centre and Fort

armagh.co.uk/navan-centre-fort
81 Killylea Road, Armagh, County Armagh, BT60 4LD | 028 3752 9644
Open daily Apr–Sep 10–6.30, Jan–Mar, Oct–Dec 10–4

For a fuller history of Armagh and its county, head to the Navan Centre, where characters in costume and audio-visual displays and exhibits bring this important archaeological site to life.

VISIT THE LIBRARY
Armagh Public Library
armaghpubliclibrary.arm.ac.uk
43 Abbey Street, Armagh,
County Armagh, BT61 7DY
028 3752 3142 | Open Mon–Fri
10–1, 2–4, other times by
appointment
Northern Ireland's oldest library dates from 1771, and is an independent research library and museum. Among its collection is a first-edition *Gulliver's Travels* marked up by Swift himself. Nearby, at No. 5 Vicars' Hill, is The Registry, an impressive building once inside that displays many of the beautiful artefacts from the library's collections.

CATCH A PERFORMANCE
Market Place Theatre & Arts Centre
marketplacearmagh.com
Market Street, Armagh, County
Armagh, BT61 7BW
028 3752 1821
This state-of-the-art facility for visual and performing arts has everything from theatre to children's shows. There's late-night entertainment on Fridays and Saturdays.

GO TO A MARKET
The Shambles Market
shamblesmarket.com
Cathedral Road, Armagh, County
Armagh, BT61 7AT | 028 3752 8192
Open Tue, Fri 10–6
Everything from radishes to ribbons are sold at this traditional variety market.

▼ St Patrick's Roman Catholic Cathedral

EAT AND DRINK

4 Vicars

4vicars.com

4 Vicars' Hill, Armagh, County
Armagh, BT61 7ED | 028 3752 7772

A modern restaurant offering
a full menu of seasonal fare,
including Sunday lunch. Visit
for a high tea of home-made
scones and cake.

McKenna's

21 Lower English Street, Armagh,
County Armagh, BT61 7LJ

028 3752 6492

This drinking place has been
owned by the McKenna family
since 1884: the current
proprietors are the fifth
generation. It's located in the
Shambles, right in the heart
of Armagh, and appeals to
both young and old.

Uluru

ulurubistro.com

3–5 Market Street, Armagh, County
Armagh, BT61 7BW

028 3751 8051

This modern local restaurant
and grill caters for everyone
from kids to vegetarians. It has
an Australian twist.

▶ PLACES NEARBY

The countryside around Armagh
contains two National Trust
properties, as well as estate
parkland and several nature
reserves. Lough Neagh (see
page 139) is to the northeast.

Ardress House

nationaltrust.org.uk

64 Ardress Road, Portadown, County
Armagh, BT62 1SQ | 028 8778 4753

House and farm: opening times
vary, check website. Lady's Mile
Walk: daily dawn–dusk

Dublin architect George Ensor
acquired Ardress by marriage
in 1760 and set about
transforming the 17th-century
farmhouse into a neoclassical
country house. He added a new
wing, a matching mock wing on
the other side and an imposing
frontage. You can still see the
original farmhouse roof peeping
over the gables and urns of the
Georgian extension. Inside,
there's stucco work in the
drawing room, fine Chippendale
furniture and Waterford crystal.
Outside is geared towards
family fun. The cobbled
18th-century farmyard attached
to the house has a collection of
agricultural tools and a variety
of farm animals, and there's a
children's play area. The walled
garden has old Irish roses, and
the orchard has old Irish apple
varieties. Farther afield,
footpaths lead through the
woods and along the Tall River.

The Argory

nationaltrust.org.uk

144 Derrycaw Road, Moy,
Dungannon, County Armagh,
BT71 6NA | Signposted off M1 at
Junction 14 | 028 8778 4753

See website for opening times

This handsome country house
in its 320 acres by the River
Blackwater presents a picture
of a well-to-do Anglo-Irish
home immediately before
Independence. Built in 1824 by
Walter McGeogh, it is entered
through a fine wide portico. The

hall, with its massive cast-iron stove, plunges visitors into the Edwardian era. Portraits hang on the walls of the reception rooms; a Steinway grand piano stands in the drawing room. Up the curved staircase is a barrel organ that was an original fixture of the house; it is played once a month (telephone for dates). There is no electricity, and lamps diffuse the soft yellow light of acetylene gas from the plant installed in the stables in 1906. Inspect the gas plant and the horse carriages in the stable yard, and then go on through the formal gardens and along the riverbank footpaths.

Gosford Forest Park

nidirect.gov.uk
7 Gosford Demesne, Markethill, County Armagh, BT60 1GD
028 3755 1277

The Gosford estate, former seat of the Acheson family, has strong literary connections. Dean Swift used to visit, as he inferred in his poem 'Lady Acheson Weary of the Dean'. Today, the estate forms Gosford Forest Park, with an arboretum, walled garden and waymarked trails. The grand mock-Norman castle has been converted to private residential use.

Peatlands Park

nidirect.gov.uk
33 Derryhubbert Road, Dungannon, County Armagh, BT71 6NW | 028 3839 9195 | Open daily 24 hours (car park Apr–May 9–7, Jun to mid-Sep 9–9, mid-Sep to Oct 9–7, Nov–Mar 9–4.30)

Peatlands Park, close to the southern shores of Lough Neagh, was specifically established to promote and facilitate awareness about peatland and the issues such areas face. It was the first park of its type in the British Isles.

The peat here has been forming for about 10,000 years. The site was acquired in 1978 from the Irish Peat Development Company (IPDC) and the park was officially opened in 1990. Visitors can explore the 655-acre site on foot along almost 10 miles of paths and wooden walkways, observing natural habitats as well as watching traditional turf-cutting techniques. There is plentiful wildlife and two National Nature Reserves within the park.

▼ Bog snorkelling at Peatlands Park

▶ Ballycastle   MAP REF 383 E1

Retaining the appearance of an old-fashioned, Georgian
seaside resort, Ballycastle is a convenient base for exploring
the Antrim Coast and Glens. Lammastide (the last Monday and
Tuesday of August) is the best time to come, for the Auld
Lammas Fair. Held since 1606, it is Ballycastle's great social
event, with music, dancing, street entertainment, food markets
and more. You're guaranteed tastings of two local delicacies:
yellowman (a kind of toffee) and dulse (an edible seaweed).

TAKE IN SOME HISTORY
Bonamargy Friary
Just south of Ballycastle on the
Cushendall Road
Built in 1500, the friary's
cloister, gatehouse, altar and
church are well preserved.
Other features include the
east window, a staircase and a
sealed burial vault. It's the final
resting place of several Earls of
Ulster and the reclusive Black
Nun, Julia McQuillan.

VISIT THE MUSEUM
Ballycastle Museum
nimc.co.uk
59 Castle Street, Ballycastle, County
Antrim, BT54 6AS | 028 2076 2024
Open Jul–Aug Mon–Sat 10–6,
Sun 2–6
To get the most out of your
explorations, learn all about
the area's history and culture
in this well-kept museum.

HEAD FOR THE BAY
Murlough Bay
see page 64

PLAY A ROUND
Ballycastle Golf Club
ballycastlegolfclub.com
2 Cushendall Road, Ballycastle,
County Antrim, BT54 6QP
028 2076 2536

A mix of terrain beside the sea,
lying at the foot of one of the
nine glens of Antrim, this
course has magnificent views.
The first five holes are parkland
with natural hazards; the
middle holes are links type and
the rest are on adjacent upland.

EAT AND DRINK
House of McDonnell
71 Castle Street, Ballycastle, County
Antrim, BT54 6AS | 07711 668 797
Established in 1766, this
traditional pub is one of the
oldest in County Antrim. You'll
find a warm welcome and
traditional music every Friday
night, with folk on Saturdays.

▶ PLACES NEARBY
There's an open farm between
Ballycastle and Cushendun,
great for a family day out. Catch
a ferry from Ballycastle and
head for the beautiful island of
Rathlin, 25 minutes away. You'll
find Loughareema, the strange
lake (see page 30), nearby too.

Watertop Open Farm
watertopfarm.co.uk
188 Cushendall Road, Ballypatrick,
Ballycastle, County Antrim, BT54
6RN | 028 2076 2576
Open daily Jul–Aug 11–5.30

▲ Rathlin Island

At this large cattle and sheep farm in the Glens of Antrim, the activities on offer include pony trekking and boating, and there are scenic walks in the surrounding area. You can also watch shearing demonstrations and visit an interesting farm museum.

Rathlin Island

rathlinballycastleferry.com
028 2076 0062
Rathlin Island has a distinctive L-shape, and a reputation as one of the friendliest of Ireland's islands. It's a good idea to rent a bicycle (reserve it in advance in peak season) to explore the island, which measures 5 miles by 3 miles. Out at the west end, the Kebble Cliffs National Nature Reserve is the largest and most remarkable cliff-nesting site in Northern Ireland – the cliffs are home to some 250,000 seabirds during the nesting season (Apr–Aug). During these months the spectacular viewing point is open under supervision (telephone beforehand to make sure the warden is there).

Bruce's Castle

Rathlin Island | Take the ferry from Ballycastle
There's really not very much to see of this ruin, which dates from before 1306, when Robert the Bruce spent the winter here. Bruce's Cave, also on the island, is allegedly where he watched the spider that inspired him to make a renewed effort to defeat the English. The castle was attacked by English forces in the 16th century, resulting in the Rathlin Island Massacre.

Kebble Cliffs National Nature Reserve

Rathlin Island, Ballycastle, County Antrim | 028 7035 9963

At the western end of the island, sheer cliffs rise 300 feet above raised beaches, while towering stacks of rock stand guard just offshore. The best time to visit the nature reserve is early May to mid-July, the height of the breeding season for many seabirds. The cliffs are crowded with thousands of fulmars, guillemots, kittiwakes and razorbills, while puffins nest in burrows dug into the cliffside grassland. Ravens, peregrine falcons and buzzards also nest on the cliff ledges. If you want to see the orchids, early summer is best, and the heathlands are in full flower in August. There's also a lake, with marshland attracting waterfowl such as coots, snipe, ducks and grebes. You'll probably see grey seals, too.

Cushleake House B&B

32 Quay Road, Ballycastle, BT54 6BH | 028 2076 3798

As well as offering accommodation, bikes are available to hire from here, as well as on Rathlin Island.

▶ Bangor   MAP REF 383 F3

With picturesque seafront promenades, a charming marina and lovely shops and restaurants, Bangor in County Down, just 12 miles from Belfast, is regularly voted the most desirable place to live in Northern Ireland. Its varied history is reflected in some of the attractions here.

This seaside town on the south side of Belfast Lough largely dates from the Victorian era with some historic buildings as well as some more modern development. It has one of the largest open-air markets in Northern Ireland and a pretty promenade walk that leads from the town centre to the impressive marina, where you can watch the many boats and water sports.

▼ Bangor Marina

TAKE IN SOME HISTORY
Bangor Abbey
Abbey Street and Newtownards
Road, Bangor, County Down,
BT20 4JB | 028 9127 0069
Open Jul–Aug Wed–Fri 2–4
St Comgall founded Bangor
Abbey in AD 558 and it grew to
be one of the most important
seats of learning in Ireland,
with almost 3,000 monks. The
main building dates from the
1830s but the tower is 15th
century. The churchyard has
many interesting gravestones,
including a memorial to John
Edward Simpson, the assistant
surgeon of the *Titanic*. Tours
should be booked via the tourist
information office.

GO ROUND THE GARDENS
Bangor Castle Walled Gardens
Valentine Road, Bangor, County
Down, BT20 4BN | 028 9127 0069
Open daily Apr–Oct 10–5.30
This beautiful garden has been
restored to its original 1840
glory and is open to the public
after years of being a lost
garden. It has a kitchen garden,
herb and topiary garden,
swamp and flower garden.

ENTERTAIN THE FAMILY
Pickie Fun Park
pickiefunpark.com
Marine Gardens, The Promenade,
Bangor, County Down, BT20 3JR
028 9145 0746 | Open Easter–Oct
daily 10–10, Nov–Easter Sat–Sun
10–dusk
For family fun, visit Pickie Fun
Park. Activities include rides on
floating swans, mini karts and
an adventure playground.

GET ACTIVE
Bangor Aurora Aquatic and Leisure Centre
bangoraurora.com
3 Valentine Road, Bangor, County
Down, BT20 4TH | 028 9127 0271
Swimming pools, fully equipped
health and fitness suites,
a great range of the latest
exercise classes and everything
from squash to a children's soft
adventure play area make this
an excellent wet-weather option
for all the family.

GO SHOPPING
Bangor Market
Castle Square, Bangor, County Down,
BT20 4SP | Open Wed 7–1
One of the largest open-air
markets in Northern Ireland,
this has over 50 stalls and
celebrated its 90th anniversary
in 2014.

Bookends
bookendsbangor.co.uk
Railway Terrace, Dufferin Avenue,
Bangor, County Down, BT20 3BX
028 9122 9783 | Open Mon–Sat
10–5
This is probably the largest
second-hand bookshop in
Northern Ireland, with over
40,000 titles. Subjects cover a
wide range, from local history
and Irish fiction to current
best-sellers, as well as
hard-to-find collectables.

PLAY A ROUND
Bangor Golf Club
bangorgolfclubni.co.uk
Bangor Golf Club, Broadway, Bangor,
County Down, BT20 4RH
028 9127 0922

This attractive golf course is a great place for Sunday lunch and the golf course has lovely views of Belfast Lough, the Irish Sea and the Antrim Hills.

EAT AND DRINK

The Boathouse Restaurant
⚝⚝⚝

theboathouseni.co.uk
1a Seacliff Road, Bangor, County Down, BT20 5HA | 028 9146 9253
Creative, complex cooking is the name of the game here. Housed in the stone-built Victorian harbourmaster's office by the marina, this pint-sized restaurant certainly punches above its weight. Spread over two floors with views of yachts bobbing at anchor, vaulted ceilings and local art on whitewashed stone walls, this charming place hums with the sound of contented diners.

Donegan's
donegansrestaurant.co.uk
37–39 High Street, Bangor, County Down, BT20 5BE | 028 9146 3928
Billing itself as a taste of the country in the centre of town, at this pub you can step back in time to enter an interior filled with items from Ireland's rich history and enjoy good food from morning to night.

Jenny Watts
jennywattsbar.com
41 High Street, Bangor, County Down, BT20 5BE | 028 9127 0401
Bangor's oldest pub is also one of its liveliest. Enjoy live jazz day and night and a friendly atmosphere. The place tends to attract a youngish crowd; there's a lower bar with live ambient music and a relaxing beer garden for lazing on a sunny afternoon.

▶ PLACES NEARBY

Nearby Newtownards has a World War I heritage centre and an arts centre. There are good pubs in Donaghadee and Groomsport. Crawfordsburn Country Park makes a great day out. Belfast (see page 84) and Strangford Lough (see page 65) are also close by.

Somme Heritage Centre
sommeassociation.com
233 Bangor Road, Newtownards, County Down, BT23 7PH
028 9182 3202 | Open Jul–Aug Mon–Fri 10–5, Sat–Sun 12–5, Apr–Jun, Sep Mon–Thu 10–4, Sat 12–4, Oct–Mar Mon–Thu 10–4
Set in the Whitespots Country Park, the award-winning Somme Heritage Centre commemorates Ireland's role in World War I. Guided tours take you back to the Home Rule crisis and you can experience life on the front line in a recreation of the trenches at the Battle of the Somme.

Ards Arts Centre
ards-council.gov.uk
Town Hall Arts Centre, Conway Square, Newtownards, County Down, BT23 4DB | 028 9181 0803
This small municipal arts centre in a restored Georgian building has two exhibition galleries and a diminutive performance space. It is also

the starting point of the Ards Sculpture Trail around the Ards Peninsula. There is an international guitar festival here every October.

Grace Neill's Bar

graceneills.com
33 High Street, Donaghadee, County Down, BT21 0AH | 028 9188 4595
A mix of music, including acoustic traditional folk and country, can be heard at this pub, one of many claiming to be the oldest in Ireland. The food is good, and famous musicians often join in a session.

The Groomsport Inn

stablesandgordonssuite.co.uk
26 Main Street, Groomsport, County Down, BT19 6JR
028 9127 1518
This inn overlooks Belfast Lough. Take in the views and watch the sun set over the water as you relax by the wood-burning stove with good pub grub and a drink. Sporting events are shown on the huge plasma screen.

Crawfordsburn Country Park

discovernorthernireland.com
Bridge Road South, Helen's Bay, County Down, BT19 1JT
Off the B20, signposted from the main Belfast–Bangor road
028 9185 3621 | Check website for opening times
With two good beaches, lovely scenery and views across Belfast Lough, this country park is a great place for walks and riverside rambles, with glens and a waterfall. The park also has a visitor centre and a cafe.

The Old Inn

theoldinn.com
15 Main Street, Crawfordsburn, County Down, BT19 1JH
028 9185 3255
Part of The Old Inn dates from the 17th century. This lavishly decorated and furnished hotel has a high level of glitz, not least in the restaurant, where a circular recess hung with lights has been set in the ornate ceiling. This is a busy dining venue offering modern European-style cooking.

▼ Cockle Row Cottages, Groomsport

▶ Belfast MAP REF 383 E3

gotobelfast.com

The capital of Northern Ireland since 1920, Belfast is a solid Victorian city with many surprises in store. Although historically it has been at the centre of the Troubles and the well-documented conflict between Republicans and Unionists, today it's a pleasant, peaceful and friendly European city.

It was built largely on the sea trading, shipbuilding and textile trades, with large public buildings that sit grandly amid fading red-brick terraces and commercial premises. Parts of Belfast are a bit shabby, but it's modernising quickly along the River Lagan and around the heart of the city. Even in the less touristy areas there is plenty of life and atmosphere. It is a city packed with attractions, most of them uncrowded, although Titanic Belfast, which opened in 2012, sees thousands of visitors. Belfast people are generous with their time and help; they may speak with black humour and they enjoy conversation.

▼ View from the top of the Stormont building

The River Lagan flows north through Belfast into Belfast Lough, cutting the city in two; most things that a visitor would want to see or do are west of the river. Most of the grand public buildings, such as St Anne's Cathedral and the Town Hall, are in the middle of the city, while along the river are Sinclair Seamen's Church, Waterfront Hall and the other attractions. Just to the west are the Falls and Shankill roads with their vivid murals – Black Taxi Tour territory (see page 94). About a mile to the south of the city lies Belfast's university quarter, with Queen's University, the Botanic Gardens, the Ulster Museum and some fine parks. Belfast is very easy to negotiate and there are a number of green and pleasant ways to get around: on foot or by bicycle, on one of the frequent city buses or cruising along the River Lagan on a boat (see page 94).

The heart of Belfast is Donegall Square, where broad pavements and flowerbeds surround the giant City Hall. Buildings to admire around Donegall Square include the Italianate sandstone Marks & Spencer, the lavishly decorated Scottish Provident Building with its cavorting dolphins and guardian lions, and the Linen Hall Library, a wonderful, hushed, old-fashioned library whose political collection offers an overview of the Troubles. There is also a tea room here that's become a Belfast institution.

ONLY IN BELFAST

City Hall

Donegall Square, Belfast, BT1 5GS
028 9027 0456 | Open Mon–Fri
8.30–5, Sat, Sun 10–4

The great green dome of City Hall (opened in 1906) rises 173 feet into the sky. Patterned Italian marble and elaborate stucco greet you in the hall, from where tours of the building ascend the dome to the council chamber. This splendid civic apartment contains two tellingly contrasted items. One is the Lord Mayor's handsomely carved throne. The other is an icon for all Orangemen: the plain and simple round wooden table at which the Unionist leader, Sir Edward Carson, signed the Solemn League and Covenant of Resistance against Home Rule on 28 September 1912. More than 400,000 Ulster Protestants were to follow him as signatories, some using their own blood.

Crown Liquor Saloon

crownbar.com
46 Great Victoria Street, Belfast, BT2 7BA | 028 9024 3187 | Open daily 11.30–11

This Victorian 'temple of intemperance' is, as its owner, the National Trust, proudly claims, 'the most famous pub in Belfast'. The Trust bought the pub in 1978 and spent

▶ City Hall, Donegall Square

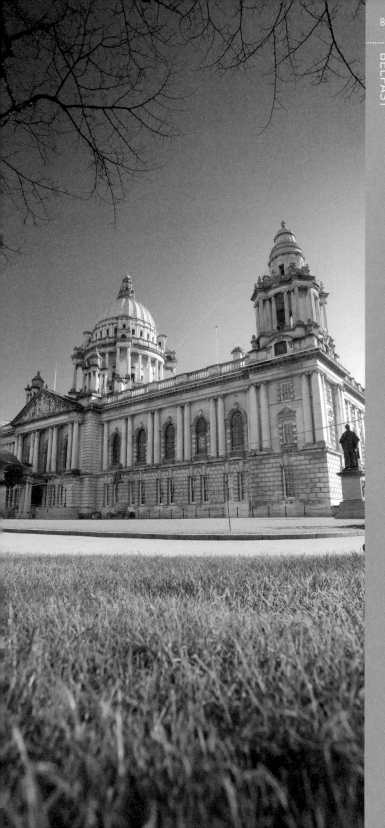

£400,000 restoring it because they recognised it as a supreme example of the golden age of public house design. From the colonnaded gilt and marble frontage to the interior with its curved bar, brightly coloured tiles, gas lamps, embossed ceiling and ornate wood snugs, with frosted glass and service bells, the Crown Liquor Saloon is gloriously over the top. Note the inlaid crown on the floor at the entrance. It was installed there in 1895 by the nationalist owner Patrick Flanagan so that all his customers could tread it underfoot.

The Entries and High Street

North of Donegall Square, the road leads to the oldest part of Belfast, which was badly damaged during World War II. Narrow alleyways called entries branch off from the High Street and Ann Street towards pedestrianised zones. Here you will find some of the best old pubs and bars, such as the Morning Star in Pottingers Entry, which serves good food.

Titanic Belfast

see highlight panel opposite

TAKE IN SOME HISTORY

St Anne's Cathedral

belfastcathedral.org
Donegall Street, Belfast, BT1 2HB
028 9032 8332 | Open Mon–Sat
9–5.15, Sun 1–3
Consecrated in 1904, St Anne's Cathedral, also known as the Belfast Cathedral, is an impressive church built of stone from all 32 counties of Ireland. Highlights include the 'Occupations of Mankind' carvings on the capitals of the nave pillars, the modern stained glass of the east window, the maple and marble of the nave floor, the 1920s mosaics by the Martin sisters, Gertude and Margaret, and the prayer book written by hand on cigarette paper by a World War II captive in a Japanese prisoner-of-war camp.

The Harbour Commissioner's Office

belfast-harbour.co.uk
Harbour Office, Corporation Square, Belfast, BT1 3AL | 028 9055 4422
The city has few grander buildings than this one, built in 1854. The interior has floors of mosaic and inlaid marble, heavy plaster mouldings and stained-glass windows. Upstairs in the barrel-roofed Barnet Room, the stained-glass windows depict the arms of old colonial partners-in-trade, such as the United States.

Stormont Castle

Parliament Buildings, Ballymiscaw, Stormont, Belfast, BT4 3XX
077 1773 2037
Seat of the Northern Ireland Assembly, Stormont Castle lies 5 miles east of the city, easily accessible by Metro bus 4A and 23. The imposing castle at the end of its mile-long drive is open to the public only by appointment, but there are walks in the woods and across the open parkland.

▶ Titanic Belfast   MAP REF 383 E3

titanicbelfast.com
1 Olympic Way, Queen's Road, Titanic Quarter, Belfast, BT3 9EP
028 9076 6386 | Open daily Jun–Aug 9–7, Apr, May and Sep 9–6,
Jan–Mar and Oct–Dec 10–5

One of the city's newest and most intriguing attractions is the Titanic Belfast, which extends over nine galleries with rides, reconstructions, interactive exhibits and special effects. It opened in 2012 to coincide with the centenary of the building of the ship.

Innovative creative techniques are used here including the 'dark ride' through the Harland & Wolff shipyard which brings to life the people involved in the construction and launch of this fated liner. Galleries tell of the lives of the passengers and crew, and the maiden voyage. Space is also dedicated to the discovery of the *Titanic* in its watery grave and gives factual information to dispell some of the myths that have grown up around this iconic ship.

Housed in a dramatic 150,000-square-foot structure, the Titanic Belfast building is now the cultural nucleus of the Titanic Quarter (titanicquarter.com), an urban waterfront regeneration project which has transformed this part of the city. Expect to find arts and entertainment, commercial and residential properties here.

▲ Belfast Zoological Gardens

VISIT THE MUSEUMS

Cultúrlann Mcadam ó Fiaich
culturlann.ie
216 Falls Road, Belfast, BT12 6AH
0208 9096 4180 | Open daily 9–6
In a converted Presbyterian
church, exhibitions, a bookshop
and music concerts promote
the Irish language and culture
in Belfast's Gaeltacht Quarter.

Home Front Exhibition
niwarmemorial.org
21 Talbot Street, Belfast, BT1 2LD
028 9032 0392 | Open Mon–Fri
10–4
The exhibition relates to the
part played by the people of
Belfast and Northern Ireland
in World War II. Footage of the
time can be seen, and displays
include the 1941 Belfast Blitz
when nearly 1,000 people lost
their lives and some 100,000
were made homeless. Other
exhibits include a striking
stained-glass memorial window
by Stanley Murray Scott.

Ulster Museum
nmni.com
College Park, Botanic Avenue, Belfast,
BT7 1LP | 028 9044 0000
Open Tue–Sun 10–5
This award-winning museum
takes an uncompromisingly
honest look at the history of
Northern Ireland, while
retaining many popular features
from its slightly musty previous
incarnation (the stuffed polar
bear continues to delight
children). From the airy central
atrium floors radiate out,
covering natural history, the
Troubles, shipbuilding, linen
and many other aspects of
Ulster's story. The top floors
house an art collection of
international importance.

▲ Botanic Gardens

GO ROUND THE GARDENS
Botanic Gardens
belfastcity.gov.uk
College Park, Botanic Avenue, Belfast, BT7 1LP | Open daily from 7.30am
These classic 19th-century gardens beside the River Lagan contain two pieces of High Victorian glass and cast-iron architecture: the great Glasshouse of 1839–40 with its Cool Wing full of bright plants, and its steamy Stove Wing and mighty central dome. There's more steam in the nearby Tropical Ravine, which contains some of the oldest seed plants around today. Here you stroll around a gallery looking down through the canopy of a miniature tropical rainforest. The wide lawns of the Botanic Gardens provide a place to relax for students from nearby Queen's University.

MEET THE ANIMALS
Belfast Zoological Gardens
belfastzoo.co.uk
Antrim Road, Belfast, BT36 7PN
028 9077 6277 | Open daily Apr–Sep 10–7, Oct–Mar 10–4
Here animals of Africa, Asia and South America live in the relative freedom of large, grassy enclosures.

SEE A LOCAL CHURCH
St Malachy's Church
saintmalachysparish.com
24 Alfred Street, Belfast, BT2 8EN
Open Mon–Fri 9.30–3; check website for times of services
The church may look unprepossessing from the outside with its dingy red brick and lurid pink paintwork but inside you'll find an early Victorian extravaganza of stucco, fan vaulting, a fine altarpiece carved by the

▲ Sinclair Seamen's church

Piccioni family (from the Tirol), and later window glass with art nouveau lilies.

Messrs Dunville's, whiskey distillers, conducted their craft next to St Malachy's Church on Alfred Street. Judging that the vibrations caused by the tolling of the bell were spoiling their product, they complained – and the bell was removed.

Sinclair Seamen's Presbyterian Church

Corporation Square, Belfast, BT1 3AJ
Open Wed 2–4.30
This L-shaped Presbyterian church of 1857 was furnished in a nautical style to attract visiting sailors. The font is a ship's binnacle; the pulpit resembles the prow of a ship; nautical themes feature in the stained-glass windows; the mast of a Guinness barge and ships' riding lights decorate the walls. Services commence with the ringing of HMS *Hood*'s brass ship's bell. Even the welcome sign by the door conveys its message by semaphore flags. Seafaring worshippers will never be turned away – 50 seats are reserved for them.

CATCH A PERFORMANCE

Belfast Empire

thebelfastempire.com
42 Botanic Avenue, Belfast, BT7 1JD
028 9024 9276 | Open Wed–Sat
11.30am–1am, Mon–Tue 11.30–11,
Sun 7pm–midnight
Anything from salsa classes to stand-up comedy is staged at the Empire, set in an old converted Victorian church in the university area.

Belfast Waterfront

waterfront.co.uk
2 Lanyon Place, Belfast, BT1 3WH
028 9033 4400
Even without its full calendar of cultural events and pop concerts, it's worth going to this stunning, multi-purpose, 3,000-seat auditorium just to enjoy the views from the bars overlooking the River Lagan and Belfast Lough.

Grand Opera House

goh.co.uk
Great Victoria Street, Belfast,
BT2 7HR | 028 9024 1919
This is a splendid example of a late-Victorian music hall. Ornate outside and overblown opulence within, it has suffered various vicissitudes down the years, from relegation to a second-class cinema in the 1950s to a brace of IRA bombs

in 1991 and 1993, which damaged, but failed to destroy, it. Yet one look at the giant gilt elephants, the angels and cherubs, and the swags of golden fruit and flowers tells you of its aspirations when it was opened in 1895. Nowadays, restored and refurbished, the Grand Opera House puts on a wide variety of entertainment that includes, of course, opera.

The Lyric Theatre

lyrictheatre.co.uk
Ridgeway Street, Belfast,
BT9 5FB | 028 9038 5685
The Lyric began as a small company specialising in the plays of W B Yeats. Many local actors, such as Liam Neeson, started their careers here. These days it has diversified, putting on a varied programme, but still with an emphasis on Irish plays. It occupies a landmark £18 million building, opened in 2011.

The MAC (Metropolitan Arts Centre)

themaclive.com
St Anne's Square, Belfast, BT1 3AJ
028 9023 5053 | Open daily 10–7
This formidable world-class arts centre, situated in the heart of the regenerated Cathedral Quarter, has been rebuilt and now hosts international art exhibitions, live theatre and experimental works in a space that includes two theatres, three visual art galleries, a rehearsal space and a dance studio.

Ulster Hall

ulsterhall.co.uk
Bedford Street, Belfast, BT2 2FF
028 9033 4455
Stately Victorian architecture and great acoustics make this popular venue the preferred home of the Ulster Orchestra. The hall is the city's premier location for classical, dance and new music.

▼ The Grand Opera House

W5

w5online.co.uk

Odyssey, Queen's Quay, Belfast, BT3 9QQ | 028 9046 7700 | Open Mon–Thu 10–5 (school holidays until 6), Fri–Sat 10–6, Sun 12–6

The five Ws are: Who? What? When? Where? Why? Enquiring young minds find learning lots of fun at this science and discovery centre, and experts are on hand to help out.

TAKE A BOAT TRIP

River Lagan explorations

laganboatcompany.com

Unit 5, The Obel, 66 Donegall Quay, Belfast, BT1 3NG | 028 9024 0124

The Lagan Boat Company runs trips from Donegall Quay: upriver past the fine new developments and out into green countryside; downriver in the area now known as the Titanic Quarter to view the shipyards of Harland & Wolff where HMS *Titanic* was built and where the twin giant yellow cranes, Samson and Goliath, are familiar landmarks.

Northern Ireland Science Park

nisp.co.uk

Queens Road, Belfast BT3 9DT | 028 9073 7813 | Tours daily Easter–Oct 11 and 2, Nov–Easter at 2

You can see the Dry Dock and Pump House at the Northern Ireland Science Park, and walk or cycle along the Lagan's towpath south to Lisburn. Useful leaflet guides are available from the Belfast Welcome Centre.

TAKE A TOUR

Black Taxi Tours

blackcabtoursni.com and belfasttours.com

028 9064 2264

Black Taxi Tours let you see West Belfast, the area where the Troubles were focused, from an insider's viewpoint, thanks to the local knowledge of the drivers. They will show

▼ The River Lagan and Waterfront Hall

you the Loyalist Shankill Road and nationalist Falls Road, the battered, graffiti-covered Peace Line that separates the two opposed communities, and the sectarian gable-end murals for which Belfast is famous. Look out for the one depicting Bobby Sands near the Sinn Féin office on Falls Road, the beautiful mural off Falls Road which commemorates the Great Famine and the one in Braemar Street dedicated to women, children and workers.

City Tours Belfast

citytoursbelfast.com
Unit 1, 143 Northumberland Street, Belfast, BT13 2JF | 028 9032 1912
Open-top bus tours of Belfast, taking in the city's sites with a commentary, are on offer from City Tours Belfast. Routes cover architecture and feats of engineering, plus the Titanic, Cathedral and Arts quarters.

GET ACTIVE
Belfast Indoor Tennis Centre and Ozone Complex

belfastcity.gov.uk
Ormeau Embankment, Belfast, BT6 8LT | 028 9045 8024 | Open Mon–Sat 9am–10pm, Sun 10–5
This newly refurbished tennis and leisure centre provides the only public tennis courts in the city. It is in a park by the river, offers classes and lessons, and there's a climbing wall too.

Dundonald International Ice Bowl

theicebowl.com
Old Dundonald Road, Belfast,

▲ On the Titanic Walking Tour

BT16 1XT | 028 9080 9123
Open Tue–Sun 11–10, Mon 11–5
Dundonald's Olympic-size ice rink is part of a popular leisure complex that includes an indoor adventure playground and a 30-lane bowling alley.

GO SHOPPING
St George's Market

12–20 East Bridge Street, Belfast, BT1 3NQ | 028 9043 5704 | Variety market Fri 6–2, food, craft and garden market Sat 9–3, Sun 10–4
This handsome 1896 building at the intersection of May and Oxford streets is Belfast's only surviving Victorian market hall. There has been a market here since 1604 and, following a major refurbishment in 1997, it is one of the most vibrant destinations in the city. Organic produce, flowers and a lively fish market, under a restored roof of glass and cast iron, are the focus for shoppers.

WATCH A MATCH
Casement Park
casementpark.ie
88–104 Andersonstown Road,
Belfast, BT11 9AN | 028 9030 0172
In the West Belfast heartland,
Casement Park is the top
stadium for Gaelic games
in Northern Ireland.

SSE Arena, Belfast
ssearenabelfast.com
2 Queen's Quay, Belfast, BT3 9QQ
028 9076 6000
The Belfast Giants ice hockey
team competes here in the
National League. The matches
are great family occasions and
worth attending for the full
US-style razzmatazz. Odyssey
Arena is also host to rock and
pop concerts, wrestling,
basketball and all kinds of
other entertainments.

Windsor Park
Donegall Avenue, Belfast, BT12 6LW
028 9024 4198
Home of the Northern Ireland
international football team and
Linfield Football Club, Windsor
Park welcomes top European
Champions League contenders,
as well as national sides and
Irish League opposition.

PLAY A ROUND
Belvoir Park Golf Club
belvoirparkgolfclub.com
73 Church Road, Newtonbreda,
Belfast, BT8 7AN | 028 9049 1693
This undulating parkland
course was designed by the
famed course architect H S
Colt. It is not strenuous to walk,
but is certainly a test of your
golf, with tree-lined fairways
and a particularly challenging
finish at the final four holes.

▼ Football at Windsor Park

Ormeau Golf Club

ormeaugolfclub.co.uk

50 Park Road, Belfast, BT7 2FX

028 9064 0700

Parkland course which provides a challenge for low- and high-handicap golfers, good shots being rewarded and those that stray offline receiving due punishment. The long par four 5th hole has an intimidating out of bounds on the right and a narrow sloping green, well protected by trees and bunkers. Two long par three holes each demand an accurate drive and when playing the 3rd and 12th holes, visitors are advised to look for the Fairy Tree which graces the middle of the fairway. Club folklore states that if a golfer hits this tree he should apologise to the fairies or his game will suffer!

Rockmount Golf Club

rockmountgolfclub.com

Carryduff, Belfast, BT8 8EQ

028 9081 2279

A cleverly designed course that offers an excellent test of golf, incorporating natural features with water coming into play as streams, and a lake at the 11th and 14th.

HIT THE DANCE FLOOR
Apartment

apartmentbelfast.com

2 Donegall Square West, Belfast, BT1 6JA | 028 9050 9777

Open daily 7am–1am

A stylish bar/restaurant with slick decor and resident and guest DJs, attracting a sophisticated crowd. It's situated right in the middle of Belfast, and window tables offer great views over the City Hall.

▼ Ormeau Golf Club

Bambu Beach Club

beachbelfast.com

Odyssey, Queen's Quay, Belfast,
BT3 9QQ | 028 9046 0011

Open Thu–Sun 9pm–1am

You can imagine you are in the sun-drenched Med in this huge, beach-themed club, which attracts a big crowd and is popular with students. Clubbers may have to wait in line, but at least they can do so under cover in the Odyssey Pavilion. Music is mainstream, and the five bars on two floors offer a choice of exotic cocktails.

Odyssey

theodyssey.co.uk

Queen's Quay, Belfast, BT3 9QQ
028 9045 8806

Several international eateries, bars, clubs, a multiplex cinema, ten-pin bowling and games rooms fill this riverside complex, Belfast's most popular nightspot for all ages.

EAT AND DRINK

Beatrice Kennedy ⊛

beatricekennedy.co.uk

44 University Road, Belfast, BT7 1NJ
028 9020 2290

There's a real buzz to the place and a relaxed bistro-style attitude all round, from the cordiality of the welcome to the warmth of the decor. Located in the university district, there's a pre-theatre menu for anyone on a budget or in a rush for curtain up, and a bespoke veggie menu if required. The menu casts a wide net with dishes that show a pan-European approach and a few Asian influences.

The Botanic Inn

thebotanicinn.com

23–27 Malone Road, Belfast,
BT9 6RU | 028 9050 9740

The Bot, as it is affectionately known, has been on the scene since 1798. Its several-hundred-year history has made it a well-known Belfast institution, while its ability to keep up with modern times by offering an ever-changing menu of food and drink makes it one of the busiest bars in the whole region.

Café Vaudeville ⊛

cafevaudeville.com

25–39 Arthur Street, Belfast,
BT1 4GQ | 028 9043 9160

Big-flavoured brasserie dishes are served in this glamorous bar and restaurant located in a historic city-centre building. There's a touch of art nouveau bling to the interior, with the appropriately named Luxebar and a 'coffee dock' serving boulangerie-style snacks. The restaurant to the rear has a domed ceiling and coloured lights that change to set the mood.

Deanes at Queens ⊛⊛

michaeldeane.co.uk

1 College Gardens, Belfast, BT9 6BQ
028 9038 2111

This lively brasserie and grill joint is in the vibrant University Quarter of the city with views over the Botanic Gardens. The cooking matches the modernity of the setting, delivering a genuine Irish flavour and some creative combinations.

Duke of York

dukeofyorkbelfast.com
7–11 Commercial Court, Belfast,
BT1 2NB | 028 9024 1062

Something of a local institution, this is a lovely little pub tucked away along a narrow cobbled alleyway in the historic Half Bap region of the city. A fine selection of Irish whiskeys and local stouts and a good atmosphere is what you will find here.

EIPIC ◉◉◉

michaeldeane.co.uk
36–40 Howard Street, Belfast,
BT1 6PF | 028 9033 1134

Michael Deane is an elder statesman of the Northern Irish dining scene. Here in the Howard Street flagship, head chef Danni Barry directs the kitchen's efforts, returning to the Deane fold after a stint with Simon Rogan at L'Enclume. The place has mellowed in recent years, becoming less serious about the fripperies that come at the high end of eating out.

James Street South Restaurant and Bar ◉◉

jamesstreetsouth.co.uk
21 James Street South, Belfast,
BT2 7GA | 028 9043 4310

Serving serious city-slicker cooking in a sharp venue, this capacious red-brick former linen mill is the hub of Niall McKenna's empire. Pristine linen-clad tables and unchallenging, contemporary colours make a serene and understated setting for refined, French-accented food.

The Merchant Hotel ◉◉

themerchanthotel.com
16 Skipper Street, Cathedral Quarter,
Belfast, BT1 2DZ | 028 9023 4888

A magnificent setting for inventive contemporary cooking served up in the Victorian former headquarters of Ulster Bank, now Belfast's grandest hotel. The kitchen has a classical-meets-modern repertoire where tip-top regional produce is treated with respect.

OX ◉◉

oxbelfast.com
1 Oxford Street, Belfast, BT1 3LA
028 9031 4121

Skilful modern cooking is dished up in a stunning location overlooking the River Lagan. OX is a collaboration between local boy Stephen Toman and Frenchman Alain Kerloc'h, who worked together in Paris under the legendary Alain Passard. The stylishly minimalistic dining room, with its open kitchen and mezzanine area, makes an unpretentious, almost retro setting for what is thoroughly contemporary food that often elevates vegetables to star billing.

Pavilion Bar

pavilionbelfast.com
The Pavilion Bar, 296 Ormeau Road,
Belfast, BT7 2GB | 028 9028 3283

Way back in 1899, wealthy Victorian-era publican Francis McGlade set up The Pavilion or 'The Big House' and it has been welcoming drinkers ever since. This is a charming Belfast pub spread over three floors that offers real Irish hospitality as well as excellent food.

Robinsons Bar

38–42 Great Victoria Street, Belfast, BT2 7BA | 028 9024 7447

One of Belfast's oldest bars offers the chance to relax with a drink in the saloon bar before enjoying folk and traditional music seven nights a week. There is even a night club as well as karaoke and a bistro serving meals.

Shu ◉◉

shu-restaurant.com

253–255 Lisburn Road, Belfast, BT9 7EN | 028 9038 1655

Contemporary Irish cooking with a buzz and good service in a thoroughly European kind of restaurant, with classical French thinking as the foundation of the sharp, modern cooking on show. Situated in a Victorian terrace in trendy Lisburn Road, the airy space with an open-to-view kitchen is served by a smartly turned-out team.

Sunflower

Union Street, Belfast, BT1 2JG
028 9023 2474

This relative newcomer to the city pub scene is unpretentious and heartfelt. Come to enjoy high quality but simple pub grub and good live music at weekends. Don't expect any gimmicks; but notice the security cage on the front door, a relic from 1980s Belfast's social history.

▶ **PLACES NEARBY**

Although Belfast itself is a busy city, the surrounding Greater Belfast area has some beautiful scenery and great open spaces, with plenty of opportunities for hiking and taking part in outdoor sports.

Cave Hill Country Park & Cave Hill Heritage Centre

Country Park: Antrim Road, Belfast, BT15 5GR | 028 9031 9629 | Open daily 7.30–dusk. Heritage Centre: 028 9077 6925 | Open daily 10–5

To the north, the city rises 1,204 feet up to Cave Hill. The walk through Cave Hill Country Park has a challenging route that skirts round the Devil's Punchbowl and goes past caves to the hill summit at McArt's Fort where you are rewarded with stunning views. The park is also home to Cave Hill Adventurous Playground, which offers a great family day out, the Cave Hill Heritage Centre in Belfast Castle on the hill's lower slopes and a wealth of archaeological and historical sites.

Down Royal Racecourse

downroyal.com

Maze, Lisburn, County Down, BT27 5RW | 028 9262 1256

See website for fixtures

Home of the Ulster Derby, held in summer, this attractive course aims to become one of the best in the whole of Ireland.

Game of Thrones Winterfell Tours

see page 108

The Gobbins Path

thegobbinscliffpath.com
Visitor Centre, Middle Road,
Islandmagee, County Antrim,
BT40 3SX | 028 9337 2318
The Gobbins Path was designed
by railway engineer Berkeley
Deane Wise and opened in
1902, creating a spectacular
coastal path along a line of dark
basalt cliffs on the Islandmagge
Peninsula, some 20 miles north
of Belfast. It has reopened after
a £6 million investment and
now up to 70,000 walkers a year
are expected to scramble
around this coast. There are
great views out to sea and the
original rock-cut steps are still
in use as well as new bridges.
Guided tours only, unsuitable
for children.

Irish Linen Centre and Lisburn Museum

lisburnmuseum.com
Market Square, Lisburn, County
Antrim, BT28 1AG | 028 9266 3377
Open Mon–Sat 9.30–5

▲ The Gobbins Path

Linen-making was once the
Lagan Valley's biggest industry,
and the Irish Linen Centre
offers a window into the trade.
You can try your hand at parts
of the manufacturing process,
learn about scutching, hackling
and retting, look at the lives of
Victorian linen workers, chat to
a weaver working on a restored
19th-century hand loom,
admire the collection of damask
linen and costumes and visit
the museum shop. Local history
is detailed in the Lisburn
Museum alongside.

Culloden Estate and Spa

hastingshotels.com/culloden-estate-
and-spa
Bangor Road, Holywood, Belfast,
BT18 0EX | 028 9042 1066
One of Northern Ireland's finest
and most distinguished hotels,
originally built as a palace for
the Bishops of Down, with its
own magnificent gardens, also

has a stand-out, state-of-the-art spa. In a beautiful coastal location, it offers exceptional service and superb food. There are several good dining options, but the Mitre restaurant is the award-winning option that does not disappoint.

The Old Schoolhouse

theoldschoolhouseinn.com
100 Ballydrain Road, Newtownards, County Down, BT23 6EA
028 9754 1182
Ensconced in the Down countryside by Strangford Lough (see page 66), though only 20 minutes' drive out of Belfast, this restaurant has been under the tutelage of the same family for over 30 years. It's an elegant conversion of the original school building, and, as at many other rural venues, the kitchen grows much of its own produce, which forms the foundation of its modern Irish cooking.

Ulster Folk and Transport Museum

nmni.com/uftm
53 Bangor Road, Cultra, Holywood, County Down, BT18 0EU | 028 9042 8428 | Open Mar–Sep Tue–Sun 10–5, Oct–Feb Tue–Fri 10–4, Sat, Sun 11–4
The Folk Museum explores Ulster history and life through reconstructed buildings, which include thatched cottages and farmhouses, a flax mill, a school and a rural Orange Hall. Traditional crafts are demonstrated by costumed guides. The Transport Museum consists of a number of galleries of beautifully maintained exhibits – gleaming steam locomotives, horse-drawn carriages, penny-farthings and racing bicycles, and a horse-drawn tram. Ulster-built cars on show here include the stylish De Lorean of *Back to the Future* fame, with its impractical gull-winged doors.

▼ The Ulster Folk and Transport Museum

▸ Belleek Pottery MAP REF 381 E3

belleek.com

3 Main Street, Belleek, County Fermanagh, BT93 3FY | 028 6865 8501

Open Jan, Feb Mon–Fri 9–5.30, Mar–Jun Mon–Fri 9–5.30, Sat 10–5.30,
Sun 2–5.30, Jul–Sep Mon–Fri 9–6, Sat 10–6, Sun 12–5.30, Oct–Dec
Mon–Fri 9–5.30, Sat 10–5.30, Sun 2–5

Since Belleek Pottery began production in the late 1850s, the
business has concentrated on high-quality products, especially
white Parian ware, famous for its hard shiny surface and
delicate shape. The factory tour reveals a fascinating process:
beating the air out of a dough-like mixture of glass and clay
with wooden paddles, teasing the material out and moulding it
into plates, cups, vases and statuettes. You also get the chance
to talk to the staff about what they are doing. These are very
skilled people, working with tools they make themselves and
hand down through the generations. The basketware, a lattice
of finely meshed clay strings, is probably the best-known of
Belleek products. Hand-painting is another remarkable skill
you can watch.

A visitor centre explains the history and techniques, and
there is a showroom where you can admire beautifully lit pieces
before parting with your money. Belleek ware is expensive, and
there are no 'seconds' for sale.

GO FISHING
Belleek Angling Centre
Main Street, Belleek, County
Fermanagh, BT93 3FX
028 6865 8181
Try your hand at course, game
and sea angling. For other
fishing opportunities, the
Northern Ireland government's
fishing department (dcal-
fishingni.gov.uk) has a wealth
of useful information.

▶ **PLACES NEARBY**
If you don't want to cross the
border, Lough Erne (see page
135) is your best bet. Here you'll
find Tully Castle (see page 136)
and Castle Caldwell Forest
(see page 137). Over in the
Republic of Ireland you can visit
Donegal, with its castle (see
page 244), to the north, and
Sligo (see page 345) to
the southeast.

▶ Bushmills Distillery   MAP REF 383 D1
bushmills.com
2 Distillery Road, Bushmills, County Antrim, BT57 8XH | 028 2073 3218
Open Mar–Oct Mon–Sat 9.15–4.45, Sun 12–4.45, Nov–Feb 10–4.45,
Sun 12–4.45

Bushmills is the oldest distillery in the world; it started
production after a licence was granted to Sir Thomas Phillips
in 1608 from King James I, and has been distilling superb malt
whiskeys ever since. Bushmills lies at the heart of a lush
barley-growing area and has the other vital ingredients
necessary for the successful distilling of whiskey: abundant
clear water, from St Columb's Rill, a tributary of the River
Bush, and plentiful supplies of peat.

The buildings, with their pagoda-style roofs, are a pleasure
to look at. The tour takes you past the huge round mash tunns,
where the wash bubbles and ferments, and the great stills
shaped like gleaming copper onions. In the cool gloom of the
warehouse, you inhale the faint, sweet smell of whiskey
evaporating from the seams of the wooden barrels in which
Bushmills matures. According to the guide, this unreclaimable
whiskey vapour is known as the 'angels' share'.

At the end of the tour you can sip a complimentary dram,
buy a bottle of whiskey and reflect on the Bushmills mantra:
'Here's to health and prosperity, To you and all your posterity,
And them that doesn't drink with sincerity, May they be damned
for all eternity!'

▶ **PLACES NEARBY**
The Giant's Causeway, a
UNESCO World Heritage Site
(see page 123), is a must-see
attraction. Portstewart (see
page 148) is to the east, and
Ballycastle (see page 78) and
the Antrim Coast (see page 60),
one of the most beautiful in
Britain, to the west.

▶ Carrickfergus Castle MAP REF 383 E3

carrickfergus.org

Marine Highway, Carrickfergus, County Antrim, BT38 7VG | 028 9335 1273

Open daily Easter–Sep 10–6, Oct–Easter 10–4

Carrickfergus, with its grey Norman stronghold, is the southern gateway to the Antrim Coast. Carrickfergus Castle was built on its shore promontory in 1180 by Sir John de Courcy to guard Belfast Lough. Its strategic position has always made it liable to attack and siege, but it has survived remarkably intact. Tableaux, effigies and explanatory plaques tell its story to visitors, and there are sometimes visiting displays.

Things to see in the town of Carrickfergus include the museum, which has a good collection of local artefacts, and 800-year-old St Nicholas Church, which is famous for its stained-glass windows.

TAKE IN SOME HISTORY
Andrew Jackson Cottage and US Rangers Centre
2 Boneybefore, Carrickfergus, County Antrim, BT38 7EQ 028 9335 8241 | Open May–Oct Thu–Sat 11–4, Sun 1–4, Nov–Apr Fri, Sat 11–3

This traditional thatched Ulster-Scots farmhouse, built in the 1750s, has been restored and decorated in 18th-century style. Although it's not the actual house that 7th US President Andrew Jackson's parents emigrated from, there's an exhibition devoted to his life.

VISIT THE MUSEUM
Museum and Civic Centre
11 Antrim Street, Carrickfergus, County Antrim, BT38 7DG | 0300 124 5000 | Apr–Sep Mon–Fri 10–6, Sat 10–4, Oct–Mar Mon–Fri 10–5, Sat 10–6

A community museum showcasing local history using interactive exhibitions.

▼ Carrickfergus Castle

SEE A LOCAL CHURCH
St Nicholas Church

saintnicholas.org.uk

3 Lancasterian Street, Carrickfergus, County Antrim, BT38 7AB | 028 9336 0061 | Open Jun–Sep Tue 2–4, Sat 11–1. Tours by appointment

This interesting church has many historic features, including a striking stained-glass window. Although it dates back to the 15th century, it has only been installed in the church for 200 years.

PLAY A ROUND
Carrickfergus Golf Club

carrickfergusgolfclub.co.uk

35 North Road, Carrickfergus, County Antrim, BT38 8LP

028 9336 3713

This is a parkland course, fairly level but still demanding, with a notorious water hazard, the Dam, at the first hole. Well-maintained, with an interesting in-course riverway and fine views across Belfast Lough.

EAT AND DRINK
Central Bar

13–15 High Street, Carrickfergus, County Antrim, BT38 7AN

028 9335 7840

The Central Bar is a busy central corner pub that has been in operation for over 50 years. It offers very reasonably priced food and beer in a no-frills atmosphere.

▶ PLACES NEARBY

Whitehead, lying midway between Carrickfergus and Larne, is a very pretty seaside village, with pastel-painted buildings on the seafront. It's known locally as 'the Town with no Streets' as there are no roads with the suffix 'street' in their names. Steam trains run from Whitehead, the home of the Railway Preservation Society of Ireland. Belfast (see page 84) is about 40 minutes away by car. Bangor (see page 80) is closer as the crow flies, but across the inlet, so you'll have to take the long way round.

In **Larne** you can visit a fun country park, or take in a performance at the theatre in **Newtownabbey**.

Carnfunnock Country Park

carnfunnock.com

Coast Road, Larne, County Antrim, BT40 2QG | 028 2827 0541 or 028 2826 0088 | Open mid-Apr to Jun, Sep, Oct Sat, Sun 11–5, Jul–Aug daily 11–5

This family-friendly park has remote-controlled boats and lorries, bouncy castles, an outdoor adventure playground, a miniature railway and other activities, including cycling, orienteering, geocaching and a 9-hole golf course, all overlooking the Irish Sea.

Theatre at the Mill

theatreatthemill.com

Mossley Mill, Carnmoney Road North, Newtownabbey, County Antrim, BT36 5QA | 028 9034 0202

A mix of dance, drama, comedy and music is on offer at this pleasing municipal arts venue, built in a converted flax mill complex, which also houses the local borough council.

▶ Castle Ward   MAP REF 383 F4

nationaltrust.org.uk

Strangford, Downpatrick, County Down, BT30 7LS | 028 4488 1204

See website for opening times

Castle Ward is an intriguing monument to an ill-matched couple. Bernard Ward, first Viscount Bangor, and his wife Anne could not agree on the architectural style of the new house they were building in the 1760s on the southern shores of Strangford Lough. So Lord Bangor designed a restrained classical frontage and set of front rooms, while his wife ordered a feast of exuberant Strawberry Hill Gothic for the back of the house. The result is both eccentric and delightful, from the austere symmetry of Bernard's music room to the frothy fan vaulting dripping down the walls of Anne's boudoir. Only in the entrance hall do whimsicality and classicism meet – for among the stucco ornamentation are a genuine hat, basket and fiddle, dipped in plaster and stuck up amid all the artifice.

In the grounds you'll find a farmyard with a sawmill, the original 16th-century fortified tower, the Strangford Lough Wildlife Centre, and Clearsky Adventure Centre, a high-tech adventure playground. There are lovely walks through bluebell woods and along the lake.

GET OUTDOORS
Strangford Lough Wildlife Centre

nationaltrust.org.uk

Strangford, Downpatrick, County Down, BT30 7LS | 028 4488 1204

To find out more about the wildlife on the estate and the lough, visit the Strangford Lough Wildlife Centre. Winter is an excellent time to see the wide range of migrating birds.

Clearsky Adventure Centre

clearsky-adventure.com
Castle Ward Demesne, Strangford,
Downpatrick, County Down
028 4372 3933

Discover more than 20 exciting adventure experiences for all ages at this centre on the Castle Ward estate. You'll need to book your adventure in advance (online is best) or check the regular events for ones that take your fancy.

TAKE A TOUR

Game of Thrones Winterfell Tours

gameofthrones-winterfelltours.com
Old Castle Ward Demesne,
Strangford, County Down, BT30 7LS
028 4372 3933

Old Castle Ward and Demesne, only 40 minutes from Belfast, was used extensively for the filming of George R R Martin's epic *Game of Thrones* novels. When you first arrive you'll realise why the location scouts chose Old Castle Ward; see the sprawling medieval walls and imposing castle tower gate, the beautiful surrounding landscapes and far-reaching views across the lough. Visitors can dress up in authentic 'Stark Family' costumes.

▸ **PLACES NEARBY**

There's plenty to do around Strangford Lough (see page 65) and Downpatrick (see page 116), plus Belfast to the north.

▸ Castlewellan Forest Park MAP REF 383 E4

forestserviceni.gov.uk
The Grange, Castlewellan, County Down, BT31 9BU | 028 4377 8664
Open daily 10–dusk

This beautiful forest park occupies the estate of the Annesley family in the northern foothills of the Mountains of Mourne. Special features are the National Arboretum of rare trees,

which surrounds an 18th-century garden; a lake in which you can fish and canoe (with permission from the park ranger); the Grange Yard, an early 18th-century farmstead; and footpaths.

SADDLE UP

Mount Pleasant Trekking and Horse Riding Centre
mountpleasantcentre.com
15 Bannanstown Road, Castlewellan, County Down, BT31 9BG
028 4377 8651
Experienced horses, expert guides and beautiful scenery combine to make a memorable visit. All levels of expertise are catered to but book ahead.

▶ **PLACES NEARBY**
The Tollymore Mountain Centre is based at Bryansford, or have a round of golf in Newcastle.

Tollymore Mountain Centre
tollymore.com
Bryansford, Newcastle, County Down, BT33 0PT | 028 4372 2158

A full range of mountain-based activities, including climbing and white-water kayaking, is offfered here. This is Northern Ireland's National Centre for Mountaineering and Canoeing.

Royal County Down Golf Club
royalcountydown.org
36 Gold Links Road, Newcastle, County Down, BT33 0AN
028 4372 3314
This championship course is consistently rated among the world's top 10 courses. Beneath the imperious Mourne Mountains, the course has a magnificent setting, stretching out along the shores of Dundrum Bay. The Annesley Links offers a less formidable yet characterful game.

▶ **Crom Estate**   MAP REF 382 C5
nationaltrust.org.uk
Upper Lough Erne, Newtownbutler, County Fermanagh, BT92 8AJ
028 6773 8118 | See website for opening times
A great variety of woodland and the presence of Upper Lough Erne in so many of the views make Crom Estate (it's pronounced 'Crumb') an ideal spot for walking, especially in late autumn when the changing leaves reflected in the lake are at their most spectacular. Paths lead to Crom Old Church, and the ruin of Crom Old Castle, which dates from 1611. With luck you'll see some of the resident deer, and the huge variety of bird life gives endless opportunities for birdwatching.

▶ **PLACES NEARBY**
Close by are two other National Trust properties – Florence Court (see page 120) and Castle Coole (see page119), both to the northwest.

◀ Slieve Croob, Castlewellan Forest Park

▶ Derry/Londonderry   MAP REF 382 C2

derryvisitor.com

Northern Ireland's lively, friendly second city of Derry has the finest city walls walk in Ireland, if not Europe (see page 112). Its monuments to hope in adversity, and the city's Loyalist relics in St Columb's Cathedral, reflect its turbulent history.

It's easy to find your way around Derry, which is still referred to by its Loyalist population as Londonderry – the name given to the city in 1613 when James I and the livery companies of London established English and Scottish settlers here. The official county name remains Londonderry.

The River Foyle shapes the east boundary, while 'old Derry', the walled city, forms a neat rectangle whose four radiating streets – Shipquay Street, Butcher Street, Ferryquay Street and Bishop Street Within – converge on The Diamond or central market square. There's a good craft market between Butcher Street and Shipquay Street, and Derry's 'street of pubs' is Waterloo Street, between Butcher's Gate and Waterloo Square, where you'll find traditional and modern music in the bars.

TAKE IN SOME HISTORY
Derry Walls
see highlight panel overleaf

CATCH A PERFORMANCE
The Guildhall
derrystrabane.com
Guildhall Square, Derry, County Londonderry, BT48 6DQ
028 7137 7335

Taking its name from historic ties with the Guilds of the City of London, Derry's neo-Gothic civic complex hosts occasional performances of classical and choral music in its great hall.

Millennium Forum
millenniumforum.co.uk
Newmarket Street, Derry, County Londonderry, BT48 6EB
028 7126 4455
This large theatre stages a variety of shows. The performance arena attracts top international stars as well as local talent, showcasing comedy, classical music, cabaret and high-quality drama along the way.

The Nerve Centre
nerve-centre.org.uk
Magazine Street, Derry,

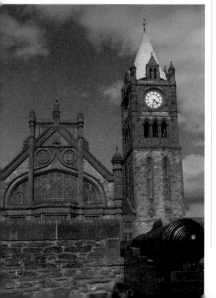

◀ The Guildhall

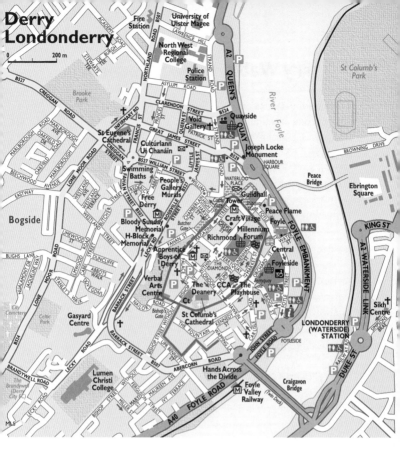

County Londonderry, BT48 6HJ
028 7126 0562
Cutting-edge music and film are major elements of this adventurous arts venue.

GO FISHING
River Foyle
loughs-agency.org
028 7134 2100
The Foyle system is one of the best salmon rivers in the world. Contact the Loughs Agency for permits and licences.

GO SHOPPING
The Craft Village
derrycraftvillage.com
Shipquay Street, Derry, County Londonderry | 028 7126 0329

Craftspeople work in this imaginative historic project right in the heart of Derry. Visitors quickly sense the great atmosphere of creative activity. The Craft Village provides a welcome alternative to the multinational chains.

PLAY A ROUND
City of Derry Golf Club
cityofderrygolfclub.com
49 Victoria Road, Derry, County Londonderry, BT47 2PU
028 7134 6369
This challenging 27-hole parkland course, founded in 1912, overlooks the River Foyle and the original nine holes were designed by prolific

▶ Derry Walls MAP REF 382 C2

44 Foyle Street, Derry, County Londonderry, BT48 6AT | 028 7126 7284

Derry is one of the finest examples of a walled city in Europe. The walls were built for defence between 1613 and 1618 by the trade guilds that had come from London to commercialise the old Celtic settlement. Their contribution was recognised by attaching 'London' to the name Derry. You can climb to the top and make the mile-long circuit, enjoying views over the old city and away to the hills. A town walls walk starting at Shipquay Gate should begin with a visit to the eye-catching Guildhall. Inside, fine stained-glass windows depict the city's history.

Numerous cannon stand on the walls, reminders of the great historic defence of Derry in 1688–89, when the Catholic army of King James II laid siege to the city. By the time the siege was lifted, in April 1689, 7,000 of the 30,000 citizens had died. At Bishop's Gate you can descend from the walls to see St Columb's Cathedral and its treasured relics of the Great Siege.

In the Tower Museum the history of Derry, including the dark, desperate days of the Troubles, is laid out in exemplary fashion. The museum's tower is a replica of a medieval round tower built by Paddy O'Doherty in 1615 as an article of faith and a pointer to better times to come (or possibly in lieu of taxes owed to the O'Donnell chieftains, depending on which story you hear).

As well as a physical barrier, the walls have been a potent symbol, representing the religious and cultural differences imposed by the building of this colonial city. Celebrations of the siege and the Protestant victory have at times proved to be problematic.

19th-century course architect Willie Park, Jr. It was extended to 18 holes in 1932 and a further nine holes were added in 1983. The clubhouse has panoramic views of the river and the hills of Donegal. The par 4 14th is the signature hole – a dogleg, with a challenging tee shot, that requires an accurate second shot, and there's a deviously sloping green to conquer along the way.

EAT AND DRINK

Browns Restaurant and Champagne Lounge ◉
brownsrestaurant.com
1 Bonds Hill, Waterside, Derry, County Londonderry, BT47 6DW
028 7134 5180

On-the-money modern Irish cooking sums up this restaurant, which has gained a reputation for its excellent food. Get in the mood with a glass of bubbly on a squidgy sofa in the champagne lounge, then head for one of the white linen-swathed tables in the dining room, where well-sourced local ingredients and unfussy execution best describes the food.

Iona House
ionainn.com
19 Spencer Road, Derry, County Londonderry, BT47 6AA
028 7134 3529

A traditional watering hole with an attitude to match. Expect good old-fashioned friendliness with a wide selection of beers. This is a family-run pub with real fires and a warm welcome.

Peadar O'Donnell's Bar
peadars.com
59–63 Waterloo Street, Derry, County Londonderry
028 71267295

Claiming to serve the best stout in the land, this bar is one of the best spots for both traditional and contemporary music in Derry. It's actually three bars in one – Peadar O'Donnells, the Gweedore Bar and Gweedore Upstairs.

Sandinos
sandinoscafebar.com
Water Street, Derry, County Londonderry, BT48 6BQ
028 7130 9927

With jazz, world, funk, folk and gypsy music, not to mention 1980s, hip-hop, soul and serious dance sounds, Sandinos is that eclectic type of bar that tries to please everyone. Live bands usually play Friday night, and there's traditional Irish sessions on Sunday evenings.

The Tea Room
no8thetownhouse.co.uk/tea-room
8 Artillery Street, Derry, County Londonderry, BT48 6RG
079 2184 1820

Coffee, croissants, herbal teas, daily papers and free WiFi are all on offer at this cosy tea house. Visit for elevenses, lunch or afternoon tea.

▶ **PLACES NEARBY**

It's not in Northern Ireland, but cross the border near Derry and head north, and you'll be on the glorious Inishowen Peninsula. If you don't have your passport to hand, there's a country park and heritage house that won't require you to cross international lines to visit.

Inishowen

visitinishowen.com

The diamond-shaped Inishowen Peninsula stretches north from Derry city, flanked on the east by Lough Foyle and on the west by Lough Swilly. Many visitors make the long journey up through Inishowen for the sake of standing on Malin Head, with its prevailing view of mountain, moor and rugged coastline.

Inishowen is a remote and underpopulated region of Donegal and once you get down to west-facing beaches such as White Strand Bay (Malin Head), Pollan Bay (Doagh Isle), Tullagh Bay (Clonmany) and Crummie's Bay (Dunree Head), you're likely to have them to yourself. The tremendous White Strand, which runs for 3 miles south from Buncrana, is better known and more frequented. Doagh Island, in reality a peninsula to the south of Malin Head, is rich in sand dunes covered in wild flowers in summer, and has the ruin of 16th-century Carnickabraghy Castle at its edge. Birdwatchers may spot waders at Trawbreaga Bay and on the mudflats around Inch Island.

The 3,700-year-old circular stone fort of Grianan of Aileach (off N13, 3 miles west of Derry) was a stronghold of the O'Neill Kings of Ulster. Stone steps climb to the top of the 18-foot walls for a fabulous view over loughs Swilly and Foyle.

Ness Country Park

doeni.gov.uk/niea

50 Oughtagh Road, Killaloo, Claudy, County Londonderry, BT47 3TR

028 7133 8417 | Open daily Jun to mid-Sep 9–9, Apr–May 9–5, mid-Sep to Mar 9–4.30

A beautiful wooded area with deep ravines thick with ferns, Ness Country Park has a spectacular walk from the parking area to where the River Burntollet makes a fine double drop of 30 feet into a pool. Above is the viewpoint of Shaun's Leap. Whether or not the famed 18th-century highwayman Shaun Crossan really escaped justice by leaping across this narrow gap, it's not a feat to try to emulate.

◀ Ness Country Park

President Wilson Ancestral Home

28 Spout Road, Dergalt, Strabane, County Tyrone, BT82 8NB
Signposted off the B72 Strabane–Newtownstewart road, just east of Strabane | 028 7138 2204 | Open Jul–Aug Tue–Sun 2–5

James Wilson, a printer by trade, was just 20 years old when he emigrated to America from this little whitewashed cottage in 1807; his grandson, Woodrow Wilson, served as the 28th President of the United States from 1913–21. You can see the family's box beds and other furniture typical of the period, and you get the chance to chat to members of the Wilson family, who still live next door.

Downhill Demesne & Hezlett House

MAP REF 383 D1

nationaltrust.org.uk

Mussenden Road, Castlerock, County Londonderry, BT51 4RP

028 7084 8728

The buildings and ruins on the cliffs near Castlerock are all that remain of the 18th-century glories of the Downhill estate, laid out in 1783–85 by the Protestant Bishop of Londonderry, Frederick Hervey, the fourth Earl of Bristol. He lived life to the full, with a string of mistresses, one of whom was reputedly installed in the cylindrical Mussenden Temple. Built in 1785, this rather bizarre building was constructed as a library with the Temple of Vesta in Italy as its inspiration. The ruins of the Bishop's Palace of Downhill, with its walled garden and ice house, lie near the Lion Gate (topped with leopard sculptures).

TAKE IN SOME HISTORY

Mussenden Temple

nationaltrust.org.uk

Built in 1785, this small circular building enjoys a dramatic position, perched on the edge of the cliffs, high above the Atlantic Ocean, offering spectacular views westwards. It was built as a library and dedicated to the memory of the Earl's cousin, Frideswide Mussenden. The National Trust has stabilised the cliffs to prevent the loss of the building, which was in some danger due to erosion.

PLACES NEARBY

Limavady, 10 miles southwest of Mussenden is a good place to go to eat. **Downhill beach** has more than 6 miles of surf, dunes and sand, with great views to Antrim and Donegal. Portstewart (see page 148), Bushmills Distillery (see page 104) and the Giant's Causeway (see page 123) are all nearby.

Greens Restaurant, Roe Park Resort ◉

roeparkresort.com

Limavady, County Londonderry, BT49 9LB | 028 7772 2222

Built as a country mansion in the 18th century, and surrounded by 150 acres of grounds beside the River Roe, Roe Park has been extended in recent years into a vast modern golfing and leisure resort. Just one of several dining options here, Greens Restaurant is a stylish, split-level space offering mostly traditional cooking and unpretentious local favourites, with the occasional modern twist.

The Lime Tree ⊛
limetreerest.com
60 Catherine Street, Limavady,
County Londonderry, BT49 9DB
028 7776 4300
The Lime Tree is a pint-sized neighbourhood restaurant in the town centre, its walls hung with vibrant artwork. It showcases the pick of the region, using seasonal local produce. There's plenty to enjoy here, particularly for lovers of ocean-fresh seafood.

▶ Downpatrick   MAP REF 383 F4

Built on two hills, Downpatrick is a market and cathedral town about 20 miles south of Belfast. Not only does Downpatrick have some interesting history but its rolling hills, known as drumlins, formed in the Ice Age, offer fine views of the surrounding scenic countryside and marshes. Its Gaelic name 'Dún Pádraig' means 'Patrick's Stronghold' and comes from the fact that the patron saint of Ireland, St Patrick, is said to be buried next to the cathedral. This is a key site for visitors, along with Inch Abbey, which also played a key part in Irish history.

Outside of town, explore the railway that follows the line of the ancient shoreline. Here an inland route leads to the lovely Strangford Lough (see page 65). Golf and healing wells provide relaxation for visitors to the surrounding area.

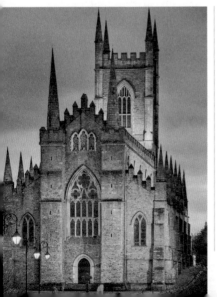

◀ Down Cathedral

TAKE IN SOME HISTORY
Down Cathedral
downcathedral.org
English Street, Downpatrick, County Down, BT30 6AB | 028 4461 4922
Open Mon–Sat 9.30–4, Sun 2–4
The site has been occupied by a cathedral since the sixth century, but the present building is mostly of the 18th and 19th centuries. Outside, a massive stone slab, inscribed 'Patric', is usually bright with

floral offerings; but whether Ireland's patron saint really does rest here, along with the remains of St Brigid and St Columcille, is open to conjecture. Down County Museum, housed in the old 18th-century jail, features the history of the county as well as offering an illuminating view of St Patrick's story.

Inch Abbey

Inch Abbey Road, Downpatrick, County Down, BT30 9AX | 028 3885 3955 | Open daily 24 hours

Sir John de Courcy, whose wife founded Grey Abbey (see page 71), was a warrior – he led the Norman invasion of East Ulster in 1177 – and also a spiritual man. He founded Inch Abbey in 1180 on marshland by the River Quoile and, until the Dissolution of the Monasteries in the 1540s, the monks proved their Anglo-Irish loyalties by rejecting all Irish applicants.

TAKE A TRAIN RIDE
Downpatrick and County Down Railway

downrail.co.uk

Railway Station, Market Street, Downpatrick, County Down, BT30 6LZ | 028 4461 5779 | Open mid-Jun to Sep Sat–Sun 2–5

Families and railway buffs will enjoy a ride on the island's only full-sized heritage railway, which travels through lovely countryside, with views of the Mourne Mountains. There's also a museum and plenty of things to see, including a collection of vintage carriages.

VISIT HEALING WELLS
Struell Wells

doeni.gov.uk/niea

Struell Wells Road, Downpatrick, County Down, BT30 6RA

Open daily 24 hours

Each of the many springs in this green valley has a reputation for healing. During the 18th century, Struell Wells became a

▼ Inch Abbey

major place of healing and of pilgrimage. Enthusiasm was spurred by the story that St Patrick had spent a night in the freezing water of the drinking well known as The Tub. From The Tub, with its domed roof, the water flows through the Eye Well (said to cure eye diseases) to reach a pair of 19th-century bathhouses: a small, now roofless, one for women, and a larger house under a vaulted roof with male and female changing rooms. There's also a men's pool fed by a fall of water.

PLAY A ROUND
Downpatrick Golf Club
downpatrickgolfclub.org.uk

43 Saul Road, Downpatrick, County Down, BT30 6PA | 028 4461 5947
A classic parkland course with spectacular views of County Down, Strangford Lough and even the Isle of Man on a clear day. Undulating fairways, strategically placed sand traps and quick but true greens make the course a testing yet pleasurable challenge.

▶ **PLACES NEARBY**
Head northeast for Castle Ward's popular Game of Thrones Winterfell Tours (see page 108), or southwest for Castlewellan Forest Park (see page 108) and the Mountains of Mourne (see page 142).

▶ **Dungiven Priory** MAP REF 382 C2
limavady.gov.uk
Priory Lane, Dungiven, County Londonderry, BT47 4PF | 028 3885 3955
Open daily 24 hours
The chancel of the 12th-century Augustinian Dungiven Priory holds one of the finest medieval tombs in Ireland, that of Cooey-na-Gal (d. 1385), a chieftain of the O'Catháin clan. His effigy lies under a canopy of carved foliage. In niches under the tomb stand six guardians, drawing their swords. Their pleated tunics may well be kilts, and they may be 'gallowglasses', or mercenaries, from Scotland. It was unwise to come upon their master without an introduction – his nickname means 'The Stranger's Bane'.

▶ **PLACES NEARBY**
Derry/Londonderry (see page 110) is the closest city. Closer is Banagher Glen.

Banagher Glen
Banagher Glen lies just 3 miles southwest of Dungiven, accessed from the B74, and is a secluded, steep wooded glen leading to Altnaheglish Reservoir and Banagher Dam. One of the oldest ancient oak woodlands in Ireland, Banagher Glen is a nature reserve and Special Area of Conservation. Walks of varying lengths are available through Banagher Forest and Banagher Glen all year round.

▶ Enniskillen   MAP REF 382 B4

enniskillen.com

Enniskillen is the bustling capital town of County Fermanagh, set on an island between two loughs. Wander along the lovely long narrow main street that is lined with individual shops and features the fascinating historic Buttermarket, filled with local crafts, many of which you can see being made. Some of the many attractions in town include the castle with its regimental and county museums; Cole's Monument in Forthill Park with a splendid view over the town from the top; and Blakes of the Hollow, a pub with traditional music.

One of Enniskillen's main attractions is its ideal situation for exploring the attractive surrounding area, including the nearby lough. Don't miss the chance to discover the pretty rivers and waterways as well as the green countryside around the town offering scenic walks and activities from boating and karting to golf and fishing.

TAKE IN SOME HISTORY

Castle Coole

nationaltrust.org.uk

Enniskillen, County Fermanagh, BT74 6JY | 028 6632 2690

See website for opening times

Legend says that if the resident flock of greylag geese ever leaves the Castle Coole estate so will the earls of Belmore. The geese still live there, however, and so does the family who built the great Palladian mansion. One of Ireland's finest neoclassical country houses, with its huge portico and long arcaded wings, stately Castle Coole was designed by James Wyatt and finished in 1798, the year after Armar Lowry-Corry was created first Earl of Belmore. He never really enjoyed Castle Coole. Apart from his money worries (he died penniless in 1802), he was devastated when his wife – a dark-haired beauty – left him. Her portrait is one of the attractions of a tour around the interior. One other poignant fact: the gorgeously appointed State Bedroom, with its red and gold canopied bed, was created for a state visit by King George IV in 1821 that never actually took place.

Cole's Monument

Forthill Park, Enniskillen, County Fermanagh, BT74 7BA | 028 6632 3110 | Open Mid-Apr to Sep daily 1.30–3.30, other times by arrangement

Climb the 180 spiral steps of this memorial tower, which is set in a pleasant park, for spectacular views.

Enniskillen Castle

enniskillencastle.co.uk

Enniskillen, County Fermanagh, BT74 7HL | 028 6632 5000

See website for opening times

Imposing and strategically important Enniskillen Castle now houses two museums:

▲ Enniskillen Castle

Fermanagh County Museum and The Inniskillings Museum. You can also find out more about your local ancestors at Fermanagh Genealogy Centre.

Florence Court
nationaltrust.org.uk
Mill Road, Enniskillen, County Fermanagh, BT92 1DB | 028 6634 8249 | See website for opening times
The Cole family, later the earls of Enniskillen, built Florence Court early in the 18th century within sight of 2,180-foot Cuilcagh Mountain. Inside you can admire the plasterwork, antique Irish furniture, portraits of generations of red-haired Coles, and a fine Belleek chamberpot with a portrait of Victorian British Prime Minister William Gladstone painted at the bottom. Gladstone supported Home Rule for Ireland; the Coles did not.

VISIT THE MUSEUM
Sheelin Lace Museum
irishlacemuseum.com
Bellanaleck, Enniskillen, County Fermanagh, BT92 2BA | 028 6634 8052 | Museum: Apr–Oct Mon–Sat 10–6. Shop: Mon–Sat 10–6
Ireland's best collection of antique lace is displayed here; some was made locally at Inishmacsaint but other pieces, from babies' caps and christening gowns to wedding dresses, have been collected from all over the country.

CATCH A PERFORMANCE
Ardhowen Theatre
ardhowentheatre.com
Dublin Road, Enniskillen, County Fermanagh, BT74 6HN
028 6632 3233/5440
This lakeside theatre has a lovely setting and presents events of broad appeal, from local artists to drama festivals.

Blakes of the Hollow

blakesofthehollow.com,
6 Church Street, Enniskillen,
County Fermanagh, BT74 7EJ
028 6632 2143
Catch traditional live music
sessions on Friday or Saturdays
in this lovely old wood-panelled
Victorian bar, which was
established in 1887 by the
Herbert family.

GO SHOPPING
The Buttermarket

Down Street, Enniskillen, County
Fermanagh, BT74 7DU | 028 6632
4499 | Open Mon–Sat 10–5
The restored Buttermarket
makes an ideal focus for local
craftworkers and some of
Ireland's top artists, who
present a fascinating range of
items. Among the many lovely
pieces for sale here are Frankie
McPhillips' classic salmon fly
collection, pottery, textile
designs, jewellery and art.

GET ON THE WATER
Fermanagh has a huge
selection of cruising
opportunities on the Erne–
Shannon waterway or loughs.
Fishing is good, too, alone or
with a ghillie (fishing guide) for
local expertise. The tourist
office has full details.

Manor House Marine

manormarine.com
Killadeas, County Fermanagh
028 6862 8100 | Open daily 10–6
Spend half a day or even a
whole day soaking up the
breathtaking scenery of Lough
Erne from a boat. Full tuition is

---

5 exquisite pieces of history

▶ *Book of Kells* page 268
▶ **Brú na Bóinne** page 187
▶ **Clonmacnoise** page 211
▶ **Derry's walls** page 112
▶ **James Joyce Centre**
page 265

---

given to first-timers and no
experience or licence is
required for rental.

EAT AND DRINK
Belle Isle

belle-isle.com and
irishcookeryschool.com
Lisbellaw, Enniskillen, County
Fermanagh, BT94 5HG
028 6638 7231
Exquisite Belle Isle is a
stunning 12th-century castle
set on its own private island,
with the whole 470-acre estate
spread over eight picturesque
islands. Stay in a cottage or
the castle or learn to cook
or improve your skills in the
purpose-built state-of-the-art
cookery school, the first of its
kind in Northern Ireland.

Catalina Restaurant, Lough Erne Resort ◉◉◉

lougherneresort.com
Belleek Road, County Fermanagh,
BT93 7ED | 028 6632 3230
Dynamic modern Irish cooking
is set off by the luxury hotel,
fully loaded with an indulgent
Thai spa and a golf course
designed by Nick Faldo. This
glossy purpose-built resort on

its own 60-acre peninsula jutting into the eponymous lough deserves every one of its five stars. When it comes to fine dining, the Catalina Restaurant is an expansive space with vaulted ceilings and views of the golf course and water, along with smart linen and swagged drapes for a refined and traditional backdrop to Noel McMeel's cooking.

▶ **PLACES NEARBY**

There's lots to do around Lough Erne (see page 135), and a spectacular cave system to the southwest.

Marble Arch Caves

marblearchcaves.net

43 Marlbank Road, Legnabrocky, Florencecourt, County Fermanagh, BT92 1EW | 028 6634 8855

Open Jul–Aug daily 10–5, Apr–Jun, Sep daily 10–4.30, Oct Mon–Fri 11–4, Sat, Sun 10–4.30

Tours of this incredible subterranean world start with the caving and mineral display in the visitor centre, then a spectacular underground route takes you by boat and on foot through the caverns, including the Moses Walk through a subterranean river. Telephone in advance and reserve a tour.

▼ Marble Arch Caves

▶ Giant's Causeway MAP REF 383 D1

A UNESCO World Heritage Site, the Giant's Causeway is a hump-backed promontory. It is formed of the wave-eroded stubs of around 40,000 mostly hexagonal basalt columns created some 60 million years ago when lava from an undersea volcano cooled rapidly on contact with the cold water. Taller columns can be seen in the cliffs behind. The viscous lava from nearby eruptions flowed into a depression, forming an inland lake of lava. As it cooled, it hardened, shrunk and cracked to form the columns of black basaltic rock running out into the sea towards Scotland that we see today.

Alternatively, legend says that the hero-giant Fionn MacCumhaill (often Anglicised as Finn McCool) laid down the causeway as a stepping stone so he could stride across the Sea of Moyle to reach his enemy Finn Gall on the Hebridean island of Staffa, where there are similar columns. Whatever created the causeway, it is a magnificent sight, especially when approached on foot from above. A coastal path can be joined at Blackrock or from the causeway visitor centre on the cliff top.

Special features

Among the many spectacular features of the Giant's Causeway are the Giant's Boot, a detached, boot-shaped formation on the shore; the Giant's Organ at Port Noffer; the Giant's Harp, above Port Reostan; and the adjacent Chimney Pots, where tottering basalt columns have become detached from the cliffs.

Worth seeing?

The Giant's Causeway has had a magnetic attraction for visitors for hundreds of years, and has also drawn its fair share of folklore and legend. Long before the Victorian novelist Thackeray travelled to see this 'remnant of chaos' in a small boat on a wild and stormy day in 1842, it had attracted the attention of Samuel Johnson, the 18th-century poet, critic and writer, and his biographer, James Boswell. In his *Life of Samuel Johnson* (1791), Boswell recalled their journey made in the late summer and autumn of 1773. Boswell had asked his companion: 'Is not the Giant's Causeway worth seeing?' to which Johnson replied rather disparagingly: 'Worth seeing? Yes, but not worth going to see.'

Shipwrecks

Many ships have foundered below these towering cliffs but none as tragically as that of the Spanish Armada galleon *Girona*. On a fateful day in October 1588, the ship was sunk by severe weather conditions within view of the Giant's Causeway. Captained by Don Alonso Martinez Levia, second-in-command of the defeated Spanish Armada, the *Girona* had taken on board the crews of two other Spanish ships, which were among 30 sunk by raging North Atlantic storms off the coast of Ireland, and they were heading north for Scotland when the tragedy occurred. Only five of the crew are believed to have survived out of 1,300 men. The wreck was discovered in 1967 by Belgian divers. The treasure that went down with the ship was salvaged in 1968 and is now on display in Belfast's Ulster Museum.

Explore the Causeway Coast

This four-day driving route running from Belfast to Derry has been rated one of the top road trips in the world and includes three Areas of Outstanding Natural Beauty.

The Antrim Coast (see page 60) is well served by its spectacular coast road, the A2, running north from Larne to hug the coast for the 25 miles to Cushendall. From here it bypasses Cushendun to take a 30-mile inland route over the moors to Ballycastle (see page 78), then about 1.5 miles inland of the basalt coast around Carrick-a-Rede (see page 128) and the Giant's Causeway. There's an enjoyable, if slow and bumpy, 'scenic route' detour on the coast road, starting in Cushendun and winding for 12 miles around Torr Head, to rejoin the A2 at Ballyvoy.

The Antrim Coast is especially striking for its cliffs, bluffs, headlands and glen mouths. Driving north you encounter white limestone cliffs around Carnlough Bay, beyond which dark red sandstone rises dramatically to 820 feet. Garron Point curves into Red Bay, where three of the Glens of Antrim (see page 130) meet the sea around the great flat-topped promontory of Lurigethan, at 1,148 feet. Farther north comes paler pudding-stone around Cushendun, before you swing west towards the basalt of the Giant's Causeway.

Each of the villages has a particular charm: Glenarm, beautifully set at the foot of its glen; Carnlough, with its sandy beach and harbour, and white limestone houses; Waterfoot or Glenariff, below the rampart of Lurigethan; and Cushendall, the 'Capital of the Glens', with its sandstone Curfew Tower jail and a huddle of houses designed by Clough Williams-Ellis.

Farms and castles

Human settlement on the Causeway Coast is confined to the small harbours and inlets and a few farmsteads further inland. On the headlands above, the ruined strongholds of Dunluce Castle, between Portrush and Bushmills, and Kinbane Castle, northwest of Ballycastle, watch over the coast. Dunluce, once home of local landowners the MacQuillans and, later, the MacDonnells, dates from the 14th century, and Kinbane, reached by a steep path and across slippery rocks, was another MacDonnell stronghold, dating from the 16th century.

Spectacular coastline

The oldest rocks in the AONB, found along the coast near Portrush and at the great sandy strand of White Park Bay, are sedimentary, dating from the Jurassic period (190 to 135 million years ago). The coast is also noted for its startlingly white chalk cliffs from the Cretaceous period (135 to 65 million years ago), but it is for the dark volcanic basalt that it is most famous. Features like the Giant's Causeway and the headlands of Benbane Head and Carrick-a-Rede Island make this one of the most spectacular coastlines in Britain.

The clifftops and ledges of the Causeway Coast provide a rich habitat for a variety of plants, such as the sea aster, sea pink and white sea campion, while the cliffs are home to seabirds such as the razorbill, guillemot and puffin, the peregrine falcon, the raven and the rare coastal member of the crow family, the chough.

CHECK OUT THE VISITOR CENTRE

Giant's Causeway Visitor Centre

giantscausewaytickets.com
On the B147 Causeway road, 2 miles from Bushmills, BT57 8SU
Open daily Apr–Sep 9–7, Feb, Mar, Oct 9–6, Nov–Jan 9–5

The visitor centre gives a good introduction to the site, and tells the story of the formation of the causeway through a 12-minute audio-visual show. There is also an exhibition area with displays on the legend of Fionn MacCumhaill and the local bird life. The area is a haven for seabirds such as fulmar, petrel, cormorant, shag, redshank, guillemot and razorbill. Rock pipits and wagtails explore the shoreline and eider ducks are found in sheltered water. Guided tours are available from the centre, and you can catch a minibus down to the causeway, or walk from the parking area in 10 minutes. Beside the centre is the Causeway School Museum, a reconstructed 1920s schoolroom complete with toys of the era.

TAKE IN SOME HISTORY

Dunluce Castle

87 Dunluce Road, Bushmills, County Antrim, BT57 8UY | 028 2073 1938
Open daily 10–5

The poignant ruin of Dunluce Castle stands on the edge of the

▼ Dunluce Castle

cliffs – so close that during a storm in 1639 the kitchens fell into the sea and the kitchen workers were killed. Steeped in myth and legend and said to be inhabited by giants, ghosts and banshees wailing through the sea mist, Dunluce is associated with many stories – the most romantic concerns its recapture from the English in 1584 by the owner, Sorley Boy MacDonnell, whose men had been hauled 200 feet up the cliffs in baskets. Look for the pretty blue flower of Dunluce and drifts of seapinks that cluster around the castle's ruined shell.

Kinbane Castle

3 miles from Ballycastle on the road to Ballintoy. Open access

Set on a narrow limestone headland that juts out to sea, there's not much left of the ruins of this castle, originally built in the mid-16th century by the brother of Sorley Boy MacDonnell. Besieged by the English in 1151 and 1555, it was damaged but rebuilt.

TEST YOUR NERVE

Carrick-a-Rede Rope Bridge

nationaltrust.org.uk

119A Whitepark Road, Ballycastle, County Antrim, BT54 6LS | 028 2076 9839 | Open daily 9.30–6

The Carrick-a-Rede Rope Bridge is the only means of crossing the 80-foot gap between the cliff and the Carrick-a-Rede basalt stack offshore. It was originally a scary fly walk with a single guide rope slung in the air by salmon fishermen to reach their offshore fishing station. The National Trust has made it more stable, but it still sways enough to raise the hairs on the back of your neck. There are no recorded instances of anyone being injured falling off the old bridge, although there have been times when visitors were unable to face the return walk and needed to be taken back by boat. Outlandish stunts have been performed on the bridge, including riding a bicycle across and doing handstands on a chair in the middle. The reward for braving the vertiginous bridge and reaching the island is witnessing a wonderful range of seabirds and experiencing a glorious view across to Rathlin Island and on towards Scotland.

TAKE A TRAIN RIDE

freewebs.com/giantscausewayrailway

Runkerry Road, Bushmills, County Antrim, BT57 8SZ | 028 2073 2844 Open Jul, Aug daily six departures, Easter–Jun, Sep, Oct Sat, Sun only six departures; see website for current timetable

The major settlement on the Causeway Coast is Bushmills, from where a narrow-gauge steam train runs to the Giant's Causeway World Heritage Site. The train travels along a magnificent two-mile coastal stretch, following the track bed of the former Giant's Causeway tram. Europe's first hydroelectric tram, designed by William Traill of Ballylough and opened in 1883, ran between Portrush and the

▲ Carrick-a-Rede Rope Bridge

Causeway Hotel. It was affectionately known as 'the toast rack' because of its quaintly shaped carriages. For many people, the rattling, leisurely journey on the tram around the spectacular coast was the highlight of their holiday but the last section of the tramway finally closed in 1951.

EAT AND DRINK

Bushmills Inn Hotel ◉
bushmillsinn.com
9 Dunluce Road, Bushmills, County Antrim, BT57 8QG | 028 2073 3000

This 400-year-old coaching inn, close to the Bushmills Distillery (see page 104), is brimming with atmosphere and history. High-class culinary standards are evident in what appears on the plate, and the menu brims with attention-grabbing ideas. Don't miss the whiskey tasting.

▶ **PLACES NEARBY**

There are plenty of attractions close by, including the Bushmills Distillery (see page 104) and the towns of Portstewart (see page 148) and Ballycastle (see page 78).

▶ Glens of Antrim MAP REF 383 E2

Only a short drive away from the crowded Antrim Coast (see page 60) at the Glens of Antrim you'll find peace and quiet amid beautiful scenery of basalt cliffs, green valleys and dense woodland. Waymarked walks for all tastes and abilities in Glenariff Forest Park take you past water in motion: fast mountain rivers, streams, rapids and waterfalls.

The nine Glens of Antrim form one of Ireland's most beautiful landscapes, but because they are close to the spectacular Antrim Coast, Northern Ireland's most popular tourist attraction, the glens see less tourist activity than they might.

The glens were formed as a result of intense glacial meltwater action at the end of the last Ice Age, perhaps 15,000 years ago. Upstream from the glens, the ice deepened existing valleys, like Glenariff and Glenballyemon, into ice-scoured hollows filled with small loughs and bogs.

The great outdoors

That is good news for walkers, birders, photographers and other lovers of quiet wide-open spaces. Not that the glens are particularly wide – great water-cut clefts in Antrim's coastal shelf, they tend to be U-shaped and high-sided, in some cases (notably Glenariff) with imposing cliffs forming their upper flanks. Iron ore was mined in the glens until the early 20th century, but now all is peaceful and green, with narrow roads winding up one glen and down the next.

Don't ignore the glens on a wet day, especially Glenariff, where rain-swollen streams are spectacular.

▼ Glenariff

The glens

The most southerly pair of glens are Glenarm, running down to Glenarm village, and Glencloy, the Glen of the Stony Dykes, which runs through a rocky defile to reach the harbour of Carnlough. North of these is Glenariff, the Queen of the Glens, and then come four close together: wide Glenballyemon descending to Cushendall, and the trio of Glendun, Glenaan and Glencorp. Glendun, the 'Glen of the Brown River', is spanned by a viaduct designed by the great architect Charles Lanyon. At the foot of the Little Blue Glen, Glenaan, the second turning left off the main Cushendall–Ballymoney road and 2 miles from Cushendall, you'll find the signposted track to Ossian's Grave, a fine 'horned cairn' burial mound perhaps 5,000 years old. Legend says this is the resting place of bold Ossian, the warrior-poet son of the giant hero Fionn MacCumhaill. North again, Glenshesk and Glentaisie run down to Ballycastle.

The narrow lane that climbs to Ossian's Grave is really too steep for a car, and there's nowhere sensible to park at the top. Walk up instead.

CHECK OUT THE VISITOR CENTRE

Glenariff Forest Park Visitor Centre

nidirect.gov.uk/glenariff-forest-park
Glenariff Road, County Antrim,
BT44 0QX | 028 2955 6000 | Open
daily 10–dusk

Glenariff, sited between Glencloy and Glenballyemon, is the most spectacular glen, and the one most geared to tourism. Waymarked trails run from the Glenariff Forest Park Visitor Centre and the Viewpoint Trail (half a mile) enables you to look down the glen to the sea. Following this walk takes you back to the car park via the ornamental gardens.

The popular waymarked Waterfall Walk Trail (3 miles) passes the lovely waterfalls of the Glenariff River, while the slightly more demanding Scenic Trail (5.5 miles) goes by way of forest, moorland and river. The Rainbow Trail (0.4 miles) is an optional detour on the Waterfall Walk Trail. Many of these paths and footbridges were laid out in Victorian times, giving the walks a period charm.

TAKE IN SOME HISTORY

Ardclinis Church

Coast Road, Cushendall, County
Antrim, BT44 0RB

The ruins of this church and its graves are in a beautiful setting overlooking Red Bay in Ardclinis. There are several legends linked to the site where there has been a church since early Christian times.

Ossian's Grave

2nd turning left off main
Cushendall/Ballymoney Road, 2
miles from Cushendall | Open access

There are great views from this megalithic court cairn on a hillside near the Glenaan River. Local folklore links this neolithic court tomb with the mythical Celtic warrior-poet, Ossian, son of giant hero Fionn MacCumhaill, but it dates to many thousands of years before he's supposed to have lived.

GET ACTIVE
Antrim Forum Leisure Centre
antrimandnewtownabbey.gov.uk
Lough Road, Antrim, County Antrim, BT41 4DQ | 028 9446 4131 | Open Mon–Fri 7.15am–10pm, Sat 9.30–5.30, Sun 2–5.30
This is one of Northern Ireland's most important leisure complexes, regularly hosting international tournaments.

Facilities include pools, a gym, tennis courts and a health suite with full spa facilities.

Ardclinis Outdoor Adventure Centre
ardclinis.com
11 High Street, Cushendall, County Antrim, BT44 0NB | 028 2177 1340
Open daily from 9am
An exciting outdoor adventure centre, offering everything from corporate team-building and solo challenges to family fun. Activities on offer include power-boating, windsurfing and abseiling.

LISTEN TO LIVE MUSIC
McMullans Central Bar
7 Bridge Street, Cushendall, County Antrim | 028 2177 1730

▼ Glenariff waterfall

Traditional and contemporary music nights cater for all tastes at this well-known County Antrim pub. Children and parties are warmly welcomed. Check first to see what music is on. A good-value menu is available while you listen.

PLAY A ROUND
Royal Portrush Golf Club
royalportrushgolfclub.com
Portrush, County Antrim, BT56 8JQ
028 7082 2311
This course, designed by Harry S Colt, is considered to be among the best six in the UK. Founded in 1888, it was the venue of the first professional golf event in Ireland, held in 1895. Royal Portrush is spectacular and breathtaking, one of the tightest driving courses known to golfers. On a clear day there's a fine view of Islay and the Paps of Jura from the third tee, and the Giant's Causeway from the fifth.

EAT AND DRINK
McCollams
mccollamsbar.com
23 Mill Street, Cushendall, County Antrim, BT44 0ST | 028 2177 1992
McCollam's is a good old-fashioned pub with a cosy atmosphere that has been running for over 200 years and welcomes tourists and locals alike. Arrive early to get a good seat for the regular live music evenings and to admire the historic interior.

▶ PLACES NEARBY
The beautiful Antrim Coast (see page 60) is a good place to carry on your explorations.

▶ Lecale Peninsula MAP REF 383 F4

Drive around the Lecale Peninsula and you'll find a quiet corner of countryside and coast that sees few tourists. From Downpatrick, go across country on the B176 to Killough, the port for the farm produce of Castle Ward in the 18th century. Turning east on the A2 you'll run through Ardglass, with its ancient fortifications around the harbour, to Kilclief. The 15th-century tower house on Park Road in Strangford was the scene of a medieval scandal when John Cely (or Sely), the Bishop of Down, was caught with a married woman and subsequently defrocked.

St Patrick is said to have landed at Saul on his return to Ireland in AD 432, and it is here he died in AD 461. You can learn of the saint's life in the church's exhibition, and climb the nearby hill of Slieve Patrick, up a path lined with Stations of the Cross, for a wonderful view.

SEE A LOCAL VILLAGE
Ardglass

This lovely coastal village, an important fishing harbour for 2,000 years, now has a marina, but it's still a major centre for marketing and processing the catch. There used to be seven castles here, but Jordan's Castle, a 15th-century defensive tower house overlooking the harbour, is the only one that remains more or less complete.

TAKE IN SOME HISTORY
Audley's Castle

Portloughan, Downpatrick, County Down, BT30 7LP

An imposing tower house, this fine example of the 'gatehouse' type of fortified dwelling was built in the 15th century. When the park at Castle Ward was landscaped in the 18th century, the ruin was perfect as that most fashionable of garden features, the romantic ruin. It still has its 'bawn' or defensive enclosure, now reduced to its foundations.

Saul Church and Round Tower

2 miles from Downpatrick, follow the A25 to Strangford. Turn onto Mearne Road and follow the signpost for the church

Built in 1932 to commemorate the 1,500th anniversary of St Patrick's arrival in Ireland, the church replaced an earlier building on the site. There's a huge statue of the saint nearby, on the crest of Slieve Patrick. Bronze panels illustrate scenes from the saint's life.

▶ PLACES NEARBY

Travel on to Downpatrick (see page 116) and Castle Ward (see page 107).

▶ Londonderry

see **Derry**, page 110

Lough Erne MAP REF 382 B4

Lough Erne's shape has been likened to a leaping dolphin scattering a shower of broken water drops behind it. It's about 50 miles long but only around 5 miles wide, and is very shallow. The surrounding soil is mostly clay and peat, poor land that has resisted agriculture and remained a beautiful mixture of moorland, forest and marsh.

Go for a drive
From Enniskillen, the hub of the Lough Erne system, you can circle Lower Lough Erne clockwise taking the A46 along the western shore to Belleek, returning down the east side of the lake on the A47 over Boa Island to Kesh, then on the A35 and B72 to Lisnarrick and the B82/A32 back to Enniskillen. Upper Lough Erne, a maze of islets and small stretches of water, is flanked on the west by the A509, which becomes the N3 as it crosses the border into the Republic and reaches Belturbet. On the east, the A4 leaves Enniskillen; a turning to the B514 runs southeast to Lisnaskea and the A34 goes on to Newtownbutler, from where you steer south by minor roads for the border. Boating is a wonderful way to get to know the lakes.

Visit the islands
The monastery established by St Molaise in the sixth century stands on Devenish Island, just north of Enniskillen (you can take a ferry from Trory jetty). Here you'll find a tall round tower, built by monks around 1120, the ruins of the beautiful little

▲ Devenish Island

15th-century abbey church and a fine high cross. There's an explanatory exhibition, and you can climb the ladders inside the tower for a wonderful view over Lough Erne. On White Island (take a boat from Castle Archdale Marina), seven extraordinary stone carvings have been built into a wall: a grinning sheela-na-gig (naked female stone figure), a seated man with a book, another holding two gryphons (griffins), a warrior and a bishop, a King David figure and a morose face. In Caldragh cemetery on Boa Island, reached by causeways on the A47, stands the Janus Man, a stumpy figure thought to be 2,000 years old, with two faces back-to-back, both with bulging eyes and pointed beards. Near him is his swollen-headed brother, the Lusty Man. It is uncertain what these figures represent.

On the causeway islands and shores of Upper Lough Erne are fine carvings of definite Christian tradition. Aghalurcher Old Church (signposted off the A34 just south of Lisnaskea), abandoned in 1484 after a murder at the altar deconsecrated the church, has elaborately carved skull-and-crossbones gravestones; so does the graveyard on Galloon Island (3 miles southwest of Newtownbutler).

TAKE IN SOME HISTORY
Tully Castle
Loughshore Road, Tully, Churchill, Derrygonnelly, BT9 6HP | 028 6862 1588 | Phone for opening times
On the shore of Lower Lough Erne, the fortified house of Tully Castle was built around 1610 by Sir John Hume. The defensive enclosure that surrounds the gaunt ruin of the house has been planted in the style of a 17th-century herb garden. Tully Castle has a tragic history. During the 1641 rebellion, Roderick Maguire, whose family had lost all their land, besieged the castle. Lady Hume, trying to protect the 16 men and 69 women and children in the castle with her, negotiated safe conduct to Enniskillen in return for surrender. But as soon as he had possession, Maguire and his men stripped the women and imprisoned them in the cellars, then tied up the male retainers and left them outside overnight. In the morning every man, woman and child was murdered; the castle was looted and burned.

TAKE TO THE WATER
Manor House Marine
manormarine.com/day-boats
Lough Erne, Killadeas, County Fermanagh, BT94 1NY
028 6862 8100
Hire a six- or eight-person boat for half or a whole day on the lough.

Lady of the Lake Tours
ladyofthelaketours.com
Killadeas, County Fermanagh, BT94 1NY | 028 6862 2200
Take a 90-minute trip or a dinner cruise on the *Lady of the Lake*.

Erne Tours Ltd
ernetours.com
Enniskillen | 028 6632 2882
Guided tours among the islands aboard the MV *Kestrel*.

Share Holiday Village
sharevillage.org
Lisnaskea | 028 6772 2122
The largest residential activity centre in Ireland offers all kinds of water activities.

GET OUTDOORS
Lough Erne is wonderful for wildlife. Three country parks around Lower Lough Erne provide lakeside and woodland walks. Castle Caldwell Forest (A47 near Kesh) has good birdwatching, and at the entrance is the Fiddler's Stone, a violin-shaped memorial to drunken fiddler Denis McCabe, who drowned in 1779. Castle Archdale Forest (A32 near Kesh) has a boating marina, fine gardens and an exhibition about the World War II flying boats based here. At Lough Navar Forest (near Derrygonnelly) a 7-mile scenic drive ends at the spectacular Cliffs of Magho viewpoint.

Castle Caldwell Forest
discovernorthernireland.com
4 miles from Belleek on A47
028 6634 3165 | Open daily
Consisting of almost 500 acres of mixed broadleaved and coniferous lowland forest along the shore of Lough Erne, the park, a bird sanctuary, offers waymarked walking trails. You can see the ruins of Castle Caldwell although it's not accessible. There's a jetty at the car park if you prefer to arrive by boat.

Castle Archdale Forest
discovernorthernireland.com
Off the B82 Enniskillen to Kesh road | 028 9082 3214 | Open daily
(see website for times)

▼ Tully Castle

Here on the shore of Lough Erne are more than 1,200 acres of lowland forest, with a mix of broadleaved and coniferous trees. Waymarked trails for walkers and cyclists begin from the car park beside the ruins of Castle Archdale, built in 1615. You can also access Davys Island by boat from the jetty.

Lough Navar Forest

discovernorthernireland.com
Signposted off the A46, northwest of Derrygonnelly, County Fermanagh
028 6634 3040 | Open daily 10–dusk

Take a 7-mile drive through the forest to an impressive panorama over Lower Lough Erne. There are picnic sites, viewpoints and various waymarked trails. You might see red deer or wild goats.

PLAY A ROUND

Lough Erne Resort

loughernegolfresort.com
Belleek Road, Enniskillen, County Fermanagh, BT93 7ED
028 6632 3230

This is the first course designed by Nick Faldo in Ireland, in a beautiful lakeland setting. It rests on its own secluded island nestling between Lower Lough Erne and Castle Hume Lough. Challenging for all levels of golfer.

EAT AND DRINK

Belleek Restaurant, Manor House Country Hotel ◉

manorhousecountryhotel.com
Killadeas, Enniskillen, County Fermanagh, BT94 1NY
028 6862 2200

Contemporary cooking is the focus of this restaurant, but there's no taking away from the view down to Lough Erne. The fine-dining action takes place in the Belleek Restaurant, housed in a conservatory extension to the old manor that gets the very best of the view.

▶ **PLACES NEARBY**

The town of Enniskillen (see page 119) is set right by the lough. Crom Estate (see page 109) is close to the southern tip.

▼ Lough Erne Resort

▶ Lough Neagh   MAP REF 383 D3

Lough Neagh is the largest freshwater lake in the British Isles. At 18 miles long and 7 miles wide it's also the third biggest in Europe. It's a haven for wildlife and a popular leisure destination. Canals linked to the lough include the Lagan Canal, the Ulster Canal, the Newry Canal and the Coalisland Canal, and there are heritage sites all round the shore. You can also see the remains of three round towers and a very fine example of a high cross, the Ardboe Old Cross. Explore on foot, by bike (the Lough Shore Cycling Trail is very popular – not just because it's lovely, but because it's mostly flat) or in the car – or follow the Lough Neagh Canoe Trail. There are two major islands, Coney Island and Ram's Island, which you can visit – boats can be hired and boat trips take in the islands as well.

TAKE IN SOME HISTORY
Ardboe Old Cross
cookstown.gov.uk

Battery Road, Ardboe, County Tyrone, BT80 0HY | Accessible daily 24 hours

On the western shore of Lough Neagh, the Ardboe Old Cross, carved in the ninth or tenth century, stands 18.5 feet tall. The shaft and head are heavily carved with biblical scenes, but weathering has blurred the finer details.

The carvings on the east and south faces are of Old Testament scenes, while the west face deals with New Testament themes. Look on the east side for Adam and Eve under a spreading Tree of Knowledge, Abraham about to sacrifice Isaac, and Shadrach, Meshach and Abednego in the fiery furnace. On the south is Cain dealing his brother Abel a thump with a flail, Samson and his lion, and a cramped David and Goliath. The west has the Adoration of the Magi, the miracles of the wine and water at Cana and the loaves and fishes at Galilee, and Christ's entry into Jerusalem on a donkey. The Passion occupies the west face of the cross head, while the east face of the head depicts the Last Judgement.

Behind the cross stands a beech tree, with thousands of coins pushed into its trunk by supplicants hoping to leave their troubles behind – or transfer them to anyone who would steal the coin. Sadly, the metal of the coins has gradually poisoned the tree. Beyond the tree is the ruin of a 17th-century church, on the site of a monastery established in the sixth century by St Colman Muchaidhe. Legend has it that when the workers building it became faint from lack of food, the saint sent his cow to walk across the lake and bring them milk. It is also said, somewhat at odds with chronology, that the leftover milk was mixed with the mortar used to build the high cross, ensuring its survival over the centuries.

GET OUTDOORS
Antrim Loughshore Park
Lough Road, Antrim, County Antrim, BT41 4DG | 028 9446 3966
Open summer 8am–9.30pm, winter 8.30–7.30
On the shores of Lough Neagh, this park hosts a variety of events, from Sunday afternoon band concerts to a dragon boat race in June. Two slipways provide access to the lough, one for jet skis and one for boats and canoes.

Oxford Island
Discovery Centre
oxfordisland.com
Craigavon, County Armagh, BT66 6NJ | 028 3832 2205 | Open Apr–Sep Mon–Sat 10–1, 2–4, Sun 2–5, Oct–Mar Mon–Sat 10–1, 2–4
For birdwatching and information and leaflets on Lough Neagh's natural history, visit Oxford Island Discovery Centre on the south shore (off Junction 10 of the M1).

EAT AND DRINK
Crosskeys Inn
40 Grange Road, Ardnaglass, Toome, County Antrim, BT41 3QB
028 7965 0694
The oldest thatched pub in Ireland is also one the most famous traditional music pubs, with sessions on Saturdays, and impromptu music other nights.

▶ PLACES NEARBY
There are several heritage properties near Lough Neagh and good places to dine in Ballymena and Galgorm.

Seamus Heaney Trail
laurel-villa.com
Laurel Villa, 60 Church Street, Magherafelt, County Londonderry, BT45 6AW | 028 7930 1459
Each of the bedrooms at this guest house is named after Ulster poets, but it is Seamus Heaney who is at the heart of the place, the starting point for an unofficial Heaney trail.

▼ Springhill, Magherafelt

Springhill

nationaltrust.org.uk

20 Springhill Road, Moneymore, Magherafelt, County Londonderry, BT45 7NQ | 028 8674 8210 | Open Easter, Jul–Aug daily 12–5, mid-Mar to Jun Tue, Sat, Sun 12–4, Sep Sat, Sun 12–4

The Conynghams, 'planters' who came from Scotland, built Springhill around 1690. The ladderback chairs, tables and cabinets were made by estate workers from the Conynghams' own timber, and the Georgian library and gunroom, with historic weaponry displayed, retain their 18th-century wallpaper. In the former laundry is a collection of costumes, and there are walks through the wooded grounds.

Wellbrook Beetling Mill

nationaltrust.org.uk

Wellbrook Road, Corkhill, County Tyrone, BT80 9RY | 028 8674 8210 Open mid-Mar to Sep Sat–Sun 2–5

Beetling (beating linen cloth smooth) played a vital part in Ulster's linen industry, and at the 18th-century Wellbrook Mill you can see the waterwheel and original machinery and learn about the industry in an enjoyable exhibition.

Newforge House

newforgehouse.com

Newforge House, Magheralin, County Armagh, BT67 0QL 028 9261 1255

The passion is palpable from the owners of this restored Georgian house, from the fine local linen and beautifully kept lawns to the lovingly decorated interior. Here you can browse in the library and take pottery lessons. The restaurant serves some of the best food in Ireland; don't miss the legendary cheese board.

Craigavon Watersports Centre

craigavonactivity.org

Lake Road, Craigavon, County Armagh, BT64 1AF | 028 3834 2669 Open Mon–Fri 9am–10pm, Sat 9–5, Sun 12–5

Waterskiing, sailing, banana boating or windsurfing on the Craigavon lakes. Tuition and equipment are provided.

Ardtara Country House Hotel

ardtara.com

8 Gorteade Road, Upperlands, Ballymena, County Antrim, BT46 5SA | 028 7964 4490

This Victorian house manages to be both welcoming and grand. The rooms are filled with antiques as well as all mod cons. The restaurant is undeniably one of the best in the area, sourcing excellent local ingredients served up with imagination and flare.

River Room Restaurant, Galgorm Resort and Spa ◉◉◉

galgorm.com

136 Fenaghy Road, Galgorm, County Antrim, BT42 1EA | 028 2588 1001

The hotel here is a superlative country house with an excellent spa. The top dining option is the River Room Restaurant, with the river floodlit at night. The menus, packed with seasonal dishes, change daily.

▶ Mountains of Mourne MAP REF 383 E5

mournelive.com

*'...I'll wait for the wild rose that's waiting for me
Where the Mountains of Mourne sweep down to the sea.'*

With these words the Victorian songwriter Percy French launched the Mountains of Mourne into the consciousness of the world's romantics. The Mournes are beautiful, a tight huddle of granite peaks that rise more than 2,100 feet from the southern coast of County Down, forming the core of the 220-square-mile Area of Outstanding Natural Beauty (AONB), which was designated in 1986. It is one of the largest and most important AONBs in Northern Ireland, and has for many years been considered the prime candidate for the region's long-awaited first national park. It contains all the peaks of the compact Mourne range, including Slieve Donard, which, at 2,789 feet (850m), is the highest point in Northern Ireland.

Most people have heard of these mountains, and many come to see them, but few bother to penetrate the narrow roads that lead up to the Silent Valley Reservoir and through the spectacularly steep-sided Spelga Pass. Fewer still pull on hiking boots for the walker-friendly paths; those who do get up to the peaks are rewarded with some breathtaking views.

The Mournes are formed of a hard, grey granite, and are among the youngest mountain ranges in the UK. They were created only 50 million years ago, when a vast block of shale

subsided deep within the earth's crust, forcing up the molten granite. Subsequent weathering and the sculpting action of Ice Age glaciers completed the majestic picture. The power of the glaciers is vividly seen at Hare's Gap – a classic mountain pass shaped by the passage of ice – between Slievenaglogh and Slieve Bearnagh.

But the AONB boundary takes in much more than the Mournes, with their sharply eroded peaks, tors and jagged rock pinnacles. To the north, the isolated outlying mountain mass of Slieve Croob (1,752 feet/532m) and Legananny Mountain (1,407 feet/429m) are separated from the main range by the forested Castlewellan Valley, while to the south, around Kilkeel, Rostrevor and Warrenpoint, the land drops away through moorland, woodland, field and farm to Carlingford Lough.

In 1993, the National Trust bought nearly 2 square miles of land in the Mourne Mountains. This included part of the highest peak of Slieve Donard and nearby Slieve Commedagh, the next highest peak in the range at 2,516 feet (767m).

Flora and fauna
The wildlife of the Mournes is dominated by the acidic moorland slopes of the hills, where the heather supports populations of red grouse and their predators, such as the peregrine falcon and buzzard. Three species of heather –

▼ The Mountains of Mourne

▲ The Cloughmore Stone, Rostrevor

cross-leaved heath, bell heather and ling – are found here, and other acid-loving plants include bog cotton, roseroot, harebell, marsh St John's wort, wild thyme and heath spotted orchid.

You are likely to meet sheep grazing high in the mountains, and the bird life includes the raven, wren, meadow pipit, grey wagtail, stonechat, snipe, red grouse and peregrine falcons. The stately golden eagle, a distinguished former inhabitant, was last seen in the Mournes in 1836.

Dark swathes of commercial coniferous forest fringe the hills at places like Tollymore, Rostrevor, Castlewellan and Donard Park. Only one small pocket of extensive native oak woodland survives: the Rostrevor Forest Nature Reserve on the mountain slopes behind Rostrevor (find it on Shore Road from Rostrevor towards Kilkeel, 875 yards from the town centre and signposted at Kilbroney Park).

Mourne granite

Mourne granite has been in demand for building stone since the 18th century, and the many quarries in the hills are said to have paved industrial Lancashire, a short journey across the Irish Sea, during the Industrial Revolution. Later, the stone was used to construct reservoirs, like the Silent Valley Reservoir, built between 1923 and 1933 to dam the Kilkeel River and provide drinking water for Belfast. Silent Valley was formerly known as Happy Valley but, since being flooded by the reservoir, it is devoid of bird life and is therefore now silent.

▲ Granite peak in the Mourne Mountains

The Mourne Wall

The granite was also used in the construction of the amazing 3-foot-wide, 5- to 6-foot-high, 22-mile-long Mourne Wall, which encloses the 14-square-mile catchment area of the reservoir and goes uphill and down dale with scant regard to the steep contours. The Wall crosses no fewer than 15 of the Mourne summits, and was constructed between 1904 and 1922 to define the boundaries of the area of land purchased by the Belfast Water Commissioners in the late 1800s. This followed a number of Acts of Parliament allowing the establishment of a water supply from the Mournes to the growing industrial city of Belfast. It is a memorial to the hungry, previously jobless men who built it.

Evocative names

Many of the Mourne Mountains have names beginning with that distinctive word 'slieve', which comes from the Irish *sliabh* and simply means mountain. Examples are Slieve Donard, Slieve Commedagh, Slieve Lamagan and Slieve Muck. There are also a number of evocatively named features among these hills, such as Pigeon Rock, Buzzard's Roost, the Cock and Hen, the Devil's Coach Road, the Brandy Pad and the curiously named Pollaphuca, which means 'hole of the fairies or sprites'.

The Brandy Pad, which winds its way from the head of the Annalong Valley to Hare's Gap before dropping down to the Trassey River, gets its name from the pedlars and smugglers of wines, spirits and tobacco who used the track during the 19th century. It is now a popular walking route through the Mournes, offering a good path and fine views.

Today, the Mourne Mountains are a playground for tourists, hillwalkers, mountain bikers and rock climbers. A countryside centre covering the Mournes AONB is located in the neat little seaside town of Newcastle, the main settlement on Dundrum Bay. Named after a now-demolished castle built in the late 16th century at the mouth of the Shimna River, Newcastle has recently benefited from a multi-million pound refurbishment. The smart restored promenade has won a number of national awards, including a Civic Trust Award for Excellence.

Immortalised in song

The song 'The Mountains of Mourne' is normally sung to the traditional Irish tune 'Carraig Donn' (or 'Carrigdhoun'), and is typical of many of songwriter Percy French's works about the great Irish diaspora of the 19th century. Contrasting the artificial attractions of the city with the natural beauty of the singer's homeland, the song is considered a little too whimsical for folk audiences today, but it will no doubt ring in your ears as you explore the famous mountains.

French, who was born in 1854 in County Roscommon, wrote his first successful song in 1877 while he was studying to become a civil engineer at Trinity College, Dublin. He is now also known for his comic songs, such as 'Phil the Fluter's Ball', 'Slattery's Mounted Foot', 'The Mountains of Mourne' and 'Are Ye Right There Michael?' – a song ridiculing the state of the rail system in rural County Clare. Having enjoyed a long and successful career as one of Ireland's best-known songwriters and entertainers, French died in Formby, Lancashire, in 1920, where he is buried.

GET OUTDOORS

Kilbroney Forest Park & Rostrevor Forest

On the A2 between Newry and Kilkeel, County Down | 028 4173 8134 | Open daily Nov–Mar 9–5, Apr, Oct 9–7, May 9–9, Jun–Sep 9am–10pm

Close to the shore of Carlingford Loch, the 97 acres of Kilbroney Forest Park lie in the shadow of the forest-clad Slieve Martin.

The impressive 4,000-acre Rostrevor Forest forms a backdrop to the park, and was planted in 1931 with mostly coniferous species. There's a 2-mile forest drive with views over the lough, an oak plantation dating from the 18th century, and the famous 40-tonne 'Cloughmore' or 'Big Stone', which legend has it was thrown across the lough by the giant Fionn MacCumhaill. In

▲ Along the Mourne Wall

fact it's an erratic, left here by a retreating glacier. You might see pine martens, badgers, red and grey squirrels, foxes, Irish jays and grouse. There are waymarked trails of varying lengths and a cafe.

SADDLE UP
Gamekeepers Lodge Equestrian Centre
270 Moyad Road, Kilkeel, County Down, BT34 4HL | 028 4176 4771

Set in the heart of the Mountains of Mourne, this centre offers activities and lessons for all ages and abilities, along with treks and horse-and-cart rides.

ENTERTAIN THE FAMILY
The Narnia Trail
visitmournemountains.co.uk Kilbroney Park, Shore Road, Rostrevor, Newry, County Down, BT34 3AA | 028 4173 8134

These trails bring the story of C S Lewis' *Narnia* to life along with other stories associated with the magical Mourne Mountains. Set in Kilbroney Forest Park, they lead to a number of interpretative stations along a short loop.

EAT AND DRINK

Brunel's Restaurant at The Anchor Bar ◉

brunelsrestaurant.co.uk
9 Bryansford Road, Newcastle, County Down, BT33 0HJ
028 4372 3951
Craft beers and a decent wine list are on offer here, along with satisfying plates of modern Irish brasserie food, with seafood a trump card.

Ghan House ◉◉

ghanhouse.com
Carlingford, County Louth
042 937 3682
The white-painted Ghan House lies just over the border on the edge of Carlingford Lough, within a pretty walled garden complete with a herb and vegetable patch. The restaurant – a traditional dining room and drawing room – has beautiful views over the Mourne Mountains and the garden. The menu has modern touches and classic partnerships and changes according to availability and the season.

Mourne Seafood Bar ◉

mourneseafood.com
10 Main Street, Dundrum, County Down, BT33 0LU | 028 4375 1377
At the foot of the Mourne Mountains, Mourne Seafood Bar is dedicated to fish and shellfish, much of which comes from the proprietors' own seafood beds.

▸ PLACES NEARBY

Close by are Castlewellan (see page 108) and Slieve Gullion (see opposite) forest parks.

▸ Portstewart   MAP REF 383 D1

colerainebc.gov.uk

This trim little Victorian seaside resort sits on a gracefully curving waterfront. Its chief attraction is the sandy beach, Portstewart Strand, stretching for 2 miles west of the town and cared for by the National Trust, which makes a good job of keeping it clean, though, unfortunately, not car-free. Here you can walk, fish, surf, swim, make sandcastles or just sunbathe. Portstewart also has the Flowerfield Arts Centre with its arts and crafts courses, exhibitions and concerts.

VISIT THE ARTS CENTRE

Flowerfield Arts Centre

flowerfield.org
185 Coleraine Road, Portstewart, County Antrim, BT55 7HU
028 7083 1400 | Open Mon–Fri 9–5, Sat 10–1
The centre, housed in a beautiful old Georgian building, aims to make creative arts

accessible for everyone and does a good job of it with music, visual arts, crafts and a host of regular events.

PLAY A ROUND
Portstewart Golf Club
portstewartgc.co.uk
117 Strand Road, Portstewart,
County Londonderry, BT55 7PG
028 7083 2015
Founded back in 1894,
Portstewart Golf Club has three
18-hole links courses with spectacular views, offering a testing round on the Strand Course in particular, with every shot in the bag required.

▶ **PLACES NEARBY**
Portstewart's next-door neighbour is the small seaside resort of **Portrush** with its three sandy beaches, and together these two towns make a good holiday spot.

▶ Slieve Gullion Forest Park   MAP REF 383 D5
Drumintee Road, Killeavy, Newry | 028 3755 1277 | Open daily 10–dusk
This lovely, partly wooded volcanic spot has a scenic drive that runs for some 8 miles. A waymarked track leads on up to the summit of Slieve Gullion at 1,886 feet (575m), with great views over South Armagh, two megalithic cairns and a dark little lake of enchanted waters – the Lake of Sorrows. The giant Fionn MacCumhaill and many other legendary characters have associations with this region.

▶ **PLACES NEARBY**
Newry has some impressive buildings, such as the 19th-century Town Hall, and the cathedral – the first Catholic cathedral built after the granting of Catholic Emancipation. It's a popular shopping destination with lots of independent shops, as well as well-known retailers. Look out for the 19th-century Russian cannon, captured during the Crimean War.

You can also have a great family day out at a fun-packed adventure playpark.

The Giant's Lair and Slieve Gullion Adventure Playpark
ringofgullion.org
89 Drumintee Road, Meigh, Newry, County Armagh, BT35 8SW | 028 3086 1949 | Open daily Apr–Oct 8am–9pm, Oct–Mar 8–4
The Giant's Lair story trail takes children on a fascinating, magical journey inspired by local myths and legends of dragons, giants, fairies and witches, and the action-packed adventure playpark, with plenty to explore and enjoy, will keep even the most energetic youngster busy.

▶ Strangford Lough
see **Ards Peninsula & Strangford Lough**, page 65

▶ Ulster American Folk Park   MAP REF 382 C3

nmni.com/uafp

2 Mellon Road, Castletown, Omagh, County Tyrone, BT78 5QY | 028 8224
3292 | Open Mar–Sep Tue–Sun 10–5, Oct–Feb Tue–Fri 10–4, Sat, Sun 11–4

Bringing Irish and American history to life, the Ulster American
Folk Park offers a multi-faceted experience. The site is divided
into Irish and American areas, linked by a reconstruction of one
of the ships in which Irish emigrants journeyed to the New
World. Costumed guides work as their ancestors would have
worked, and are always ready to explain and to answer
questions. The park came into being thanks to the generosity of
the Mellon family of the United States, whose ancestor Thomas
emigrated from the Omagh area with his family in 1818 when
he was just five years old. Like many Irish emigrants he
prospered, becoming a judge; his son Andrew founded
Pittsburgh's steel industry. The park's large collection of
original buildings has been assembled from locations all over
Northern Ireland and also from America.

In the Irish area you'll find the Mellon house, with its dark
interior smelling of turf smoke, its cosy kitchen, and ducks and
hens in the yard outside. The family houses of other eminent
Americans are here, too: the Hughes house, birthplace of John
Joseph Hughes, the first Catholic Archbishop of New York; and
the McKinley house, ancestral home of William McKinley, US
president from 1897 until his assassination in 1901. There's a
simpler peasant cabin, too, with just a single room and a total
lack of privacy, the state in which most Irish people were living

◀ Feeding the birds at the Ulster American Folk Park

back then. You'll also find a weaver's cottage complete with costumed spinner at her wheel; a Mass House from the era of the Penal Laws; a blacksmith's forge where the fire often glows red and the sparks fly; and a splendid schoolhouse where visiting schoolchildren experience Victorian-style lessons.

A replica of a 19th-century Ulster street leads to the dockside and the cramped, dark, frightening hold of a ship, similar to that in which emigrants made their dangerous three-month crossing of the Atlantic. On the far side is the American area with another replica of a street, this one in an American port. Beyond are the buildings encountered or built by the Irish in America: log cabins and barns, a smokehouse for preserving food, and the 18th-century house built by Samuel Fulton of Donegal Springs, Pennsylvania, with stones from his fields, exactly as he would have built it in Ireland.

The Centre for Migration Studies at the park has a specialist reference library available to any member of the public wishing to research any aspect of emigration and genealogy.

▸ **PLACES NEARBY**

Nearby attractions are as diverse as classic cars and castle ruins.

The Abingdon Collection

theabingdoncollection.com
16 Gortnagarn Road, Omagh, County Tyrone, BT78 5NW | 028 8224 3373
Open by appointment only
A far-reaching collection of classic cars and motorcycles, The Abingdon Collection is complemented by over 500 die-cast model cars.

Castlederg Castle

Castlederg Main Street, Castlesessagh, Strabane, County Tyrone, BT81 7BF
028 9054 3051 | Open daily
24 hours
Castlederg was the setting for a feud between the O'Neill and the O'Donnell lordships. Excavations have found the remains of a 15th-century O'Neill tower house which it is thought was taken by Henry Og O'Neill from the O'Donnells. The rivalry between the two families continued until the 16th century. The castle ruins you see at Castlederg are a plantation-era house and bawn (defensive wall).

▸ Costumed demonstrator

VISIT THE MUSEUMS | GET OUTDOORS | EXPLORE BY BIKE | GO BACK IN TIME | TAKE A TRAIN RIDE | MEET THE WILDLIFE

TAKE IN SOME HISTORY | HIT THE BEACH | EAT AND DRINK | GET INDUSTRIAL | VISIT THE GALLERIES | GO CANOEING

TRY HORSE-RIDING | PLACES NEARBY | CATCH A PERFORMANCE | GO ROUND THE GARDENS | TAKE A BOAT TRIP

A–Z of
the Republic
of Ireland

▶ Abbeyleix MAP REF 378 C3

Abbeyleix is a handsome Georgian town that was laid out by Viscount de Vesci, the 18th-century Lord of Abbeyleix House, at the gates of his park. Found on the old main road between Dublin and Cork, it is a good base to explore the midlands of Ireland, and a pleasant place to visit in its own right. The town is also home to Morrissey's, established in 1775, one of the oldest pubs in Ireland.

TAKE IN SOME HISTORY
Abbeyleix Heritage House
abbeyleixheritage.com
Ballyroad Road, Abbeyleix,
County Laois | 057 873 1653
Open May–Sep Mon–Fri 9–5,
Sat–Sun 1–5, Oct–Apr Mon–Fri 9–5
At Abbeyleix Heritage House in the former boys' school built in 1884, you can learn about the development of the town from its origins as a huddle of houses around a 12th-century Cistercian monastery. There's also a display on the town's long-defunct carpet industry (when the ill-fated RMS *Titanic* set sail on her disastrous maiden voyage in 1912, her stateroom floors were covered with Abbeyleix carpets).

GO ROUND THE GARDENS
Abbey Sensory Gardens
Dove House, Main Street, Abbeyleix,
County Laois | 057 873 1325
Open Jun–Sep Mon–Fri 9–4, Sat,
Sun 2–6, Oct–May Mon–Fri 9–4
In the old walled garden of Abbeyleix's former Brigidine convent at Dove House are delightful gardens designed for sensory stimulation – touching, seeing, hearing, smelling and tasting. There are scented plants, and plants with interesting textures.

PLAY A ROUND
Abbeyleix Golf Course
abbeyleixgolfclub.ie
Rathmoyle, Abbeyleix, County Laois
057 873 1450
A pleasant parkland course. Undulating terrain with water features at five holes.

EAT AND DRINK
EJ Morrissey's
Main Street, Abbeyleix, County Laois,
057 873 1281
This cave-like place was once a grocery shop and the old jars of sweets and the slicing machine remain, along with the bar's own brand of tea. Coming here is like stepping back in time.

▶ PLACES NEARBY
Nearby attractions include a ruined castle, beautiful gardens and a lakeland area perfect for outdoor fun.

Rock of Dunamase
Dunamaise, County Laois
Rising dramatically from the countryside is the Rock of Dunamase, with its ruined mid-12th-century castle. It was built by Dermot MacMurrough, King of Leinster, who eloped with Dervorgilla, wife of Tiernan O'Rourke, and who later invited the Normans to Ireland. The

▲ The Sunken Garden at Heywood House Gardens

alliance was cemented when his daughter Aoife married their leader Richard de Clare (Strongbow), who turned the fort into a stronghold. It lasted nearly 500 years, until Cromwell's men blew it up in 1650. You can climb the steeply sloping wards to reach the sturdy keep, from where there are views from the Slieve Bloom Mountains to the Wicklow Hills.

Heywood House Gardens

Ballinakill, County Laois. Off R432 outside Ballinakill, 4 miles from Abbeyleix | 057 873 3563
Open May–Aug 8.30am–9pm, Apr, Sep 8.30–7, Oct–Mar 8.30–5.30
Nothing remains of Heywood House – the 18th-century mansion was burned to the ground in 1950 – but the gardens are remarkable. They were designed in 1909 by celebrated architect Sir Edwin Lutyens and planted in the subsequent three years by his frequent collaborator, garden designer and plantswoman supreme, Gertrude Jekyll. The well-tended landscape includes fine terraces and garden 'rooms' and there's a lovely lime walk and a scatter of pavilions.

Laois Angling Centre

laoisanglingcentre.ie
Clonoghil House, Coolrain, Portlaoise, County Laois
057 873 5091
This area is a fisherman's dream. The Laois Angling Centre, based at Clonoghil House in the heart of the countryside, boasts four tranquil lakes which are surrounded by woodland and are regularly stocked with fish – brown and rainbow trout, bream and carp. The centre caters for all abilities and you can enjoy a half-day or full-day's fishing. Other facilities at the centre include a nature trail, a picnic area and barbecue, refreshments and equipment rental.

▶ Achill Island (Oileán Acla) MAP REF 380 B4

achilltourism.com

Achill is Ireland's largest island, with a spectacular landscape and some of the best beaches in the country. An irregular chunk of mountainous land, it is 14 miles wide and 12 miles from north to south, and connected to the mainland by Michael Davitt Bridge. The mountains of Knockmore (1,115 feet/340m) and Minaun (1,322 feet/403m) dominate the southern half, while the peaks of Croaghaun (2,191 feet/668m) and Slievemore (2,204 feet/671m) rise in the north. Around 2,500 people live here.

The narrow coast road signposted 'Atlantic Drive', which runs south along the sound, is the best introduction to the island. It passes austere 15th-century Kildavnet Castle, one of the strongholds of County Mayo's famed and feared pirate queen Grace O'Malley (c 1530–1600).

The Atlantic Drive turns north for a beautiful run up the wild west coast. Towards the top of the island you reach the village of Keel, with its long beach and spectacular view of the lofty Cliffs of Minaun. Just beyond lies Dooagh, where, on 4 September 1987, Don Allum, the first man to row the Atlantic both ways, came ashore after 77 days at sea. The road ends 3 miles beyond Dooagh at Keem Strand, a lovely unspoilt beach in a deep bay with a memorable cliff walk.

GET OUTDOORS
Annagh

On the north side of Achill Island, and only accessible by boat or on foot, Annagh is a local beauty spot with a freshwater lake – the lowest corrie (glacial) lake in Ireland – and a grey sandy beach. Here you can also find a megalithic tomb, evidence of habitation in this remote part of the island.

▼ Keel Beach, Achill Island

TAKE IN SOME HISTORY

Kildavnet Castle

achilltourism.com

Kildavnet, Achill Island, County
Mayo | 098 20705 or 098 20400

Open daily 10–5

This perfect example of a
15th-century tower house is
located on the southeast of the
island, and is thought to have
been built by the Clan O'Malley
around 1429. Its strategic
importance is the reason for its
local association with Grace
O'Malley, as it was one of her
coastal strongholds.

Grace O'Malley, also known
as Granuaile, was a 16th-
century pirate queen whose
family motto was 'Invincible on
land and sea'. Granuaile
harassed the English by land
and sea in Tudor times, and
few, if any, got the better of her.
Fearing that enemies would
steal her ships by night, she
slept with one end of a silk
thread tied to her toe and the
other running through the
window out to hawsers
(mooring ropes) of her fleet.

Kildownet Church

achilltourism.com

Kildavnet, Achill Island,
County Mayo

Next to the castle stands the
ruin of Kildownet church. A map
of the graveyard on the wall of
the church locates several
poignant sites that reflect hard
times on Achill.

The Deserted Village

Southern slopes of Slievemore
mountain

Another of Achill Island's
remarkable sites is the
deserted village of 74 roofless
houses on the southern slope of
Slievemore. The village was
abandoned during the Great
Famine, but was used as a
'booley' village – a summer
grazing and milking settlement
– until the 1940s. It is an
emotional and atmospheric
place; spend an hour or so here
and contemplate this:

'No one knew enough to
relate when and why the village
was forsaken' (Heinrich Böll,
The Irish Journal, 1957).

PLAY A ROUND

Achill Island Golf Club

achillgolf.com

Sandybanks, Keel, Achill, County
Mayo | 098 43456

This is a nine-hole links course
with a scenic location by the
Atlantic Ocean overlooking Keel
Strand, with panoramic views of
the Minaun Cliffs.

EAT AND DRINK

Alice's Bar

achillislandhotel.com

Achill Sound, County Mayo

098 45138

Alice's Bar at Óstán Oileán Acla,
(Achill Island Hotel) carries on
the tradition of its predecessor,
Alice's Harbour Inn. The
interior, featuring local stone,
is part of the appeal; having a
drink overlooking the Atlantic
is another.

▶ PLACES NEARBY

Clare Island (see page 207) lies
to the south of Achill Island.

▶ Adare MAP REF 377 D3

adarevillage.com

One of the prettiest towns in Ireland, Adare is a charming spot with its green park, brick houses and thatched cottages. Much of the town's charm is the result of remodelling carried out by the earls of Dunraven towards the end of the 19th century. Adare's history goes much further back than that, however; evidence of the settlement's status in medieval times can be seen in several ruined abbeys here.

TAKE IN SOME HISTORY

Holy Trinity Abbey

adareparish.ie

Adare, County Limerick

061 396 172

Holy Trinity Abbey was founded in 1230 for monks of the Trinitarian Order, which had been set up to rescue hostages seized during the Crusades. It was known as the White Abbey, for the colour of the monks' habits, and its low square tower, restored and battlemented in 1852, dominates the high street. Tucked behind is a circular dovecote, unusual in Ireland, which would have provided a useful additional food source for the monks.

Black Abbey

ireland.anglican.org

The Rectory, Adare, County Limerick

061 396 227

The Augustinians built a friary known as the Black Abbey, due

▼ Thatched cottage in Adare

to the colour of the friars' habits, on the riverbank opposite the castle around 1314, and the elegant church was restored and reopened as the Church of Ireland parish church in 1937. The extensive ruins of a Franciscan friary, dating from 1464, lie in the parkland of Adare Manor, to the south of the river. This 19th-century mansion was the seat of the earls of Dunraven and is now a luxury hotel.

Desmond Castle
heritageireland.ie
Limerick Road, Adare, County Limerick | Open daily Jun–Sep 10–5
The massive remains of Desmond Castle, sometimes called Adare Castle, lie on the north bank of the River Maigue, a short walk from the middle of the town. The castle dates back to 1326 and the second Earl of Kildare, though there was an earlier O'Donovan structure on the same site. The castle withstood several sieges but was finally demolished by Oliver Cromwell's men in 1657. Book a guides tour at the Adare Heritage Centre.

VISIT THE HERITAGE CENTRE
Adare Heritage Centre
adareheritagecentre.ie
Main Street, Adare, County Limerick
061 396 666
Tours of Desmond Castle can be booked here. There are also shops and tourist information, plus an exhibition exploring Adare's history from the arrival of the Normans.

PLAY A ROUND
Adare Manor Golf Club
adaremanorgolfclub.com
Adare, County Limerick | 061 396 204 | Open daily 10am to one hour after sunset
This fine parkland course surrounds the extensive ruins of a Franciscan abbey and Desmond Castle.

▶ PLACES NEARBY
If you're looking for a great place to eat, try the Mustard Seed in Ballingarry.

Mustard Seed
mustardseed.ie
Echo Lodge, Ballingarry, County Limerick | 069 68508
The Mustard Seed is an award-winning restaurant in a charming country house set in its own orchard and herb garden. The classic four-course dinner is recommended, but the stand-out tasting menu, with eight courses, shouldn't be missed and is incredible value.

▶ Aran Islands (Oileáin Árann)

MAP REF 376 B1

visitaranislands.com

The Aran Islands are only 20 minutes by plane from the mainland but they could be in a different world. All three Aran Islands share the same distinctive landscape of bleak grey limestone, devoid of grass in most parts but supporting sheets of wild flowers. The islands are weather-beaten, sleepy and full of character, lying in line across the mouth of Galway Bay. The largest and most seaward of the group is Inishmore (Inis Mór), 9 miles long. In the middle lies Inishmaan (Inis Meáin; 3 miles long), while the smallest and roundest island, Inisheer (Inis Óirr; 2 miles wide) is the most easterly.

Narrow *boreens*, or lanes, thread through the islands and, like the small rocky fields, are bounded by stone walls that are sturdy but so loosely constructed that you can see blue sky or green sea between each individual stone. Life on these windswept, barren islands has always been hard, and still is. The houses are low with small windows to give maximum protection from bad weather. Traditional hide-covered boats (*currachs*) are still used for fishing, and transport is mostly on foot or bicycle. The pace of life is determined by the tides and winds, and by tasks completed, rather than by the clock. Irish Gaelic is spoken throughout the islands, but principally on Inishmaan, the most isolated of the three. Here you'll find plenty to photograph.

▼ Fields bounded by limestone walls, Inishmaan

▶ Inishmaan (Inis Meáin) MAP REF 376 C1

Of the three islands, Inishmaan is the quietest and least
affected by tourism. The famous Irish playwright J M Synge
stayed here each year between 1898 and 1902, researching his
definitive book *The Aran Islanders*. It is also a popular centre
for diving on account of its marine wildlife and clear waters.
The island co-operative works hard to maintain employment
and to encourage a sympathetic understanding of Inishmaan
among visitors.

TAKE IN SOME HISTORY
Teach Synge
Ms Theresa Ní Fhatharta Inishmaan
(Inis Meáin) Aran Islands
099 73036
This charming 300-year-old
cottage is where J M Synge
stayed when he visited
Inishmaan, and is now a
museum dedicated to his life
and work. It has been restored
as closely as possible to how it
would have been when he
visited the island.

▶ Inisheer (Inis Óirr) MAP REF 376 C1

Inisheer is close to The Burren (see page 194) and the Cliffs of
Moher (see page 208) and is easily reached from Doolin. It is
small enough to walk around in a morning. You may recognise
the remains of the MV *Plassey*, from its appearance in the
opening credits of the television series *Father Ted*. It was
wrecked off the island during a severe storm in the 1960s, and
thrown above the high tide mark by the waves. Loch Mór, the
island's only freshwater lake, is close by.

▼ O'Brien's Castle, Inisheer

▶ Inishmore (Inis Mór) MAP REF 376 B1

Inishmore has the most striking archaeological remains, the largest village, Kilronan (Cill Rónáin), and more visitors than the other two islands put together. There's an excellent heritage centre and island museum in Kilronan, and you can buy genuine handknitted Aran sweaters in An Púcán craft shop before taking a pony-and-trap from the pier, or a minibus tour of the island.

The main attraction is Dún Aonghasa, a large Iron Age stone fort perched on the edge of a 295-foot cliff. Its sister stronghold of Dún Dúchathair, the Black Fort, stands on its own lonely cliff top. Near the western tip of the island is the Seven Churches, a gathering of ruined chapels and fragments of a cross dating from the 8th to 15th centuries, reminders of Inishmore's early Christian history.

GO BACK IN TIME

Dún Aonghasa
heritageireland.ie
Aran, County Galway | 099 61008
Open daily 9.30–4 (9.45–6 during peak season)

The most famous and dramatic of the prehistoric forts on the island, Dún Aonghasa stands at the edge of a 295-foot cliff. The fort dates in part from around 1100 BC and consists of four concentric drystone walls, 13 feet wide in places, and restored to 19 feet high. Some of the fort has been eroded. You will also see an arrangement of upright stone slabs, known as a cheval de frise.

Cill Éinne, Inishmore
The ruins of one of Ireland's earliest monasteries, founded by St Enda in the 5th century,

▼ Traditional Aran sweaters

can be seen here, and the village takes its name from the monastery. Apparently St Enda and 120 other saints are buried in the churchyard.

The Seven Churches (Na Seacht dTeampaill)

West Inis Mór at the village of Eoghanacht

This was once one of the largest monastic foundations on the west coast of Ireland, and a centre of pilgrimage. There are in fact only two churches here – the name probably comes from the pilgrimage circuit of Rome, which did include seven. St Brecan's Church dates from the 8th to the 13th centuries, while the Church of the Hollow is 15th century. There are also fragmentary decorated crosses.

TAKE A TOUR OF THE ISLAND

Inismór Tours

inismortours.com

087 693 5101; call to book

Join Rory for a guided mini-bus tour of the island. You'll see pretty much everything, from beautiful beaches and dramatic scenery to churches, cottages and ring forts.

BUY AN ARAN SWEATER

An Púcán Craft Shop

Kilronan, Aran Islands, County Galway | 091 757 677

Buy a traditional Aran sweater hand-knitted by local women in their own homes.

EAT AND DRINK

Tí Joe Wattys

joewattys.ie

Kilronan, Aran Islands, County Galway | 099 20892 or 086 049 4509

This is a lovely, welcoming local bar on the island where the food is good and there is a great programme of live music. There is a nice beer garden for warm summer evenings and real fires in winter.

▼ Aerial view of Inisheer

▲ Beach on Arranmore

▶ Arranmore (Árainn Mhór) MAP REF 381 E1

Arranmore is the largest inhabited island in County Donegal, and the second largest in all Ireland. It is also called Aran Island, but is generally referred to as Arranmore to prevent confusion with the Aran Islands in Galway Bay. It is served by two ferry services: Arranmore Ferry and Arranmore Ferry Service; both operate from Burtonport (Ailt an Chorráin) and the crossing takes just 15 minutes.

Most visitors come for the day but it's best to stay overnight – especially in August during Arranmore's annual country music festival, which is centred on the cultivated eastern side in the bars and shops of Leabgarrow. From here you can wander narrow lanes towards the west coast, or turn aside to climb one of the three modest peaks for the view from 745 feet. There is a variety of accommodation including guest houses, self-catering and small hotels. The island has been settled since pre-Celtic times and there is a promontory fort in the south of the island and some shell middens along the beaches.

▶ Athlone MAP REF 378 B1

athlone.ie

On the border of counties Roscommon and Westmeath, and the commercial and social hub for a wide rural area, Athlone is a lively base for boating and fishing on the River Shannon. The best place for a pint, a tune and all the local information is Sean's Bar on Main Street, one of the oldest pubs in Europe. The world-renowned tenor John McCormack (1884–1945) was born in The Bawn at the heart of Athlone. From the castle battlements there's a good view of the town and the River Shannon towards Lough Ree.

TAKE IN SOME HISTORY
Athlone Castle and Visitor Centre
athloneartsandtourism.ie
Castle Street, Athlone, County Westmeath | 090 644 2130
Open Jun–Aug Mon–Sat 10–6, Sun 12–6, Mar–May, Sep, Oct Tue–Sat 11–5, Sun 12–5, Nov–Feb Wed–Sat 11–5, Sun 12–5
The castle visitor centre offers an interesting journey through history with replica weapons and the chance to dress in period costumes.

Jump 4 Joy
jump4joyathlone.com
Unit 6, Monksland Business Park, Tuam Road, Athlone, County Westmeath | 090 649 8450
Open Mon–Wed 10–6, Thu–Sat 10–7, Sun 11–7
Parents can relax for a couple of hours while the kids go wild with slides, climbing frames, a bouncy castle and a ball-pool.

CATCH A PERFORMANCE
Dean Crowe Theatre and Arts Centre
deancrowetheatre.com
Chapel Street, Athlone, County Westmeath | 090 649 2129
There's plenty of entertainment for all ages at this theatre and arts centre, one of Ireland's largest provincial theatres, on Athlone's very own 'left bank' not far from the centre of town. The All-Ireland Drama Festival is held here annually for nine days in May; it also includes poetry, puppetry, exhibitions and dance. The theatre has been a favourite venue for dancing and entertainment since its days as the church hall in the 1950s. Classes, workshops and exhibitions relating to the arts are also held at the theatre.

GET ACTIVE
Athlone Sports Centre
athlonesportscentre.ie
Ballymahon Road, Athlone, County Westmeath | 090 647 0975 | Open Mon–Fri 7am–10pm, Sat, Sun 9–6
The best-equipped sports complex in the region, with a big swimming pool, children's pool, state-of-the-art gym, jacuzzi and sauna. There are over-50s and adults-only sessions, an activity club for children and a childcare facility.

GET ON THE WATER
Adventure Viking Cruise
vikingtoursireland.ie
7 St Mary's Place, Athlone, County Westmeath | 086 262 1136
Open daily Easter–Oct
Dress up in full Viking gear and cruise the waters of the River Shannon in a replica Viking longship, from The Strand in Athlone upriver into Lough Ree, or travel downstream to Clonmacnoise.

PLAY A ROUND
Glasson Country House Hotel and Golf Club
glassongolfhotel.ie
Glasson, Athlone, County Westmeath 090 648 5120
Opened in 1993, the course has a reputation for being one of the most challenging and scenic in Ireland. Designed by Christy

O'Connor Jnr, it is reputedly his best yet. As it is surrounded on three sides by Lough Ree, the views from everywhere on the course are breathtaking.

EAT AND DRINK

Sean's Bar

seansbar.ie

Main Street, Athlone, County Westmeath | 090 649 2358

Right in the very heart of Ireland, this bar hosts visitors from around the globe and lays claim to being not only the oldest pub in Ireland but in Europe. It is certainly worth a visit if you are in town.

▸ **PLACES NEARBY**

Nearby attractions include a castle, a cathedral and a family-friendly farm. Kilbeggan and Lough Ree have much to offer, and there is the West Meath Way for walkers.

Charleville Forest Castle

charlevillecastle.com

Tullamore, County Offaly

057 932 1279

Charleville Castle is said to be the finest example of Gothic revival architecture in the country. Five beautiful avenues of Irish yew trees radiate from the castle, which was built with grand spires, turrets and pinnacles in 1798, and walled as if to shut out the world. There is elaborate stucco in the gallery, which runs the whole width of the house; and it was here that the Bury family could promenade and admire the gardens in bad weather.

Charles William Bury, Earl of Charleville, had the castle built by Francis Johnston, one of the leading architects of his time. Thickly tangled oak woods, adding to the eerie atmosphere, surround what is called 'the most haunted house in Ireland' – a little girl died here in 1861 and it has since been the subject of numerous paranormal investigations and has featured in TV shows.

Clonfert Cathedral

Clonfert, County Galway

Open daily

St Brendan's Cathedral at Clonfert is an architectural gem with masterful stonework. The site was originally occupied by a monastery founded in AD 563 by St Brendan the Navigator, the putative discoverer of America. The Cathedral of St Brendan was built around 1160, with a 13th-century chancel and a 15th-century tower added. The monastery was burned by Vikings three times during the 12th century and rebuilt by the monks, but was finally destroyed in 1541. A 1900s restoration accounts for its excellent state of repair. The cathedral is locked but a key is available from the house to its right-hand side.

Glendeer Open Farm

glendeerpetfarm.ie

Curryroe, Drum, County Roscommon | 090 643 7147

Open Mon–Sat 11–6, Sun 12–6

This family farm has cows, sheep, chickens, ostriches,

emus, deer, peacocks and rabbits. Some of these can be petted. There is also an indoor skywalk and playground and an outdoor play area with ziplines. Plus lots of slides and soft play.

Hodson Bay Water Sports Centre

baysports.ie

Hodson Bay, Lough Ree, County Roscommon, 5 miles north of Athlone via N6 Galway road and N61 | 090 649 4801; call for activity times and details

Fishing, powerboat driving, boardsailing, boat handling and more are available at this marina on Lough Ree. There is also a large inflatable waterpark for more aquatic fun.

Kilbeggan

Kilbeggan is a good example of the kind of wayside settlement that grew into a flourishing town by virtue of its position on the Grand Canal. Now it is a charming town with a couple of attractions worth a look – namely the distillery museum and the local racecourse.

Kilbeggan Distillery Experience

kilbeggandistillery.com

Lower Main Street, Kilbeggan, County Westmeath | 057 933 2134

Open daily Apr–Oct 9–6, Nov–Mar 10–4

Locke's Distillery was in production for a full 200 years, until 1957, and is now a fine museum of whiskey. Exhibits include an old steam engine and a working millwheel. You can still buy Locke's whiskey – among the range sold here are bottles of Locke's single malt, which nowadays is made at Cooley's Distillery in County Louth. Devotees say it's one of the smoothest whiskeys in Ireland. You can guide yourself, or opt for the guided sessions, which take you around the site in about 40 minutes, followed by a quick taste at the end.

Kilbeggan Racecourse

kilbegganraces.com

Kilbeggan, County Westmeath | 057 932 176 | Race meets Apr–Sep

Irish National Hunt meetings are held on this nine-furlong track. The punters of Offaly and Westmeath turn out in force, and it's a great occasion.

Lough Ree

Lough Ree is the third-largest lake in Ireland (it's 16 miles long) and is full of oddities including Hare Island, where Viking gold was found, and Inchbofin, which has only one inhabitant.

Islands dot this mighty stretch of water, and many were occupied by farming families as late as the 1950s. You can rent boats and fishing tackle at various places around the lake, and Athlone has several tackle shops. The most rewarding island is Inchcleraun, or Quaker's Island, towards the north end of Lough Ree (you can anchor near red lake navigation marker No. 7). Explore the ancient churches of Teampull Diarmuid and

Teampull Mór, the tiny 12th-century Chancel Church and the Church of the Dead near the shore, and, near the middle of Inchcleraun, the 12th-century Clogás Oratory with its bell tower. Take a stroll along the 1.5-mile looped walk near Lecarrow. Here is an ivy-covered ruin of a Norman castle which looks out onto Lough Ree.

Athlone Golf Club

athlonegolfclub.ie

Hodson Bay, County Roscommon

090 649 2073

Founded in 1892, this is a picturesque parkland course with a panoramic view of Lough Ree. Its treelined fairways and undulating terrain make it a true test of golfing ability.

West Meath Way

irishtrails.ie

The Westmeath Way is a 20-mile-long, low-level walking route from Kilbeggan to Mullingar. The lovely route follows a section of the River Brosna and then public roads northwards to Lilliput on the shores of pretty Lough Ennell, where writer Jonathan Swift is said to have stayed and used the name for his fantasy island in his novel *Gulliver's Travels*.

▶ Avoca Handweavers MAP REF 379 E2

avoca.ie

Old Mill, Avoca, County Wicklow | 040 235 105 | Open daily Jun–Sep 9–6, Oct–May 9.30–5.30

Whether you're shopping on Grafton Street in Dublin or browsing in craft outlets, you'll see the name of this little Wicklow Mountains village on high-quality mohair and cashmere garments that are manufactured in the tiny weaving shed at the Old Mill on the edge of the village. Established in 1723, it is one of the oldest factories in continuous use in Ireland. Visitors can get a feel for the clatter of the weaving shed, with its array of working handlooms and machine looms, and take a mill tour before visiting the factory shop. Its excellent cafe is a must for lunch or tea.

▶ Baltimore MAP REF 376 C6

baltimore.ie

It is difficult to believe that the pretty seaside town of Baltimore was once the scene of pirate raids, kidnaps and murders. This was once a wealthy fishing village, sheltered from the Atlantic by a rocky headland. In 1537, fishermen from rival Waterford burned it down after one of their boats was seized, and in 1631 Algerian pirates pounced, killing dozens of people and kidnapping hundreds more to sell as slaves in North Africa.

After the second outrage, many inhabitants moved upriver to the relative safety of Skibbereen, but it suffered worse than most in the famines. Today, visitors come for the rocky bays and seabirds, for access to the islands of Roaringwater Bay (see page 171) and to drive out to the headland for extensive views, as well as for great local food.

TAKE IN SOME HISTORY
Dún na Séad Castle
baltimorecastle.ie
The Square, Baltimore, County Cork
028 20735 | Open daily Mar–Oct 11–6
Dún na Séad Castle, in the heart of Baltimore, was built in 1215 but lay in ruin for many years until restoration began in 1997. The restoration was completed in 2005 and the castle is now inhabited again for the first time since the middle of the 17th century. It has been restored following the original design, which was revealed through a study of the remaining features. Visitors learn about all its occupants from the Normans to the O'Driscoll family and Oliver Cromwell's troops, who used it as a garrison.

TAKE TO THE WATER
Baltimore Sailing Club
baltimoresailingclub.com
The Pier, Baltimore, West Cork
020 820 426
The large natural harbour at Baltimore is perfect for both windsurfers and dinghy sailors, and also provides a safe anchorage for visiting yachts. Charter yachts with experienced skippers are available for beginners.

Scuba diving
Conditions for diving are ideal in the seas around Baltimore,

▼ Baltimore harbour

thanks to the influence of the Gulf Stream which gives clear waters, pleasant temperatures and abundant sea life. Visit the reefs around Fastnet rock or some of the many wrecks here, from the wartime German submarine U260 to the ore carrier MV *Kowloon Bridge*, which sank in 1986. There are a number of dive centres in the area providing trips, training and equipment.

Shark fishing

Sharks are plentiful during summer and the popular Baltimore Deep Sea Angling Festival takes place in August. The four-day competition attracts anglers from around the world.

▼ Whale-watching off Baltimore

Whale-watching

whalewatchwestcork.com
Carrigillihy, Union Hall, County Cork | 086 120 0027
Whales and dolphins can be spotted in the waters around Baltimore. The season usually starts in spring, with giant fin whales spotted from late summer onwards. Boat tours leave Baltimore Harbour daily at 9.30 and 2.15 (weather permitting) and last about four hours.

EAT AND DRINK

Bushe's Bar

bushesbar.com
Baltimore, West Cork | 028 20125
Sailors still pop in for a pint and to enjoy the panoramic view of the harbour. Originally known as Salters, the pub is one of the oldest bars in Baltimore. It has been in the Bushe family since 1970 and is famous around the world.

Rolfs Country House ⍟

rolfscountryhouse.com
Baltimore Hill, Baltimore, West Cork
028 20289
Rolfs Country House is set in beautiful subtropical gardens overlooking Baltimore Harbour to Roaringwater Bay and Carbery's 100 isles. Johannes Haffner is the current incumbent at the stoves, and he runs the culinary side of the operation with his sister Frederica. They ensure that produce is locally grown, reared and caught, organic whenever possible, and pastries and breads are all home-baked.

▲ Roaringwater Bay

▶ PLACES NEARBY

Close by is vast Roaringwater Bay. From here you can take a boat trip to the outlying islands and a lighthouse.

Roaringwater Bay
baltimore.ie

In the far southwest corner of Ireland, Roaringwater Bay is around 7.5 miles long and up to 5 miles wide. Of the 15 islands within the bay, Sherkin and Cape Clear are the largest. Distinctive features of the bay are the buoys and snaking black lines of the mussel- and oyster-culture industries. Both species thrive here in the plankton-rich waters.

Sherkin
sherkinisland.ie

Sherkin, a 10-minute boat ride from Baltimore, has a 15th-century abbey, a ruined castle, good beaches – try Silver Strand – and rare plants.

The Abbey
The Pier, Sherkin | Open access

The Abbey is actually a Fransciscan friary. Dating from the 15th century, the tiny ruin was established by the island chieftain, Fineen O' Driscoll.

Cape Clear Bird Observatory
capeclearisland.ie/birdobservatory
birdwatchireland.ie
Trá Chiaráin, Cape Clear
028 39181

Cape Clear is a stop-off point for migratory birds, and its observatory is well established.

Fastnet Lighthouse
fastnettour.com

Fastnet Rock Lighthouse marks Ireland's most southerly point. It is the tallest and widest lighthouse anywhere in Ireland and Great Britain and is of great importance to shipping. Several operators from Baltimore and Cape Clear offer boat trips around the rock.

▶ Bantry House MAP REF 376 C6

bantryhouse.ie

Bantry, County Cork | 027 50047 | Open Jun–Aug daily 10–7, Apr, May, Sep, Oct Tue–Sun 10–5

On the southwestern edge of bustling Bantry town, just off the N71, the pink and white Bantry House makes the very best of its views over the wooded islands of Bantry Bay. The mansion dates from 1700 and is still owned by the White family, who acquired it in 1739. In 1945, it became the first great house in Ireland to open its door regularly to the public, who have flocked here ever since to admire the treasures amassed by the earls of Bantry. Richard White, the second earl, was the chief collector and brought back much of what is on show today from his wide travels in Europe. Look for the Aubusson tapestries in the Rose Drawing Room, reputedly made for French queen Marie Antoinette, and the portraits of George III and Queen Charlotte by Allan Ramsey in the Blue Dining Room.

The house stands on the third of seven terraces, a feature of the extensive formal gardens also created by the second earl. Highlights include the Italianate garden, and the glorious Wisteria Circle. Walk up the Stairway to the Sky, 100 restored stone steps, for the best views over the house to Bantry Bay. The house hosts a chamber music festival in late June or early July and a world-class festival of traditional music, Masters of Tradition (westcorkmusic.ie/mastersoftradition) in mid-August.

In the courtyard of the house, the Armada Exhibition Centre tells of the attempted French invasion of December 1796, in

▼ View of Bantry House from the Stairway to the Sky

support of the United Irishmen. The 48 ships made it from Brest, in France, but were prevented from landing in the bay by stormy weather and forced back. It was Richard White (1765–1851) who raised the alarm, and was made an earl for his pains. Nationalist Wolfe Tone (1763–98) was one of those on board the failed fleet, and a statue of him stands in Bantry's town square, which is also named after him.

VISIT THE TOWN
Bantry
The town of Bantry, in the heart of West Cork, is a region of lush vegetation, palm trees and semi-tropical flowers. Hemmed in by high mountains and clear seas, the Gulf Stream assures a lovely climate and this is a popular destination for tourists, with a tourist office at the east end of town. Bantry is lively, with plenty of good restaurants and pubs, especially around the Wolfe Tone Plaza. Walk around town to Bridge Street where you can see the old waterwheel by the library.

EXPLORE AN ISLAND
Whiddy Island Ferry
whiddyislandferry.com
Top of Bantry Bay, County Cork
086 862 6734
If you would like to explore one of West Cork's islands, a ferry leaves Bantry pier for Whiddy Island and takes just 10 or 15 minutes. The island has an interesting history and rich wildlife, and bicycles can be hired while there.

EAT AND DRINK
Ma Murphy's Bar
mamurphys.com
New Street, Bantry, County Cork
027 50242

Both a pub and off licence, this cosy bar in the centre of town always gets rave reviews. Visitors can expect a warm welcome and a great Guinness and should try to arrange a visit when one of their many events or tastings are happening.

▶ PLACES NEARBY
A little further west along the Atlantic coast is the Mizen Peninsula, which offers great sea and sealife views. Glimpse the mountains from Ballingeary or look out over Bantry Bay from Ballylickey.

Mizen Peninsula
mizenhead.ie
This beautiful rugged peninsula stretches southwest between Dunmanus and Roaringwater bays, with the high point of 1,334-foot (407m) Mount Gabriel at its landward end, and 75-foot-high cliffs at its seaward end. **Ballydehob** has a statue of local wrestling hero Dan O'Mahony on the main street and a disused 12-arch tramway viaduct. **Schull** is an amiable fishing village, with a planetarium. At the tip of the peninsula, beyond Goleen and the beaches of Barley Cove, lies **Cloghane Island**, linked to the mainland by a bridge. Beyond

Enjoy tried-and-true country cooking in a hauntingly beautiful setting. Those views over the lake towards the mountains look especially magnificent from the ample windows of the dining room, where fine seasonal artisan produce takes centre stage but there are no airs and graces to the cooking.

the bridge is Mizen Head Signal Station. Look out for wildlife in the Atlantic – home of seals, whales and dolphins.

Mizen Head Signal Station

mizenhead.ie

The Harbour Road, Goleen, West Cork | 028 35115

Open daily mid-Mar to May, Sep, Oct 10.30–5, Jun–Aug 10–6, Nov to mid-Mar Sat–Sun 11–4

This former signal station is now a visitor centre and cafe in a lighthouse.

Schull Planetarium

schullcommunitycollege.com

Schull Community College, at Colla Road, Schull, West Cork | 028 28315

Evening shows in summer; see website for details

Part of the local community college, this 26-foot dome is Ireland's only planetarium.

EAT AND DRINK

Gougane Barra Hotel ◉

gouganebarrahotel.com

Ballingeary, off R584 between N22 at Macroom and N71 at Bantry, West Cork | 026 47069 | Open Apr–Sep

The Heron's Cove ◉

heronscove.com

The Harbour, Goleen | 028 35225

This is an exceptionally easy-going, friendly place, where you can eat out to sublime sea views on the balcony overlooking the tiny inlet in summer. The kitchen takes time to source the best local ingredients that are the backbone of its output.

Seaview House Hotel ◉◉

seaviewhousehotel.com

Ballylickey, 3 miles north of Bantry, West Cork | 027 50073 and 027 50462

The grand white-painted Seaview has the promised vista over Bantry Bay, glimpsed through the trees in the pretty gardens. The restaurant is decorated in a traditional manner, traversing three well-proportioned rooms, one of which is a conservatory with lush garden views. There's a good deal of local produce on the menu, and everything is handled with care and attention to detail.

▶ Beara Peninsula MAP REF 376 B6

bearatourism.com

Wild and rugged, with dramatic explosions of tiny islands and spectacular coastline, Beara is the third 'ring' in Ireland, after Kerry and Dingle. Although lesser known, it is perhaps even more beautiful and has less traffic – a real plus in peak season – and forms part of the Wild Atlantic Way driving route. The peninsula juts out into the Atlantic joining the counties of Cork and Kerry and is one of the most scenic areas in the country, with fishing villages, archaeological sites and farms, as well as crafts, retreats and workshops.

The villages can be explored via the 82-mile Ring of Beara driving route or the Beara Way walking route (123 miles). The massif of the Caha Mountains forms the spine of the peninsula, with Hungry Hill (2,247 feet/685m) its highest point. It is crossed by the scenic Healy Pass (1,082 feet/330m), a famine road completed by Bantry-born Timothy Healy and encircled by the Beara Ring drive, which begins at Glengarriff and ends at Kenmare. Make a stop at nearby Bantry Bay (see page 172) to admire the view and perhaps take a trip to Garnish Island. The road from here flanks jagged cliffs and ambles through the Caha Mountains.

EXPLORE THE PENINSULA
Dursey Island
durseyisland.ie
Dursey Island lies just off the western tip and is linked to the mainland by Ireland's only cable car. See the website for times.

Castletown Berehaven
Castletown Berehaven (or Castletownbere) is the main town and a fishing port sheltered by the hills of Bear Island. No visit is complete without a visit to the legendary McCarthy's Bar.

Eyeries
The picturesque village of Eyeries, on the northern shore, is the home of Milleen cheese, a soft washed-rind cheese which is one of Ireland's best-known farm cheeses.

GO TO A SPA
Samas Park Hotel
parkkenmare.com
Kenmare | 064 664 1200
One of the best spas in the world, Samas is an incredible sanctuary with an indulgent number of treatments to choose from. Don't miss the chance to use the outside hot tubs surrounded by trees and overlooking the water.

GO SHOOTING
Sheen Falls Lodge
sheenfallslodge.ie/activities
Kenmare | 064 664 1600
Clay pigeon shooting is just one of the activities on offer at this erstwhile hunting lodge, which is now a standout hotel.

Shoot clays in the forest, or try falconry, horse riding or a spot of salmon fishing.

VISIT THE RETREAT
Dzogchen Beara Garranes, Allihies
dzogchenbeara.org
Garranes, Allihies, West Cork
027 73032 | Open daily 10–4.30
Sitting high on atmospheric cliffs plunging into the Atlantic, this peaceful retreat was set up under the spiritual direction of Tibetan Buddhist master Sogyal Rinpoche, author of *The Tibetan Book of Living and Dying*. With sweeping views of the sea and sky, this charitable trust welcomes everyone. Come for the twice-daily meditations (see the website for details), to visit the lovely cafe and giftshop, or for a retreat or 'rest and renewal' break if you are seeking a bit of respite from your daily life. Nearby, Allihies, known as the artists' town, has a beach of crushed quartz which is the spoil from old copper mines.

VISIT THE ISLAND
Garnish Island
garnishisland.com
Glengariff, Bantry, County Cork
027 63040 | Open Apr–Sep Mon–Sat 10–6.30, Sun 11–6.30, Oct Mon–Sat 11–4, Sun 1–5
Of all the islands in Bantry Bay, Garnish Island (also known as Garinish, or Ilnacullin), is the most intriguing, for it is the site of a wondrous Italianate garden. The 37-acre island was a barren rock when Annan

▲ Italianate garden, Garinish Island

Bryce bought it from the British War Office in 1910 and hired garden designer and architect Harold Peto. Bryce's planned house was never started, but his semi-tropical gardens survive, and were gifted to the nation in 1953. Rhododendrons, camellias and magnolias thrive in the mild climate. Ferries leave from Glengarriff.

EAT AND DRINK
The Mews
themewskenmare.com
Henry Court, Henry Street, Kenmare, County Kerry | 064 664 2829
Within a few months of opening in 2015 this restaurant had become known as one of the best in town. This is modern Irish cuisine at its best. Be sure to make a reservation and don't miss the desserts.

Park Hotel Kenmare ◉◉
parkkenmare.com
Kenmare | 064 664 1200
Set against a backdrop of the Cork and Kerry Mountains, with stunning views over Kenmare Bay, this landmark Victorian hotel dates from 1897 and is justifiably regarded as the best in Ireland. Fine crystal glassware, gleaming silver cutlery and polished silver cloches, combined with formal service from immaculately attired staff, add an air of traditional elegance to a meal here and the cooking suits the grand surroundings. Produce sourced from the surrounding area dominates the menu.

Sheen Falls Lodge ◉◉
sheenfallslodge.ie
Kenmare, N71 to Glengarriff
064 664 1600
A stately country house that makes the most of its location. The River Sheen cascades past as it falls towards the bay, and the hotel's drape-framed picture windows overlook floodlit surrounding woodland. A refined tone of soft lighting and piano accompaniment is maintained in La Cascade restaurant, which is enhanced by helpful, informative staff.

▶ Bective Abbey MAP REF 379 D1

meathtourism.ie

Bective, Navan, County Meath | 046 943 7227 | Open daily dawn–dusk

Founded in 1147 as a daughter abbey to Mellifont, Bective was an Anglo-Norman, Cistercian foundation, but little survives from that period. What you see today, in a field by the River Boyne, is largely the 15th-century defensive additions. A square tower rises above the remaining walls of the cloister, nave and chapterhouse. Also discernible are the fireplaces, chimneys and windows of the fortified mansion that the site became after the monastery's dissolution in 1543. A medieval bridge across the river indicates the abbey's former importance.

▶ Belvedere House MAP REF 378 C1

belvedere-house.ie

Mullingar, County Westmeath | 044 934 9060 | Open daily May–Aug 9.30–8, Apr, Sep 9.30–7, Mar, Oct 9.30–6, Nov–Feb 9.30–4.30

With its fine plasterwork ceilings and decoratively carved woodwork, the 18th-century fishing and hunting lodge of Belvedere House and its gardens make an enjoyable excursion. Pride of place among the many follies in the grounds goes to the Jealous Wall, a large sham castle frontage, complete with turrets, Gothic arches and 'shattered' windows. It was built in 1760 on the orders of the 'Wicked Earl', Robert Rochfort, first Earl of Belvedere, to block his view of Tudenham Park, the home of his younger brother, with whom he had quarrelled. The Wicked Earl also suspected his other brother, Arthur, of having an affair with his wife, Mary, in 1743. Lord Belvedere sued Arthur for £20,000, and eventually had him imprisoned, where he eventually died. Mary was shut away in another of the earl's houses, where she remained under lock and key for more than 30 years. After the earl's death in 1774, one of her sons released her, still clad in a dress she had worn before her incarceration and still protesting her innocence.

LISTEN TO LIVE MUSIC
The Stables

Yukon Bar, Dominic Street, Mullingar, County Westmeath
044 934 0251

Great evenings happen at this club. There's a very eclectic bill – everything from rock and cover bands to indie outfits and cutting-edge hip-hop sounds.

PLAY A ROUND
Mullingar Golf Club

mullingargolfclub.com
4 miles from Mullingar on the N52/R400 towards Belvedere
044 934 8366

The wide rolling fairways between mature trees provide parkland golf at its very best. The course, designed by the great James Braid, offers a tough challenge. It has been the venue of the Irish Professional Championship, and is also the host to the Annual Mullingar Scratch Trophy. One advantage of the layout is that the clubhouse is never far away.

▸ PLACES NEARBY

If the children tire of visiting houses, close by are a couple of more active attractions.

Irish Farm Safari Park

Ballinea, Mullingar, County Westmeath | 044 935 5200
Open by appointment only
An all-weather fun and educational facility, where enthusiastic owner Greg takes visitors on a safari tour in his bus. Animals include red deer, donkeys, emus, llamas, pot belly pigs and more.

Lilliput Adventure Centre

lilliputadventure.com
Lilliput House, Lough Ennell, Mullingar, County Westmeath
044 922 6789 | Call ahead for tours
Children get their thrills under careful supervision at this activity centre. Day activities might include kayaking, abseiling, rock climbing, canoeing, pier jumping, gorge walking, orienteering, archery, hill walking or even a manhunt.

Lilliput Boat Hire

lilliputboathire.com
Lilliput House, Lough Ennell, Mullingar, County Westmeath
087 649 2866 | Open Mar to mid-Oct

▲ Belvedere House

Lough Ennell is one of the Midlands' best fishing lakes, with plentiful trout, pike and perch, as well as many other species. Rent a boat, either with an engine or with oars, and cast off and out to see what luck you'll have. Fishing gear can also be rented here.

Mullingar Arts Centre

mullingarartscentre.ie
Lower Mount Street, Mullingar
44 934 7777 | Open Mon–Fri 9am–9.30pm
Mullingar Arts Centre presents a wide variety of entertainment. There are regular exhibitions in its art gallery, as well as art workshops and a whole range of performance events that include clubbing dance nights, early music, plays, comedy, party nights and films.

▶ Birr   MAP REF 378 B2

Birr is one of the most attractive towns in the middle of Ireland with wide streets of colourful Georgian houses, but its greatest attraction is the imposing Birr Castle Demesne, its Science Centre and the Giant Leviathan telescope. There is also a lively nightlife with music and good restaurants in Birr, making it well worth a visit.

The Parsons family settled at Birr in 1620, and the earls of Rosse directed the fortunes of the area from then on. During the 18th century, they laid out a model Georgian town with a central square and wide tree-lined streets or 'malls' flanked with well-built houses and neat gardens. The Birr Town Trail, set out in a little leaflet obtainable from the tourist information office, takes you around the best parts. Notice the carved surrounds of the shopfronts here.

GO ROUND THE GARDENS
Birr Castle Demesne
birrcastle.com
Birr, County Offaly | 057 912 0340
Open daily mid-Mar to Oct 9–6,
Nov to mid-Mar 10–4
The chief attraction of the town is undoubtedly the castle itself, founded in 1170 and altered in the succeeding centuries. It is still the private residence of the Earl and Countess of Rosse, and the castle itself is not open to the public all year round, but you can book a tour during the summer months. The family has developed the demesne (grounds), with woodland walks, formal and informal gardens and water features. There are rose gardens and a very fine collection of magnolias, and a path between gigantic hedges of box that date back to the 17th century.

Plenty of experimental plant work has been carried out at Birr Castle Demesne. The earls and countesses of Rosse seem always to have had enquiring, scientific minds. The Science Centre in the castle stables gives a very accessible account of the family's various achievements in science, including the development by the third earl, William Parsons (1800–67), of the huge telescope which is still kept in the grounds and is demonstrated three times a day. This 70-foot-long telescope contains the largest cast-metal mirror ever made. The photographs taken of the newly installed telescope by the earl's wife, Mary, are really remarkable.

EAT AND DRINK
Dooly's Hotel
doolyshotel.com
Emmet Square, O'Connell Street,
Birr, County Offaly | 057 912 0032
The much-loved Dooly's is the best example of Birr's hospitality industry, combining good food in the fine Emmet restaurant with live music in the coach house bar and a nightclub in the basement.

▶ PLACES NEARBY

A short drive south is Leap Castle and slightly further on is the village of Roscrea, with its 13th-century castle and historic buildings and heritage centre.

Leap Castle

North of Roscrea on the R421, County Offaly | 086 869 0547
Entry by appointment only
Ireland's most haunted castle was built in the 1500s by the O'Connells and is said to be the scene of many grisly goings on.

Roscrea

Roscrea, noted for its medieval architecture, is dubbed Ely O'Carroll Country, after the two ancient Irish families who dominated its history until their lands were seized by the English in the 17th century. In the middle of town is a huge 13th-century castle, with a Queen Anne mansion and formal walled garden.

Roscrea Castle and Damer House

heritageireland.ie
Castle Street, Roscrea, County Tipperary | 050 521 850 | Open 2 Apr–23 Sep daily 10–6
The castle dates from the 1280s and the gate tower, curtain walls and two corner towers remain. The rooms are furnished and there are also exhibitions. Damer House is an early 18th-century Queen Anne-style pre-Palladian building, with one room furnished in period style. You can also see a restored mill and the original St Cronan's high cross and pillar stone.

Roscrea Heritage Centre

Castle Street, Roscrea, County Tipperary | 050 521 850 | Open Apr–Oct daily 10–6
See the exhibitions about the town's history and there's a heritage walk taking in the weathered 12th-century wheel cross and round tower of St Cronan's, and the tower of a 15th-century Franciscan friary.

Shannon Adventure Canoeing Holidays

The Marina, Banagher, County Offaly 509 51411
Being the master of your own craft is by far the best way to explore the Shannon and its lakes. Renting a two-person canoe gives you that freedom.

Thatch Pub

Crinkill
057 912 0682
A couple of miles outside Birr, this pub takes its name from the thatched roof on the 200-year-old inn, which is a lovely spot for a pint or a meal.

▶ Birr Castle

▶ Blarney Castle   MAP REF 377 D5

blarneycastle.ie
Blarney, County Cork | 021 438 5252 | Open daily Jun–Aug 9–7, May, Sep
9–6.30, Oct–Apr 9am–dusk

The word 'blarney' has become almost synonymous with Ireland,
but there's more to do at Blarney Castle than kiss its famous stone.
The castle is a romantic 15th-century ruin beside a pretty village,
set in landscaped gardens with 18th-century grottoes. In summer,
visitors from every nation thread their way around the tower and
through the park. Out of season it has a magical peace about it.

A square stone tower, the castle is perched on a rocky hillock
framed by trees, with broken battlements and two separate
watchtowers. As you enter, above your head is the good-natured
banter surrounding that Irish cliché, the kissing of the blarney
stone. Entry through the thick stone walls is via a double outer
door, complete with murder hole and right-handed spiral staircase
to confound attackers. Follow the red arrows and keep to the
one-way system that is vital with so many narrow winding stairs
and awkward doorways. You'll pass chambers described as the
great hall, bedrooms, kitchen and so on. They are mostly damp and
crumbling, but the views from the windows make it all worthwhile.

'Blarney' means 'eloquent nonsense', a term said to have been
coined by Elizabeth I, who wearied of the successful stalling tactics
of owner Cormac McCarthy when she tried to take over his castle.
There are many legends surrounding the Blarney Stone: one says
that it was the pillow used by Jacob when he dreamt of angels in
the desert; the best known is that it is allegedly half of the Stone of
Scone, presented to McCarthy by Robert the Bruce after his
support at Bannockburn in 1314. Kissing the stone involves lying
down and leaning backwards over a parapet. A photograph is
taken, and you'll be given a ticket to collect your picture later (there
are no previews). To avoid the crowds, it is best to arrive early and
head straight up the steps to the roof, where the stone lies.

In the 18th century, the castle came into the hands of the
Jeffereys, who created the gardens, which can be accessed on a
path south from the tower, passing through a narrow stone tunnel.
A network of paths leads through carefully crafted woodland,
ornamented with lumps of naturally sculpted limestone. A grotto,
artfully constructed beneath a giant yew, is named the Witches'
Kitchen. Nearby, the Wishing Steps lead down to a murky pool
(walk down and up backwards for your wish to come true). Rocky
outcrops have such fanciful names as Druids' Circle.

The Tudor-style village of Blarney is also worth a visit and has
some pleasant pubs and restaurants.

▶ PLACES NEARBY

The city of Cork (see page 229), 5 miles southeast of Blarney, is well worth a visit. Closer to home is the legendary Blarney Woollen Mills.

Blarney Woollen Mills
blarney.com
Blarney, County Cork | 021 451 6111 | Open Mon–Fri 9.30–5.30

Packed with high-quality Irish gifts such as delicate crystal goods, Belleek pottery and dramatic Celtic jewellery, as well as a whole host of colourful rugs and knitwear, such as Aran sweaters, this enormous shop is housed in one of Ireland's oldest and wonderfully authentic Irish woollen mills.

▶ Boyle MAP REF 381 E4

By far the most important and striking building in the town of Boyle is Boyle Abbey, standing magnificently beside the River Boyle on the eastern edge of town. Boyle has an attractive mix of Victorian and Georgian architecture and is home to an arts festival which takes place each summer, featuring Irish artists, classical and traditional musicians, poetry, drama and children's events.

TAKE IN SOME HISTORY
Boyle Abbey
heritageireland.ie
Boyle, County Roscommon | 071 966 2604 | Open daily Apr to mid-Sep 10–6
Founded in 1148 by the Cistercian community, the remains of the old monastery cloister garden, kitchens and refectory are in a very good state of preservation, as is the abbey church itself. The humorous carvings, floral capitals and decorative pillars are unusual for the austere Cistercian order.

There's an exhibition in the gatehouse, where jambs are scored with sword cuts and graffiti from the garrison that occupied the abbey from 1603 until 1788. In that year, the Connaught Rangers, or 'The Devil's Own' as the roughneck militia were called, moved to King House elsewhere in Boyle.

King House
kinghouse.ie
Military Road, Boyle, County Roscommon | 071 966 3242
Open Apr–Sep Tue–Sat 11–4
This lovely early Georgian mansion had just been vacated by the King family in favour of their grand Rockingham Estate (now Lough Key Forest Park) when the Connaught Rangers moved in. King House is a wonderful place for children, with storytelling, activities and dressing-up to help bring history to life; adults can watch audiovisual displays on the history of the King family and the area, and also on the Great Famine. The Boyle Origin Farmer's market is held in the courtyard of the mansion every Saturday from 10 to 2.

GET CREATIVE
Boyle Arts Festival Office
boylearts.com
Bridge Street, Boyle, County Roscommon | 071 966 3085
See website for details
Visitors can take part in everything from creative

◀ Boyle Abbey

workshops to popular poetry competitions. See the website for details of the following year's programme.

▶ PLACES NEARBY

Close to Boyle are several managed forest parks and a historic burial tomb.

Drumanone Dolmen
megalithicireland.com
On the R294 from Boyle
Just over a mile from Boyle is an excellent example of a megalithic portal tomb, one of the largest in Ireland. It measures 15 feet by 11 feet and was constructed before 2000 BC. It is located in pasture with good views of the surrounding landscape.

Lough Key Forest Park
loughkey.ie
Signposted on the N4 Carrick-on-Shannon road, 3 miles east of Boyle, County Roscommon | 071 967 3122
Open Jul, Aug Mon–Fri 10–6, Sat, Sun 10–7, Apr–Jun daily 10–6, Mar, Sep, Oct Wed–Sun 10–6, Jan, Feb, Nov, Dec Fri–Sun 10–5
Lough Key Forest Park comprises 870 acres of woodlands with footpaths and the island-dotted Lough Key. It forms part of the once-grand Rockingham Estate. Activities on offer include the Lough Key Experience: an audio trail describes the park's history, flora and fauna as you walk through underground tunnels to the top of the five-storey Moylurg viewing tower and along the unique tree canopy walk. Boda Borg is an adventure house (for visitors aged over 10 years) where a minimum of three people is needed to solve puzzles while moving from room to room. The Adventure Play Kingdom is a safe outdoor play area.

Kilronan Castle Estate and Spa
kilronancastle.ie
Ballyfarnon, County Roscommon
071 961 8000 and 086 021 0542
Kilronan certainly looks like an authentic medieval castle complete with a business-like crenallated turret, but it is actually a mere pastiche, dating from the early 19th century. In the Douglas Hyde restaurant, the kitchen looks to French classicism for its inspiration, spiked here and there with oriental notes.

▶ Bray MAP REF 379 E2

Once promoted as a resort for wealthy Dubliners, Bray is now a desirable commuter town, backed by Bray Head and the distinctive cones of the Great and Little Sugar Loaf hills. The town has an interesting cultural and artistic tradition and is home to Ardmore Studios, the centre of Ireland's film and television production industry.

Bray sits on a long sweep of beach at the south end of Killiney Bay and the cliff walk from the town to Greystones is one of the area's most popular attractions. The long expanse of grey stones between the two town beaches are what gives this one-time fishing vilage its name. The walk is about 4 miles and has great views of the east coast. On the slopes of the Little Sugar Loaf is Killruddery House and Gardens.

GO ROUND THE GARDENS
Killruddery House and Gardens
killruddery.com
Southern Cross, Bray, County Wicklow | 087 419 8674
Open May–Sep daily 9.30–6, Apr, Oct Sat, Sun 9.30–6
Killruddery House and Gardens have been in the Brabazon family since 1618. The gardens were designed in French classical style in the 1680s by Bonet. The 17th-century house, redesigned in Elizabethan style in 1820, contains a mantelpiece by Grinling Gibbons and bookcases by Chippendale.

CATCH A PERFORMANCE
Mermaid Arts Centre
mermaidartscentre.ie
Main Street, Bray, County Wicklow
01 272 4030
Dance, drama and a wide range of musical performances have made the Mermaid a success as County Wicklow's arts centre. It's a good place to catch the big names in traditional music and professional theatre without paying Dublin prices.

MEET THE SEA LIFE
National Sea Life Centre
visitsealife.com
Strand Road, Bray, County Wicklow
01 286 6939 | Open Mar–Oct daily 10–6, Nov–Feb Mon–Fri 11–4, Sat, Sun 10–6

This all-weather attraction on the seafront, with over 24 displays, offers insight into Ireland's freshwater and marine world and the opportunity to view sea creatures from the world's oceans.

PLAY A ROUND
Bray Golf Club
braygolfclub.com
Bray, County Wicklow
01 2763 200
A USGA-standard parkland course of nearly 200 acres to the south of Bray, combining stunning scenery with a classic layout. The 11th par-four signature hole provides a fine view of the coastline.

EAT AND DRINK
Holland's
hollandsofbray.com
78–80 Main Street, Bray, County Wicklow | 01 286 7995
Craft beers, popular toasted sandwiches and Guinness (which the owners say is the best in town) are all on offer here. Coffee, afternoon tea, lunches and pizza are also available here.

▶ PLACES NEARBY
Head west to visit the Avoca Handweavers (see page 168) or, further on, stop at Powerscourt to admire the stunning gardens (see page 337).

▶ Brú na Bóinne   MAP REF 383 D6

heritageireland.ie

Brú na Bóinne Visitor Centre, Donore, County Meath | 041 988 0300

Open daily Jun to mid-Sep 9.30–7, Oct 9.30–5.30, Nov–Jan 9–5, Feb–Apr 9.30–5.30, May 9–6.30

Older than Stonehenge and the Pyramids of Giza, Brú na Bóinne, the 'palace of the Boyne', is the name given to an important and extensive group of neolithic remains in the Boyne Valley, 7 miles west of Drogheda. The huge, white-fronted passage tomb of Newgrange is the best known, but the nearby mounds of Knowth and Dowth were probably of equal importance historically. These great tombs are more than 5,000 years old. We can only guess at the significance of their swirling rock art but the impact of the winter solstice sun, which stunningly lights up the tombs' darkest recesses, was clearly important. You can visit the main site only with an organised tour from the visitor centre, but it is worth spending time in the centre itself, learning about the culture that created these extraordinary monuments.

There are more than 50 lumps and bumps with ritual significance around Brú na Bóinne. Of the three major tombs, you can visit the interiors of Knowth and Newgrange on organised tours but visitor numbers are restricted. Some of the stops on these tours are assigned to tour operators coming from Dublin so if you want to guarantee a visit to the tombs

▼ Knowth passage tomb

▲ The entrance stone at Newgrange

themselves you may be better joining one of those. Otherwise, arrive early and be prepared to wait. Once you have bought your ticket you can explore the surrounding countryside until your tour is due to leave. Your ticket buys you a seat on an allotted minibus, which leaves from beneath the visitor centre.

The whole Brú na Bóinne area is designated a World Heritage Site by UNESCO, putting it on equal footing with Stonehenge (which is 1,000 years younger) and the Pyramids of Giza (which are 100 years younger). The antiquity of the site means it is difficult to know who began the structures and what their cultural significance was. The pre-Celtic founders may have come from the Iberian Peninsula, as some experts have suggested their swirling artwork indicates, but other authorities claim this is a specifically Irish phenomenon. Early Christians also occupied the site, adding their dead to the prehistoric tombs. By the ninth century this was an important stronghold of the Uí Néill clan, but the Middle Ages saw its decline and eventual abandonment. The tombs remained untouched until 1699, when renewed interest in antiquities brought them back into public knowledge.

The visitor centre

The visitor centre is more than just a conduit to the tomb visits – it deserves at least an hour's attention in its own right. There are detailed touch-screen explanations of how the site evolved, who built it and how it was discovered. Among the life-size

▲ Knowth passage tomb

reconstructions are a cross-section of an archaeological survey, showing the painstaking methods used by the researchers investigating the site, and a recreation of the main passage inside the Newgrange tomb, crucially widened so that wheelchairs can fit all the way in (the actual site is not accessible to wheelchair users because the passages are too narrow). A seven-minute audiovisual presentation shows you what the solstice light looks like and there are even hands-on demonstrations of carbon dating. In addition to viewing the cabinets displaying finds from the sites, you are invited to share your theories on the meanings behind the swirling artforms. The viewing area includes the free use of telescopes and there is a good bookshop, cafe and tourist information desk.

Dowth

Dowth is the least known of the three great tombs, and though it contains some of the finest rock art to be seen anywhere in Ireland, its interior is out of bounds to visitors. However, you are free to roam about its grassy site, a freedom not allowed at the other tombs, Newgrange and Knowth. The mound is over 200 feet across and about 46 feet tall; the crater on its summit is the result of enthusiastic Victorian excavations. Some early Christian remains were found within, and one of the passages connects to an early Christian souterrain (underground chamber). There are two principal neolithic tombs inside and the mound is outlined by 115 edging stones.

Knowth

Knowth was certainly already built when the 'beaker people' (named after their characteristic pottery) arrived from mainland Europe and occupied the site around 1800 BC. It featured heavily in the lives of the Iron Age Celts from around 500 BC, and plays a part in the dazzling array of legends that was passed down in the Irish language from these people.

Knowth is the most westerly of the great tombs, and is accessible only by tour, although it can be seen from the nearby road. The mound is outlined by 127 huge edging stones. Surrounding the main tomb are at least 18 smaller tombs, some of which pre-date the larger tomb. There has been human activity here from far back in prehistory through to the early Christian period, and understanding the complex story of the site's development has not been easy. Inside the tomb are two passages, both lined with upright stones, their faces adorned with swirling patterns and lines. The eastern passage contains a large ditch. This was added in the early Christian era and demonstrates the mound's lasting spiritual importance across the millennia. Knowth tends to attract fewer visitors than Newgrange, so you may find it easier to get a ticket for this site than for the better-known tomb.

▶ **PLACES NEARBY**

There are several other places of historical interest around Brú na Bóinne. Slane Castle (see page 344) is 5.5 miles west, and the Hill of Tara (see page 304) is 17 miles southwest. The town of Drogheda (see page 246), which was established by the Vikings, is 5 miles east, and for a great family day out you can visit the open farm at Corballis.

Red Mountain Open Farm

redmountainopenfarm.ie
Corballis, Donore, Drogheda, County Meath | 041 982 3221 | Open Easter, Jul, Aug Tue–Sat 11–5, Sun 1–5, Apr–Jun, Sep, Oct Sat 9–5, Sun 1–5, Dec Sat, Sun 11–5
The farm is a family-run mixed farm with sheep, poultry and horses, set in the open

countryside of the Boyne Valley near the village of Donore, and not far from the entrance of Newgrange. There are tractor rides, farm walks and play and picnic areas.

▼ Knowth passage tomb

▶ Newgrange MAP REF 383 D6

Newgrange was supposedly the home of Tuátha Dé Danann, troglodytic followers of the goddess Danu. Legend claims that warrior hero Cúchulainn was conceived here, the kings of Tara were buried here and Diarmuid, the wounded lover of Finn McCool's wife Gráinne, was carried here to be brought back to life.

The mound is fronted by white quartzite. This is actually the result of restoration work in the 1960s but the effect is truly stunning. The nearest source for quartzite is 40 miles away, so whoever built this tomb had the ability to transport materials to the site over long distances. The whole mound is 330 feet across and about 33 feet high. There are 97 boulders forming an edging ring and, until the 17th century, a large standing stone stood at the summit. At the entrance, one of these edging stones is adorned with the distinctive spiral and line motifs that characterise the rock art that has been found in the surrounding area. Above it stands the rectangular opening known as the roof box.

Studies of the site between 1962 and 1975 revealed that the midwinter sun penetrates a slit in this chamber, sending a narrow shaft of light up the main passageway to illuminate the recess at the back of the north chamber. To witness the magic of this moment on the morning of the winter solstice, you must win a lottery draw, which you can enter at the visitor centre. The experience is reconstructed using an accurately positioned electric light. Astronomical calculations reveal that this effect would have been even more dramatic 5,000 years ago. Subtle shifts in the earth's axis and orbits have left the light falling slightly short of illuminating the whole chamber; when it was constructed the dawn light would have filled the back wall during the winter solstice.

Another remarkable feature of the tomb is the construction of its roof. The massive stones above the chambers are interlaced in such a way as to make them watertight, even after 5,000 years. The best examples of rock carving are on the roof and walls of the right-hand chamber as you go in.

▶ Bunratty Castle and Folk Park MAP REF 377 D2

shannonheritage.com and bunrattybanquet.com

Bunratty, County Clare | 061 360 788 | Open daily 9–7

Bunratty Castle, a tall tower house, was built around 1425 by the MacNamara clan on the site of a former castle, before passing into the hands of the O'Briens, who later became Earls of Thomond. The castle has been very thoroughly and expertly restored, and fitted out with furniture, paintings and tapestries from the 15th and 16th centuries. The Main Guard, a vaulted feasting hall with a minstrels' gallery, now hosts entertaining medieval banquets twice an evening (reservations required).

The Folk Park recreates a corner of 19th-century Ireland with carefully reconstructed buildings and workplaces, some of them forming a 'village street'. These include cottages and farmhouses, where visitors are welcomed by guides in period costume, and, at the other end of the social scale, the fine Georgian country residence of Bunratty House, into which the last resident owners of Bunratty Castle moved in 1804.

There's a working watermill producing flour for sale, and a forge, as well as a church, a pub and a teashop and bakery. Garden-lovers will be delighted by the restored walled garden of Bunratty House, and also by the other gardens, laid out in authentic vernacular style.

There are plenty of domestic and farm animals in the 25-acre Folk Park, along with working thatchers, weavers, churners of fresh butter and other costumed guides.

▼ Bunratty Castle

EAT AND DRINK

Carrygerry Country House ◉

carrygerryhouse.com

Carrygerry, Shannon, County Clare

061 360 500

Dating back to the 1790s, Carrygerry is a charming country house, its elegant dining room extending into a conservatory space overlooking the Shannon estuary. It's a family-owned place that offers traditional country-house cooking using much artisan and organic produce.

▶ PLACES NEARBY

Nearby Ennis town, with its abbey and creative influences, is well worth a visit.

Ennis

visitennis.com

Ennis, county town of Clare, is the bustling heart of social and commercial life for a wide rural region, where old-fashioned shopfronts line the streets. A column in O'Connell Street commemorates Daniel O'Connell (1775–1847), who swept to parliament in 1828 after holding a mass meeting in Ennis. In the town park near the courthouse is a bronze statue of Eamon de Valera.

Ennis Friary

Abbey Street, Ennis, County Clare

065 682 9100 | Open Mar–Oct

The 13th-century abbey contains the beautifully carved McMahon tomb. It also has an impressive sacristy, with a barrel-vaulted ceiling, leading to the cloister.

Dromoland Castle ◉◉

dromoland.ie

From Shannon take the N18 towards Ennis | 061 368 144

Turrets and ramparts are present and correct at this top-end country-house hotel, with a golf course on the vast estate, a spa within its 15th-century walls, and plenty of good eating to be had. The Earl of Thomond restaurant, in a spectacular room filled with antiques, has an unmistakably French accent and top-notch produce drawn from the estate itself and local suppliers.

Glór Theatre

glor.ie

Friar's Walk, Ennis, County Clare

065 684 3103

A superb purpose-built concert venue, Glór Theatre, formerly Glór Irish Music Centre, presents the cream of Ireland's artists and performers and their work, especially in the field of traditional music. Performances feature the best Irish bands, individual musicians and singers, plus theatre, children's plays, film and dance. Exhibitions held at the theatre include paintings and photography.

wallcandy.ie

Professional artists in Ennis have grouped together to create the Wallcandy project, an exhibition of art displayed in unlikely locations around the town. Grab a map from one of the local shops or download it from the website.

▶ The Burren MAP REF 376 C1

The Burren is like nowhere else in Ireland. From the northwest
corner of County Clare it rises as a cluster of grey-domed hills
with terraced sides, whose western feet slope to the sea at
Galway Bay. There are no bogs and very few pastures. Instead
there are huge pavements of limestone called clints, their
vertical fissures known locally as grikes. However bleak it
appears, it is home to some wonderful plant life and there is
evidence that people settled here as long ago as the Stone Age.
Villages are scattered around the fringes: Ballyvaughan on the
north coast, Doolin and Lisdoonvarna to the west, and Kilfenora
with its Burren Visitor Centre in the south, connected by the
R477 coast road and the R476 and R480. The N67 crosses
the interior from Ballyvaughan to Lisdoonvarna. There are
no settlements here, but this is where many of the most
interesting historical sites are to be found.

Limestone landscape

The porous, almost waterless limestone of the Burren, scraped
smooth by glaciers, has never provided easy living conditions
for humans, although it makes ideal bedrock for plant life. By

▲ Poulnabrone portal dolmen

the mid-17th century, General Ludlow was reporting to Oliver Cromwell that the Burren possessed 'not any tree to hang a man, nor enough water to drown him, nor enough earth to bury him'. Cattle herding still takes place, though, keeping the scrub down and aiding the spread of wild flowers. Tourism is an ever-stronger factor in the growth of the local economy.

Attractive flora

The Burren supports Ireland's richest flora. In spring, you'll find the royal blue trumpets of spring gentians and the sulphur-yellow of primroses; in summer, the hills flush crimson with bloody cranesbill and are dotted white with eyebright. Orchids of many kinds grow here: spotted, early purple, marsh, bee, butterfly and frog orchids. Plants that wouldn't normally be found within a thousand miles of each other grow contentedly in neighbouring cracks and hollows in the limestone pavements and on the hill slopes: northern species such as mountain avens, southern species such as the bright yellow hoary rockrose; alpine saxifrages flourish down at sea level; woodland ivies and violets thrive in this exposed and treeless place.

Pieces of history

The middle of the Burren is deserted today, but evidence of former human settlement is plentiful with two impressive Stone Age tombs standing beside the R480 Ballyvaughan to Corofin road and later examples from Burren settlers of stone ring forts. Towers and fortified houses of note include Newtown Castle and Leamaneh Castle, east of Kilfenora (closed to the public, but visible from the road).

GO BACK IN TIME

Poulnabrone portal dolmen

Field east of the Ballyvaughan–Corofin road, County Clare
One of Ireland's most photogenic portal tombs (burial chambers) and easily accessible from the road, this square stone chamber (c 4000 BC), is topped by a huge capstone. Human remains of both adults and children have been found here.

Gleninsheen wedge tomb

2 miles south of Ballyvaughan on the road to Corofin, County Clare
This is a classic example of a wedge tomb (c 2500 BC). It was constructed with two large slabs on each side topped with a large flat stone for the 'roof'.

Caherballykinvarga

East of Kilfenora beside Ballyvaughan to Kilfenora road, County Clare
An excellent example of a stone ring fort still standing up to 15 feet high in places, the poignant ruin of Caherballykinvarga is well worth a visit.

Corcomroe Abbey

Bellharbour, County Clare
01 647 2300
Perhaps one of Ireland's most well-known ecclesiastical sites, the 12th-century abbey is in a wonderful state of repair with some fine carvings and tombstones to be seen.

Kilfenora Cathedral

Kilfenora, County Clare | Open daily Jun–Aug 9.30–5.30, Mar–May, Sep, Oct 10–5
Four heavily carved 12th-century high crosses, notably the Doorty Cross, stand in the partly re-roofed Kilfenora Cathedral, built on the site of an early monastery and dedicated to St Fachtnan.

Newtown Castle

Just southwest of Ballyvaughan, County Clare | 065 707 7200
Open Mon–Fri 9.30–5.30
This cylindrical 16th-century fortified tower house has been beautifully restored. There are great views from the Main Hall. Now part of the Burren College of Art, it houses a facsimile copy of the *Book of Kells*.

CHECK OUT THE VISITOR CENTRE

Burren Visitor Centre

theburrencentre.ie
Kilfenora, County Clare
065 708 8030
Find out more about the Burren in this purpose-built centre,

which houses an audiovisual film theatre and a fascinating exhibition, as well as a craft shop and tea room. You can explore the archaeology, history, folklore, geology and natural history of this remarkable area. There's also plenty of information on walks, hiking trails and cycle routes.

TOUR THE CAVES
Aillwee Cave
aillweecave.ie
Ballyvaughan, County Clare
065 707 7036 | Open daily Jul, Aug 10–6.30, Mar–Jun, Sep 10–5.30, Nov–Feb 10–5
One of Ireland's oldest caves, this show cave leads you into the subterranean world of the Burren, a honeycomb of caverns and passages eaten out of the rock by the chemical action and the friction of rainwater on limestone. You'll see some huge stalactites and stalagmites, sheets of glittering calcite, open caverns of churchlike size and a rushing underground waterfall.

EXPLORE THE VILLAGES
Lisdoonvarna
Near Doolin, Lisdoonvarna is Ireland's only spa whose waters are still drunk for medicinal purposes. The village is chiefly known for its Matchmaking Festival in August/September when lonely and not-so-lonely hearts get together, although really it is just an excuse for a party. Try the Roadside Tavern (see page 198) for traditional live music.

Kilfenora
South across the hills lies Kilfenora, where you can get an overview of the region in the Burren Visitor Centre (see opposite), and find great music in Linnane's (see below) and Vaughan's (see page 198).

Doolin
On the coast to the west, Doolin is the best known village for music in Ireland; you'll find tunes in McDermott's (see below) and lively songs in O'Connor's (see page 198).

LISTEN TO LIVE MUSIC
The Burren villages are great places for traditional music, for which County Clare is famous. In particular, Ballyvaughan on Galway Bay is the 'capital' of the north Burren.

Greenes Bar
Ballyvaughan, County Clare
065 707 7147
This is a classic Clare pub with traditional music on Mondays and Wednesdays.

Linnane's
Main Street, Kilfenora, County Clare
065 708 8157
A really traditional and welcoming pub with live music at 9.30pm on Wednesdays until late September. Expect talented musicians and singers and a lively atmosphere.

McDermott's
mcdermottspubdoolin.com
Doolin, County Clare
065 707 4328

▲ Gealain Lough in the Burren

This award-winning pub is not only in a spectacular location but has been in the same family since 1867. Visit for live music for much of the year or for one of the many events.

Monk's Bar
monks.ie
High Street, Ballyvaughan, County Clare | 065 707 7059
This is the place to go for music on Fridays, as well as probably the best seafood in town.

O'Connor's
gusoconnorsdoolin.com
Doolin, County Clare
065 707 4168
The *craic* is here in this pub, as well as a high standard of traditional live music and very decent pub grub.

The Roadside Tavern
roadsidetavern.ie
Lisdoonvarna, County Clare
065 707 4084
This is not only a really good gastro pub, but a great spot for traditional live local music and a wide selection of stouts and ales.

Vaughan's
vaughanspub.ie
Kilfenora, County Clare
065 708 8004
This pub is as traditional and as Irish as it gets. Home-cooked food is on the menu and as well as live music there is set dancing in the nearby barn.

WALK THE BURREN WAY
The Burren Way
theburrencentre.ie
This is one of Ireland's official Waymarked Ways, a 28-mile walk from Ballyvaughan southwest through the Burren to Liscannor. Old country roads, tracks and walled *boreens* (lanes) take you across the hills and valleys to Doolin. From here, a coastal path leads to the Cliffs of Moher (see page 208).

EAT AND DRINK
Cullinan's Seafood Restaurant and Guest House ◉◉
cullinansdoolin.com
Main Street, Doolin, County Clare
065 707 4183
The Cullinan's guest house overlooks the Aille River meadow, the sumptuous views captured by floor-to-ceiling windows on two sides of the dining room. It's a charming setting but it is chef-proprietor James Cullinan's skilful French-influenced modern cooking that is the showstopper.

Gregans Castle ◉◉◉
gregans.ie
On the N67, 3 miles south of Ballyvaughan, County Clare
065 707 7005

The restaurant is a romantic and refined room where picture windows open on to a view across the gardens to Galway Bay. Candlelight flickers in the evening and, as the summer sun sets, diners are treated to an eerie light show as the dying rays ignite the grey limestone rocks. If it's a light show you're after, there are some fireworks on the plate too, for David Hurley's sharp modern cooking is out of the top drawer.

Monk's Seafood Restaurant and Pub

monks.ie

Coast Road, Old Pier, Ballyvaughan, County Clare

This is a charming, family-run place with long and ongoing connections with the sea. Part pub, part restaurant, stop here for fresher-than-fresh seafood and a great pint, as well as a cracking atmosphere.

Moy House ◎◎

moyhouse.com

0.5 miles from Lahinch on the Miltown Malbay road, County Clare

065 708 2800

Seasonal cooking with panoramic views of the bay are on offer at this gleaming-white hotel on the Clare coast, which was the ancestral home of the Fitzgerald family, having originally been built for Sir Augustine in the mid-Georgian era. The food draws on unimpeachable local supply lines for four-course seasonal dinner menus that have much to entice.

Sheedy's Country House Hotel ◎◎

sheedys.com

Main Street, Lisdoonvarna, County Clare | 065 707 4026

Flavour-led cooking in a small rural hotel comes from chef-patron John Sheedy, who is the latest in a long line of Sheedys who have run the family business since the 18th century. The small country-house hotel is the oldest house in the village, and exudes the sort of family-run tradition that keeps a loyal fan base returning again and again. John Sheedy has long-established local supply lines to support his passion for authentic ingredients: the kitchen garden provides fresh herbs and vegetables to supplement local organic meat and fish landed at nearby Doolin.

Wild Honey Inn ◎◎

wildhoneyinn.com

Kincora Road, Lisdoonvarna, County Clare | 065 707 4300

Wild Honey has been around since 1860 and, although a makeover in recent years has grafted on a smart contemporary sheen, this convivial family-run inn oozes cosy character. Arrive early to dig into the kitchen's no-nonsense modern bistro cooking. Driven by the splendid larder of the rugged west coast, the culinary emphasis is on wild, free-range and seasonal ingredients, delivered in a hearty repertoire that is simplicity itself.

▶ **Cahir** MAP REF 378 B5

The busy little 18th-century town of Cahir has two main attractions – Cahir Castle and the Swiss Cottage. It is the castle that dominates, though, dwarfing the surrounding buildings, as it's one of the largest in Ireland. This pleasant compact town with a long-standing market can easily be explored in an hour or two. Its lovely location on the River Suir, which is situated at the eastern end of the Galtee Mountains, means it is a good jumping-off point for explorations and activities in the surrounding countryside. The tourist information office in the castle car park can provide more information.

TAKE IN SOME HISTORY

Cahir Castle

Castle Street, Cahir, County Tipperary
052 41011 | Open daily mid-Jun to Aug 9–6.30, mid-Mar to mid-Jun, Sep to mid-Oct 9.30–5.30, mid-Oct to mid-Mar 9.30–4.30

Cahir Castle stands on a crag beside the River Suir and is one of the best-preserved Norman castles in Ireland, with a keep, a tower and its outer wall still largely intact.

Swiss Cottage

Kilcommon, Cahir, County
Tipperary 052 41144
Open Mar–Nov daily 10–6

The Swiss Cottage is a great contrast to the castle – a rustic building with a thatched roof, stickwork verandas and elegant interiors, set in parkland. It was built in 1810 to designs by John Nash, and reflects a vogue for the cottage orné. Admission is by guided tour.

GO FISHING

cahiranddistrictanglersassociation.
com
052 744 2729

The salmon weir, on the opposite side of the bridge from the castle, is a popular location to fish. Angling guides are available with vast experience of the river and its tributaries. The Cahir and District Anglers' Association is one of the oldest in Ireland.

▶ **PLACES NEARBY**

The Knockmealdown Mountains are south of Cahir, and the Mitchelstown Cave is to the southwest. The nearby Galtee Mountains form the largest inland range in Ireland. Here, you'll find Glengarra Wood, with two looped walking trails, a beautiful variety of trees and sweeping views, which is very popular with walkers.

Mitchelstown Cave

mitchelstowncave.com
Burncourt, Cahir, County Tipperary
052 746 7246 | Open daily Apr–Sep 10–5.30, Oct–Mar 10am–dusk

Although Mitchelstown Cave is one of Europe's major show caves, the entrance to this spectacular natural wonder is about as low key as you can get. If it weren't for the flagstaff outside the farmhouse, it would be easy to miss. A grey metal door in the rock leads to the 88 concrete steps that descend into a wonderland of limestone, created over millions of years by dripping water depositing limestone to form the translucent stone curtains, stalactites, stalagmites and even sideways-growing halectites. The temperature is a steady 12°C, and the air feels dry and fresh. For half a mile, successive caverns open out, revealing ever more fantastic formations, and culminating in the Tower of Babel.

▶ Carlow   MAP REF 378 C3

carlowtourism.com

Carlow is the county town of County Carlow, with good shopping off its wide open square. Away from the heart of town is a pleasing tangle of early 19th-century streets. Hidden gems on the doorstep are found among beautiful countryside, mountains and rivers in Ireland's sunny southeast. The courthouse is a striking replica of the Parthenon, and was supposedly intended for Cork city until a mix-up of documents bestowed upon Carlow one of its grandest buildings.

TAKE IN SOME HISTORY

Carlow Castle

carlowcountymuseum.com

College Street, Carlow, County Carlow | 059 917 2492

Open Mon–Sat Jun–Aug 10–5, Sep–May 10–4.30

Carlow's castle lies stranded amid modern housing schemes by the Barrow River. The two remaining round towers and a section of curtain wall date from the 13th century. The rest was, bizarrely, destroyed in 1814 by a local doctor trying to convert the site into a hospital for the mentally ill with the aid of high explosives.

Carlow Cathedral

carlowcathedral.ie

Dublin Road, Carlow, County Carlow

059 916 4086

The early 19th-century Gothic Cathedral of the Assumption, one of the first Catholic churches built after the Emancipation Act, was designed by Thomas Cobden and is topped by an impressive lantern tower. The Parish Shop is open Monday to Friday 9–1 and 2–5.

▶ PLACES NEARBY

The area around Carlow has much to offer, not least a prehistoric portal tomb 2 miles east of the town. Religious sites dot the countryside as well as gardens to visit; driving trails are available to guide you.

Brownshill Dolmen

The dolmen stands in a field opposite a car showroom about 2 miles out of town on the R726. A surfaced track leads from a parking area to the stones, which date from 2500 BC and would once have been covered in earth. The precarious capstone is believed to be one of the largest in Europe.

Carlow Garden Trail

carlowgardentrail.com

Identifiable road signs make the Carlow Garden Trail an easy-to-follow and interesting tour. The trail can be driven in a day and covers more than 20 gardens, ranging from grand and mature to small and newly established grounds.

Trail of the Saints

trails.carlowtourism.com

Three separate driving routes take you around some 51 religious sites in the county of Carlow, which include St Patrick's, St Moling's and St Laserian's trails.

Lord Bagenal Inn

lordbagenal.com

Main Street, Leighlinbridge, County Carlow | 059 977 4000

This riverside restaurant offers appealingly unpretentious cooking. The menu includes oriental, international and modern Irish dishes made with local ingredients.

Mount Wolseley Hotel, Spa and Country Club ◉

mountwolseley.ie

Tullow, County Carlow

059 918 0100 and 059 915 1674

Enjoy modern Irish cooking in this sumptuous hotel and country club, with plenty of golf. In keeping with the chic surroundings, the place encompasses a stylish split-level dining room where seafood is a forte.

▶ Carrick-on-Shannon   MAP REF 381 E4

irelandnorthwest.ie

Carrick-on-Shannon is one of Ireland's fastest-growing inland resorts and has thrived since the reopening of the Ballyconnell and Ballinamore Canal as the Shannon–Erne Waterway in 1994. It provides the missing link between Upper Lough Erne and the Shannon, opening up a 236-mile boating route from Belleek to Limerick and the Shannon Estuary. Carrick's situation on the River Shannon has resulted in it becoming one of the most popular destinations for leisure cruising in Ireland. Within a 6-mile radius are 41 lakes, so water activities are high on the agenda here.

The Dock Arts Centre occupies the former courthouse. Also in the town you'll find Ireland's smallest chapel, said to be the second-smallest chapel in the world. The Costello Memorial Chapel on Bridge Street was commissioned by bereft local widower Edward Costello after the death of his wife Mary Josephine in 1877. When she passed away he had her body embalmed and commissioned the beautiful tiny chapel for her final resting place.

▲ Walkway on the River Shannon

SEE A LOCAL CHURCH
Costello Memorial Chapel
Main Street, Carrick-on-Shannon,
County Leitrim
This tiny, intimate chapel is
sometimes described as
Ireland's Taj Mahal, which was
also erected to honour the early
death of a beloved wife.

CATCH A PERFORMANCE
The Dock Arts Centre
thedock.ie
St Georges Terrace, Carrick-on-
Shannon, County Leitrim
071 965 0828
This multi-purpose arts centre
puts on a lively programme of
evening entertainment, as well
as various art exhibitions and
community workshops.

TAKE A BOAT TRIP
Moon River Cruise
moonriver.ie
Marina, Carrick-on-Shannon,
County Leitrim | 071 962 1777
You can rent boats for the day
or for a longer trip from various
companies at the Carrick
marina. With Moon River, you
float gently from Carrick Quay
along the starlit Shannon with a
drink in your hand, serenaded
by the cream of local singers
and bands.

PLAY A ROUND
**Carrick-on-Shannon Golf
Club**
carrickgolfclub.ie
Woodbrook, Carrick-on-Shannon,
County Leitrim | 071 966 7015
An 18-hole course with a
delightful diversity of scenery.
Extended from nine holes on
preserved marshland that
sweeps down to a lake and the
Boyle River. The original nine
holes are set in mature
parkland and constitute the first
five and last four holes of the
course. Two of the most
spectacular holes are the
eighth, where the tee is
surrounded by water which
requires a carry over the river,
and the 13th, a scary par three.

▶ PLACES NEARBY

Paintball enthusiasts will love the facility at Battlebridge.

Battlebridge Paintball and Zorbing

battlebridgepaintball.ie
Battlebridge, County Leitrim | 086 166 4959 | Open daily 9am–dusk
Close to Carrick-on-Shannon, Battlebridge is a purpose-built paintball and zorbing site.

▶ Castletown House MAP REF 379 D2

castletown.ie

Celbridge, County Kildare | 01 628 8252 | Open Easter to mid-Nov
Tue–Sun 10–6

Castletown is the largest and earliest Palladian-style house in Ireland. Constructed between 1722 and 1729 for William Conolly, who was once speaker of the Irish House of Commons and the wealthiest commoner in Ireland, it is approached by an avenue of lime trees half a mile long. With a view over meadows to the River Liffey and the mountains, the main hall has detailed stucco work by the Lafranchini brothers and an enormous painting, *The Boar Hunt*, by Paul de Vos (1596–1679). Conolly made his fortune buying and selling forfeited property after the Battle of the Boyne, but never lived to see his great house completed, a task left to Lady Louisa Conolly, the wife of his great-nephew, who moved there in 1759. The interiors have been left virtually untouched since her death in 1821. One particular room, the Print Room, is lined with paper taken from 18th-century magazines. The house was acquired by the Irish state in 1994.

▶ PLACES NEARBY

Dublin and the pretty east coast villages of Howth (see page 308) and Dún Laoghaire (see page 289) are just a half-hour drive from this imposing house.

▼ Castletown House

▶ **Cavan** MAP REF 382 C5

thisiscavan.ie

This pleasant town in Ulster is the county town of County Cavan and has a narrow main shopping street, Farnham Street, which is a lovely place to linger. The shops are mostly independently owned, their bright frontages harking back to an older Ireland, all but vanished this far east. Of the 14th-century Franciscan friary, to which the town owes its origin, the belfry tower remains in a run-down churchyard near the bus station. The huge green rotunda and neoclassical facade of St Patrick's Roman Catholic Cathedral, built in 1942, stand out in the north of the town.

The whole county has a rich music and dance scene and many of the pubs and bars in Cavan, such as Blessings on Main Street (see below), have live traditional Irish music every week.

TAKE IN SOME HISTORY
St Patrick's Roman Catholic Cathedral
kilmoredpc.ie
Cullies, Cavan, County Cavan
049 433 1496
There was a cathedral in the diocese from 1454, but after the Reformation it was taken over by the Church of Ireland and, after a new Anglican Cathedral was built, became a parochial hall. There was no Catholic cathedral for almost 300 years. The current neoclassical cathedral was constructed between 1938 and 1942. The single spire is 230 feet tall and the stained glass is from Harry Clarke's studios.

GET INDUSTRIAL
Cavan Water Mill
cavanwatermill.ie
The Mill Block, Cavan, County Cavan
087 456 4375 | Tours Jun–Sep 3pm
This 19th-century famine-era mill has been restored and is now a museum and visitor centre. Step back in time as you are introduced to this intriguing place by an authentic miller and learn the secrets of the oat milling process just as it was carried out 170 years ago. Entry is only by pre-booked tour.

PLAY A ROUND
County Cavan Golf Course
cavangolf.ie
Drumelis, Cavan, County Cavan
049 433 1541
A parkland course with a number of mature trees, some over 100 years old. The closing six holes are an exacting challenge for handicap and professional golfers alike.

EAT AND DRINK
Blessings
Main Street, Cavan, County Cavan
049 433 2140
It may have been recently modernised, but this pub has lost none of its traditional charm. With a hundred-year-old history, it boasts artefacts such as an old telephone box and a red-painted petrol pump.

10 Wild Atlantic Way highlights

Botanica Restaurant, Radisson Blu Farnham Estate Hotel ◉

farnhamestate.com

Farnham Estate, County Cavan

From Cavan take Killeshandra road for 2 miles | 049 437 7700

Enjoy Irish produce in French-influenced cooking while you are surrounded by lakes, rivers and ancient oak forests on this massive 1,300-acre, 16th-century estate. A friendly service team is well versed in the ins and outs of each dish and the kitchen places its faith in local ingredients, bringing it all together with French-inspired flair.

The Keepers Arms

Bridge Street, Bawnboy, Cavan, County Cavan | 049 952 3318

This is a simple hostelry with a good old-fashioned welcome, great beer and a lovely location.

McGinnity's

38 Bridge Street, Cavan, County Cavan | 049 436 8042

This is a much-loved and well-established spot in the centre of town that has a lively atmosphere day and night.

▶ **PLACES NEARBY**

The county museum can be found in Ballyjamesduff, to the southeast of town, and further afield, south of Blacklion, is the remarkable limestone plateau of Cavan Burren Park.

Cavan County Museum

cavanmuseum.ie

Virginia Road, Ballyjamesduff, County Cavan | 049 854 4070

Open Jun–Sep Tue–Sat 10–5, Sun 2–6, Oct–May Tue–Sat 10–5

This museum has some interesting local exhibits, particularly on archaeology, the Great Famine and the songwriter Percy French.

Cavan Burren Park

cavanburren.ie

Just outside Blacklion in West Cavan 071 985 3941 | Open daily 24 hours

This is one of the most spectacular integrated prehistoric landscapes of its kind in the whole of the country. Visitors can explore a rich landscape featuring ancient megalithic tombs, rock art and impressive stone walls, as well as wonderfully preserved glacial erratics and pre-bog walls. There are spectacular views over Lough MacNean, Cavan and Fermanagh and the wider Global Geopark. There is a visitor centre with imgainative displays, and four walking trails.

▶ Clare Island   MAP REF 380 B5

clareisland.ie

Clare Island lies at the mouth of Clew Bay. The gaunt castle at the harbour was the chief stronghold of the 16th-century pirate queen Grace O'Malley, who probably lies buried in the ruined abbey on the island's south coast road. The climb to the Knockmore summit (1,512 feet/461m) is rewarded by the view over Clew Bay. If you stay overnight in summer, note that the pub often doesn't open until midnight. There's plenty to do, including boat tours, yoga retreats and numerous events and festivals throughout the year. There are a number of important archaeological sites here including promontory forts and a megalithic tomb – signposted from the harbour – dating from 4000–3000 BC.

HIT THE BEACH
The Harbour
blueflagireland.org
Clare Island, County Mayo
01 400 2202
On the eastern side of the island by the harbour, this is a lovely spot for a swim and sandy walks along the shore.

GET AWAY FROM IT ALL
Macalla Farm
macallafarm.ie
Clare Island, near Westport, County Mayo | 087 250 4845
At Macalla Farm, visitors can book retreats in yoga, horses, food and mindfulness.

TAKE TO THE WATER
Clare Island Ferry Company
clareislandferry.com
098 23737
Call for sightseeing sailings around Clare, as well as nearby islands and diving excursions.

EAT AND DRINK
Sailor's Bar
Clare Island, Clew Bay, County Mayo
Known for its live music, this is the perfect spot for a Guinness overlooking the bay.

▶ PLACES NEARBY
Westport (see page 363) is to the east on the mainland.

▼ Granuaile's (Grace O'Malley's) Castle

▶ Cliffs of Moher MAP REF 377 C2

The Cliffs of Moher are one of Ireland's most spectacular sights. Shale, sandstone and silt form an extraordinary rampart 682 feet high, facing Galway Bay. In summer, this is generally crowded with visitors, taking in superb views of the Aran Islands and along the Clare coastline for 30 miles southwest to Loop Head. The cliff edge is unguarded so take care, especially in windy weather.

CHECK OUT THE VISITOR CENTRE

The Cliffs of Moher Visitor Experience

cliffsofmoher.ie

Cliffs of Moher, Liscannor, County Clare | 065 708 6141 | Open daily 9am–dusk

Make the visitor centre your first stop, which is the starting point for walks of varying difficulty as well as the 12-mile Cliffs Coastal Trail. The underground centre at the heart of the cliffs houses an exhibition with displays and interactive experiences for old and young. It's also a good stop to pick up maps, guides and snacks for your journey.

ENJOY THE VIEW

O'Brien's Tower

cliffsofmoher.ie

Cliffs of Moher, Liscannor, County Clare

In 1835, Sir Cornelius O'Brien, the local member of parliament and descendant of Brian Boru, the High King of Ireland, built the tower known as O'Brien's Tower that stands on the cliffs. From the roof on a clear day, you may see the mountains of County Kerry to the southwest, Connemara's Twelve Bens to the northeast and the three Aran Islands to the west.

GO BIRDING

The Cliffs of Moher are ideal for birdwatching. In fact, they are home to Ireland's largest mainland seabird nesting colony. Look out for clown-like puffins, as well as guillemots, razorbills and choughs.

▶ PLACES NEARBY

You can follow a coastal path to get to Doolin in the Burren (see page 198).

▼ The Cliffs of Moher

▶ Clonakilty MAP REF 377 D6

clonakilty.ie

The lively little market town of Clonakilty was once known for linen manufacture but is now best remembered for its associations with patriot Michael Collins (1890–1922), whose statue stands on Emmet Square. Collins was born 5 miles west at Sam's Cross. Clon, as it is often known, is proud of its community spirit and well-known music scene.

VISIT THE MUSEUM

Michael Collins Centre Heritage Park

michaelcollinscentre.com
Castleview, Clonakilty, West Cork
023 884 6107 | Open mid-Jun to Mid-Sep Mon–Fri 10.30–5, Sat 11–2
Learn more about Collins on the 1921 Trail at the Michael Collins Centre Heritage Park at Castleview.

GO ROUND THE GARDENS

Lisselan Estate Gardens

lisselan.com
Clonakilty, West Cork | 023 883 3249 | Open daily dawn–dusk
Lying just to the east of the town are the attractive Lisselan Estate Gardens, which also offer golf and fishing.

ENTERTAIN THE FAMILY

West Cork Model Railway Village

modelvillage.ie
Inchydoney Road, Clonakilty, County Cork | 023 883 3224
Open daily 11–5
Children and railway buffs will love this attraction with its fully scaled handmade model of the 1940s West Cork Railway Line, with working model trains and an interpretative room about the railway towns and those who lived and worked there.

PLAY A ROUND

Dunmore Golf Course

dunmoregolfclub.ie
Dunmore, Muckross, Clonakilty, West Cork | 023 883 4644
A hilly, rocky nine-hole course overlooking the Atlantic.

EAT AND DRINK

De Barra's

debarra.ie
55 Pearse Street, Clonakilty, West Cork | 023 33381
This is a muso's paradise. The whole interior is covered with musical instruments for a start, and most of the bar staff are talented musicians.

▶ PLACES NEARBY

Close to Clonakilty is a Bronze Age site, a sandy beach and the ruins of an old abbey.

Drombeg Stone Circle

megalithicireland.com
At this popular Bronze Age site, 17 stones form one of the best prehistoric circles in the country. During excavations in the 1950s, the cremated remains of a body were found in an urn in the middle of the circle. The remnants of two round huts stand to the west of the circle, with a lined pit from around AD 368.

Inchydoney Island

inchydoneyisland.com

If you prefer a break from sightseeing, there is a sandy beach at Inchydoney Island, as well as a lovely spa.

Timoleague Abbey

timoleague.ie

Timoleague, Cork, County Cork

Timoleague Abbey is on a bend of the Argideen River, renowned for its fish and bird life, where it runs into Courtmacsherry Bay.

The ruin dates from 1312, when Franciscans moved in at the behest of Donal Glas MacCarthy. Forced out at the Reformation, they returned in 1604 but were burned out again in 1642 by Cromwell's men. Of the two later churches in the village, the Church of the Ascension reflects in miniature the square tower of the abbey; the Catholic church has a window dating from 1929 by artist Harry Clarke.

▶ Clonalis House MAP REF 381 E5

clonalis.com

On the N60, just west of Castlerea, County Roscommon | 094 962 0014

Open Jun–Aug Mon–Sat 11–5

Ancestral home of the O'Conor family, who are direct descendants of the last kings of Ireland, Clonalis House is a late-Victorian Italianate country house. Its interest lies in the antiquity of its owners. One, Ruaidri Ua Conchobair (Rory O'Conor), reigned from 1166 to 1186 as the last High King of Ireland. The O'Conors preserve a huge archive of family papers and historical documents. You can also see the great stone on which the O'Conor chiefs were inaugurated since pre-Christian times, and the harp that belonged to Turlough O'Carolan (1670–1738), the blind harpist and poet known as the last of the traditional court bards. The O'Conor Don (clan chief) at the time was a keen patron of O'Carolan. Visitors can opt to stay in the house or in one of the cottages, or simply come for the day.

▶ PLACES NEARBY

The famous Knock (Marian) Shrine is a short drive to the west. At Castlerea just to the east there is a treasure trove for railway enthusiasts.

Knock (Marian) Shrine

knockshrine.ie

Knock, County Mayo | 094 933 8100

Open daily 9–6

This is a National Shrine visited by Roman Catholic pilgrims from all over the world.

Hell's Kitchen Railway Museum and Bar

hellskitchenmuseum.com

Main Street, Castlerea, County Roscommon | 087 230 8152 |

Open daily 12–6

Ireland's largest collection of rail memorabilia and equipment is on display here.

▶ Clonmacnoise MAP REF 378 B2

heritageireland.ie/en/clonmacnoise
Clonmacnoise, Shannonbridge, Athlone, County Offaly | 090 967 4195
Open daily Jun–Aug 9–6.30, mid-Mar to May, Sep, Oct 10–6, Nov to
mid-Mar 10–5.30

One of Ireland's most popular tourist destinations, the historic
monastery of Clonmacnoise lies on a great bend of the River
Shannon, some 7 miles downstream of Athlone, near the meeting
point of three counties: Offaly, Westmeath and Roscommon. It also
has its own jetties on the riverbank for foot-passengers arriving by
water: the most impressive view of Clonmacnoise is had this way.

Whether you arrive by road or by boat, you'll enter through the
visitor centre, essential to your appreciation of Clonmacnoise.
The monastic site lies immediately east of the centre, with the
round tower and churches huddled compactly together inside their
surrounding wall. As you enter, O'Rourke's Tower lies to the left
beyond the copy of the Cross of the Scriptures. Ahead is the copy of
the South Cross, with the cathedral just beyond it. At the far side
of the site you can follow a marked path to the Nuns' Church.

A site with mixed blessings

When he founded the monastery of Clonmacnoise around AD 548,
St Ciarán chose the site extremely well. The monastery stood not
only on Ireland's largest navigable river, but also on the glacial
ridge called Esker Riada, the King's Highway, the main east–west
high road of the kingdoms of Connacht and Leinster.

Clonmacnoise enjoyed more than six centuries of prosperity and
pre-eminence as Ireland's chief religious and educational centre.

Monks from all over Europe came and kings of Ireland were buried here. Yet things were tough. The Vikings attacked at least eight times; the locals outdid them, attacking on nearly 30 occasions and setting the monastery on fire a dozen times. After the arrival of the Normans in 1180, Clonmacnoise began to decline, and in 1552 English soldiers stole every treasure, and smashed what they could not carry away.

By far the most enjoyable way to arrive at Clonmacnoise is to rent a boat at Athlone and cruise here. The view is of towers, churches and a drift of gravestones, enclosed within a protective wall on a green bank and reflected in the river. Altogether this aspect of Clonmacnoise forms an unforgettable ensemble and a perfect subject to photograph.

Cross of the Scriptures

The high crosses facing wind and weather on the monastic site are copies; the originals, too precious to be exposed to the elements, are on display in the visitor centre. The best-preserved, the Cross of the Scriptures, stands 15 feet high. It is often called Flann's Cross – an inscription on the base attributes it to King Flann, High King of Ireland at the turn of the 10th century when the cross was carved. Abbot Colman Conailleach probably erected the cross around AD 910. It is richly carved with biblical scenes: St Anthony besting the devil, the Saved called to eternal life, and Christ in his tomb being awoken by a peck on the lips from a bird that might be the Holy Dove.

The Cross of the Scriptures may be the most striking of the Clonmacnoise high crosses, but don't ignore the other two great crosses on display. The ninth-century South Cross, badly weathered, shows a crucifixion with the identifiable figures of Longinus the lance-bearer and Stephaton the sponge-bearer; while the North Cross, perhaps dating back as far as AD 800, has stiffly posed lions and a motif of spiralling foliage. The cross-legged figure here might be Cernunnos, the horned god of the woods and of virility, revered in Celtic pagan mythology.

Grave slabs

Also in the visitor centre exhibition is a unique collection of grave slabs. Dating from the eighth century to the twelfth, they represent Europe's largest collection of early Christian burial markers. Some are decorated with interlace carving and incised crosses of various shapes. One of the slabs is clearly marked 'Colman'; another implores, 'Ior do thuathal saer', a prayer for Thuathal the Craftsman.

O'Rourke's Tower (Round Tower)

Once out of the visitor centre and into the roughly circular walled site of the monastery, most visitors turn left past the copy of the Cross of the Scriptures and head for O'Rourke's Tower, the most obvious landmark. The O'Rourke in question was probably Fergal O'Rourke, King of Connacht, who died in AD 964, roughly the same time that the tower was built for protection against the frequent attacks of the Danes. The tower, 65 feet high, is built of beautifully shaped, slightly curved stones, but the top is incomplete. The cap was blasted off by a lightning strike in 1135, as was meticulously recorded by the monks.

The Cathedral or Macdermot's Church

East of O'Rourke's Tower is Clonmacnoise Cathedral, a neat incorporation of the original church built in AD 904 by Abbot Colman and High King Flann Sinna within a 12th-century rebuilding. Many ancient fragments of carved stones lie in a side chapel. The Gothic arch of the north door is made up of a whole nest of recessed courses carved with barley-sugar fluting and foliage, in which the sculptor has set the dragons of sin to writhe helplessly. This formidable door has a special property – if you bring your mouth close to the stonework on one side and whisper, the sound will be carried right round the top of the arch and down to a listener's ear pressed against the opposite door jamb. In medieval times, priests could thus hear the confession of a leper without risk of contamination. Nowadays, children rejoice in the secret of the Whispering Door.

St Ciarán's Church (Temple Ciarán)

Immediately east of the cathedral lies the diminutive St Ciarán's Church, from around AD 800. The founder of Clonmacnoise is said to be buried at the far end. For centuries farmers would anoint the corners of their fields with earth scraped from the floor of St Ciarán's Church to protect their corn and cattle. Eventually, the floor became so hollowed that stone slabs were laid. But old beliefs die hard, and you may still see pilgrims furtively collecting a handkerchief of earth from just outside the church. Those who suffer from warts anoint them with rainwater from the hollow of the bullaun (ancient quernstone) inside St Ciarán's Church.

MacCarthy's Church (Temple Finghin)

Against the monastery's surrounding wall, due north of St Ciarán's Church, stands the 12th-century MacCarthy's Church, or Temple Finghin, unmistakable because of the miniature round tower with its herringbone cap of stone tiles that rises from the south wall of the church. The tower, which was probably a belfry rather than a defensive stronghold as its door is vulnerably placed at ground level, was built around 1124, some say by Big Finian MacCarthy. The Romanesque chancel arch is decorated with weathered but still beautiful chevron carving.

The Nuns' Church

Many visitors miss this exquisite little church because it lies a short walk east of the main site. The carvings are superb, far richer than in any of the other Clonmacnoise churches, with Romanesque chevrons, faces, beaked beasts and other grotesques. The church was built in 1167 as an act of penance by Dervorgilla O'Rourke, a powerful princess, who was married off to one of the most powerful kings in Ireland as a political move. Whether she was subsequently abducted or eloped, Dervorgilla played a key if indirect role in the end of the golden age of Celtic Ireland as it was one of the events that led to the Norman invasion of Ireland.

Among the carvings around the west door and the chancel arch of the Nuns' Church is another pagan symbol: you can pick out a couple of 'green men'. These enigmatic figures are always shown with foliage emerging from one or more of their facial orifices. They seem pagan in character yet are found in medieval church decoration all over Europe and beyond.

▶ **PLACES NEARBY**

They might not sound glamorous, but boglands in Ireland are special places. Read Seamus Heaney's evocative poem 'The Boglands' to get a sense of these magical landscapes. Boglands make up 5 per cent of Ireland's landscape and are home to many rare plants and animals. The old Irish word for soft, 'bogach' is spongy ground containing decaying peat moss.

Blackwater Bog

The Blackwater Bog covers some 19,770 acres of counties Offaly, Westmeath, Roscommon and Galway, some untouched, other parts exploited for fuel and fertiliser. The practice of cutting peat (turf) for domestic fuel makes little impression on the bog, but commercial exploitation for industrial fuel and gardening by the Peat Board since World War II has seen damage on a vast scale. Destruction of the bogs over the past 50 years has been on such a scale that an international outcry by conservationists ensued, and exploitation is due to cease by 2030.

Bord na Móna (the Peat Board) operates miles of railway across the peatlands. At Clonmacnoise a section was used as a tourist attraction, but it was closed in 2008 because tourist traffic was interfering with the movement of peat. You can appreciate the scale of the peat industry by glimpsing the huge West Offaly Power station complex (not open to the public) near Shannonbridge, on the way to Clonmacnoise. The old machinery used in the closed railway, as well as a number of railway engines, is still on display, although you may have to be a serious railway or bog buff to visit.

Bog of Allen

The great Bog of Allen stretches some 62 miles from County Kildare through County Offaly to the River Shannon. This is a 'raised bog', formed when water trickles down from higher ground and collects on an impermeable base which, in this case, is a thick sheet of clay spread by the retreating glaciers of the last Ice Age. The bog holds up to 20 times its own weight of water and the peat can be 32 feet or more in depth. At first glance it appears lifeless, but closer inspection reveals abundant plant life, including many kinds of sedges, sundews and the brilliant orange stars of bog asphodel.

Lough Boora Discovery Park

On the R357 near Kilcormac, off the N52 between Birr and Tullamore, County Offaly | 057 934 0010
Open daily; check the website for times

Learn all about the conversion of the bog into wildlife and amenity parks at Lough Boora Parklands near Kilcormac, which has walking trails, a cycle path, birdwatching, a sculpture park, fishing opportunities and special events.

▶ Clonmel   MAP REF 378 B5

visitclonmel.ie

Considered to be one of the most beautiful towns in Ireland, the county town of Tipperary, Clonmel, dates back to the 12th century. It was once a stronghold of the important Butler family, the Earls and Dukes of Ormonde. The best way to see the town's historic buildings is via the Heritage Trail (leaflet available from the tourist office). Highlights include the arcaded Main Guard of 1684 and the blue-painted Town Hall on Parnell Street. Hearns Hotel is where Italian Charles Bianconi (1786–1875) established what would become the most famous bus company in Ireland in 1815. It is interesting to note its architectural features from the exterior, but it is not open to general visitors.

Laurence Sterne, author of *The Life and Opinions of Tristram Shandy*, was born in Clonmel in 1713, and Anthony Trollope and George Borrow also lived in the town. A literary festival in September recalls local authors.

TAKE IN SOME HISTORY
The Main Guard
Sarsfield Street, Clonmel, County Tipperary | 052 612 7484
Open 2 Apr to 16 Sep Tue–Sun 9–5
This significant building, a central landmark in the town, was originally constructed as the courthouse for the Palatinate, or administrative region, for the county of Tipperary. Its role in regional history has been recognised and it has been restored to its former glory.

VISIT THE MUSEUM
Museum of Transport
Richmond Mill, Emmet Street, Clonmel, County Tipperary
052 612 9727 | Open Jun–Aug Mon–Sat 10–6, Sun 2.30–6, Sep–May Mon–Sat 10–6
Around 20 gleaming antique cars are on display at the Museum of Transport on Emmet Street.

GO TO THE RACES
Clonmel Racecourse
clonmelraces.ie
Powerstown Park, Clonmel, County Tipperary | 052 618 8508
Horse racing took place here for at least a century before the racecourse was properly enclosed in 1913. Around 120 horses will race at any meeting at this renowned track, and these take place most months (not July or August).

PLAY A ROUND
Clonmel Golf Club
clonmelgolfclub.com
Lyreanearla, Mountain Road, County Tipperary | 052 612 4050
Set in the scenic, wooded slopes of the Comeragh Mountains, this is a testing course with lots of open space and plenty of interesting features. It provides an enjoyable round in exceptionally tranquil surroundings.

EAT AND DRINK

Hotel Minella ◉

hotelminella.com

Coleville Road, Clonmel, County
Tipperary | 052 612 2388

The restaurant is at ground-floor level in the original house, so has plenty of character and a traditional, period feel, as well as views across the garden, which runs down to the River Suir. The kitchen team keep things simple with a good choice of unchallenging fare with a local flavour.

▶ PLACES NEARBY

North of Clonmel, the quaint town of **Fethard** has a tiny folk museum housed in its former railway station, and a market on Sundays.

There are good hikes to be made in the Comeragh Mountains, which rise to the south of the town.

▶ Cobh MAP REF 377 E5

The town of Cobh (pronounced 'Cove'), on the south side of Great Island, east of Cork city, is a naturally sheltered harbour. This made it a significant embarkation point for naval fleets during the Napoleonic Wars of the 18th century, for emigration and prison ships in the 19th century, and for the glamorous transatlantic liners of the 20th century. Today it is a seaside resort, with brightly painted Regency frontages above little shops and restaurants. Popular with sailors, Cobh is also a leading venue for sailing.

Between 1791 and 1853, almost 40,000 convicts passed through Cobh on their way to Australia and other distant penal colonies, banished for crimes that ranged from as little as petty theft to murder. In the 1820s prison hulks were moored here, dealing with overspill from the crowded land jails. Between 1815 and 1970 more than three million people took their last view of Ireland here, as they emigrated to the US, Canada and other countries.

Approaching Cobh by road, turn left at ruined Bellvelly Tower and take the shorter route through rolling farmland and over the crest of the ridge to emerge directly behind St Colman's Roman Catholic Cathedral.

The town was renamed Queenstown in honour of Queen Victoria, who visited in 1849, but reverted to Cobh in 1920. A statue on the quay by sculptor Jeanne Rynhart depicts three children who left here on the SS *Nevada*. The girl, Annie Moore, was the first to enter the US through Ellis Island, on 1 January 1892. The *Titanic* called into Cobh on 11 April 1912, taking on a final 123 passengers before heading west. The daily Titanic Trail walking tour highlights the town's links with the notorious liner. Survivors from the *Lusitania*, which was sunk by a

German submarine off the Old Head of Kinsale in May 1915, were brought ashore here, and around 150 bodies from the wreck lie in the old cemetery, 2 miles north of town. A poignant memorial dominates the town centre.

TAKE IN SOME HISTORY

Queenstown Story Heritage Centre

cobhheritage.com

Western end of the seafront, Cobh, County Cork | 021 481 3591 | Open Mon–Fri 9.30–5, Sat 9.30–6

The interesting stories of local emigrants, as well as local history, are well told at this heritage centre.

St Colman's Cathedral

cobhcathedralparish.ie

5 Cathedral Terrace, Cobh, County Cork | 021 481 3222

St Colman's Cathedral was completed in 1915 and stands high above the town. The graceful spire, 300 feet tall, conceals a carillon of 49 bells, including Ireland's largest bell, which ring out tunes on summer Sunday afternoons. Inside, note the rose window framed by dummy organ pipes, and the mosaic floors. Mass takes place at 8am and 10am Monday to Friday, at 6pm on Saturday and at 8am, 10am, 12 noon and 7pm on Sunday.

GET ON THE WATER

SailCork

sailcork.com

East Hill, Cobh, County Cork

021 481 1237

In these sheltered waters you'll see little sailboats and sailboards out at all times of the year – instructors come here in winter to train. Lessons and charters are available from this well-established, family-run company, including dinghy sailing, canoes and powerboats. All abilities – from novice to expert – are welcome, and there's a multi-activity course for children.

GO WALKING

Titanic Trail

titanic.ie

Departs from Commodore Hotel, Cobh, County Cork | 021 481 5211

Check website for opening times

See some of the sites associated with the *Titanic* and her first and last fateful voyage. This fascinating 90-minute walking tour of the town provides lots of information about Cobh's rich maritime and emigrant heritage, and there's a spooky Ghost Trail on offer too for groups of eight or more.

EAT AND DRINK

Mansworth's Bar

4 Midleton Street, Cobh, County Cork | 021 481 1965

This magnificent pub, dating back to the 19th century, lives and breathes Cobh's maritime heritage. Founded in 1868, this is officially Cobh's oldest pub and in 1912 some of the

◀ St Colman's Cathedral

Titanic's passengers would have had their last pint here before getting on board the doomed liner.

▶ **PLACES NEARBY**

Whiskey buffs will enjoy a visit to Jameson's distillery in Midleton, just to the northeast of Cobh.

Jameson's Old Midleton Distillery

jamesonwhiskey.com
Old Distillery Walk, Midleton, County Cork | 021 461 3594
Open daily; see the website for seasonal variations

Midleton is a small town, 10 miles from Cobh, dominated by the silver-grey spire of its cathedral and the massive bulk of the distillery, which took over whiskey production in 1975. The original 1825 distillery has been restored. A gleaming copper still stands before the visitor centre, and a 10-minute film, followed by a 50-minute guided tour (largely out of doors), gives an insight into the history and skills of whiskey manufacture. You see the progress of the grain through malting, fermenting and blending, and the world's biggest pot still (32,000 gallons). At the end of the tour you can participate in a whiskey tasting.

▼ Cobh harbour

▲ The Mweelrea Mountains

▶ **Connemara** MAP REF 380 B6

connemara.ie

Connemara's wild romantic landscape is one of the top sights in the country, with rugged mountains, deep valleys and a beautiful coastline. It is the westernmost part of County Galway, between the great Lough Corrib in the east and the ragged, wild Atlantic on the west. To the north, it slopes to the narrow fiord of Killary Harbour, while the southern border is formed by Galway Bay.

The heart of Connemara is a vast stretch of lonely bog, broken by the dramatic rise of twin mountain ranges – the Maumturks (Sléibhte Mhám Toirc) to the east, and the Twelve Pins (Na Beanna Beola) farther west. The N59 runs west from Galway city through the Connemara heartland, bordering the wild, lonely and beautiful area known as Iar Connacht, the 'back of Connacht', on its way to Clifden, the region's capital and sole town of any size. Then it bends back through northern Connemara. Buses are few, trains non-existent. The narrow, winding roads are good for slow drivers, excellent for cyclists, and best of all for walkers.

▲ Clifden

The most romantic place name in Ireland, Connemara evokes images of steep mountains, ragged coasts, turf cutters, horse-and-donkey carts, fishermen in black *currach* canoes – a landscape for poets, artists and dreamers that's wildly, extravagantly beautiful. But the poor soil, stony bogs, harsh mountains and rocky coasts reveal that this has always been a poor region. Many of the long, straight bog roads, the lonely jetties and causeways were built as famine relief works in the 19th and early 20th centuries. As a result of geographical and cultural isolation in the past, much of Connemara is a Gaeltacht or Irish-speaking region. People still struggle to make a living, and tourism is a cornerstone of the economy.

The only town in Connemara, Clifden has everything you could want, from banks, supermarkets and music pubs to the excellent tourist office in the old station buildings. Its focus is the town square and Main and Market streets, teeming with visitors in summer. The town comes fully alive in mid-August when it hosts the Connemara Pony Show.

CHECK OUT THE VISITOR CENTRES

Clifden Tourist Office
connemara.ie
Galway Road, Clifden, County Galway | 095 21163 | Open Mon–Sat 9.30–5
Pop in for tips and advice on things to do and see in the area.

Letterfrack Visitor Centre
connemaranationalpark.ie
076 100 2528 | Open daily 10–5
The visitor centre in Letterfrack gives information about guided walks, self-guided nature trails pony trekking, exhibitions and talks. There are also tea rooms, and a play area.

TAKE IN SOME HISTORY
Kylemore Abbey
kylemoreabbey.com

Kylemore Abbey, grey and impressive, dominates Pollacappul Lough just east of Letterfrack. The house was built as a grand Gothic country seat in the 1860s by Manchester businessman Mitchell Henry, and in the late 19th century was the heart of a 13,850-acre estate. After World War I it became a convent for nuns who had fled from Belgium. The house is not open to the public, but the beautiful Walled Garden is a major attraction.

VISIT THE MUSEUMS
Leenane Sheep and Wool Museum
sheepandwoolcentre.com
Leenane, Connemara, County Galway
095 42323 and 095 42231 | Open mid–Mar to Oct daily 9.30–5

The Leenane Sheep and Wool Museum displays spinning and dyeing techniques, and information on rare breeds.

Pádraig Pearse's Cottage
heritageireland.ie
Inbhear, near Rosmuc Village, County Galway | 091 574 292
Open daily mid-May to Aug 10–6, late Mar to mid-Apr 10–5

On the shores of Lough Oiriúlach near Gortmore (Angort Mór) stands the thatched, whitewashed cottage built by poet, teacher and ardent nationalist Pádraig (or Patrick) Pearse between 1903 and 1904, now a national monument. In these small, simply furnished rooms, and out in the rocky countryside round about, Pearse perfected his Gaelic, taught the language to students from Dublin, and formulated his ideas for Irish national independence. It was Pearse who proclaimed the infant Irish Republic from the stone steps of Dublin's impressive General Post Office building on Easter Monday 1916. A few days later Pearse was shot as a traitor in Kilmainham Gaol.

VISIT A MUSIC WORKSHOP
Roundstone Musical Instruments
IDA Craft Centre, Roundstone, County Galway | 095 35808
Open daily 10–6, later if busy

Malachy Kearns, known as 'Malachy Bodhrán' to one and all, is Ireland's Master Maker of *bodhráns*, or traditional goatskin drums. Since he established his workshop here in the old monastery buildings at Roundstone his fame has spread worldwide. You can buy a beautifully made *bodhrán* (Malachy's wife adds the lovely Celtic designs) or other musical instruments, and browse in the gift and craft shop.

GET OUTDOORS
Connemara National Park
connemaranationalpark.ie

Around 7,400 acres of blanket bog and four of the Twelve Pins peaks are protected as the Connemara National Park. It's a paradise for birdwatchers and nature lovers as bird life and flora are rich and varied here; red deer have been reintroduced and a herd of wild Connemara ponies was presented to the park by the late President Childers. The herd is currently managed under agreement with the Connemara Pony Breeders' Society. Common songbirds include skylarks, meadow pipits, stonechats, chaffinches, robins and wrens, and birds of prey such as kestrels, sparrow hawks, merlins and peregrine falcons are sometimes spotted.

In recent years both pine marten and non-native mink have been seen; the latter is a threat to some of the native wildlife species.

Twelve Pins (Na Beanna Beola), the Maumturks (Sléibhte Mhám Toirc) and the Inagh Valley

Much of the drama and beauty of Connemara derives from the mountain ranges that rise from the central bogs of the region: the amorphous mass of the Maumturks, and on their western flank the more shapely peaks of the Twelve Pins. Guided walks in the mountains, including the ascent of Benbaun (Binn Bhán), at 2,392 feet (729m) the highest of the Twelve Pins, are offered by the Connemara National Park Visitor Centre; you can also climb the 1,437-foot (438m) Diamond Hill by a waymarked track. Bisecting the Twelve Pins/Maumturks massif is the Inagh Valley with its long lake. The N59 road encircles the mountains, while the R344 runs through the valley.

HIT THE BEACH
An Trá Mhóir, the Great Beach
There is great swimming to be enjoyed in the sea all along the Connemara coast, provided you know which beaches have gently shelving sand and are free of clogging seaweed. An Trá Mhóir, the Great Beach, below the Connemara Golf Club, is one that fits this bill exactly.

From Clifden, turn right off the R341 in Ballyconneely, and follow the road for 3 miles; turn right just before reaching Bunowen Pier at a Connemara Golf Club sign and follow the lane across the golf course to the club house.

Eyrephort Beach
The drive to this beach is one of the main attractions apart from the white sands. Looking out onto the islands of Inishturbot and Inishturk South, this is a popular spot so expect crowds on a sunny day.

Omey Strand
The tidal island of Omey can be reached at low tide from the mainland village of Claddaghduff, and Omey Strand, one of the island's most interesting beaches, hosts horse-riding along the sands, and the famous Omey Races.

EXPLORE THE AREA
Killary Harbour
Killary Harbour, lying between counties Galway and Mayo, is the northern boundary of Connemara. The fiord-like inlet is 150 feet deep; mountains rise dramatically on both sides – south, the bulk of the Maumturks (Sléibhte Mhám Toirc; 1,800 feet/549m); north, the flanks of Mweelrea (2,687 feet/819m) and Ben Gorm (2,460 feet/750m).

Killary once served as a base for the British Navy. At the eastern end lies the popular angling centre of Leenane,

huddled under the mountains. There are good walking trails in the surrounding countryside, one leading to the Ashleag Waterfall at the eastern tip of Killary Harbour.

Northern Connemara
The N59 runs from Clifden to Leenane through northern Connemara, with side roads leading north to a beautiful coast of deeply indented bays. Letterfrack, a neat little 19th-century village built by Quakers, is home to the Connemara National Park Visitor Centre. North of Letterfrack there are some superb white-sand beaches, Rusheenduff and Glassillaun being especially striking.

Out at Renvyle Point, the Renvyle House Hotel was formerly the country retreat of Dublin surgeon and man of letters Oliver St John Gogarty ('Buck Mulligan' in James Joyce's *Ulysses*), who entertained W B Yeats, George Bernard Shaw and other Irish literary luminaries.

Roundstone (Cloch na Rón)
On the shores of Bertraghboy Bay, Roundstone has a tiny harbour and a scatter of pubs and small shops. A track leads to the summit of Errisbeg, the hill that rises 985 feet behind the village.

GO FOR A DRIVE
Romantic roads
The beautiful switchback road that runs west out of Clifden to

encircle the Kingstown Peninsula is called the Sky Road, while the drunkenly twisting and bumping road between Ballyconneely and Roundstone is known as the Brandy and Soda Road. Another, built between Cashel and Rosmuck as a famine relief measure using turf and grass, is *Bóthar na Scrathóg*, the 'road of the top-sods'.

PLAY A ROUND

Connemara Championship Links

connemaragolflinks.com
Ballyconneely, Clifden, County Galway | 095 23502

This championship links course has a spectacular setting by the Atlantic Ocean, with the Twelve Pins Mountains in the background. Established in 1973, it is a tough challenge, due in no small part to its exposed location, with the back nine the equal of any in the world. The last six holes are exceptionally long and offer a great challenge to golfers of all abilities. When the wind blows, club selection is crucial. Notable holes are the 13th (200-yard par three), the long par five 14th, the 15th with a green nestling in the hills, the 16th, guarded by water, and the 17th and 18th, both par fives over 500 yards long.

EAT AND DRINK

Abbeyglen Castle Hotel ◉

abbeyglen.ie
Sky Road, Clifden, County Galway
095 21201

Abbeyglen Castle lies ensconced in 12 acres of lovely grounds. In the restaurant at dinner, the decor is bold and bright with artworks on cherry-red walls and crystal chandeliers, and a pianist tinkles away on a grand piano. Expect classic cooking built on excellent local materials. As you'd hope, given the closeness to the sea, fish and seafood makes a good showing.

Cashel House ◉◉

cashel-house-hotel.com
Cashel, Connemara, County Galway
095 31001

The restaurant here offers a repertoire of French-accented classics, served in either an airy conservatory extension, or a polished traditional setting amid antiques and artworks. Connemara's lakes, rivers, hillsides and the ocean supply the kitchen with the finest produce it could wish for.

O'Dowds Seafood Bar & Restaurant

odowdsbar.com
Roundstone, County Galway
095 35809

The oldest bar in town is still one of the best. It has a basic interior, but a great atmosphere and a lovely view of the harbour. Five generations of the same family have run this place.

▶ PLACES NEARBY

Close to Connemara on the R341 is an aviation memorial, and not far offshore are the rugged Causeway Islands.

Alcock and Brown Monument

Two signposted routes lead from the crossroads on the R341. A right turn will bring you to the Alcock and Brown monument, a tall splinter of dark stone silhouetted on a hillside between Mannin Bay and Ardbear Bay, with wonderful views over west Connemara. The memorial commemorates Sir John Alcock and Sir Arthur Whitten Brown, who accomplished the first non-stop transatlantic flight in June 1919. They flew from St Johns (Newfoundland) to Clifden in Ireland, where their flight ended in a crash landing. The rough road on the left from the crossroads (better walked than driven) leads in about one mile to the site where they landed their Vickers Vimy bomber plane nose-down in Derrygimlagh bog.

Causeway Islands

At Costelloe (Casla) on the R336 Galway city–Maam Cross (An Teach Dóite) road, a left turn goes west across the islands of Lettermore (Leitir Móir), Gorumna (Garumna) and Lettermullan (Leitir Mealláin). They are linked by causeways that were built as part of a famine relief scheme. Well off the beaten tourist track, these Irish-speaking islands have thatched cottages, sprawling villages and tiny stone-walled fields in a windswept landscape.

▶ Alcock and Brown landing site

Inishbofin

inishbofin.com

Inishbofin lies some 3 miles north of Aughrus Point, 45 minutes by ferry from the fishing village of Cleggan, and has a population of just 200. There is a great view from the top of Cleggan Hill. The islanders are very welcoming, and the pace of life here is easy. Inishbofin is ideal for exploring on foot, and is particularly attractive to birdwatchers for its huge population of seabirds. The best guidebook is *Inis Bó Finne/Inishbofin, A Guide to the National History and Archaeology* by David Hogan and Michael Gibbons (available on the island). Sites include a heritage centre at the pier, a star-shaped Cromwellian fort built in 1656 to house Catholic gentry condemned to transportation, and the ruins of a 14th-century church on the site of the seventh-century monastery of the hermit St Colman.

▶ Coole Park and Gardens MAP REF 377 D1

coolepark.ie

Coole Nature Reserve, Gort | 91 631669 | Open access

Coole Park is where Lady Augusta Gregory (1852–1932), patron of the Irish literary revival of the late 19th and early 20th centuries, entertained writers and artists. The house was demolished in 1941, but the wooded grounds and 'glittering reaches of the flooded lake' – as W B Yeats wrote in 1931 – now form a forest park. The Autograph Tree is a lovely copper beech which bears the signatures of many literary and artistic figures of the past. Coole Park is one of the locations on the Lady Gregory Yeats trail (ladygregoryyeats.trail.com), run by a not-for-profit group aiming to promote wider awareness of Lady Gregory and W B Yeats and their influence on the area.

▶ PLACES NEARBY

Close to Coole Park you will find the ruins of a monastery and a tower house.

Kilmacduagh Monastery

Open access (ruins)

Sometimes called 'Ireland's Pisa' because of its leaning tower, Kilmacduagh monastic site, founded around AD 610, stands against a backdrop of the domed limestone hills of the Burren in County Clare. The impression is of a close-knit community, which reflects a thousand years of Christian occupation of Kilmacduagh, despite Viking attacks in the ninth and tenth centuries. The most striking feature is the 11th-century round tower, 111 feet tall, which leans noticeably. The roofless cathedral nearby predates the coming of the Normans to Ireland, though it was rebuilt in graceful Gothic style in the 14th century.

Nearby is the Abbot's House or Bishop's Castle, a two-floor, square block of a fortified tower house. Also on the site are O'Hyne's Abbey, founded in the 10th century, and St John's Oratory, a lovely little building that might date back to St Colman's time.

Thoor Ballylee

yeatsthoorballylee.org

Signposted off the N66, 3 miles northeast of Gort | 091 631 436

Open mid-Jun to Aug daily 11–6, Sep Mon–Fri 10–1, Sat–Sun 12–4

'I the poet William Yeats... / Restored this tower for my wife George.'

William Butler Yeats characteristically celebrated in verse his restoration of the 16th-century tower house that became his country retreat and preferred writing spot. He bought it in 1917 for £35. You can wander through the four floors, viewing Yeats's first editions and memorabilia, while listening to recordings of the man reading his own works, including extracts from his 1928 collection *The Tower*, inspired by Thoor Ballylee.

▶ Cork MAP REF 377 E5

cork-guide.ie

Today, Cork, in County Cork, is a vibrant, modern industrial and university city. Its status as a European Capital of Culture in 2005 resulted in major refurbishment, visible throughout the city's shopping streets and increased pedestrianisation. The city's heart lies between the north and south channels of the River Lee, and waterways and its many bridges have given it the soubriquet of Ireland's Venice. Three-spired St Fin Barre's Cathedral (1870) lies to the south.

Ireland's third-largest city has a lively buzz and plays host to a number of international festivals covering jazz, film and folk. Walking round the compact town is a pleasure and you'll hear many of the locals call Cork the 'real capital of Ireland'.

Ancient history

Cork's history dates back to the founding of a monastery on marshland here by St Finbarr in the mid-seventh century. The Vikings built a town, and walls were constructed around the core; these were demolished in the 17th century, after a siege by William of Orange's men. Cork's 19th-century prosperity was founded on sea trade, notably by shipping butter to Australia and South America. Part of the city was burned by the English in 1921 during the nationalist uprisings. You can learn more at the Cork Vision Centre on North Main Street and the Public Museum in Fitzgerald Park.

▼ View over Cork from St Patrick's Hill

Cork is second only to Dublin for the quality and variety of its shopping. Patrick Street is the hub, curving south from the North Channel, and you'll find all the big-name shops and department stores here (within Merchants Quay Shopping Centre), including Dunnes, Penneys and Brown Thomas, and all the usual high-street chain stores. Step off the main drag and pedestrianised lanes branching north to Paul Street and south to Oliver Plunkett Street (named after a 17th-century martyr) are lined with classy independent retailers and appealing eateries. There is also lively nightlife and, with the entire Cork area known for its musicians and artists, expect to be joining in a ballad or two in the local taverns.

TAKE IN SOME HISTORY

Church of St Anne Shandon
shandonbells.ie
Church Street, Shandon, Cork
021 450 5906 | Open Jun–Sep
Mon–Sat 10–5, Sun 11.30–4.30,
Mar–May, Oct Mon–Sat 10–4, Sun
11.30–3.30, Nov–Feb Mon–Sat 10–3
The red and white sandstone tower, capped by a gilded weathervane in the shape of a salmon, is one of the city's great landmarks. Built in 1722, St Anne's is the oldest parish church still in continuous use in Cork, and is affectionately known for its famous bells, which were popularised in the 19th-century ballad 'The Bells of Shandon'. The name Shandon comes from Séan Dún, the Irish for 'old fort'.

Cork City Gaol
Heritage Centre
corkcitygaol.com
Sunday's Well, Cork | 021 430 5022
Open daily Mar–Oct 9.30–5, Nov–
Feb 10–4
Whatever time of year you visit, it's always bone-cold inside the walls of this grim, castle-like structure on a steep hillside northwest of the city. Inside, the cells and corridors resonate with the unhappiness of the men and women incarcerated here between 1824 and 1928. Cells are furnished in 19th- to early 20th-century style, and the audio tour and audiovisual presentation bring it all to life. In the early days felons were isolated in single cells to avoid further corruption, and left in silence (even the warders' boots were muffled) to contemplate their crimes. In reality, such treatment often led to madness. Dusty dummies portray a sense of waste and decay.

In the 1950s the empty buildings became the unlikely headquarters of the budding Radio Éireann. A separate radio museum is housed upstairs.

Red Abbey
Red Abbey Street, Cork | Open access
The Red Abbey's tower stands on the site of an Augustinian abbey thought to have been founded in the 13th or 14th century. Its name comes from the reddish sandstone used in its construction.

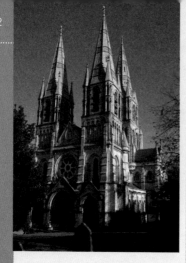

▲ St Fin Barre's Cathedral

St Fin Barre's Cathedral

corkcathedral.webs.com

Dean Street, Cork | 021 496 3387

Open Mon–Sat 9.30–5.30, Sun 1–5.30

Consecrated in 1870 St Fin Barre's Cathedral occupies a site which has seen Christian worship since the seventh century. Tour guides are available to take visitors around the cathedral, and performances take place here throughout the year.

VISIT A GALLERY

Crawford Art Gallery

crawfordartgallery.ie

Emmet Place, Cork | 021 480 5042

Open Mon–Sat 10–5

This outstanding municipal collection is housed in a red-brick building, erected in 1724 as the Custom House, when Emmet Place was the King's Dock. As well as rotating exhibitions from the permanent collection of paintings, and the Sculpture Room, there is a modern space for temporary

shows. Up the big staircase (with brilliant stained glass by James Scanlon, 1993) the displays on the upper floor include depictions of Aran islanders by Charles Lamb (1893–1964) and a portrait of actress Fiona Shaw by Victoria Russell (1964–). There's a historical image of the local sport of road bowls, *Bowling Match at Castlemary, Cloyne*, by Daniel MacDonald (1821–53), and James Humbert Craig's Lowryesque figures huddled against the rain in *Going to Mass* (c 1935). Séan Keating's icon of Irish nationalism, *Men of the South* (1921), is also here.

VISIT A MUSEUM

Cork Butter Museum

corkbutter.museum

The Tony O'Reilly Centre, O'Connell Square, Shandon, Cork

021 430 0600 | Open Mar–Oct daily 10–5, Nov–Feb Sat, Sun 11–3

This unique museum in the Shandon area of Cork city celebrates Ireland's butter trade and explores the country's dairy culture from early practices of preserving butter in bogs through to the evolution of the Cork Butter Exchange, which became the largest butter market in the world.

GET OUTDOORS

Bishop Lucey Park

One of the very few green spaces in Cork city, Bishop Lucey Park was officially opened in 1985. The park is bounded by the Grand Parade, Tuckey Street, the South Main

Street and Christ Church Lane, and is named after Bishop Cornelius Lucey, who was the Roman Catholic bishop of Cork for over 30 years. The park opened to commemorate Cork 800, a celebration of Cork's 800 years as a chartered city.

You can see a section of Cork's old city wall, excavated during the park's construction, near the park entrance; the entrance archway used to be the entrance to the former corn market in Anglesea Street. The park has two notable sculptures: the *Onion Seller*, Seamus Murphy's bronze commemorating the street traders on Cornmarket Street, and John Behan's bronze fountain with eight swans, again symbolising Cork 800.

CATCH A PERFORMANCE
City Limits Comedy Club
thecomedyclub.ie
Coburg Street, Cork | 021 450 7744
One of the top venues for UK, Irish and American comedians, there is always plenty of laughter at this intimate venue.

Cork Opera House
corkoperahouse.ie
Emmet Place, Cork | 021 427 0022
Musical drama and family entertainment, from jazz concerts and pantomime (vaudeville-style fairy tales) to international touring ballet, set the scene at this modern venue. The backstage door gives access to the Half Moon Theatre, with more drama, live music and a nightclub.

Everyman Palace Theatre
everymanpalace.com
15 MacCurtain Street, Cork
021 450 1673
A lively mixture of comedy, touring theatre and opera productions, with pantomime over the Christmas period, are staged in this Victorian listed building. Irish plays dominate the programme during the summer season.

TAKE A CITY TOUR
Cork City Tours
corkcitytour.com
A good way to explore the stories and history of Cork city is on a tour. Cork City Tours operates open-top double-decker buses, which run regularly during the day. The route is through the main streets, along the quays and past city-centre landmarks with a guide who will regale you with tales of the city.

The Cork Fabulous Tasting Trail
fabfoodtrails.ie
Led by a guide on Saturday mornings and lasting three hours, this relaxed tour stops off at outdoor and indoor markets, cafes, restaurants and pubs – so you may not need lunch!

Literary Tour
corkcitylibraries.ie
For the literary minded, pick up a free audio walking literary tour of Cork, or download one onto your MP3 player at the Cork City Library.

ENJOY THE NIGHTLIFE
The Oliver Plunkett
theoliverplunkett.com
106 Caroline Street, Cork, County
Cork | 021 422 2779
Formerly known as Scotts, this
is an elegant and streamlined
bar. There's a nightclub
upstairs, open Friday and
Saturday; patrons under 21
must produce photo ID.

Thomond Bar
2 Marlborough Street, Cork
021 427 9747
A lively Irish pub which serves
good local food all day and by
romantic candlelight in the
evening. There are live bands
most nights; this is the place to
hear traditional Irish ballads.
Sport is also shown here.

GO SHOPPING
English Market
englishmarket.ie
Enter at Grand Parade, St Patrick's
Street, Princes Street and Oliver
Plunkett Street, Cork
Open Mon–Sat 8.30–6
For the very essence of the
city, visit this covered food
emporium. In the early morning
you'll see some top local
restaurateurs in here, picking
out the best of the produce.

Buy your black or white
puddings from the array of
butchers' stalls, or go for the
traditional Cork dish of tripe
and drisheen (cow's stomach
lining). Iago sells the best range
of Irish cheeses. The market
holds other delights, such as
the tiny Good Yarns bookshop;
and the barber shop (for a hot

towel, shave and massage). The
upstairs cafe is a great place to
people-watch.

Butlers Chocolate Café
butlerschocolates.com
30 Oliver Plunkett Street, Cork
021 427 8866
These delectable cafe-and-
chocolate-shops are now found
all over the world, including in
Dublin and Galway city. The
chocolates can be gift-wrapped
to take away, or bought singley
to enjoy with a coffee.

Merchants Quay Shopping Centre
1 Patrick Street, Cork
021 427 5466
This large complex is one of the
premier shopping destinations
in the city.

PLAY A ROUND
Cork Golf Club
corkgolfclub.ie
Little Island, Cork | 021 435 3451
Some 6 miles east of the city
centre, this championship-
standard course is playable all
year round. Memorable and
distinctive features include
holes at the water's edge and
in a disused quarry. The fourth
hole is considered to be among
the most attractive and testing
holes in Irish golf.

EAT AND DRINK
The Mutton Lane
corkheritagepubs.com
3 Mutton Lane, Cork | 021 427 3471
This is one of the oldest pubs in
Cork. Just around the corner
from the Buttermarket, live

sheep were once run past it to the market, hence its name. The dark interior is candle-lit and the pictures on the walls tell great stories.

Roundy Bar

1 Castle Street, Cork | 021 422 2202
Another old pub that is also situated in one of the oldest buildings in Cork. Come for a coffee, a toasted sandwich and for some lively conversation as much as the great Guinness.

Sin É

8 Coburg Street, Cork
021 450 2266
You could easily while away an entire day at this atmospheric old place. There's music most nights, much of it traditional, but with the odd surprise.

▶ PLACES NEARBY

The county of Cork has a number of key attractions, all easily accesssible from Cork city. These include Blarney with its famous stone (see page 182), Sheep's Head Peninsula (see page 341) and Mizen Peninsula (see page 173). You can visit a wildlife park, just 20 minutes away, and find great places to eat in Castlelyons and Douglas.

Fota Wildlife Park

fotawildlife.ie
Carrigtohill, County Cork
021 481 2678 | Open Mon–Sat 10–5, Sun 11–5
More than 90 species of exotic animals live in this wildlife park, 6 miles east of Cork city. It was established in 1983 to breed endangered species, and the cheetahs are a particular success story, with more than 150 cubs born here. Ostriches, giraffes, zebras, kangaroos and ringtailed lemurs are some of the animals in the 70 acres of lush countryside. Fota House, dating from 1825, has beautiful gardens and an arboretum. Stories of its residents are brought to life with little films.

Ballyvolane House

ballyvolanehouse.ie
Castlelyons, near Fermoy, County Cork | 025 36349
Ballyvolane is an exquisite country home, run with love and commitment by its owners. Dinner here is more house party than a formal dinner, with guests of the house all sitting at a communal table. The food – from Ballyvolane's walled garden, farm, river and the local area – is invariably excellent and in 2015 they started making a superb local gin, named Bertha's Revenge (ballyvolanespirits.ie), with no less than 18 botanicals.

Maryborough Hotel and Spa ◉

maryborough.com
Maryborough Hill, Douglas, County Cork | 021 436 5555
There's a whiff of glamour at this country-house hotel, surrounded by well-maintained gardens and woodland. In contrast, there's a sharp look to the bar and restaurant, called Bellini's, where locally sourced produce is used to create the menu's modern dishes.

▶ Craggaunowen Project   MAP REF 377 D2

shannonheritage.com

Quin, County Clare | 061 367 178 | Open Easter–Sep daily 10–5

Irish history is brought to life at fascinating Craggaunowen – one of the best 'step-into-the-past' open-air sites in Ireland. It's easy to gain a mistily romantic notion of life in pre-Christian Celtic Ireland but at Craggaunowen costumed guides interpret the warts-and-all realities of the fifth and sixth centuries in the cleverly recreated buildings here. Exhibits include a fenced dwelling built on a *crannóg* or artificial island in a lake; a ringfort with a round, solid earth rampart protecting a huddle of cylindrical thatched huts; a *fulacht fiadh* or cooking pit used for boiling meat over fire-heated stones; and a length of planking road that crossed the bog some 2,000 years ago. You can also see the leather-hulled currach *Brendan*, which explorer Tim Severin built and sailed to Newfoundland in 1976–77 to substantiate the claim that St Brendan once made the journey. It was this voyage that showed how St Brendan may have discovered America back in the sixth century AD. Look for the patched-up hole that an iceberg tore in her side. The lake walks are charming and there is a good cafe selling home-made food.

▶ PLACES NEARBY
Bunratty Castle and Folk Park (see page 192), lying to the southeast of Craggaunowen, offers a good family day out, and further on is the lively city of Limerick (see page 329), founded by the Vikings.

▶ Croagh Patrick   MAP REF 380 C5

croagh-patrick.com

County Mayo | 098 64114

The cone-shaped peak that overlooks Clew Bay is Ireland's holy mountain, Croagh Patrick. In AD 441 St Patrick preached at the summit and allegedly banished all the snakes from Ireland. A steepish path leads up from Campbell's Bar in Murrisk to a saddle at 1,475 feet (450m), then there's a scramble up a very steep boulder slide to the summit chapel at 2,500 feet (762m). The reward is a superb view, especially south towards the Twelve Pins, and north across island-studded Clew Bay.

The Croagh Patrick Visitor Centre is located near the National Famine Monument in Murrisk. This impressive piece of sculpture, which commemorates Ireland's Great Famine, was created by John Behan and is in the form of a haunting Coffin Ship with skeleton bodies.

▲ Croagh Patrick mountain

The mountain is still very much a holy place today and attracts around one million pilgrims every year. Reek Sunday (the mountain is known affectionately by locals as the 'Reek'), on the last Sunday in July, sees over 25,000 pilgrims of all ages visit. Many of them come barefoot as an act of penance. St Patrick's Chapel, erected in 1928 by Reverend Father Patterson, is where Mass is celebrated and confessions are made by worshippers.

CHECK OUT THE VISITOR CENTRE

Croagh Patrick Visitor Centre
croagh-patrick.com
Murrisk, on Pilgrim's path at base of Croagh Patrick, opposite National Famine Monument | 098 64114
In the visitor centre, as well as displays on local history and the archaeology of Croagh Patrick, there is a craft shop, coffee shop and guided tours in summer on request. Sturdy boots or shoes and rain gear are advisable if you are going to walk to the summit.

▶ **PLACES NEARBY**
Westport (see page 363) is 5 miles west of Croagh Patrick.

▶ Dingle Peninsula (Corca Dhuibhne) MAP REF 376 A4

Artists, film-makers and photographers are all drawn to the barren but magical Dingle Peninsula, with its changing colours, moods and weather. Seen from anywhere along this coast, it is the mountains which first define the Dingle Peninsula: the Slieve Mish Mountains to the east rising to 2,791 feet (851m), and the peaks of Mount Eagle (Sliabh an Iolair; 1,686 feet/ 514m) and Mount Brandon (Cnoc Bréanainn; 3,122 feet/950m) to the west. In the middle are green valleys becoming steadily stonier towards the western tip and Dunquin. Follow the Slea Head Drive clockwise for the great views at Clogher Head. Gaelic is still widely spoken here, so road signs may be in Irish.

Headlands and viewpoints

There are rocky cliffs at Slea Head (Ceann Sléibhe) and Brandon Head (Pointe an Chorra Dhóite), and superb sandy bays on the north shore around Castlegregory, and on the northwest tip around Ballyferriter (Baile an Fheirtéaraigh). One of the best viewpoints is at the top of the Connor Pass (1,496 feet/456m), reached by a hair-raising narrow and winding road. The N86 is a more direct route between Tralee and Dingle. The Slea Head Drive is a scenic loop from Dingle; follow it clockwise for the best views. The Dingle Way long-distance path goes from Tralee for 111 miles around the peninsula. Dingle, on the southern shore, is the only significant town.

Ancient history

The earliest inhabitants of this area left plenty of signs of their habitation, from cup-marked boulders, Iron Age forts and Ogham-inscribed stones to the distinctive drystone cells (beehive huts) of the early Christians who, from the fifth century on, sought refuge here. In the sixth century, St Brendan sailed from Brandon Creek, on the northern coast, at the start of his epic voyage. In 1579, a Spanish army supporting the Desmonds (see Youghal, page 373) built a fort, Dún an Óir, at Ferriter, only to be wiped out the following year by the English.

Dingle (An Daingean)

Dingle started out as the site of a fort and trading port, developed into a fishing town, and is now the main tourist hub for visitors to the peninsula.

▶ The road to Dunquin harbour

TAKE IN SOME HISTORY
Gallarus Oratory
heritageireland.ie
6 miles from Dingle (R559)
066 915 5333 | Open Mon–Sun 9–8
Apart from a minor sag in the roofline, this deceptively simple stone church looks much as it did when it was first built, some time between the seventh and 12th centuries, and it is outstanding among the ancient sites of Ireland. The walls of this serene and beautiful structure are of thick, pinkish sandstone and constructed entirely without mortar. Its form resembles the keel of an upturned boat and echoes the shapes and hues of the hills around. The visitor centre below offers a video interpretation, a restaurant and gift shop.

VISIT A MUSEUM
Celtic and Prehistoric Museum
Kilvicadowning, Ventry (Ceann Trá), County Kerry | 066 915 9191
Open daily Mar–Oct 10–6
Just west of Ventry Strand, the traditional-looking building on the left holds a few surprises. First is its bright, modern interior and relaxed mood with music playing, and next is the guidebook that comes on loan with your ticket – a huge spiral-bound affair, mixing *Far Side* cartoon humour with detailed information about the exhibits. What you go on to see, simply displayed in six small rooms, is a fabulous collection of antiquities from across the globe. They include a nest of fossilised dinosaur eggs, a genuine mammoth skull with tusks 10 feet long fished out of the North Sea, Stone Age hand-tools of chipped flint and Bronze Age brooches. Through it you get a real insight into the sort of people who were the early settlers on the Dingle Peninsula.

ENTERTAIN THE FAMILY
Dingle Oceanworld Aquarium
dingle-oceanworld.ie
The Wood, Dingle, County Kerry
066 915 2111
Also along the waterfront here, the Dingle Oceanworld Aquarium celebrates local marine life; it features a tunnel that goes 30 feet through the middle of the ocean tank.

MEET THE DOLPHIN
Dingle Dolphin
dingledolphin.com
Unit 2, The Tourist Office, The Pier, Dingle, County Kerry
066 915 2626
Separated from Dingle Bay (Bá an Daingin) by a long, hilly spit of land, the town has a sheltered harbour which is home to Dingle's most famous resident – Fungi, a wild Atlantic bottlenose dolphin who has made the area his home since 1983, and who seems to love the company of visitors. Daily tours are on offer here to see Fungi the dolphin, as well as harbour tours.

HIT THE BEACH
Inch Strand
Inch, the most famous beach in Ireland, stretches 3 miles south

of Dingle. To the east, a ridge covered with marram grass shelters the marshy shallows of Castlemaine Harbour, beloved of oystercatchers, ringed plovers and other waders. To the west, there seems to be a permanent mist of spray from the waves, softening a view punctuated by people fishing, flying kites and picnicking. A lifeguard is on duty in summer. The 1972 movie *Ryan's Daughter*, filmed here, is credited with putting Dingle on the world map and the movie has its own memorial stone at a windswept picnic spot above a tiny harbour west of Slea Head.

GET ON THE WATER
Jamie Knox Watersports
jamieknox.com
The Maharees, Castlegregory, County Kerry | 066 713 9411
Towards the tip of the sandy spit north of Castlegregory, Jamie Knox Watersports offers tuition in all kinds of water sports, including activities such as surfing, boardsailing and kite-surfing.

SADDLE UP
Longs Horse Riding and Trekking Centre
longsriding.com
Ventry, County Kerry | 066 915 9034
If the idea of a canter along the sands has always appealed, this friendly riding centre to the west of Dingle (An Daingean) town is the place to go. The emphasis here is on safety and fun, and there is a range of equine activities on offer.

GO SHOPPING
Dingle Crystal
dinglecrystal.ie
Green Street, Dingle, County Kerry
066 915 1550
Browse the beautiful items of individually cut crystal from local craftsmen and perhaps purchase one for a souvenir. Prices are relatively reasonable.

PLAY A ROUND
Dingle Links Golf Club
dinglelinks.com
Ballyferriter, County Kerry
066 915 6255
This most westerly course in Europe has a superb scenic location. It is a traditional links course with beautiful turf, many bunkers, a stream that comes into play on 14 holes and, usually, a prevailing wind.

Waterville House and Golf Links
watervillegolflinks.ie
Waterville, County Kerry
066 947 4102
On the western tip of the Ring of Kerry, this course is highly regarded by many top golfers. The feature holes are the par five 11th, which runs along a rugged valley between towering dunes, and the par three 17th, which features an exceptionally elevated tee. Needless to say, the surroundings are beautiful.

EAT AND DRINK
Coastguard Restaurant ◉
dingleskellig.com
Dingle Skellig Hotel, and Peninsula Spa, Harbourside, County Kerry
066 915 0200

The main dining option is the Coastguard Restaurant (food is also available in the bar, bistro and cocktail lounge), with its stunning view over the bay through capacious picture windows. The kitchen works with the excellent produce from around these parts, with locally landed fish and West Kerry lamb stealing the show, to create modern Irish fare.

Gormans Clifftop House and Restaurant ⊚

gormans-clifftophouse.com

Glaise Bheag, Ballydavid (Baile na nGall), County Kerry | 066 915 5162

This stone-built house perches on the clifftops above Smerick harbour. Chef-proprietor Vincent Gorman has a passion for sourcing as much as possible of his materials from the local farms and ports. Simplicity is the key to this delightful restaurant with rooms: there's nothing to get in the way of the dining room's views across the Atlantic, produce is spankingly fresh and the concise menu offers five choices at each stage.

Dick Mack's

Greene Street

066 915 1787

This is very much a family pub with a little bit of star quality. Dick Mack's has seen various famous faces order a drink over the years from Dolly Parton to Robert Mitchum. Current owner Oliver was born in one of the rooms over the pub and has lived there his whole life.

South Pole Inn

Main Street, Anascaul, County Kerry

066 915 7388

A more surprising find is the South Pole pub, by the bridge. It was bought and named by sailor Tom Crean (1877–1938), a remarkable and modest man who took part in three of the most famous voyages of Antarctic discovery with Robert Falcon Scott and Ernest Shackleton. In the early 1920s he retired here and opened the pub with his wife, Nell. Today it is full of photographs and memorabilia, a popular haunt of modern explorers for whom the ice presents the ultimate challenge – and the Guinness is good, too. A statue of Crean with two husky pups stands in the little park opposite, and an 8-mile walk in the area is named after him.

Sammys Bar

inchbeach.com

Inch, County Kerry | 066 915 8118

Right on the beach in a spectacular location, this bar is also a cafe and restaurant. It's a traditional family-run Irish pub with a warm welcome and good, locally sourced food.

▶ PLACES NEARBY

Well worth visiting, and just 2 miles off the western end of the Dingle Peninsula, lie the green humps of the Blasket Islands.

Blasket Islands

blasketislands.ie

The green humps of the Blasket Islands (na Blascaodaí) have

▲ The Blasket Islands

captured a very special place in the Irish consciousness for their remarkable literary heritage that depicts them as a world apart. The village on An Blascaod Mór (Great Blasket) was abandoned in 1953 but in summer you can visit by ferry from Dunquin (Dún Chaoin) or Dingle town to see the sandy beach of Trágh Bhán and colonies of seals.

Blasket Centre

Dunquin, Dingle, County Kerry
066 915 6444 and 066 915 6371
Open Apr–Oct daily 10–6
The struggle for, and the celebration of, life on these isolated islands is revealed in the Blasket Centre, built in 1993. With framed views of the Blaskets, stained glass by Róisín de Buitléar and sculptures, the building itself is a work of art. Exhibitions tell of island life in this remarkable community, focusing on the autobiographies written by three people who lived there: Tomás Ó Criomhthain (1855–1937, *The Islandman*), Peig Sayers (1873–1958, *Peig*) and Muiris Ó Súileabháin (1904–50, *Twenty Years A-Growing*).

Blasket Islands Ferry Co

Dunquin, Dingle, County Kerry
087 231 6131
Now the abandoned farmsteads and villages of the islands can be explored on day trips. The ferry runs from Dunquin and takes about 20 minutes. You can also choose a three-hour eco tour of the surrounding waters, rich with basking sharks and dolphins.

▶ **Donegal** MAP REF 381 E2

Although it's the county town, Donegal is a modest little place with attractively small-scale streets overshadowed by the gabled walls and turrets of Donegal Castle. The town in its present form was laid out in the early 17th century around a central square known, as in many of the northerly Irish towns, as 'the Diamond'. Looming up on its rocky knoll behind the Diamond is Donegal Castle, a great Jacobean mansion.

When wandering through the ruins of the friary, a mile south of the town by the River Eske (open access), try to picture the learned Michael O'Clery and his assistants Peregrine O'Clery, Peregrine O'Duignean and Fearfeasa O'Maolconry laboriously compiling their *Annals of the Four Masters*. This wonderful document (copies can be seen in the National Library in Dublin) is a vivid history of the island from 2958 BC (apparently 40 years before Noah's flood) until AD 1616.

TAKE IN SOME HISTORY
Donegal Castle
heritageireland.ie
Tirchonaill Street, Donegal, County Donegal | 074 972 2405 | Open Mar to mid-Sep daily 10–6, mid-Sep to Feb Thu–Mon 9.30–4.30
You can tour Donegal Castle, which is furnished in mid-17th-century style. It was built in 1623 on what remained of a 15th-century fortress belonging to the O'Donnell clan, who demolished it late in the 16th century rather than let it fall into the hands of the English. In 1601, the legendary Red Hugh O'Donnell also caused the ruin of Donegal Friary while besieging his cousin Niall Garbh, who was holed up inside with some English allies. The bombardment ignited barrels of English gunpowder.

VISIT THE MUSEUM
The Donegal Railway Heritage Centre
donegalrailway.com
Tirchonaill Street, Donegal, County Donegal | 074 972 2655 | Open Jul, Aug Mon–Fri 10–5, Sat, Sun 2–5, Sep–Jun Mon–Fri 10–5
The centre recalls a now defunct scenic local line, with a simulator and rail exhibits.

TAKE A BOAT TRIP
Donegal Bay Waterbus
donegalbaywaterbus.com
Donegal Pier, County Donegal
074 972 3666

◀ Donegal's Church of Ireland

This purpose-built, luxury passenger boat with an open-top deck operates an 80-minute sightseeing cruise that explores the wildlife, history and environment around Donegal Bay. There is an on-board bar and the boat is fully wheelchair accessible. The boat is moored at Donegal Pier, three minutes' walk from the town centre.

EAT AND DRINK
Harvey's Point Hotel ⊚⊚
harveyspoint.com
Lough Eske, 2 miles from Donegal towards Lifford, County Donegal
074 972 2208
It was the heavenly setting that brought the Swiss family Gysling here to the shore of Lough Eske in the Donegal Hills to build their sprawling luxurious hotel complex. Harvey's Restaurant's open kitchen has a split-level layout and allows everyone to bask in the splendid lough views.

Olde Castle Bar
oldecastlebar.com
The Diamond, Donegal, County Donegal | 074 972 1262
The Olde Castle Bar & Red Hugh's Restaurant Donegal is well known among locals and loved by visitors. Right in the centre of town, this is a local landmark next to Donegal's famous historical monument, Red Hugh O'Donnell's Castle, and near the River Eske.

▶ **PLACES NEARBY**
Bundoran has an excellent beach and adventure centre for a great family day out.

Donegal Adventure Centre
donegaladventurecentre.net
Bayview Terrace, Bundoran, County Donegal | 071 984 2418; see website for more details
Thrill seekers of all ages will love this centre offering surfing, high-rope climbing, archery, zip wire, abseiling, cliff jumping, body boarding and much more.

▼ Donegal Castle

▶ **Drogheda** MAP REF 383 D6

drogheda.ie

Drogheda was established by Viking traders in AD 911. Spanning both banks of the River Boyne, its Gaelic name, Droichead Atha, means 'bridge by the ford'. The outskirts of the town were the site of one of the most infamous battles in Irish history in 1690 (see page 24). The industrial heart is undergoing a Renaissance and Drogheda has been improved since the M1 toll bridge diverted traffic out of the town. The north side of the river has the main shopping area and medieval remains such as St Laurence's Gate, a four-floor barbican, and Magdalene Tower, a remnant of a Dominican friary from 1224.

TAKE IN SOME HISTORY
Battle of the Boyne
battleoftheboyne.ie

Visitor Centre, Oldbridge House and Estate, Drogheda, County Meath 041 980 9950 | Open daily; call to check times as they change according to weather conditions

You can learn all about the bloody battle at the visitor centre before walking on the actual battle site. Some 1,500 men were slaughtered there although the armies of Prince William of Orange and King James II totalled thousands. Colour-coded and self-guiding walking trails are available.

Millmount Museum
millmount.net

Millmount Drogheda, County Louth 041 983 3097 | Open Mon–Sat 9.30–5.30, Sun 2–5

On the south side of the river, accessed from the riverside by steep steps, is the Millmount fortification. A Martello tower crowns an Anglo-Norman motte from the 12th century. A museum, craft centre and restaurant are in the next-door barracks, with splendid views.

ENTERTAIN THE FAMILY
Funtasia Waterpark Drogheda
funtasia.ie

1 Donore Road Industrial Estate, Drogheda, County Louth | 041 989 8000 | Waterpark open Fri 3–7.30, Sat–Sun 10–6; other attractions see website for full details

This Egyptian-themed entertainment centre is said to be the first of its kind in Ireland, with a Pirates' Cove interactive waterpark, super bowl speed slide and the Boomerang. Other attractions include the Atlantis Cove play area, a bowling alley, rollerskating rink, crazy golf, rock climbing, a casino, Pharaoh's fast food restaurant, video games and simulators.

EAT AND DRINK
Scholars Townhouse Hotel ◉◉
scholarshotel.com

King Street, Drogheda, County Louth 041 983 5410

The interiors are extraordinary: the panelled walls are crammed with landscape pictures, and potted plants, lamps and elliptical mirrors are everywhere you look. Ceiling frescoes of the Battle of the

Boyne in the interlinked dining rooms add a historical note that is thrown into relief by the lively modern Irish cooking.

▶ **PLACES NEARBY**

To the northwest of Drogheda lie Monasterboice and the remains of Mellifont Abbey.

Monasterboice

Monasterboice, County Louth

This much-pictured monastic site seems smaller than you might imagine. What you'll find, one mile from the intersection with the M1, is a neat, working cemetery, a splendid 110-foot round tower without its cone, and magnificent high crosses. Little remains of the rest of the monastic settlement that was first established by St Buithe in the fifth century. There are some extant walls from a church building, originating in the eighth or ninth century.

Also visible are the remains of a 13th-century church. The crosses are among the best in Ireland. The 16-foot-tall Cross of Muiredach is an elaborate wheel-head cross from the 10th century. On its base the inscription translates as 'A prayer for Muiredach, by whom this cross was made'.

Mellifont Abbey

mellifontabbey.ie

Tullyallen, County Louth | 041 982 6459 | Open Jun–early Sep daily 10–6

Only a gatehouse and an octagonal lavabo (wash house) remain above head height at

7 literary landscapes

▶ **Ben Bulben, Sligo (Yeats)** page 38

▶ **Blasket Islands (Tomás Ó Criomhthain's works)** page 243

▶ **The Burren (Tolkien's *The Lord of the Rings*)** page 194

▶ **Cave Hill (Swift's *Gulliver's Travels*)** pages 38, 100

▶ **Glens of Antrim (John Hewitt's works)** page 130

▶ **Magherafelt, County Londonderry (Seamus Heaney's works)** page 37

▶ **Mountains of Mourne (C S Lewis's *Narnia* novels)** pages 38, 147

Mellifont, an important medieval abbey on the banks of the Mattock River. It was founded in 1142 by monks from Clairvaux, France. In the 17th century, the abbey became the country mansion of Edward Moore, saw the surrender of Hugh O'Neill in 1607, suffered a Cromwellian siege, and became headquarters for William of Orange during the Battle of the Boyne in 1690. By 1723 it was abandoned, and by the middle of the 19th century its ornate ruins were doubling as a pigsty. Four sides of the Romanesque lavabo remain from 1200, and the 14th-century chapterhouse has been re-roofed and contains a collection of glazed tiles. On a bank above the visitor centre stands the roofless shell of a Protestant church dating from 1542.

▶ Dublin MAP REF 379 E2

It is often visited on a weekend trip but rushing around is not the best way to experience Dublin. One of the city's irresistible charms is its welcoming people; so take time to relax in the pubs and cafes while absorbing the craic that is synonymous with the Irish. Slide away from the touristy themed pubs to discover the real heart of Dublin in its less well known taverns and in conversation with the locals.

Boom town

When Ireland joined the European Union, an economic boom began that flourished in the 'Celtic Tiger' years of the 1990s – fashion, the arts, food and Irish culture all blossomed, turning Dublin into one of the world's hottest city destinations. Its transformation has continued into the 21st century with a technology boom. There is something very special about this small city with its split personality – exhilarating and chic on one side but traditional, with an older generation still hanging on to pre-EU values, on the other.

Fair city

Situated on the Irish Sea at the mouth of the River Liffey, Dublin's 'Fair City' is everything a cosmopolitan capital should be – with excellent shopping, fascinating museums and galleries, lively nightlife, a thriving arts and cultural scene, fine parks and gardens, great pubs and restaurants and a strong

▲ Ha'penny Bridge

sense of history. Architecture is at its best in the Georgian quarter around Merrion Square and in James Gandon's buildings, such as the Four Courts and Bank of Ireland. Visitors flock south of the Liffey to the trendy Temple Bar area with its busy bars and cool arts scene. The Irish Film Centre (IFC), the experimental Projects Arts Centre and around a dozen galleries are here.

A major rejuvenation project has also breathed new life into the north area around O'Connell Street, reputed to be Europe's widest urban street and home to the Spire, the world's tallest piece of sculpture. That process continues around the docks and Grand Canal, where Google has expanded its European HQ.

City tours

There is plenty to see in the city centre, from the world-famous ninth-century illuminated Book of Kells at Trinity College to Christ Church Cathedral and the iconic Guinness Storehouse. The best way to see central Dublin is on foot but to reach several key attractions, such as Kilmainham Gaol and the Irish Museum of Modern Art, you will need a taxi or public transport. Take the open-top bus tours that allow you to jump on and off at significant points on the route, or try the Dublin Bikes scheme. Only a few stops away on the DART (local railway line) you can find yourself beside the sea at Dalkey and Malahide or in the little fishing village of Howth (see page 308).

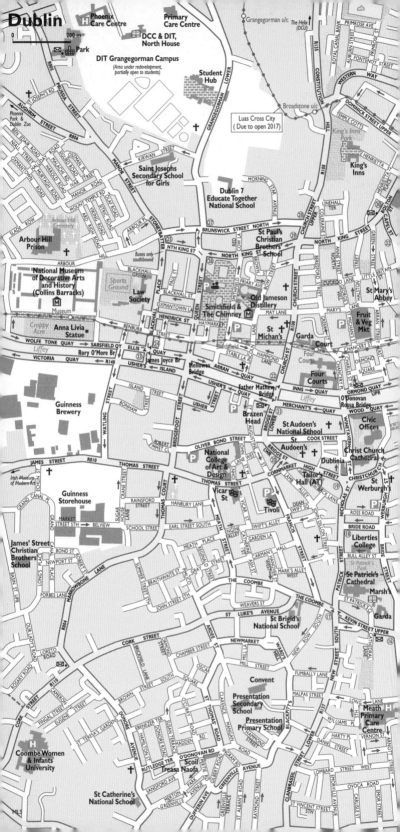

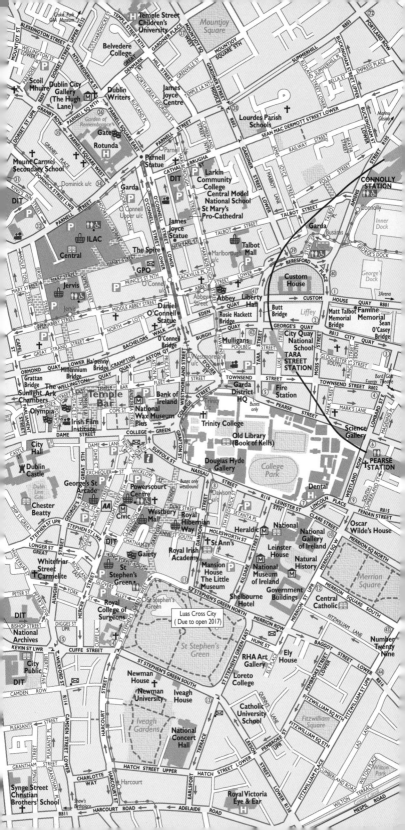

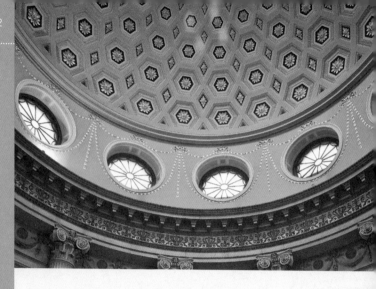

▲ City Hall's dome

TAKE IN SOME HISTORY
City Hall
dublincity.ie

Cork Hill, Dame Street, Dublin 2

01 222 2204 | Open Mon–Sat
10–5.15

The magnificent Corinthian portico of Thomas Cooley's 1779 Royal Exchange, in front of Dublin Castle on Lord Edward Street, has been the public face of the Dublin Corporation since 1852 and is still the City Hall, its principal meeting place. An outstanding example of the Georgian architecture for which Dublin is famous, the City Hall is testimony to the prosperous merchants who flourished here in the 18th century. 'The Story of the Capital' is an exciting exhibition on the ground floor which relates the city's history from Viking times to today, while the restored rotunda has statues of various Dublin worthies, and an Arts and Crafts mural depicting Dublin's past. Ireland's first president, Arthur Griffiths, lay in state here, as did Michael Collins after his assassination in 1922.

Croke Park GAA Museum
crokepark.ie

St Joseph's Avenue, Dublin 3

01 819 2323 | Open Jul, Aug Mon–Sat 9.30–6, Sun 12–5, Sep–Jun Mon–Sat 9.30–5, Sun 12–5; on match days the museum opens at the same time as the turnstiles

The heart of Irish sporting life for over 100 years, iconic Croke Park provides a fascinating insight into the passion that sport arouses here. That Ireland's capital city should have the third-largest sports stadium in Europe is no surprise in this sports-mad country. The 85,000 capacity Croke Park is the home of the Gaelic Athletic Association (GAA), the governing body of Gaelic games – Gaelic football, hurling, handball and rounders. It fills up every year for the dramatic All-Ireland finals,

▲ Fireworks at Croke Park

the excitement of which is portrayed in the film *A Day in September*, which is shown in the stadium's museum.

The museum explains the different codes (game rules) and the political and historic context of the GAA, and you can catch up on missed games through computer-accessed video highlights.

The Croke Park Stadium Tour allows visitors to walk in the footsteps of legends as they visit the teams' dressing rooms, sit in the VIP area and enjoy panoramic views from the top tier of the stand, 30 yards above the pitch. If you feel like testing your skills, you can try your hand at hurling and football in the interactive games zone.

Croke Park plays an important part in modern Irish history, not least because of the notorious incident in November 1922, when British troops opened fire on the crowd and players, killing 12 people.

Custom House
Custom House Quay, Dublin 1
01 888 2538
Thought by many to be the most impressive piece of architecture in Dublin, the Custom House was designed by James Gandon and completed in 1791. It is one of the most prominent buildings on the waterfront, and its classical facade is best appreciated from the opposite bank of the river downstream from O'Connell Bridge. It is 375 feet long, and the huge green copper cupola is 125 feet high. The exterior is adorned with sculptures and coats of arms. The building of the Custom House marked a high point in the development of the port of Dublin, but it was made virtually redundant only 10 years later when the Act of Union robbed Ireland of her income from duties. Today, the Custom House contains government offices and is closed to the public.

Drimnagh Castle

drimnaghcastle.org

Long Mile Road, Drimnagh, Dublin
12 | 01 450 2530 | Mon–Thu 9–4,
Fri 9–1, weekends by appointment

Drimnagh Castle hides behind
a school complex in the west
Dublin industrial estates, but it
is a hidden gem – a medieval,
moated castle with a restored
17th-century garden. The tower
gateway leads into a walled
courtyard, a world away from
its immediate surroundings.
Inhabited for more than 500
years, the castle was then
abandoned in the 1950s and
left to slide into ruin.

Restoration began in the late
1980s, using traditional craft
skills to bring the masonry and
woodwork back to their former
condition, and 5,500 tiles were
specially made for the great
hall in 1991. The fireplace is
built of English sandstone,
creating a striking effect
against the white of the
predominant local limestone.
Outside, the moat once more
flows with clear water. The
castle is said to be haunted by
Lady Eleanor Barnewell, who
tragically died around 500 years
ago on the grave of her lover;
he had been killed by Lady
Barnewell's father because she
was betrothed to someone else.

Dublin Castle and the Chester Beatty Library

dublincastle.ie

Dame Street, Dublin 2 | 01 677 7129
Open Mon–Sat 9.45–4.45, Sun
12–4.45. Closed during state
business

Dublin takes its name from the
Dubh Linn, the Black Pool at
the confluence of the Liffey and
Poddle rivers. The gardens of
Dublin Castle now occupy that
site and their Celtic-design
parterre cleverly doubles as
a helicopter pad for visiting
dignitaries. The castle was built
for King John in the 13th
century and was renovated for
use as a vice-regal palace in
the 16th century.

Long the symbol of Anglo-
Norman power, the Dublin
Castle complex is a mix of
vice-regal classicism, medieval
buildings, modern offices and a
world-renowned museum. The
Chester Beatty Library and
Gallery of Oriental Art contains
a collection of early religious
manuscripts including
fragments of second-century
biblical tracts and ninth-century
Koranic texts.

On view at the castle itself
are the fine State Apartments,
its undercroft, showing traces
of the Viking fortress that was
the earliest incarnation of the
city of Dublin, and its Chapel
Royal, a neo-Gothic gem of a
church, designed by Francis
Johnston and built in 1814.

The oldest remaining part
of Dublin Castle is the Record
Tower, once used as a top-
security prison. Red Hugh
O'Donnell, son of a Donegal
chieftain, was held here in 1592
for rebelling against the Crown.
He escaped and, together with
Hugh O'Neill, led the Nine Years
War. Today the Record Tower
houses a simple museum

documenting the history of Ireland's police force.

The State Apartments were designed to reflect the extravagant and fashionable lifestyle of the vice-regal court. Following a disastrous fire in 1684, they were remodelled by Sir William Robinson, who also designed the Royal Hospital at Kilmainham. He planned the Upper and Lower courtyards to complement the remaining buildings. From the entrance in the Upper Yard, a guided tour visits the Throne Room, dating from 1740, where the throne is said to have been presented to William of Orange to commemorate his victory at the Battle of the Boyne.

St Patrick's Hall is hung with banners of the old order of the Knights of St Patrick. Its ceiling, painted by Vincenzo Valdré in 1778, depicts links between Ireland and Britain. The apartments, with Killybegs carpets and Waterford crystal

chandeliers, are used for presidential inaugurations and other ceremonial occasions.

The undercroft was revealed when work was done on the Lower Yard in 1990. The city walls join the castle here and a small archway allowed boats to land provisions at the Postern Gate, also visible. In the base of the Norman Powder Tower, the original Viking defensive bank can be made out.

The Chapel Royal (officially the Church of the Most Holy Trinity) was designed by Francis Johnston and is best known for its ornate plaster decorations by George Stapleton and Richard Stewart's woodcarvings.

The Garda Museum moved to the Record Tower in 1997. The museum displays uniforms and equipment charting policing in Ireland from the days of the Royal Irish Constabulary to the Civic Guard of 1922 (later renamed Garda

 Dublin Castle

Síochána na h'Éireann). The top floor has the best view of the Dubh Linn Garden, and exhibits on the worldwide role of the Garda, working for the United Nations.

The Chester Beatty Library and Gallery of Oriental Art houses the interesting collection of Sir Alfred Chester Beatty, a wealthy North American mining magnate of Irish descent, who died in 1968. Chief among the exhibits are the fragments of early religious texts. There are more than 300 Korans, Babylonian tablets over 6,000 years old, Coptic Bibles, Jewish texts, Confucian scrolls and Buddhist literature, with explanations on these religions. The displays and exhibits are supported by touch-screen computers giving more information about the world's religions and the artwork inspired by them. Popular exhibits are the exquisite Burmese and Siamese parabaiks describing folk tales and drawn on paper made from mulberry leaves. There are also exhibition spaces here, housing collections of contemporary work. Don't miss the Pauline letters from AD 180–200, and the Gospels from AD 250 – the oldest full collections in the world; the delicate papyrus fragment of St John's Gospel, taken from the Bodmer codex, the oldest New Testament scripture in existence; and the beautiful Chinese jade books, first intricately engraved then filled with gold.

Dublinia
dublinia.ie
St Michael's Hill, Christchurch, Dublin 8 | 01 679 4611 | Open daily Mar–Sep 10–6.30, Oct–Feb 10–5.30
This popular museum presents a different perspective on Viking and Medieval Dublin, with multimedia presentations which include the arrival of Anglo-Norman leader Richard de Clare (Strongbow), the Black Death, a merchant's house and the dockside at Wood Quay, plus a scale model of the city in 1500. There are skeletal remains, the opportunity to experience the smells and sights of a medieval street and many other interactive activities. There's a wonderful view from St Michael's Tower.

Four Courts
Inns Quay, Dublin 7 | 01 888 6000
Open Mon–Fri 10–4 when courts are in session
Designed by Thomas Cooley and James Gandon, the Four Courts was built between 1786 and 1802 and has been at the epicentre of the Irish legal

▲ The Four Courts

system ever since. A statue of Moses stands on the six-columned portico, flanked by Justice and Mercy in front of the great lantern tower. Four Courts takes its name from the old legal divisions: the courts of Common Pleas, Chancery, Exchequer and King's Bench.

This is still Ireland's main criminal court and public access is allowed when it is in session. What you see now was mostly restored in the 1930s after the building was gutted during the Civil War. It was held by anti-treaty forces and, when the government troops attacked, the resulting fires destroyed many of Ireland's historic legal records, some dating back to the 12th century.

General Post Office

O'Connell Street, Dublin 1 | 01 705 7000 | Open Mon–Sat 10–5

The main stronghold of the Irish Volunteers in the historic 1916 Rising, The General Post Office (GPO) building still continues to fulfil its original purpose. The impressive structure, built in the Greek revival style, was seized by Pádraig Pearse and his rebel army in Easter 1916. From the steps outside he proclaimed the Irish Republic and then settled down to a week-long siege by the British Army. The building was destroyed, the rebels rounded up and their leaders executed at Kilmainham Gaol, but the new Irish state adopted their struggle and the GPO became something of a national icon. It was restored in 1929, but traces of bullet marks can still be identified on the outside.

Inside, a remarkable bronze sculpture by Oliver Shepherd from 1935 depicts the death of the legendary Irish hero Cúchulainn, and is dedicated to the participants in the Easter Rising. The GPO also houses the An Post Museum. And you can post a letter there too!

Trinity College & The Book of Kells

see highlight panel on page 267

▶ **Kilmainham Gaol** MAP REF 379 E2

heritageireland.ie

Inchicore Road, Kilmainham, Dublin 8 | 01 453 5984 | Open Apr–Sep daily
9.30–6, Oct–Mar Mon–Sat 9.30–5.30, Sun 10–6

This sinister place is where the leaders of the 1916 rising were
executed and is saturated with some of Ireland's painful history.
Its last prisoner, released in 1924, was Eamon de Valera, who went
on to become Taoiseach (prime minister) and two-time president.
Viewing is by guided tour only. After a video presentation in the
basement you are led through the east wing, the chapel, the west
wing and then the prison yards. A museum contains some grim
exhibits illustrating the lives and deaths of former inmates. The

thought-provoking tours, accompanied by an enthusiastic and knowledgeable curator, last around 60 minutes and run every half hour. The gaol's history is put in context, not just as a place for political prisoners but also as a prison for common criminals. It closed in 1924.

The east wing is a painstakingly restored example of a 19th-century cell block. A three-floor shell, open to skylights in the roof, is ringed by tiny cells opening onto iron lattice landings. From the central ground floor, where the prisoners would eat, every cell door is visible and from the landings observation hatches allowed warders to see inside every cell. Unlike older prisons, inmates here could not hide in the shadows; their behaviour was monitored 24 hours a day.

There's a stark contrast in the west wing, with its labyrinth of dank, dilapidated corridors and tight, dimly lit cells. Recent graffiti in some corridors enhances the sense of squalor. Connecting the two is the prison chapel, where Joseph Plunkett married Grace Gifford the night before his execution in 1916. They spent 10 minutes together as a married couple before he was led away. Each cell is labelled with the names of the most significant occupants. With risings against British rule in 1798, 1803, 1848, 1867, 1883 and 1916, it is easy to understand the gaol's reputation as the place to hold political prisoners, and graffiti over one doorway threatens the gaolers with the 'vengeance of the risen people'. Charles Stewart Parnell was held here in 1883, in a pleasant suite of rooms that befitted his political standing. Other prisoners were not so lucky and overcrowding was a significant problem. During the famine years, when thousands flocked to Dublin to find food, more than 7,000 men and women were crammed into the cells.

The exercise yards are where the 14 leaders of the Easter Rising were executed by firing squad; a cross marks the spot where the injured James Connolly was strapped to a chair so he could be upright when he was shot. However, the 1916 rising was not well supported at the time, and its leaders were not portrayed as heroes until much later. In the Civil War that followed independence, the Free State government dispatched a further 77 anti-treaty fighters against these grey walls.

Among the grim items in the museum are memento mori of each of the 14 executed. You can also see the block of wood on which Robert Emmet's head was removed following his hanging in 1803. Emmet had hoped to bring Napoleonic firepower to the fight against the British, but it didn't materialise in the way he had planned. On a lighter note, there are many fine banners from the various struggles; a charming home-made selection from the Irish Land League in 1879 declares 'the land for the people'.

VISIT THE MUSEUMS

Leinster House

oireachtas.ie

Kildare Street, Dublin 2

01 618 3781

Designed by Richard Cassels in 1745, Leinster House, originally known as Kildare House, is the seat of the Oireachtas, the Irish parliament. It was once the palace of the Dukes of Leinster. Today, the Dáil (lower house) meets in the former lecture theatre of the Royal Dublin Society. The Seanad (upper house) meets in the North Wing Saloon. Tours are available when parliament is not in session; make reservations a week in advance.

The Little Museum

littlemuseum.ie

15 St Stephen's Green, Dublin 2

016 611 000 | Open Fri–Wed 9.30–5, Thu 9.30–8

A recent addition to the capital's museums, The Little Museum should be top on the list for anybody wishing to grasp Dublin's recent history. The museum grew organically from a 'meet and greet' service for visitors and quickly became what we see today. On permanent exhibition are such items as the lectern used by John F Kennedy during his visit to Ireland in 1963 and a U2 exhibition, which contains mementoes donated by band members themselves.

National Museum of Ireland

museum.ie

The National Museum safeguards some of Ireland's most precious and important treasures – gold and silverware found in bogs, caves and burial mounds, and memorabilia from the 20th-century struggle for independence. The Kildare Street site, the National Museum of Archaeology and History, is based around a glorious marble-halled rotunda, and the Benburb Street site, the National Museum of Decorative Arts and History, is the old Collins Barracks.

National Museum of Archaeology and History

Kildare Street, Dublin 2 | 01 677 7444 | Open Tue–Sat 10–5, Sun 2–5

Opened in 1896, the Kildare Street site was designed by Cork architects Thomas Newenham and Deane and his son Thomas Manley Deane in a style known as Victorian Palladian. Its dome is modelled on the Pantheon in Rome and rises to 62 feet.

◀ Dáil Chamber, Leinster House

The Prehistoric Ireland displays include tools and weaponry from the Stone Age and Bronze Age, with explanations of burial customs and reconstructed graves. One of the most impressive exhibits is the Lurgan Bog Boat, more than 43 feet long, pulled from a Galway bog in 1902 and dated to around 2500 BC.

There is a huge collection of sheela-na-gigs here too. These weird, often comically explicit, stone carvings of women date from a pre-Christian era. The discovery of Iron Age bodies in the bog at Oldcroghan, County Offaly and Cloncavan, County Meath in 2003 and the subsequent research examining the human remains resulted in a major exhibition. Along with other bog bodies in the collection, the final analysis gives an insight into the lives of the early inhabitants of Ireland. Information on Iron Age burial rituals, along with objects including weapons, textiles and utensils, help to evoke life and ritual in prehistoric Ireland.

Bronze Age Ireland produced a wealth of gold, jewellery and other items, on display in 'Ór – Ireland's Gold'. The collection includes gold lunulae dating back to 2000 BC, and more sophisticated works made around 700 BC.

The best-known pieces of ancient Irish craftsmanship are preserved in the treasury. The Tara Brooch, only 2 inches across yet intricately patterned with Celtic motifs, is believed to have been made in the eighth century AD of white bronze, silver gilt, amber and glass, and symbolises the inspirational early Christian design that flourished here while much of the British Isles languished in the Dark Ages. The superb Ardagh Chalice is also from that period – gilded and studded in multi-coloured glass and decorated in gold filigree.

▼ National Museum of Ireland

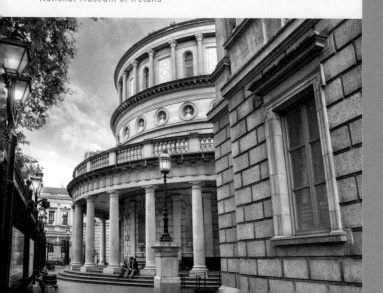

The exquisite crozier from Clonmacnoise shows the wealth and power of the early church. Be sure to see the rare Tully Lough Cross, the only intact example of a metal-encased cross on a wooden core to be found in Ireland. Located in pieces at the bottom of Tully Lough, County Roscommon, the cross was conserved and reconstructed by conservation staff at the museum. It depicts a human figure between two animals and dates from the eighth or ninth century. The only intact comparison is an eighth-century example at Bischofshofen in Austria.

Viking Ireland is explored upstairs, particularly the peaceful trading aspects of the Scandinavians who established their port at Dublin. The Medieval Ireland section feels a bit thin by comparison, perhaps reflecting the decline in indigenous culture during this period. Also on this floor is the permanent Ancient Egypt exhibition. This comprises some 3,000 objects taken mainly from excavations between the 1890s and 1920s. A highlight is the beautifully decorated mummy case of Tentdinebu, dating from the 22nd dynasty (945–716 BC). There is the rare chance to see some excellent ceramics and glass from Ancient Cyprus, most of which are from tombs unearthed in the 19th century. There is also a full programme of temporary exhibitions.

National Museum of Decorative Arts and History

Collins Barracks, Benburb Street, Dublin 7 | 01 677 7444
Open Tue–Sat 10–5, Sun 2–5

The striking 18th-century Collins Barracks are the administrative headquarters for all the National Museums of Ireland. They began life as the main barracks for the British garrison in Dublin and were built in 1700. The Irish Free State took them over in 1922 and they remained in military hands until the 1990s, renamed after Michael Collins. In the courtyard, which doubled as a parade ground, you can see 100 marching paces marked against the wall.

The layout is a little more confusing than at the Kildare Street site, with 13 galleries on four floors around two sides of the central courtyard, but there's a leaflet from the reception desk to help you navigate. The section devoted to Irish Silver takes the silversmith's craft from the early 17th to the 20th century, and another section deals with coinage. It was the Vikings who first brought the concept of currency to Ireland's shores and this exhibition follows its history, from 10th-century hoards to the ATM.

'The Way We Wore' displays 250 years of Irish clothing, and the influence of European trends on local materials. 'Curator's Choice' is an eclectic selection chosen for interesting stories or significance, and includes a wedding gift from Oliver Cromwell to his daughter, and King William's gauntlets from the day of the Battle of the Boyne in 1690. Of particular interest in this gallery is the Fonthill Vase, an early example of Chinese porcelain and highly regarded by the museum. Its well-documented history tracks the vase's travels around Asia and Europe from the 14th century to its final resting place in the museum.

Opened in 2006, in a three-storey, purpose-built space, the exhibition 'Soldiers and Chiefs: The Irish at War at Home and Abroad, 1550–2001' uses original material including letters, audio accounts and authentic objects to trace the lives of Irish soldiers and the effect of war on the Irish people. The large space enables the display of aeroplanes and armoured vehicles, along with descriptions of those who have flown or driven them. The social history surrounding the men and women of the armed forces brings to life their activities at home as well as in action, from early times right up to date with peacekeeping duty with the United Nations.

Ongoing improvements and additional building has seen the museum grow rapidly in recent years. The former riding school now houses temporary exhibitions and a new conservation laboratory has also been added. Further building will accommodate new exhibitions and permanent galleries for the ethnographical and earth science collections.

'The Easter Rising: Understanding 1916' puts the events of 1913–23 into context, concentrating on the ill-fated rising in 1916. There's an original copy of Pádraig Pearse's Proclamation of the Irish Republic from the steps of the GPO, and exhibits on the individuals involved in the struggle for independence.

National Wax Museum Plus
waxmuseumplus.ie
4 Foster Place, Dublin 2
01 671 8373 | Open daily 10–7
This surprisingly engaging exhibition brings you face-to-face with some of the most familiar characters from Irish history, with some alarmingly realistic portrayals of Michael Collins and Eamon de Valera, Phil Lynott (from Thin Lizzy), U2 and St Patrick. The Chamber of Horrors isn't for younger children. At the end of the tour is a series of hands-on exhibits celebrating Irish contributions to technology and science.

Natural History Museum
museum.ie
Merrion Street, Dublin 2 | 01 677 7444 | Open Tue–Sat 10–5, Sun 2–5
On the southern flank of Leinster House, the Natural History Museum contrasts markedly with the up-to-date museums that abound in modern Ireland. Known irreverently as the 'dead zoo', it is an excellent example of

▲ Bedroom suite at Number Twenty Nine

old-school museum values, showing the preserved bodies of animals with no real attempt at context. It is virtually unchanged since its opening in 1857 as the museum of the Royal Dublin Society. The first room you encounter is devoted to Irish animals, starting with the skeletons of huge Irish deer, now extinct. Around the walls, display cases are full of other stuffed creatures, such as martens, otters and bats. There are birds and fish too, and, at the far end, insects and invertebrates. Upstairs, the emphasis is on creatures from the rest of the world. On the main floor are monkeys, bears, rhinos and marsupials. There are two gallery floors above this, the first devoted to vertebrates – the dodo is particularly popular – while the second covers invertebrates: worms, insects, jellyfish, crabs and so on. A huge skeleton of a humpback whale is suspended from the ceiling, while the giraffe skeleton rises up from the floor below. Also featuring on the top floor are the delightful animal models in glass by Blaschka of Dresden, using refraction in light to recreate the shades of nature.

Number Twenty Nine

esb.ie/numbertwentynine
29 Lower Fitzwilliam Street, Dublin 2 | 01 702 6165 | Open Tue–Sat 10–5, Sun 12–5
A visit to this well-preserved example of Dublin's elegant Georgian terraced houses gives a clear insight into the lives of the upper middle classes who lived in them. Every room is authentically furnished with items from 1790 to 1820.
A short video presentation is followed by the tour, beginning with the kitchen and housekeeper's quarters then going upstairs to the dining room (set for dessert), the drawing room with its Dublin

crystal chandeliers and huge windows overlooking the street, and the impressive marble-floored hallway. Upstairs again, you see the boudoir, the master bedroom and the dressing room then, on the top floor, the schoolroom and nursery, with toys and educational games.

VISIT THE LITERARY MUSEUMS

Dublin Writers Museum

writersmuseum.com
18 Parnell Square North, Dublin 1
01 872 2077 | Open Mon–Sat 10–5, Sun 11–5

Irish literature is renowned all over the world and this legacy is celebrated in a magnificent 18th-century mansion in the heart of Dublin. The Dublin Writers Museum reflects the important contribution the city has made to world literature, covering the lives and works of many notable authors. A portable audio commentary leads you around displays telling the story of Dublin's literary heritage, including Patrick Kavanagh, Flann O'Brien, Roddy Doyle, Oscar Wilde, W B Yeats, Jonathan Swift, George Bernard Shaw and Samuel Beckett.

Notable first editions here include Joyce's *Ulysses* and *Dubliners*, and Bram Stoker's *Dracula*. There is also a random collection of memorabilia, which includes the phone from Samuel Beckett's Paris apartment, Brendan Behan's typewriter and press pass, and Oliver St John Gogarty's flying goggles. The annex has a room devoted to children's literature, a comprehensive bookshop, which hosts regular book readings, lunchtime theatre performances, special exhibitions and a cafe.

James Joyce Centre

jamesjoyce.ie
35 North Great George's Street, Dublin 1 | 01 878 8547
Open Tue–Sat 10–5, Sun 12–5

Joyce never lived in this restored Georgian terraced house just a few minutes from O'Connell Street but he did live nearby, in a succession of squalid houses, from 1893 to 1904. You can join a tour of Joyce's Dublin and see the exhibition of memorabilia upstairs, including the furniture from Paul Leon's apartment in Paris, where Joyce and Leon would discuss the progress of *Finnegans Wake* in the 1930s. A good introductory video presentation makes this accessible to both true Joyce fanatics and literary novices and there is a bookshop where you can buy almost everything he ever published. The centre is also the co-ordinating body for the Bloomsday festival in June (see page 54).

Marsh's Library

marshlibrary.ie
St Patrick's Close, Dublin 8
01 454 3511 | Open Mon, Wed–Fri 9.30–5, Sat 10–1

Virtually unchanged for three centuries, Marsh's Library behind St Patrick's Cathedral is the oldest public library in Ireland. Opened in 1707, and taking its name from Archbishop Narcissus Marsh (1638–1717), this is one of the few buildings in Dublin still used for its original purpose and is a perfect example of a late Renaissance and early Enlightenment library. The smell of the 25,000 ancient volumes, from the 15th to the early 18th century, hits you as you walk in.

The farthest room contains the caged reading areas where scholars could view the most valuable of the library's books but not take them out of the building. Among the prized volumes on display is Clarendon's *History of the Rebellion*, complete with anti-Scottish scrawl in the margins by Jonathan Swift, and signed copies of works by Laud, Swift himself, John Donne and Hugh Latimer. The library's guest book includes the signatures of James Joyce and Daniel O'Connell.

National Library

nli.ie

Kildare Street, Dublin 2 | 01 603 0200 | Open Mon–Wed 9.30–7.45, Thu–Fri 9.30–4.45, Sat 9.30–12.45

People from all over the world who believe they can trace their roots to Ireland visit the National Library housed in a 19th-century Renaissance-style building on the northern flank of Leinster House. The library is best known for its genealogical service, helping to trace Irish origins through its records and archives, and giving information about other research facilities across the country. A large quantity of Irish-related material can be consulted without charge.

The National Library is the home of the Chief Herald, who can grant arms to those who fulfil the appropriate criteria. The impressive domed reading room counts James Joyce among its historic scholars. Although viewing is free, a reader's ticket is required for research. Changing exhibitions reflect the library's huge collection. The library also runs the National Photographic Archive in Temple Bar.

Shaw's Birthplace

33 Synge Street, Dublin 8
01 475 0854 | Open Jun–Aug Mon, Tue, Thu, Fri 10–1, 2–5, Sat 2–5

The plaque on 33 Synge Street records George Bernard Shaw as the 'author of many plays', which is how the Nobel Laureate wanted his birthplace to be commemorated. He was born in this modest terraced house in 1856 and left for London in 1876. His house, which opened to the public in 1993, has been restored to reflect the life of a middle-class family in Victorian Dublin.

Shaw didn't write any of his works (*Pygmalion, Arms and the Man, Man and Superman* to name just a few) in Dublin but, like James Joyce, he drew heavily on his experiences of the city and its characters.

▶ Trinity College & The Book of Kells MAP REF 379 E2

tcd.ie/library

College Street, Dublin 2 | 01 896 2320 | Open May–Sep Mon–Sat 9.30–5,
Sun 9.30–4.30, Oct–Apr Mon–Sat 9.30–5, Sun 12–4.30

No visit to Dublin is complete without seeing one of the most
famous illuminated manuscripts in the world. The intricate beauty
of the *Book of Kells* has been imitated countless times, but to see
the pages themselves, and those of the similarly ornate books of
Durrow and Armagh, is a really memorable experience. But there
is much more to see in Trinity College Library than these revered
texts alone. The exhibition 'Turning Darkness into Light' brings a
context to the works, and upstairs the barrel-ceilinged Long Room
is filled with the intoxicating musk of more than 200,000 ancient
leather-bound books.

The entrance to the Old Library is through the gap in the square
on the right-hand side. It faces a group of modern buildings
including the Berkeley Library, which was designed by Paul
Koralek in 1967. The exhibition is reached through the shop at
street level.

University life

Trinity College is a modern working university and so, unless you
visit on Sunday morning or in high summer, its courtyards are
usually teeming with students and their bicycles. Founded by
Queen Elizabeth I in 1592, it is Ireland's oldest university. Although
this Georgian building (1759) is grand in its own right, its impact is
lessened by the proximity of the traffic and the more overt
classicism of James Gandon's east front of the Bank of Ireland
across the road. This dates from 1785 and was added to an older
building, which once housed the Irish parliament.

▼ Library Square, Trinity College

Past the Porter's Lodge you come out into Parliament Square, with the chapel, built in 1798, to the left and the Examination Room, of 1791, to the right. Ahead of you is the Campanile, a bell tower 98 feet high added to the square in 1853. Beyond it, the red-brick building is known as the Rubrics. With its origins around 1700, this is the oldest surviving building on the campus. The playwright Oliver Goldsmith had chambers on the top right-hand side next to the Old Library.

The Book of Kells

Before the rebuilding work of the 1980s, the *Book of Kells* was kept upstairs in the Long Room, and the area known as the Colonnades below, where the shop, exhibition and treasury are now, was a crowded storage area for the library's overflowing collection of books. When the building was originally constructed, this area had been left open to prevent damp rising into the library. It was filled in to house more books in the 1860s.

'Turning Darkness into Light' is the name of the exhibition in the Old Library that leads you up to the displayed pages of the *Book of Kells*. It explains the context of the book, follows the development of writing and illuminating manuscripts and has examples of Ogham and Ethiopian scripts. Pages and individual illustrations have been enlarged to the size of a person, so you can stand back and identify the truly stunning detail of the monastic scribe's art.

The *Book of Kells* itself is displayed in a darkened room known as the treasury. Its 680 pages were rebound during the 1950s into four separate volumes, two of which are always on display, so you are able to see two double-page spreads at a time, and these are turned every three months. It was written, if that is the right word for its spectacularly ornate pages, in the ninth century by monks at St Columba's monastery on Iona on the west coast of Scotland. It was transferred to the monastery at Kells in County Meath for safekeeping during the Viking raids and then its history is less certain until it arrived in Dublin in 1653, during the Cromwellian upheavals, and was acquired by Trinity College in 1661.

Its brilliantly elaborate pages reveal both the craft and the wit of its scribes. The text is the four Christian Gospels, written in Latin. Each evangelist is portrayed in minute detail and each Gospel begins with just a few words on a magnificently decorated page. Some of the pages, known as 'carpet pages', have no words at all, just the swirling abstract ornamentation which has become the hallmark of this incredible era of Celtic art.

A book lover's delight

Also on display in the treasury are the equally fabulous, but less well-known books of Durrow and Armagh, which may originate

▲ The Long Room

from the seventh century. They too demonstrate the tremendous scope and vision of the monastic scribes, again displaying an intricacy of penmanship that could scarcely have been visible in that distant age before electric lighting and artificial magnification.

The cathedral-like Long Room, which measures nearly 213 feet in length and houses almost a quarter of a million books, is up the stairs from the treasury. As in Marsh's Library at St Patrick's Cathedral, the smell of old books hits you as you walk in. They are piled high to the ceiling, which was extended in 1860 to fit more in. The gallery bookcases were added at this point. The central aisle is lined with busts of scholars and there is also a beautifully carved harp on display, believed to be the oldest in existence, though its 15th-century provenance means it can't be the legendary harp of Brian Boru, the 11th-century High King of Ireland, as one story claims. It is, however, the harp that appears on Irish coins. Another display has a rare copy of the original Proclamation of the Irish Republic, as read out by Pádraig Pearse from the steps of the General Post Office in 1916, Robert Emmet's arrest warrant and other papers from the struggle for independence.

VISIT THE GALLERIES

Dublin City Gallery, the Hugh Lane

hughlane.ie

Charlemont House, Parnell Square North, Dublin 1

01 222 5550 | Open Tue–Thu 10–6, Fri–Sat 10–5, Sun 11–5

This modern art gallery on the north side of Parnell Square may look inauspicious but it conceals some important works by Monet, Degas, Pissarro and Renoir, as well as over 2,000 examples of modern and contemporary Irish art, including those by Jack Butler Yeats, Walter Osborne, Sarah Purser, Frank O'Meara, William Orpen and Norman Garstin.

The gallery is traditional in its layout, though the Henry Moore figure in the foyer and the bizarre man in a mangle (*The Wringer* by Patrick O'Reilly, 1996) add some three-dimensional interest. In the Francis Bacon Studio, the entire contents of his studio have been painstakingly relocated from London, and illustrate the notoriously chaotic working lifestyle of this distinctive Irish artist.

The house dates from 1762 and the core collection was bequeathed to the nation by Hugh Lane in 1908. A new extension to the building houses some impressive Sean Scully paintings donated by the Dublin-born artist.

There is a kids' club and learning resource centre, and concerts are held on Sundays during the summer months.

Irish Museum of Modern Art (IMMA)

imma.ie

Royal Hospital, Military Road, Kilmainham, Dublin 8 | 01 612 9900 | Open Tue, Thu–Sat 10–5.30, Wed 10.30–5.30, Sun, 12–5.30

The Irish Museum of Modern Art, known as IMMA, can be found inside the magnificent buildings of the old Royal Hospital at the end of a long castellated gateway.

Based on Les Invalides in Paris, this is one of the finest remaining 17th-century buildings in Ireland. A formal garden in the French style stretches away on its northern side, while to the west there are smooth lawns extending to the little graveyard of Bully's Acre, where there is a 10th-century cross shaft amid the graves of the hospital's military pensioners. Inside, a small exhibition explains the building's history and the main galleries display current works by leading contemporary artists and the national collection of modern art. Don't miss the shop and its cafe in the original crypt of the Royal Hospital. The museum's excellent website contains up-to-date information about upcoming exhibitions.

National Gallery

nationalgallery.ie

Merrion Square and Clare Street, Dublin 2 | 01 661 5133 | Open Mon–Wed, Fri–Sat 9.30–5.30, Thu 9.30–8.30, Sun 11–5.30

Ireland's National Gallery exhibits an important collection

of European art from the 15th century to the present. Forming the western arm of the Leinster House complex, it was established by an Act of Parliament in 1854, and opened to the public 10 years later. With over 2,500 paintings and more than 10,000 works in other media, there is a great deal to see, though obviously they are not all on display at once. The acquisition of works has been helped by numerous bequests; the legacy of one-third of George Bernard Shaw's residual estate enabled the gallery to acquire important works by Fragonard and JL David, among others.

Everyone will find their own favourites among the works of Canaletto, Rembrandt, Caravaggio, Rubens and El Greco. There are huge collections of Irish works too, with an entire section devoted to the Yeats family: the work of Jack Butler Yeats and his father John Butler Yeats. A popular collection is the portraits of Irish men and women who have made significant contributions to the social, cultural and political life of the country. Free audio guides help explain the works and there is a special audio tour for children. The Millennium Wing, specialising in 20th-century art and themed exhibitions, opens onto Clare Street and includes two restaurants and a shop, contrasting markedly with the

▶ Glasnevin Cemetery

quiet Beit, Milltown and Dargan wings of the old Merrion Square side of the building.

GET OUTDOORS
Glasnevin Cemetery
glasnevintrust.ie
Finglas Road, Glasnevin, Dublin 11
01 882 6500 | Cemetery open daily 8–6, museum 10–5
The list of occupants of Glasnevin Cemetery, established in 1832 when Catholics were finally allowed to conduct funerals, reads like a roll-call of the key players in Ireland's story from the last 180 years. Daniel O'Connell is commemorated by a round tower standing 160 feet high, Charles Stewart Parnell by a big lump of granite. Here, among the Victorian Gothic memorials, you will also find the last resting place of Eamon de Valera. Michael Collins, Countess Markiewicz, Alfred Chester Beatty and Brendan Behan are among the other names familiar to any visitor to Dublin. There are sad

reminders of famine and poverty in the many paupers' graves, and sections devoted to the Irish army and other services. Controversial sites include the grave of Roger Casement (there is some debate as to whether his real remains were returned by the British after his execution for treason), and a plot of more recent Republican activists. Glasnevin Museum is the world's first cemetery museum, holding events, exhibitions and talks.

Dublin Docklands

dublindocklands.ie

Just a short stroll from O'Connell Street, Dublin Docklands is fast becoming an exciting and energetic part of the city around the Grand Canal, which was an important means of transport during the 18th century. You can take a boat down the canal or walk along the banks, stopping to rest alongside the bronze of poet Patrick Kavanagh, who loved this piece of leafy calm. In complete contrast, the huge piazza at Grand Canal Dock is a hub of activity surrounded by tinted-glass shops and restaurants. The centrepiece is the diamond-shaped Grand Canal Theatre, fronted by red-glass paving covered with glowing light sticks and green polygon planters. Look out for the Jeanie Johnston tall ship and the Famine Museum at Customs House Quay. A number of events take place

during the year, from Irish beer and food markets to concerts at the 3 Arena, which is housed in a former Victorian warehouse, and a big summer festival each May.

Iveagh Gardens

heritageireland.ie
Clonmel Street, Dublin 2
01 475 7816 | Open May–Oct
Mon–Sat 8–6, Sun 10–6, Nov–Apr
Mon–Sat 8–4, Sun 10–4

This lovely park lies hidden behind the huge bulk of the National Concert Hall. It looks like a private garden and to get in you'll need to locate entrances on Clonmel Street, off Harcourt Street and Hatch Street. The gardens were designed by Ninian Niven for the International Exhibition of Arts and Manufactures on Earlsfort Terrace in 1865, and are in three thematic sections. The central parterre, with its lawns, statues and fountains, echoes the Bois de Boulougne in Paris. The southern end has rocky outcrops reflecting North American landscapes. There is a miniature maze and a lovely manicured lawn.

Dublin Zoo

dublinzoo.ie
Phoenix Park, Dublin 8
01 474 8900 | Open Mar–Oct
Mon–Sat 9.30–6, Sun 10.30–6,
Nov–Feb Mon–Sat 9.30am–dusk,
Sun 10.30am–dusk

Committed to conservation and education, Dublin Zoo opened in 1831 and today houses more than 700 animals. The Gorilla

▲ Houses on Merrion Square

Rainforest, the Kaziranga Forest Trail and the Asian Forest all offer memorable animal experiences. The 'African Plains' area allows African animals to roam with greater freedom.

Merrion Square
merrionsquare.ie

Merrion Square is the heart of Georgian Dublin and these days is home to a number of events which take place around the year, from Christmas carols to summer opera and fashion shows. It has a fascinating history evident in a reclining statue of Oscar Wilde in the corner of the square which gazes across the street to his former home at 1 Merrion Square. The gifted writer lived here from 1855 to 1878 in what is now the American College. The house, with its superb Georgian architraves and cornices, has been restored, but is not currently open to the public.

The square itself was laid out by John Ensor in the 1770s, with Leinster House and its attendant galleries on the western side. In the 1930s it passed from the family of the Earls of Pembroke to the Catholic Church, who planned to build a cathedral here. However, the cost was prohibitive and the plan was dropped. Many of the fine Georgian buildings around the remaining three sides are still private houses. Daniel O'Connell once resided at No. 58, W B Yeats at No. 82, and the Duke of Wellington was born around the corner on Merrion Street Upper. The impressive Georgian museum piece, No. 29 Lower Fitzwilliam Street, is just off the square on the south side.

National Botanic Gardens
botanicgardens.ie
Glasnevin, Dublin 9 | 01 804 0300
Open daily mid-Feb to mid-Nov
9–6, mid-Nov to mid-Feb 9–4.30

A few miles north of the heart of the city, the National Botanic Gardens line the south bank of the Tolka River. They were founded by the Royal Dublin Society in 1795 and have benefited from extensive restoration work in recent years. The latest project was the Victorian Great Palm House, reopened in 2004. The impressive curvilinear glasshouses date from the middle of the 19th century and were restored in the mid-1990s; they house orchids, ferns, succulents and tropical water plants. Outside are 48 acres of specimen trees, bedding plants and rockeries. The Burren Garden recreates in miniature the limestone-loving flora of northwest County Clare. There is usually something worth seeing here, though spring and summer are the most striking periods.

Phoenix Park

phoenixpark.ie

Visitor centre, Phoenix Park, Dublin 8 | 01 611 0095 | Open daily Mar–Oct 10–6, Nov–Feb 9.30–5.30

Often claimed to be the largest city park in the world, Phoenix Park stretches west from Parkgate, near the Collins Barracks, for nearly 3 miles. Within this huge open space, the most visible feature is the 205-foot Wellington obelisk, commemorating the Battle of Waterloo in 1815. Nearby is Dublin Zoo, which is one of the oldest in the world (see page 272), and deer can be seen roaming freely in the park. On the northern side of the park, the stately home of the British Viceroys of Ireland became the Áras an Uachtaráin, official residence of the President of Ireland, in 1937. Guided tours are available every Saturday except at Christmas. The park passed into notoriety when the British chief secretary, Lord Frederick Cavendish, and his undersecretary, T H Burke, were assassinated here in 1882 by a radical Republican group known as the Invincibles.

On the southern side, an area known as the Fifteen Acres is popular for Gaelic sports; Pope John Paul II greeted more than a million people here on his visit in 1979. To get the most from a visit to the park, head for the visitor centre, next to Ashtown Castle, which traces the area's history from 3500 BC.

O'Connell Street

There's no avoiding O'Connell Street, which is not only a key thoroughfare in central Dublin leading down to the River Liffey and the always-busy O'Connell Bridge, but is said to be the widest street in Europe. Dublin's famous store, Easons, is here, and there are busy shopping areas off Henry Street to the west, including another famous Dublin store – Arnott's. In the street opposite the GPO is the Monument of Light, also called The Spire, a 394-foot spike of stainless steel. The site was formerly occupied by Nelson's Pillar (demolished by a rogue IRA man in 1966), and then by a depiction of Anna Livia. The spire was raised in 2002 and, despite problems with its lighting, has become a symbol of modern Dublin.

Upper O'Connell Street was originally laid out in the 1740s and was connected to Lower O'Connell Street, then known as Sackville Street, in 1784. O'Connell Bridge, formerly the Carlisle Bridge, was completed in 1790 and is overlooked by a statue of Daniel O'Connell, 'the Liberator', still bearing bullet marks from 1916. O'Connell Street is now home to a number of fast-food chains and can be noisy at night.

St Stephen's Green

Dublin 2 | Open Mon–Sat 8am–dusk, Sun 10am–dusk
An oasis of calm and greenery in the city centre, this pleasant public park is perfect for picnics and walks and is probably Ireland's favourite Victorian public park. Its peace was shattered in the Easter Rising of 1916 when a group of insurgents established themselves here.

The park was enclosed in 1669, and surrounding land was sold off to property developers. Trees and paths soon followed and Dubliners were charged for access. However, in 1877, Sir Arthur Guinness secured an Act of Parliament to make access free for all, and today it is a popular haven from the din of the surrounding traffic. It includes a duck pond, children's play area and a sensory garden for the visually impaired. The main entrance is through Fusiliers' Gate on the corner facing Grafton Street. Nearby is a small Huguenot Cemetery established in 1693 by French Protestant refugees.

SEE THE CHURCH AND CATHEDRAL

St Michan's Church

stmichans.com
Church Street, Dublin 7 | 01 872 4154 | Open Mar–Oct Mon–Fri 10–12.45, 2–4.45, Sat 10–12.45, Nov–Feb Mon–Fri 12.30–3.30
The main, if macabre, attraction of the church of St Michan's lies in its crypt. Here in the dry atmosphere of its grim vaults, the corpses became mummified rather than decomposed. The casket lids are off, revealing the taut yellow skin of a number of men and women, including a nun. This is definitely not a tourist stop for the faint-hearted!

Guided tours point out ancient remains and bodies of the 18th-century dead, including those of Henry and John Sheares, leaders of the rebellion in 1798. There is also a death mask of Wolfe Tone, and some believe Robert Emmet was buried in the churchyard. The church can trace its origins back to 1095 but the present structure is mostly from 1686. The organ is also of interest as it is believed to have been played by Handel and is one of the oldest still in use in Ireland.

St Patrick's Cathedral

stpatrickscathedral.ie

Patrick Street, Dublin 8 | 01 453 9472 | Open Mar–Oct daily 9.30–5, Nov–Feb Mon–Sat 9.30–5, Sun 9–3

One of three cathedrals in Dublin, St Patrick's is the largest and is also the national cathedral of Ireland. It is a bit of a walk from the city centre, and is not situated in a particularly pleasant part of town, but this is definitely one of Dublin's key sights, especially for lovers of literature. It was built on a site where St Patrick himself is supposed to have baptised converts and the local area has a Christian history dating back to around AD 450.

Although it was built in 1191, today's building mainly dates from the 1860s, when it was rebuilt using money from the Guinness family to reinterpret its original Gothic and Romanesque features.

Inside you will find the grave and some memorabilia of its most famous dean, Jonathan Swift. The author of *Gulliver's Travels* became dean of St Patrick's in 1713. The cathedral organ is the largest in Ireland, and in the south choir aisle are two of Ireland's rare 16th-century monumental brasses. Look for the tomb and effigy of the 17th-century adventurer Richard Boyle, Earl of Cork, and a memorial to the great Irish bard and harpist Turlough O'Carolan (1670–1738).

One notable curiosity is a wooden door, originally from the chapterhouse but now mounted at the junction of the north transept. Through a hole in this, the Earl of Kildare stretched out his hand to make peace with the Earl of Ormond, the supposed origins of the phrase 'chancing your arm'.

SAMPLE A GUINNESS

Guinness Storehouse

guinness-storehouse.com

St James's Gate, Dublin 8

01 408 4800 | Open daily Jul–Aug 9.30–7, Sep–Jun 9.30–5

No trip to Dublin would be complete without a taste of the 'Black Stuff' and a search for that mythical 'best pint of Guinness'. The Dublin brewer's status as a world brand ensures that a ready stream of visiting drinkers arrive to take up the challenge. The Guinness Storehouse off St James's Gate is a good place to start. Here, an old warehouse next to the vast brewery has been transformed into a cathedral to the creation of this ale.

The building was originally constructed in 1904 to house the Guinness fermentation process, in the style of the Chicago school of architecture, with massive steel beams providing the support for the structure. The Storehouse building served the purpose of fermenting this famous beer until 1988, and in 2000 it was transformed into one of Dublin's major attractions. The focus of the building is a giant pint glass, stretching up from reception on the ground floor to the Gravity Bar on the top floor.

Seven floors of dramatic exhibits take you through the process, from the water (it doesn't really come from the Liffey as the legends say), Irish barley, hops and yeast to the finished product. On the way you learn how the beer developed from dark porter-style ale popular among Irish migrant workers in London to the distinctive global superbrand it is today.

Escalators connect the floors in a pleasingly futuristic style redolent of Fritz Lang's classic 1920s film *Metropolis*. The labyrinthine displays include sections dedicated to the transport that has carried Guinness around the world. You get a free pint in the seventh floor Gravity Bar, now reputed to be the best pint in Dublin. The views over the city to the docks and the mountains are impressive. Back on the ground floor is a large, comprehensive Guinness merchandise shop.

EXPLORE THE QUARTERS
Smithfield
Smithfield Village, Dublin 7
This corner of Dublin is reinventing itself since its initial redevelopment in the 1990s. You can still find traces of the old Smithfield, even if the old horse market has long gone, but modern apartment blocks

▼ St Patrick's Cathedral

now dominate and retail spaces are beginning to fill up. The Jameson Distillery is in Bow Street. The company moved most of its operations to Cork in the 1960s, so is no longer in production, but tours show how whiskey was made from the sixth century and end with a tasting session. The old distillery chimney had a viewing platform on top, 184 feet above the street, accessed via an external glass lift, offering a 360-degree view of the city but it has been closed for several years now – a visible reminder of the end of the Celtic Tiger years. The Lighthouse Cinema is just across the Market Square. There is a lively outdoor market here every Friday in the summer months. Don't miss some of the traditional old pubs, such as The Cobblestone, which still remain in this area, many completely unchanged by modern development.

Temple Bar
temple-bar.ie
Promoted as 'Dublin's Cultural and Creative Quarter', Temple Bar takes its name from Sir William Temple, who owned much of the land in the 17th century. It is actually one of the oldest parts of the city, with history dating back to Viking times. These days you will find boundless energy within this block of narrow streets and countless pubs popular with drinking parties, traditional music, cafes, theatres and nightclubs. Ireland's smallest

theatre is also here, The New Theatre, and the Victorian Olympia theatre.

By the 1970s the site was earmarked for a bus station, and the bus company began letting out the buildings to artists and musicians. Temple Bar established a bohemian reputation for its buzzing nightlife and in doing so won a reprieve from the wrecking ball. The most evocative entrance is over the iconic Ha'penny Bridge (there used to be a toll of a halfpenny to cross the bridge), which was built in 1816 and is now the best known of Dublin's bridges with its lamps and distinctive ironwork. Open-air performances often take place in Meeting House Square, where there is also a food market on Saturdays.

TAKE IN SOME ARCHITECTURE
Marino Casino
heritageireland.ie
Off Malahide Road, Marino, Dublin 3 | 01 833 1618 | Open May–Oct daily 10–5
Incongruous amid housing estates, the casino is all that remains of the 18th-century neoclassical estate of the Earl of Charlemont. Nothing to do with gambling, it was an extravagant summer house to complement the now-demolished Marino House. Despite its outward appearance, it has 16 rooms on three floors, and a host of architectural tricks retain the exterior integrity, such as drainpipes being hidden in pillars.

CATCH A PERFORMANCE

3 Arena

3arena.ie

3 Arena, North Wall Quay, Dublin 1

01 819 8888

This dockside, state-of-the-art mega-venue, with world-class acoustics, replaced the much smaller, former Point Theatre on the same site. With a standing capacity of 14,000, it attracts star performers such as Bob Dylan, U2, David Bowie and Lady Gaga.

Abbey Theatre

abbeytheatre.ie

26 Lower Abbey Street, Dublin 1

01 878 7222

The original Abbey Theatre was founded in 1904 in a former morgue by W B Yeats, Lady Augusta Gregory and others. The present purpose-built home of the National Theatre of Ireland dates from 1966. The main, fan-shaped auditorium seats 628, nearly 100 of which are in a shallow balcony. The diminutive and intimate Peacock stage is dedicated to brand new works.

The Ark

ark.ie

11a Eustace Street, Temple Bar, Dublin 2 | 01 670 7788

This is a purpose-built, cultural venue for 3- to 14-year-olds. It stages varied performances by children and for children in both the indoor theatre and the outdoor amphitheatre. There is a gallery space and workshops concentrating on arts and activities for young people.

Bord Gáis Energy Theatre

bordgaisenergytheatre.ie

Grand Canal Square, Dublin 2

01 677 7999 (info), 0818 719377 (box office)

The newest addition to the Dublin theatre scene is attracting interest as much for its architecture – a spectacular wedge of glass and steel overlooking a new quayside plaza – as for its performances.

Civic Theatre

civictheatre.ie

Blessington Road, off Belguard Square East, Tallaght, Dublin 24

01 462 7477

The Civic is a community arts centre in the southwest suburbs of Dublin which opened in 1999 to provide mainstream drama and classical music concerts, as well as some traditional and contemporary music. There is an art gallery upstairs and a small studio space, a popular cafe that's open during the day and a bar.

Gaiety Theatre

gaietytheatre.com

South King Street, Dublin 2

01 677 1717

Affectionately known as The Grand Old Lady of South King Street, this theatre in the vicinity of the northwest corner of St Stephen's Green is one of Dublin's oldest and has played host to a number of international stars. It is famous for its winter pantomimes and also has a lively calendar of events, featuring a mixture of popular drama and music.

Gate Theatre

gate-theatre.ie

1 Cavendish Row, Parnell Square,
Dublin 1 | 01 874 4045

One of Ireland's foremost
theatres, staging new works
and the standards in a beautiful
Georgian-fronted building that
has been a theatre since 1928.
This was an early showcase for
the actors Orson Welles and
James Mason.

The Helix

thehelix.ie

Dublin City University, Collins
Avenue, Glasnevin, Dublin 9
01 700 7000

Opened in 2002, this complex
at City University has three
auditoria – the 1,260-capacity
Mahony Hall, the 450-seat
Theatre and the 150-seat Space
– serving up classical concerts,
drama and mainstream rock
and pop music.

Irish Film Institute

irishfilm.ie

6 Eustace Street, Temple Bar,
Dublin 2 | 01 679 5744

A state-funded art-house
cinema showing retrospectives,
foreign-language films (with
subtitles) and new works that
are most unlikely to make it to
the multiplexes.

National Concert Hall

nch.ie

Earlsfort Terrace, Dublin 2
01 417 0000

Dublin's biggest classical music
venue was built for the
International Exhibition of Arts
and Manufactures in 1865. As

well as hosting the greatest
visiting musicians of the day,
it is home to the RTÉ National
Symphony Orchestra.

TAKE A TOUR

Dublin City Tour

dublinsightseeing.ie

DublinBus Head Office, 59 Upper
O'Connell Street, Dublin 1
01 703 3028

Dublin City Tours are operated
by DublinBus and run around
the middle of Dublin all day.
There is live commentary, and
tickets, which you can buy on
board, are valid for 24 hours, so
you can get on and off to visit
the sights. The route takes in
Phoenix Park, the National
Museum of Decorative Arts
and History, the Dublin Writers
Museum, Henry Street/GPO,
Trinity College, the National
Gallery, Dublin Castle and the
Guinness Storehouse.

The brave can opt for The
Dublin Ghost Bus Tour,
operated by the same company,
which takes in some of the
city's most haunting sights,
such as the College of
Surgeons, the Hellfire
Clubroom, the Christchurch
crypt and St James' Graveyard.

Hidden Dublin

hiddendublinwalks.com

085 102 3646

These walks take visitors to
some unique locations around
the city, focusing on the stories
and some of the more
interesting and colourful
characters that lie beneath
Dublin's history.

Historical Walking Tours of Dublin

historicalinsights.ie

64 Mary Street, Dublin 1

087 688 9412

These historically themed walking tours are led by knowledgeable history graduates from Trinity College. A two-hour 'seminar on the street' includes Wood Quay in the heart of Viking Dublin, the Four Courts, Trinity College, Christ Church Cathedral and Dublin Castle.

Viking Splash Tour

vikingsplash.ie

64–65 Patrick Street, Dublin 8

01 707 6000

This ex-World War II amphibious vehicle tours Viking Dublin before driving into the Grand Canal.

EXPLORE BY BIKE

Dublin bikes scheme

dublinbikes.ie

A full list of stations throughout the city centre is given on the website. A 3-Day Ticket costs €5 and the first 30 minutes is free on every bike.

DANCE THE NIGHT AWAY

The Button Factory

buttonfactory.ie

Curved Street, Temple Bar, Dublin 2

01 670 9202

In the heart of Temple Bar, this club has built a very respectable reputation for its eclectic mix of music. Come for live modern big-band jazz on a Monday evening, or the club nights on Thursday through to Sunday. Saturday nights are a little bit indie, while Sundays are reggae.

Fitzsimons

fitzsimonshotel.com

21–22 Wellington Quay, Temple Bar, Dublin 2 | 01 677 9315 | Open daily 10.30am–late

Part of a popular hotel, this is a vibrant nightspot, with bars over four floors, Irish dancing shows and a nightclub where DJs play a mix of pop and dance. Big, busy and bustling, it has a great atmosphere. There is a roof terrace.

The George

thegeorge.ie

South Great George's Street, Dublin 2

01 671 3298

The George is both a bar and a nightclub and has long been Dublin's main gay and lesbian venue.

Laughter Lounge

laughterlounge.com

6 Eden Quay, Dublin 1

01 874 4611

At O'Connell Bridge, Laughter Lounge is Ireland's top comedy venue, hosting Irish and international comedians and it also has an After Lounge where you can dance after the show.

Sugar Club

thesugarclub.com

8 Lower Leeson Street, Dublin 2

01 678 7188

A theatre-style venue hosting comedy events, cabaret and film evenings. From 11pm it is a buzzing nightclub.

▲ Leopardstown Racecourse

Viperoom

5 Aston Quay, Temple Bar
01 672 5566

A late-night venue on two floors with a bar and music, especially salsa and rhythm 'n' blues.

Whelan's

whelanslive.com
25 Wexford Street, Dublin 2
01 478 0766

A bar and venue of the type you might hope to find in any big city – live rock bands play at the back, while at the front is a cracking traditional Dublin bar. Look out for performers from around the world, and up-and-coming local bands.

GO TO THE RACES

Leopardstown Racecourse

leopardstown.com
Leopardstown Road (off the Stillorgan road), Foxrock, Dublin 18
01 289 0500

Leopardstown has a modern and popular course. The track is in the southern suburbs and there are one or two meetings a month, mostly National Hunt (steeplechase), but some flat racing too.

WATCH A MATCH

Gaelic Athletic Association (GAA)

gaa.ie
Croke Park, Dublin 3 | 01 836 3222

There are dozens of teams in County Dublin playing Gaelic football, hurling, camogie and handball. The easiest place to see football and hurling is the Fifteen Acres area of Phoenix Park, where many local teams in these strictly amateur sports play. The headquarters of the GAA is Croke Park (see page 252). You can get tickets for these games only through local clubs, but semi-final games are also played at Croke Park and tickets are usually available in advance.

Irish Rugby Football Union

irfu.ie; irishrugby.ie
10–12 Lansdowne Road, Ballsbridge, Dublin 4 | 01 647 3800

The best rugby in Ireland is played in the RBS Six Nations tournament, in which an all-Ireland side plays against England, Wales, Scotland, France and Italy. The Aviva Stadium, built on the site of the former Lansdowne Road Stadium, also hosts international football matches.

PLAY A ROUND

Luttrellstown Castle Golf and Country Club

luttrellstown.ie

Castle Knock, 10 miles west of Dublin via the R148 | 01 860 9600

Set in the grounds of the magnificent 560-acre Luttrellstown Castle estate, this championship course has been redesigned to enhance the golfing experience. The layout respects and retains the integrity of the mature and ancient parkland. The course is renowned for the quality of its greens and facilities.

The Royal Dublin Golf Club

theroyaldublingolfclub.com

Dollymount, 3 miles northeast of Dublin | 01 833 6346

A popular course with visitors, for its design subtleties, the condition of the links and the friendly atmosphere. Founded in 1885, the club moved to its present site in 1889 and received its royal designation in 1891. A notable former club professional was Christy O'Connor, who was appointed in 1959 and immediately made his name. Along with its many notable holes, Royal Dublin has a fine and testing finish. The 18th is a sharp dog-leg par four, with out-of-bounds along the right-hand side. The decision to try the long carry over the 'garden' is one many visitors have regretted.

EAT AND DRINK

Ashling Hotel ◉

ashlinghotel.ie

Parkgate Street, Dublin 8

01 677 2324

The Ashling is a large, modern and glitzy hotel near Phoenix Park and Dublin Zoo, where Chesterfields Restaurant occupies a spacious, softly lit room with plushly upholstered dining chairs and a busily patterned carpet. The kitchen has some success with its combinations of flavours and textures, and the modern dishes are notable for their accurate timings.

Balfes at The Westbury Hotel ◉

balfes.ie

Grafton Street, Dublin

01 679 1122

The second dining option at the Westbury Hotel (after the main restaurant named after Oscar Wilde), Balfes is a buzzy all-day operation with a creative menu that takes its inspiration from Paris and New York.

The Cellar Restaurant ◉◉

merrionhotel.com

Upper Merrion Street, Dublin 2

01 603 0600

Down below one of the finest Georgian town houses in the capital is the award-winning Cellar. Enjoy beautifully crafted, modern Irish dishes that are made with love from local ingredients. If you're expecting crepuscular gloom down here, think again. A vision of white-linened tables and fresh flowers is in prospect.

Coppinger Row ◉◉

coppingerrow.com
1 William Street South, Dublin
01 672 9884
With its burnished copper bar
and elegant ambience, this
restaurant has a New York-style
buzz that attracts visiting
celebrities and hip Dubliners.
It serves European and Middle
Eastern food.

Doheny and Nesbitt

5 Lower Baggot Street, Dublin 2
01 676 2945
One of the most photographed
pubs in the city, this is a
distinguished old pub away
from usual tourist drinking
spots, and a protected example
of Victorian pub architecture.
Doheny and Nesbitt attracts
politicians and media people to
its three floors and bars, which
are well stocked with whiskeys
and stouts. Its mirrored walls,
high ceilings and intimate
snugs are a step back in time.

Drury Buildings

drurybuildings.com
5-55 Drury Street, Dublin 2
01 960 2095
A red-brick building with a good
bar for weekend brunch and a
restaurant on the first floor,
plus a garden area at the back.
Also serves pre-theatre menus.

McDaid's

3 Harry Street, Dublin 2
01 679 4395
Just off Grafton Street, this is
a classic Dublin pub that has
changed little since Brendan
Behan and Patrick Kavanagh

stood at the bar. With no frills,
it offers good beer and friendly
service. It is cramped and noisy
most nights of the week.

Mulligans

mulligans.ie
8 Poolbeg Street, Dublin 2
01 677 5582
A pub since 1820, Mulligans is
a Guinness drinkers' institution.
Retaining its Victorian
mahogany furnishings, it has
steadfastly resisted change
over the decades.

O'Neill's

oneillsbar.com
2 Suffolk Street, Dublin 2
01 679 3656
A licensed bar for more than
300 years, this complex of
snugs and alcoves, near Temple
Bar, is believed to have been
built on the site of the Norse
parliament or 'thingmote'.

The Porterhouse

porterhousebrewco.com
16–18 Parliament Street, Dublin 2
01 679 8847
One of Ireland's oldest
microbreweries, they make
great ales that are perfect for
washing down a portion of their
Irish stew. You can try their own
brand of acclaimed oyster stout
ale, which is actually made with
oysters. There is live music
most nights.

Restaurant Patrick Guilbaud
◉◉◉◉

restaurantpatrickguilbaud.ie
Merrion Hotel, 21 Upper Merrion
Street, Dublin 2 | 01 676 4192

Paris-born Monsieur Guilbaud opened his restaurant in 1981 with the aim of bringing outstanding haute cuisine to Dublin at a time when it probably seemed like a brave move. Bravery is rewarded sometimes and that is very much the case here, for Restaurant Patrick Guilbaud has been at the forefront of Irish fine dining ever since.

The Shelbourne Dublin, a Renaissance Hotel ◉◉
theshelbourne.ie
27 St Stephen's Green, Dublin 2
01 663 4500
At the Saddle Room a menu of modern brasserie dishes specialises in seafood (including generously loaded platters) and 32-day aged beef (two of you might set about a pound of Chateaubriand).

The Temple Bar
templebarpubdublin.ie
47–48 Temple Bar, Dublin 2
01 672 9286
With its warm welcome, huge selection of whiskeys, live traditional music sessions and crowds of drinkers, this is perhaps the epitome of tourists' Temple Bar, but the *craic* can be good and there's room enough for all.

Trocadero
trocadero.ie
4 St Andrew Street, Dublin 2
01 677 5540
This theatrical dining establishment has been popular with the acting set for many years. Its red-painted walls and banquettes create an intimate atmosphere and there are photographs on the walls of all the stars that have passed through.

The Westbury Hotel ◉◉
doylecollection.com
Grafton Street, Dublin | 01 679 1122
This prestigious city-centre hotel has a fine-dining restaurant that is dedicated to Oscar Wilde, with a bust of the writer and poet, and references continuing into the artworks dotted around the swishly decorated and furnished room. Waterford crystal chandeliers above tables laid with crisp white linen, sparkling silver and glassware make a glossy setting for a wide-ranging menu of comfort-orientated modern brasserie dishes. The kitchen picks the cream of Ireland's produce and showcases it.

▶ PLACES NEARBY
As well as Dublin's many attractions there are plenty of other places to visit in the area, some right on the doorstep. Dalkey is a seaside resort just south of Dublin, while Dalkey Island can easily be visited by boat. Howth (see page 308) is 8 miles northeast of the city. Malahide Castle is 9 miles north and Killiney 10 miles southwest. You are also well placed to visit excellent restaurants in Clontarf and Swords, and the hotel spa at the Talbot Hotel Stillorgan.

Dalkey

dalkeycastle.com

Now a suburb of Dublin, Dalkey (pronounced 'Daw-key') was once an important port. On its main street the fortified mansions of 15th-century trading families face each other. Of these, Archbold's Castle is little more than a three-floor shell, but Goat Castle contains a heritage centre with displays and live reconstructions of the town's history, and you can walk around the castle's battlements. Above the harbour stands Bulloch Castle, built in the 12th century by monks from St Mary's Abbey in Dublin to protect the harbour. Granite quarries on Dalkey Hill are popular with climbers and offer good views.

Goat Castle

dalkeycastle.com

Castle Street, Dalkey, County Dublin

01 285 8366 | Mon–Fri 10–5.30, Sat, Sun 11–5.30

Dating back to the 13th century, the castle was built as a fortified town house to store goods before transport to Dublin, at a time when the Liffey was silted up and unnavigable for large ships. The castle is named for the Cheevers family who owned it in the 17th century, 'Chèvre' being French for goat.

Dalkey Island

ilovedalkey.com

Boat trips run to Dalkey Island, which has, among other things, a Martello tower and monastic oratory. Much of the island is now a bird reserve. It is also home to a colony of seals.

Dollymount Strand

Bull Island, Causeway Road, off James Larkin Road

A tidal lagoon separates this island beach, also called Bull Island, from Dollymount and Clontarf. Stretching for 3 miles and now an important nature reserve, it was created by the construction of the North Bull sea wall, protruding 1.75 miles into Dublin Bay. Before the wall

▲ Malahide Castle

was completed in 1821, the maximum depth in Dublin's harbour at low tide was barely 6 feet but the scouring effect of the River Liffey's waters rushing around the obstacle has increased this to 16 feet or more, allowing passage for much larger ships. You can drive onto the sand via a bridge at the west end and a causeway in the middle. There are views across the bay to the two Sugar Loaves and Wicklow Mountains, and an interpretative centre (summer only) illustrates the island's wildlife.

Malahide Castle

malahidecastle.com
Malahide, County Dublin | 01 846 2184 | Open Apr–Sep Mon–Sat 10–5, Sun 10–5, Oct–Mar Mon–Sat 10–5, Sun 11–5. No tours 12.45–2
Malahide Castle, in 249 acres of grounds, was home to the Talbot family from 1185 to 1976 and incorporates a mixture of styles, from its 12th-century core to the 18th-century embellishments. Family portraits are hung alongside works on loan from the National Gallery. In the stable block is Tara's Palace, a doll's house museum recreating the 18th-century golden age of Irish great houses at one-twelfth scale. Next door, the Fry Model Railway is a reconstruction of a transport system begun by engineer Cyril Fry in the 1930s.

Killiney

This is an affluent suburb of villas and embassies, with exceptional views across the bay to Bray Head and the mountains, and to the north. The pebbly strand is reached through a dark tunnel beneath the DART railway line. From here a bracing seafront stroll stretches 4 miles to Bray; alternatively you can climb for about 30 minutes through trees and gardens to the summit of Killiney Hill.

Fahrenheit Restaurant ◉◉
clontarfcastle.ie
Clontarf Castle Hotel, Castle Avenue, Clontarf, County Dublin | 01 833 2321 and 01 852 3263
Ten minutes out of the city centre, Dublin's Clontarf Castle Hotel is a beguiling mix of ancient structure and modern boutique luxury. It dates from the 12th century. The Fahrenheit is the destination restaurant, a dramatic showcase room for some striking modern Irish cookery.

Fitzpatrick Castle Hotel ◉
fitzpatrickcastle.com
Killiney, Dublin Bay | 01 230 5400
A range of hospitable dining venues includes the Grill at the Castle, located in the former dungeons of this 18th-century castellated house, where wine-red banquettes and exposed stone walls are the background for a menu of modern brasserie cooking. There's no wild experimentation here, just honest preparations of prime materials.

Radisson Blu St Helens Hotel ◉
radissonblu.ie/sthelenshotel-dublin
Stillorgan Road, Blackrock, County Dublin | 01 218 6000 and 01 218 6032
This grand old house dates from the middle of the 17th century but has all the expected 21st-century mod cons of a Radisson Blu. The Talavera, restaurant serves up smart Italian food in a series of rooms with either traditional country-house decor or rather more contemporary chic. There's also an all-day Orangery Bar, ideal for a cocktail or afternoon tea. The main restaurant focuses on the cooking of Lombardy, where the chef comes from.

Roganstown Hotel and Country Club ◉
roganstown.com
Naul Road, Swords, County Dublin
01 843 3118
A sprawling resort with golf, spa and conference facilities, Roganstown is also home to the impressive McLoughlins Restaurant. Located in a wood-panelled room within the hotel (the original part of the structure was a farmhouse in a former life), there's plenty of room between well-dressed tables. The kitchen seeks out first-class ingredients and delivers a menu that has ambition and a contemporary feel about it.

The Talbot Hotel Stillorgan ◉
stillorganpark.com
Stillorgan Road, County Dublin
01 200 1800 and 200 1822
A hotel with a spa, Stillorgan Park is also home to the Purple Sage restaurant, with its breezy vibe and contemporary finish. There are plenty of nooks and crannies in the split-level room if you're after a bit of privacy. The menu takes a gently modern tack, nothing too wacky, and with classic combinations at the heart of the action.

▶ Dún Laoghaire MAP REF 379 E2

Part modern port facility and part seaside resort, Dún Laoghaire (pronounced 'Dún Leary'), 8 miles from central Dublin, is where the Holyhead car ferries have berthed since 1966. The massive stone piers of the harbour were built of Wicklow granite from the quarries on Dalkey Hill in the first half of the 19th century and enclose not only the ferry terminal but also the grand marinas of the Royal Irish Yacht Club. A walk along the piers of this former small fishing village is a popular seaside stroll of a couple of hours each, and affords splendid views back along the coast to Sandycove, Dalkey Island and hill and across Dublin Bay. The spire of the former Mariners' Church dominates the town; it now contains the National Maritime Museum.

VISIT THE MUSEUM
National Maritime Museum
mariner.ie
Haigh Terrace, Dún Laoghaire, County Dublin | 01 280 0969
Open daily 11–5
Among the National Maritime Museum's most popular exhibits are the SS *Great Eastern* display, the largest ship in the world when it was built in 1857, and the original optic, worked by clockwork and still functioning, from the Baily lighthouse on the Howth peninsula.

▶ PLACES NEARBY
Some 8 miles south of Dublin is a former home of James Joyce which still contains some of the author's personal effects.

Sandycove and Joyce Tower
Joyce Tower, Sandycove
01 280 9265 | Open Apr–Aug
Tue–Sat 10–1, Sun 2–6
A tiny cove near Dún Laoghaire gives this affluent suburb its name. James Joyce lived briefly in the Martello tower overlooking a rocky peninsula. It features in the opening chapter of *Ulysses* and now houses a museum of Joycean memorabilia: his letters to Nora Barnacle, a 1935 edition of *Ulysses* illustrated by Matisse, a guitar and a waistcoat. Nearby Forty Foot Pool is a sea-bathing facility, popular even in winter, with changing areas cut in the rock. Contrary to the old sign, mixed bathing is allowed.

▶ Dublin Bay from Dún Laoghaire

▶ **Fore** MAP REF 382 C6

Signposted off the R195 near Castlepollard, on the R394, 13 miles north of Mullingar

The village of Fore is famous for the legendary Seven Wonders of Fore, evidence of which lies in the fields on the outskirts. Pilgrims visit regularly, and though the Wonders may look rather unremarkable to sceptics, local belief is strong.

The first of them is 'the monastery in the quaking scraw', a fine range of monastic buildings, complete with gatehouse and dovecot, which were built on a rock that's surrounded by a quaking bog. Then comes the 'water that flows uphill' and the 'mill without a race' – the ruin of a mill that is said to have been founded here by St Fechin in a then-waterless place; the stream, apparently defying gravity by flowing uphill, appeared with a stroke of his staff. 'The tree that won't burn' is next – a stump that has been poisoned by the thousands of copper coins pushed into its trunk as offerings by miracle-seekers. Then there's the 'water that won't boil' – but nobody's going to try when legend has it that the water of the muddy remnants of St Fechin's holy well brings bad luck to anyone even attempting to boil it.

On the other side of the road you'll find 'the stone raised by St Fechin's prayers'. The massive lintel of a 12th-century church, carved with a Greek cross in a circle, reputedly rose into place on the saint's prayers. Lastly, there's the 'anchorite in a stone', which is actually the cell of 17th-century hermit Patrick Begley, within what looks like a church but is in fact the mausoleum of the Greville Nugent family. Should the mausoleum be locked when you arrive, collect the key for it from the Seven Wonders pub in the village.

▼ Fore Abbey

▶ **PLACES NEARBY**

Tullynally, 13 miles north of Mullingar, has a fine castle, or you can visit Crookedwood or Lough Derravaragh.

Tullynally Castle and Gardens

tullynallycastle.ie

Castlepollard, County Westmeath

Signposted off the R394 | 044 966 1159 | Gardens and tea rooms open Apr–Sep Thu–Sun 11–5

Tullynally Castle has been the seat of the Pakenham family (now Earls of Longford) since 1655, and they still live in the house that was rebuilt during the 19th century into a full-scale Gothic castle. There are tours of the house, and outside are lovely gardens.

The Church of Taghmon

Crookedwood, County Westmeath

The Church of Taghmon is a charming 14th-century church and well-preserved ruin. It is a fortified building, making it appear more like a castle. Also in the village overlooking Lough Derravaragh is Crookedwood House, a former rectory that is now a restaurant.

Lough Derravaragh

County Westmeath

Also known as Donore Lake, Lough Derravaragh is one of the highest in Ireland. Sitting at about 210 feet above sea level, this delightful freshwater lake is popular with anglers and water-sport enthusiasts.

▶ **Galway** MAP REF 381 D6

Galway is the liveliest city in the west of Ireland with winding lanes filled with shops, cafes and bars from which drift the strains of Irish music. Thanks to its university and the number of job-providing industries that have come to the town, Galway combines traditional appeal in areas such as its Latin Quarter with modern-day attractions. It is also one of the places where you are more likely to hear Irish spoken. July is particularly atmospheric, as that's when the Galway International Arts Festival (see page 54) takes place. If you're going to be in the city in the last two weeks of July or the first week in August, when the Galway Races are on, reserve accommodation well in advance.

Medieval Galway enjoyed great prosperity through trade not only with the rest of Ireland but also with Spain and with other continental countries. It all came to an end after the city was attacked by Oliver Cromwell in 1652, and again by King William III in 1691, but you can see evidence of this former wealth in embellishments to ancient doorways, window frames and walls. Rich merchants would employ the best stone-carvers to adorn their town houses with their coats of arms, and with grotesque sculptures and heraldic beasts. Lynch's Castle, an impressive 15th-century tower house (now a bank; ground-level display open during business hours), at the intersection known as the Four Corners where William Street becomes Shop Street, is especially well provided with sculptures, as is the Collegiate Church of St Nicholas in Church Lane, with its grave slabs adorned with bas-reliefs showing the tools of the trade followed by the departed. Overlooking the River Corrib, the grand 1965 Roman Catholic cathedral topped by a huge copper dome is dubbed the 'Taj Michael' by locals after the then-Bishop of Galway, Michael Brown.

TAKE IN SOME HISTORY
Lynch's Window
Behind Lynch's Castle on Market Street, a 17th-century window is preserved to mark the spot where in 1493 Mayor James Lynch Fitzstephen personally hanged his own son Walter for murdering a visiting Spaniard. Lynch's Window is at the side of St Nicholas' Church.

Spanish Arch
The famous Tudor-era Spanish Arch is located on the left bank of the Corrib, where Galway's river meets the sea. The Spanish Arch was originally a 16th-century bastion, which was added to Galway's town walls to protect merchant ships from looting.

VISIT THE MUSEUMS
Galway City Museum
galwaycitymuseum.ie
Spanish Parade | 091 532 460
Open Tue–Sat 10–5, Sun 12–5
Parts of the Spanish Arch now form the modern Galway City Museum, a fascinatingly random collection of mementoes, from ancient fishing tools and traps for badgers to the orations of heroes and the pikestaffs of rebels. A highlight is the Claddagh Exhibition.

Nora Barnacle House Museum
Bowling Green, Galway City, County Galway | 091 564 743 | Open mid-May to mid-Sep Mon–Sat 10–5
Number 8 Bowling Green is the home of Nora Barnacle before she eloped with writer James Joyce in 1904.

Thomas Dillon's Claddagh Gold
claddaghring.ie
Quay Street, Galway | 091 566 365
Open Mon–Sat 10–5 Sun 12–4
On Quay Street near the River Corrib you'll find this jewellery shop where you can browse through a small museum and learn the story of the Claddagh Ring, Galway's world-famous love token of two hands clasping a heart.

EXPLORE ON FOOT
John F Kennedy Memorial Park
Galway is a great city to explore on foot. At its heart is the John F Kennedy Memorial Park, an inner-city public park formerly named Eyre Square and still widely known by that name. It is a popular meeting place and

Galway

200 m

hub of activity, and the Eyre Square shopping centre is filled with top-name shops. From here, Galway's chief thoroughfare runs south through the city.

GO SHOPPING

Galway Market

galwaymarket.com

Church Lane, Galway | Open Sat 8–6 (some stands Sun in summer 2–6) This is one of the liveliest street markets in the west of Ireland. You'll find everything from paintings and pottery to fruit and flowers, from local meat and cheeses to olives, toys, herbs and crafts.

CATCH A PERFORMANCE

The Crane

thecranebar.com

2 Sea Road, Galway, County Galway 091 587 419

The Crane hosts Galway's best traditional music sessions. There are two bars, one featuring Irish music every night. An upstairs concert venue features acts three or four nights a week.

Druid Theatre

druid.ie

Flood Street, Galway, County Galway 091 586 660

One of Ireland's best modern theatre companies, Druid is

based in a refurbished former warehouse. This dynamic company puts on Irish classics, and also premieres up-and-coming young playwrights.

SAMPLE THE NIGHTLIFE

Carbon

carbongalway.ie

19–21 Eglinton Street, Galway

091 449 204

Featuring top names in music and guest DJs, Carbon is just a short stroll from Eyre Square.

Róisín Dubh

roisindubh.net

Dominic Street, Galway

091 586 540

Róisín Dubh (it means Black Rose in English) is one of the best known pubs in Galway and this intimate venue is a great place to catch a live gig or even see a comedy show.

PLAY A ROUND

Galway Golf Club

galwaygolf.com

Blackrock, Salthill, Galway

091 522 033

This course is inland by nature, although some of the fairways run close to the ocean. The terrain is of gently sloping hillocks with plenty of trees and furze bushes to catch out the unway. Although not a long course, it continues to delight visiting golfers.

EAT AND DRINK

Ardilaun Hotel and Leisure Club ✹

theardilaunhotel.ie

Taylor's Hill, Galway | 091 521 433

Alternatives of bistro or full-on restaurant dining keep things flexible here, with the main dining room offering cooking in the European country-house manner.

Front Door & Sonnys Bar and Restaurant

frontdoorpub.com

High Street & Cross Street, The Latin Quarter, Galway | 091 563 757

This pub is full of history and has plenty of original features and character. There are actually no less than five bars here – all spread over two floors in this large venue which also includes a restaurant.

The G Hotel ✹✹

theghotel.ie

Wellpark, Dublin Road, Galway

091 865 200

Gendered lounges are in blue for boys, and screaming pink with black-and-white concentric circles for girls. You might think the contemporary Irish brasserie cooking would struggle to keep up but there's plenty of vivacity here too, from laden sharing boards of charcuterie to seafood.

Kellys

kellysbar.ie

5 Bridge Street, Galway

091 563 804

A modern offering, Kelly's is a good place to go for decent food and drink as well as live music. Look out for changing DJs and don't miss the menu offering interesting meat and seafood dishes.

Park House Hotel and Restaurant ◉

parkhousehotel.ie
Forster Street, Eyre Square, Galway
091 564 924
The traditionally inspired cooking here is classically underpinned, while making good use of local ingredients on a menu with broad appeal.

▶ **PLACES NEARBY**

Outside Galway is a 12th-century abbey, a village full of history and great places to eat.

Cong Abbey

megalithicireland.com
Main Street, Cong, County Mayo
Open daily
Cong Abbey consists of 12th-century limestone buildings with elaborately carved pillars. Beside the river is the monks' fishing house – when a fish entered the net, a bell rang in the kitchen.

Quiet Man Heritage Cottage

museumsofmayo.com
Circular Road, Cong, County Mayo
094 954 6089 | Open Easter–Oct daily 10.30–4
Most visitors come to Cong to see the abbey but the village is where John Ford shot most of his 1952 film *The Quiet Man*. The thatched Quiet Man Heritage Cottage has a display on the archaeology and history of the area. You can follow a dry canal dug as a relief project during the Great Famine of 1845–49. It was intended to connect the two lakes but the limestone is so porous that it never held water.

Abbey Hotel Glenlo ◉

glenloabbeyhotel.ie
Kentfield, Bushypark | 2 miles from Galway city centre on the N59 to Clifden | 091 519 600
Float four miles or so upstream on the River Corrib from Galway to find Glenlo, a grandiose country house built in the early Georgian era. It's a splendid design concept, and makes an elegant setting for the traditionally based European cooking on offer.

Lough Inagh Lodge

loughinaghlodgehotel.ie
Inagh Valley, Recess, Connemara, County Galway | 095 34706 and 095 34694
Dating from 1880, when it was built as a fishing lodge, this boutique hotel is in a lovely spot on the shore of Lough Inagh, surrounded by wild mountains. There's an oak-panelled bar, a library with a log fire, and a restaurant where silver and glassware reflect candlelight and an oval window gives wonderful views.

The Pins at The Twelve

thetwelvehotel.ie
Barna Village, County Galway
091 597 000
The Pins is actually an unusual amalgam of bar, bakery, bistro and pizzeria. If you want to keep things simple, the Dozzina pizzeria turns out authentic Neapolitan-style pizzas made in an oven hewn from Vesuvian stone, or you can enjoy the uncomplicated modern dishes of the gastro pub.

▶ Glencolumbkille (Gleann Cholm Cille)

MAP REF 381 D2

gleanncholmcille.ie

There's something special about the atmosphere here in Glencolumbkille, tucked away in a hidden cleft among remote seaward mountains, 6 miles along the R263 from Carrick. This peaceful green valley is where St Columba (born in Donegal in AD 521) established a monastery. Columba is one of Ireland's three patron saints, along with St Patrick and St Brigid.

VISIT THE MUSEUM

Father McDyer's Folk Village Museum

glenfolkvillage.com

Gleann Cholm Cille, County Donegal
074 973 0017 | Open Easter–Sep
Mon–Sat 10–6, Sun 12–6

Also known as the Glencolmcille Folk Village, this folk museum, with its traditional thatched homes, gives an insight into local life. It consists of several small cottages making up a *clachan*, or settlement, on a hillside overlooking Glen Bay Beach, and is one of Ireland's best living-history museums. There is also a lovely tea room.

GO FOR A WALK

Walkers can follow An Turas Cholmcille, Columba's Journey, for 3 miles around 15 stations or sacred sites, to St Columba's Chapel, Bed and Well.

▶ PLACES NEARBY

The surrounding countryside includes dramatic cliffs and gentle, managed parkland. There are also sandy beaches to enjoy, and some atmospheric pubs where you can listen to some music, and have a pint and a chat with the locals.

Slieve League cliffs

Seen from the little parking bay high on a windy ledge at Bunglass, the Slieve League cliffs are hugely impressive – a great wall of multicoloured rock that plunges 1,952 feet into the sea below, claiming the title of 'highest sea cliffs in Europe'. Walkers can teeter along the very narrow 'One Man's Path' to the summit of Slieve League, but not in windy conditions or when the ground is slippery.

The Fleet Inn

fleetinnkillybegs.com

Bridge Street, Killybegs, County Donegal | 074 973 1518

This small, family-run business offers accommodation as well as a bar, and a restaurant with a menu serving fresh local fish and seafood.

Slieve League Lodge

slieveleaguelodge.com

Main Street, Carrick, County Donegal | 074 973 9973

Enjoy a drink in the bar or a great meal in the restaurant at this friendly holiday hostel in Carrick, at the heart of the Slieve League Peninsula. It makes an ideal base for exploring the area.

▶ Glendalough & the Wicklow Mountains MAP REF 379 E3

The combination of a well-preserved monastic settlement with a beautiful lake and mountain setting makes Glendalough and the Wicklow Mountains one of eastern Ireland's premier attractions. The reclusive St Kevin first established a monastic presence in this U-shaped glacial valley in AD 570. The remote location was ideal for his hermitic tendencies, but he emphasised them still further by spending time in a cave (St Kevin's Bed), accessible only by boat, on the cliffs above the Upper Lough. St Kevin came from one of Leinster's ruling families and was abbot here until his death in AD 618. He encouraged Glendalough's reputation for learning and its renown spread across Europe.

Place of pilgrimage

This was a place of pilgrimage too; seven trips here were equivalent to one trip to Rome even as late as 1862. Though it survived Viking and Norman raids, as well as those of indigenous bandits, the settlement began to decline in importance with the wave of French monastic foundations that followed the Anglo-Norman occupation of Ireland. But there were still monks in residence here when the monastery was dissolved in the 16th century. St Kevin's feast day (3 June) continued to draw visitors to Glendalough into the 19th century, by which time the monks had acquired a rather bawdy reputation. The middle of that century saw an increased interest in archaeology and the site was taken over by the Commissioners of Public Works in 1869.

▼ The Upper Lough at Glendalough

Church and cathedral

Glendalough means 'Valley of the two loughs', although the
principal site is below the Lower Lough on slightly raised land by
the confluence of the Gledasan and Glenalo rivers. Here are the
ruins of St Ciarán's Church and St Kevin's Church, often called
St Kevin's Kitchen because its tower resembles the chimney stack
of a bakehouse. A double arch by the Glendalough Hotel leads you
into the churchyard where the remnants of the cathedral stand, its
ninth-century nave and chancel now roofless. The Priest's House
contains carvings of St Kevin and dates from the 12th century. The
110-foot tower would have served as a belfry, lookout and treasury.

Cross and cemetery

Although the conical roof has been restored, the rest of the tower
is in its original condition, an indication of how well this site has
been preserved. There's a high cross here, though its impact is
lessened somewhat by the proliferation of wheelhead motifs
adorning the surrounding graves – this is still a working cemetery
for the residents of the glen and the nearby village of Laragh. On
the far side of the churchyard, the 10th-century St Mary's Church
may have housed St Kevin's tomb.

Ancient history

Between the visitor centre and the bridge stands the Deerstone,
which despite its spurious legend of a doe squirting milk into its
hollow to feed Kevin's disciples, is actually a much older grinding
stone from the glen's prehistoric inhabitants. Beyond the Lower
Lough, another group of important sites includes the 10th-century
Reefert Church, with its tombs of local chiefs, and St Kevin's Cell,
the beehive-style hut where the settlement began.

Waterfalls and mines

Above here, you can walk up past the tumbling Poulanass Waterfall
into the surrounding mountains, or follow the old miners' road up

along the northern shore of the Upper Lough to see the remains of the lead and silver mines that were established in the rocky outcrops at the head of the valley. These were part of a larger 19th-century mining operation in the next glen.

Take a walk

The free visitor centre parking area is the best spot to start from to see all the sites on foot. There are clearly waymarked paths between the principal sites, and the two lakes and the mountains that surround them are superb walking territory, whether you're looking for a woodland stroll or a more challenging upland circuit.

On the cliffs on the south side of the lough, the peculiar Teampull na Skellig is a platform cut into the rock, the site of the very early Church of the Rock. Near St Kevin's Bed is a Bronze Age burial site, later associated with Kevin's escape from Kathleen, a temptress whom he allegedly threw in the lough to drown. The tale conveniently bolsters the early fathers' belief that women were the source of all corruption.

CHECK OUT THE VISITOR CENTRE

Glendalough Visitor Centre
Glendalough, Bray, County Wicklow
0404 45325 | Open daily mid-Mar to mid-Oct 9.30–6, mid-Oct to mid-Mar 9.30–5

At the entrance to the glen, just beyond the site of the Trinity Chapel at Glendalough, is the visitor centre for the monastic settlement and Wicklow Mountains National Park. The visitor centre helps you to understand not just what you can see on the ground but also its place in Irish history. The main audiovisual presentation lasts for 17 minutes and concentrates on Glendalough's Christian heritage. The interactive displays are more balanced, and explain the key features: the high cross, the carvings and the round tower, one of the most recognisable landmarks in the area. A scale model shows what the monastic settlement might have looked like in the 12th century.

GET OUTDOORS
Wicklow Mountains National Park

wicklowmountainsnationalpark.ie

The Wicklow Mountains National Park rises from the suburbs of south Dublin and covers some 49,420 acres of high granite moors, wooded valleys and lakes. The highest point is 3,035-foot Lugnaquilla, a rounded peak rising above Glenmalur. The mountains are traversed by the spectacular military road from Dublin to Laragh, and crossed by the high passes of the Wicklow Gap and the Sally Gap. In the western foothills, several valleys have been flooded to form Blessington Lake, sometimes called Pollaphuca Reservoir.

GET ACTIVE
Kippure Estate

kippure.com

Manor Kilbride, Blessington, County Wicklow | 01 458 2889 | Open sessions May–Sep Sat, Sun 1.30–4.30

On a 240-acre site just over the River Liffey from the Wicklow Mountains National Park, this adventure centre specialises in rope-based activities. There's a high ropes course, zip-line and plenty of opportunities for climbing and abseiling, as well as orienteering, mountain walking, geocaching, archery and even a family treasure hunt. There is also paintballing and golf. Bed-and-breakfast and self-catering units are available in the grounds and staying there earns a discount on the activities.

PLAY A ROUND
Tulfarris Hotel and Golf Resort

tulfarris.com

Blessington, County Wicklow

01 045 867 609

This course, designed by Paddy Merrigan, is on the Blessington lakeshore with the Wicklow Mountains as a backdrop. The use of the natural landscape is evident throughout the course, the variety of trees guarding fairways and green approaches.

▶ PLACES NEARBY

The beautiful gardens of Mount Usher are worth a visit.

Mount Usher Gardens

mountushergardens.ie

Ashford, County Wicklow

040 440 205 | Open daily 10–6

There is a deliberately natural style to the delightful Mount Usher Gardens, which are one of Ireland's best-loved gardens. Lining the banks of the Vartry River on the southern edge of Ashford, they were begun in 1868 by Edward Walpole, a Dublin businessman, who used Mount Usher as a base for walking in the Wicklow Mountains. There are more than 5,000 plant specimens from all over the world across the estate's 19 acres, including azaleas, Chinese conifers, bamboos, Mexican pines and pampas grasses. The maples are particularly fine in autumn and the river acts as a unifying feature. The charming Avoca Garden Café, nestled in the trees, is well worth a visit.

▲ Glenveagh Castle

▶ **Glenveagh National Park**   MAP REF 382 B2

glenveaghnationalpark.ie

Churchill, Letterkenny, County Donegal | 076 100 2537 | Open daily
Mar–Oct 9–6, Nov–Feb 9–5

Ireland's second-largest national park, Glenveagh covers some
40,000 acres in the Derryveagh Mountains and was previously
a private deer forest. These days, the park offers a range of
walks, from family-friendly to more demanding, and the chance
to spot local wildlife such as hares, falcons and ravens.

The visitor centre on the northern end of Lough Veagh has
a number of interesting displays and information on the park's
history and the walking trails. There is also a restaurant.

TAKE IN SOME HISTORY
Glenveagh Castle

glenveaghnationalpark.ie

Glenveagh National Park, Churchill,
Letterkenny, County Donegal | 076
100 2537 | Gardens open from dawn
until dusk all year round. Access to
the castle is by guided tour

Queen Victoria had popularised
Scottish Baronial style when
John George Adair built
Glenveagh Castle in 1870–73.
Adair, a harsh, evicting
landlord, bought a vast area of
Donegal and chose the most
scenic spot for his granite
castle and its gardens and
grounds, looking across Lough
Beagh to the rugged backbone
of the Derryveagh Mountains
(Sléibhte Dhoire Bheatha).
Adair's American wife Cornelia
introduced the rhododendrons
that now flower so vividly here
in early summer.

Later, American owner
Henry Plumer McIlhenny
improved and landscaped the
gardens, so that today, after a
tour of the chic but comfortable
rooms of the castle, visitors
can stroll through a judicious
blend of native and exotic
plants and trees.

Mount Errigal (An Earagail)
The quartzite cone of Mount Errigal is a landmark in northwest County Donegal. At 2,468 feet (752m) it is the highest of Donegal's many mountains, and its peak of naked quartzite gleams like snow. Approaching along the R251 from Bunbeg you see the rugged screes, corries and cliffs of the mountain's west face at their most formidable. Once you have passed the bulk of Errigal it seems much less daunting.

Errigal is in fact an easy mountain to climb if you are sensibly shod, reasonably fit and prepared for a sudden change in the weather. The path up the eastern ridge leaves a pull-off on the R251 at a 'walking man' waymark and makes a steady ascent of around 1,738 feet, following a clear track over heather and then broken quartzite. There's a surprise at the top – the mountain has a twin summit, with the two peaks linked by a very narrow ridge. Wonderful views over the lakes and mountains of Donegal, and south to Sligo's Benbulben, on a clear day, amply reward the effort of the climb.

GET OUTDOORS
Glenveagh National Park Visitor Centre
glenveaghnationalpark.ie
Churchill, Letterkenny, County Donegal | 076 100 2537 | Open daily Mar–Oct 9–6, Nov–Feb 9–5
Located at the northern end of Lough Veagh, near the edge of the National Park, the visitor centre has a living heather roof to mimic its surroundings. Inside are extensive displays explaining the park's natural and built history and providing information on events and walking trails. The duty guides can also provide information about the park, as well as tickets for the park buses.

▼ Glenveagh National Park

▶ **PLACES NEARBY**

Within striking distance west of the National Park is the coast with views to Tory Island. To the east is Letterkenny, an attractive former market town.

Bloody Foreland (Cnoc Fola)

The best time to visit Bloody Foreland is an hour before sunset, when the sun tips the cliffs around Altawinny Bay and makes them glow blood-red to dramatic effect. With the cone of Bloody Foreland rising behind, you look out across the sea towards the long, low bar of Tory Island (Toraigh) on the northern horizon. The headland is signposted off R257 between Bunbeg (An Bun Beag) and Gortahork (Gort an Choirce).

An Grianán Theatre

angrianan.com
Port Road, Letterkenny, County Donegal | 074 912 0777
County Donegal's biggest and most versatile theatre offers a varied performance schedule that includes plays, stand-up comedy, dance, children's plays and shows, musicals and a wide range of music, from rock to jazz and cabaret to crooners.

Radisson Blu Hotel Letterkenny ◉

radissonblu.ie/hotel-letterkenny
Paddy Harte Road, Letterkenny, County Donegal | 074 919 4444
This outpost of the Radisson Blu group is in the centre of Letterkenny and has facilities aplenty. The Port Bar and Grill can sort you out for a quick lunch, but the TriBeCa Restaurant catches the eye.

Arnolds Hotel ◉

arnoldshotel.com
Dunfanaghy, County Donegal
074 913 6208
Arnolds Hotel is a comfortable and comforting place, with open fires in the winter, and a restaurant capitalising on those coastal views. The kitchen takes a fuss-free approach, relying on quality raw materials and sound technique to make the most of flavours.

▶ **Hill of Tara** MAP REF 379 D1

hilloftara.org

Near Navan, County Meath | 046 902 5903 (May–Oct), 041 988 0300
(Nov–Apr) | Main site: open mid-May to mid-Sep daily dawn–dusk
Visitor centre: mid-May to mid-Sep daily 10–6

Bathed in Celtic myth, Tara is one of Ireland's historical treasures.
It has played a central role in early Irish history and has more than
30 visible monuments, part of a ritual landscape with an unbroken
history of 4,000 years up to the sixth century AD. Located near the
River Boyne, this archaeological complex runs between Navan and
Dunshaughlin. Among the more impressive remains is the Mound
of the Hostages, a passage grave which contained 40 Bronze Age
cremations. Tours and an audiovisual display are available in
summer from the visitor centre in St Patrick's Church on the site. If
it's closed, a tea-and-gift shop sells books with explanations of the
monuments. Names recall the site's importance as home of the
High Kings of Ireland – the Royal Enclosure, Rath of the Synods,
Banquet Hall. In a ring feature known as Cormac's House, the Lia
Fáil is the stone on which High Kings were crowned. On a clear
day it is claimed that you can see half the counties of Ireland
from Tara and from the east the view reaches all the way to the
Mountains of Mourne.

▶ PLACES NEARBY

Bective Abbey (see page 178),
another place of historical
religious interest, lies to the
west of the Hill of Tara. Still
standing are some of the
15th-century additions and
a medieval river bridge.

▼ Aerial view of the Hill of Tara

▶ Holy Cross Abbey MAP REF 378 B4

Holycross, Thurles, County Tipperary | 086 1665 869 | Tours Wed, Sun at 2

In a landscape dotted with ruined abbeys, Holy Cross Abbey is a surprise – restored and very much alive. It is considered to be one of Tipperary's gems. It was founded as a Cistercian house in 1180 by Donal Mór O'Brien, and extensively rebuilt in the mid-15th century by James Butler, fourth Earl of Ormond. Its fragment of the True Cross made it Ireland's top pilgrimage site, until the effects of the Dissolution took their toll in the 16th century and it was abandoned. An Act of Parliament in 1969 enabled its reconstruction, and it reopened in 1975.

Functional buildings form two sides of the cloister, with the mighty limestone church on the north side. Inside, the church feels cool and modern, with its whitewashed walls, vaulted roof of grey stone, plain glass windows, modern altar and raked floor. Look for the faint traces of a medieval mural on the west wall, and the Gothic stone sedilia (canopied seats) in the chancel. Michael, a 750-year-old bell, is said to be the oldest church bell in Ireland. The modern Padre Pio gardens have bronze Stations of the Cross by Enrico Manfrini.

▶ PLACES NEARBY

The town of **Thurles** is just northeast of the abbey.

Thurles Farmers' Market

Thurles, County Tipperary

A lively farmers' market takes place on Saturdays outside the greyhound track in Thurles.

Turtulla Garden

Turtulla, Thurles, County Tipperary
050 421 839

This award-winning garden has over 30 varieties of daffodils and many trees, shrubs and roses. Some plants are for sale.

Inch House Country House and Restaurant ◉

inchhouse.ie
Thurles, County Tipperary
050 451 348 and 050 451 261

Inch House is the hub of a working farm run by the Egan family. They run the hotel and farm the land, and the land provides a lot of the ingredients for the restaurant – they make their own black pudding, too – and what isn't home-grown won't have travelled very far. This is country-house cooking.

▼ Holy Cross Abbey

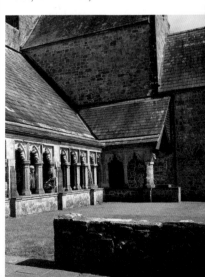

▶ Hook Head Peninsula MAP REF 379 D5

County Wexford points a finger into the crashing waters of the Atlantic Ocean at Hook Head. The lighthouse at the end of the peninsula is one of the oldest working lighthouses in the world. Records show its origins to be in the fifth century AD and its red sandstone base dates from 1172.

Hook Head is a strange place. A walk along the water's edge reveals blowholes – best seen on a blustery day as long as you exercise caution – and dangerous rocky ledges. It's no place for a swim: even on calm days there can be freakishly large waves. Two abbeys were founded at the base of the peninsula. A tour of Hook Head should also include Duncannon, a seaside resort with a huge sandy beach and an excellent star-shaped fort from the 16th century, and Slade, where the ruins of a 15th-century castle guard a tiny fishing harbour.

TAKE IN SOME HISTORY

Hook Lighthouse and Heritage Centre

hookheritage.ie
Hook Head, County Wexford | 051 397 055 | Open daily for guided tours Jun–Aug 10–5.30, every 30 min, Sep–May 11–5, every 30 min

This is the oldest intact operational lighthouse in the world; the structure is around 800 years old. You can take a tour and climb the 115 steps to the top – the view, as you would expect, is spectacular. You might see seals, dolphins and even whales. There are visitor facilities, including a shop and cafe, in the former lighthouse-keeper's cottages.

Tintern Abbey

hookpeninsula.com
Saltmills, New Ross, County Wexford
051 562 650 (winter 056 772 4623)
Open 2 Apr–28 Oct daily 10–5
A Cistercian monastery named after Tintern Abbey in Wales, this was one of the most powerful monastic foundations

◀ Wild flowers at Hook Head ▲ Hook Head Lighthouse

in southeast Ireland. It was founded around 1200 by William, the Earl Marshall. In the 1790s part of the abbey was converted and used as a residence by the Colcough family. The remains include the nave, chancel, chapel, tower and cloisters.

Duncannon Fort
duncannonfort.com
Duncannon, New Ross,
County Wexford

This star-shaped fortress is ideally located in a strategic position in Waterford Harbour. It dates from 1588 and was built as a defence against attack by the Spanish Armada. It has a 30-foot dry moat, and the outer ramparts have impressive views across the estuary and down to Hook Head. It's currently closed for renovation.

TOUR THE VILLAGES
Duncannon
Duncannon is dominated by its 16th-century fort, and also has a small, busy harbour. The beach is very popular – unusually, you can take your car down onto it.

Slade
Slade is a charming little fishing village. There's not much here except the castle (not open to the public) and the quaint harbour, which was built as a famine-relief project in the 1860s. The castle was built by the Laffan family, who were among the first colonists to arrive in the Norman invasion of the 12th century. They became wealthy merchant traders who prospered in late medieval times. Parts of the castle probably date from the 15th century.

HIT THE BEACH
Duncannon beach
The sand here is supposed to be particularly superior – and to prove it, the town is host to a sand-sculpting festival which takes place in August.

▶ Howth   MAP REF 379 E2

The peninsula of Howth (rhymes with 'both') Head forms the northern arm of Dublin Bay, and is visible from many parts of the city. It is heavily developed, but the shore itself is mostly cliff and has therefore escaped the middle-class housing that spreads around its central hill. A waymarked path stretches for 5 miles around the head itself, passing the Baily lighthouse, and makes an invigorating walk (you can catch a bus back).

Howth town is a fishing port, its harbour facing the rocky islet of Ireland's Eye. Boat trips to view its puffin colony, Martello tower and sixth-century monastic ruins are available. Little remains of St Mary's Abbey except a shell rising above the steep streets of the town but, about half a mile to the west, signs to the Deer Park Hotel also lead to the grounds of Howth Castle (not open) and the National Transport Museum. The best views are from 510-foot Ben of Howth, near The Summit Inn.

VISIT THE MUSEUM
National Transport Museum
nationaltransportmuseum.org
Heritage Depot, Howth Castle
Demesne, County Dublin | 01 832
0427 | Open Jun–Aug Mon–Sat
10–5, Sep–May Sat, Sun 2–5
The transport museum, with its collection of public service and commercial road transport vehicles, contains lovingly restored trams, buses, fire engines and more.

GET ON THE WATER
Howth Boats
Howth-boats.com
43 St Nessan's Terrace, Howth,
County Dublin | 085 813 5193
Half- and whole-day trips for sea-angling (including winter fishing and summer evenings), birdwatching and sightseeing. Explore Dublin Bay and Ireland's Eye bird sanctuary.

EAT AND DRINK
Summit Inn
summitinn.ie
Howth, County Dublin
01 832 4615
Located on the summit of Howth Hill, the pub is cosy and traditional, with a turf fire in the bar and wonderful views. Pub grub includes fresh local fish.

▶ PLACES NEARBY
Dún Laoghaire (see page 289) lies to the south, and Dublin (see page 248) to the west.

◀ The cliffs at Howth

▶ Kildare   MAP REF 379 D2

The low-lying county of Kildare is horse-racing territory: more than 140 registered stud farms breed world-class, flat-racing horses and, in Punchestown and the Curragh County, Kildare has two of the country's leading racecourses. For this reason, Kildare town's principal attractions are related to the National Stud, a state-owned venture breeding some of the most famous horses in the world. Next to the stud, a pair of renowned gardens have been planted. The Japanese Garden reflects the passion of the Edwardian era for Eastern religious design. The more recent St Fiachra's Garden follows modern concepts, allowing a more natural habitat to develop. Kildare is also a favourite destination for serious shoppers, with a thriving outlet nearby, and the town has a good cultural and social scene.

Kildare's central square is pleasantly quiet, with a heritage and information centre in the restored 18th-century Market House. In the early Christian period there was a monastic settlement in Kildare, dedicated to St Brigid. It was badly damaged in a Viking raid in AD 835, but its surviving round tower is the second tallest in Ireland.

For centuries Kildare was a frontier town on the edge of the English Pale (area controlled by England). At times its position was so precarious that it almost vanished completely as a settlement. However, with the development of the Curragh, and the construction of the turnpike road from Dublin to southwest Ireland in the middle of the 17th century, the town's fortunes revived. You can see the last vestiges of Kildare Castle behind the Silken Thomas public house.

Although a motorway cuts across its heart, the area known as the Curragh, which begins on the eastern edge of town, is still the largest tract of semi-natural grassland in Europe.

▼ The gardens at the National Stud

The space and grass attracted the attentions of horse breeders in the 13th century and racing enthusiasts from the 18th century. The racecourse is now the headquarters of flat racing in Ireland and stages up to 20 meetings a year.

The wide open space of the Curragh has also always appealed to soldiers. The British established military bases here, which are still in use by the modern Irish army. The main hub of military life is at the Curragh Camp, 5 miles to the east.

TAKE IN SOME HISTORY
St Brigid's Cathedral
Market Square, Kildare, County Kildare | 045 530 672 | Open Mon–Sat 10–1, 2–5, Sun 2–5

Kildare's Cathedral has had a chequered past. Its Gothic predecessor was destroyed by Cromwell's troops in 1641 and it wasn't until 1896 that its restoration was completed. Today it houses religious artefacts that include a 16th-century vault, religious seals and a medieval font. It is open to the public by arrangement (tel 045 530 672). The structure reflects the defensive function of the cathedral, with Irish parapets and walkways a distinctive feature of the roof. In the grounds are the foundations of an ancient Fire Temple that was surrounded by a ring of twigs, inside which no man was allowed to enter. The flame was extinguished in the 16th century but has been recreated in the Market Square. In 2006, President Mary McAleese presented the St Brigid's Flame to the people of Ireland on St Brigid's feast day, 1 February. Also in the grounds is a fine Celtic stone cross. Check out the visitor centre.

Kildare Town Heritage Centre
Market Square, Kildare, County Kildare | 045 530 672 Open Mon–Sat 9.30–1, 2–5

Here you can watch a 12-minute video explaining the area's history and read about the significance of the Curragh for horse-racing and the military.

VISIT THE HORSES
The National Stud
irishnationalstud.ie
Irish National Stud, Tully, Kildare, County Kildare | 045 521 617 Visitor centre open mid-Feb to mid-Dec daily 9.30–5

The National Stud was founded at Tully on the edge of Kildare town by Colonel William Hall-Walker in 1900. This was once the site of the 12th-century Black Abbey and its scant remains can still be seen. Hall-Walker was the heir to a Scottish brewing family and had theories about the astrological influences on stock breeding. The stable buildings have lantern roofs designed to ensure the correct parts of the night sky would illuminate the stallions. He gave the whole complex to the British government and was rewarded with a title, Lord Wavertree. In the 1940s, the complex was transferred to the Irish state. Today there are up to 10 stallions at work per season, with each one able to service more than 70 mares at around €85,000 each.

The best time to visit is between February and July, when there will be foals in the stables and paddocks. As well as guided tours of the paddocks and stable blocks, you can visit the Horse Museum, which contains memorabilia and the skeleton of Arkle, one of the stud's most famous racehorses.

GO ROUND THE GARDENS
The Japanese Gardens
irishnationalstud.ie
Irish National Stud, Tully, Kildare, County Kildare | 045 521 617
Gardens open Feb–early Nov daily 9–6

There's more to the stud than horses. It was here that Colonel Hall-Walker established the Japanese Gardens on reclaimed bogland between 1906 and 1910. They were designed by Tassa Eida, a renowned Japanese gardener, and his son Minoru. Their significance is not purely horticultural for they also portray the journey of a man through life, from his birth to the afterlife. The set pieces have names such as the Hill of Ambition, the Marriage Bridge, the Hill of Learning, the Island of Joy and Wonder and the Tunnel of Ignorance. As you might expect, there are pagodas and little red bridges alongside some important specimen trees and bushes.

St Fiachra's Garden
Irish National Stud, Tully, Kildare, County Kildare | 045 521 617
Open mid-Feb to mid-Dec daily 9.30–5

There is a spiritual feel to St Fiachra's Garden, built to commemorate the millennium – the sixth-century Irish cleric St Fiachra is the patron saint of gardeners. Designed by Martin Hallinan, it uses limestone and water to create an island hermitage. Its woodland, wetland and rock give it a much more natural feel than the other-worldly atmosphere of the Japanese Gardens. An inner subterranean garden is decorated with Waterford crystal, lighting the darkness of the hermit's cave. A statue of St Fiachra himself, holding a symbolic seed of creation, sits on a rock that juts into the lake.

CATCH A PERFORMANCE
Cunningham's
Main Street, Kildare, County Kildare
045 521 780

There's live traditional music most nights of the week in Kildare's bright, welcoming pubs. Cunningham's is a pretty Victorian pub with a warm welcome and open fire, offering good music, food and *craic*.

GO TO THE RACES
The Curragh
curragh.ie
Curragh Racecourse, County Kildare
045 441 205

The word Curragh may derive from the Irish Gaelic for 'racecourse', such is the pedigree of this famous flat-racing venue. The headquarters for flat racing in Ireland, there are five classic meets here every year and as many as 18 others between March and October.

Naas Racecourse
naasracecourse.com
Tipper Road, Naas, County Kildare
045 897 391

Naas is one of two horse-racing circuits near this small Kildare town. It's an important course for spotting this year's National Hunt hopefuls in February.

Punchestown Racecourse
punchestown.com
Punchestown, Naas, County Kildare
045 897 704

The Punchestown National Hunt horse-racing festival, held in April or May, draws visitors from all over Europe, and the course has been redeveloped to reflect this international popularity, with new stands and hospitality facilities.

GO SHOPPING
Kildare Shopping Village
kildarevillage.com
Nurney Road, Kildare, County Kildare | 045 520 501

Designer clothes, jewellery and luxury goods are all to be found in this chic outlet that offers discount prices on top brands.

PLAY A ROUND
Royal Curragh Golf Club
royalcurraghgolf.com
Curragh, County Kildare
045 441 714

A particularly challenging course, well wooded and with lovely scenery all around.

EAT AND DRINK
Ballyfin Demesne ◉◉
ballyfin.com
Ballyfin, County Laois
057 875 5866

Possibly Ireland's most opulent Regency house, standing in over 600 acres, Ballyfin makes a grand country hotel, with only 20 guest rooms, so you won't need to feel shoehorned in. A walled garden supplies the kitchen with plenty of produce, as do the resident bees, and lucky human residents are regaled with menus of French-inspired contemporary cooking of considerable dazzle.

▶ **PLACES NEARBY**

Places of fact and folklore can be found not far from Kildare. Emo village has a stunning mansion and Rathbridge lays claim to a holy well.

Emo Court

heritageireland.ie

Emo, County Laois | Signposted from the N7 Kildare–Portlaoise road 057 862 6573 | Open Easter–Oct daily 10–6

Emo Court is a neoclassical mansion designed by architect James Gandon, who is best known for great public building works such as Dublin's Custom House (see page 253). He designed it for the Earl of Portarlington in 1792. The family was in residence here until 1920, when it became a Jesuit seminary. The house was restored during the 1970s, and it was acquired by the Irish nation in 1996.

The focal points as you approach are the green dome that tops the building and the imposing colonnaded portico through which you enter. The inside is full of fine plasterwork and *trompe l'oeil* decoration.

The gardens are divided into two principal parts – the Grapery, with a path leading through the shrubberies down to the lakeshore, and the Clucker – so called because it was laid out on the site of a former nunnery – where rhododendrons and azaleas bring a riot of early summer colours among the cedars, pines and maples.

Father Moore's Well

Rathbridge, between Kildare and Milltown, County Kildare

One of Ireland's holy wells, the story of Father Moore's well was recorded by Lord Walter Fitzgerald in 1918. Father Moore had a reputation for curing various ailments and he blessed this well before his death in 1826.

Irish Parachute Club

skydive.ie

Clonbullogue Airfield, on the R401, 7 miles south of Edenderry, County Offaly | 046 973 0103

Experience the ultimate adrenalin thrill, if you have the nerve. An hour's instruction is followed by the jump from a plane, attached to an instructor.

Riverbank Arts Centre

riverbank.ie

Main Street, Newbridge, County Kildare | 045 448 327 | Open Mon–Fri 10–2, 2.30–5.30, Sat 10–1

A modern complex for the arts in one of Kildare's fast-growing towns, the Riverbank promotes all forms of popular, classical and traditional music, stages plays and has gallery space.

The Dew Drop

dewdropinn.ie

Main Street, Kill, County Kildare 045 877 755

Enjoy the best in local as well as international drinks at this traditional pub with some very modern ideas. There is a high standard of food on the menu which makes it one of the best gastro pubs in the area.

▶ **Kilkenny** MAP REF 378 C4

Regularly voted Ireland's friendliest city, Kilkenny is a welcoming and historic place, famous for its beer and castles. There are also a number of local gold- and silversmiths here who make lovely jewellery.

The area rose to prominence in the 13th century along with the powerful Anglo-Norman Butler family, the Earls of Ormond. Their castle rises above a bend in the River Nore, looking out over a modern urban core with plenty of historic nooks. The local limestone produces a black stone known as Kilkenny marble, seen on many of the city's public buildings.

St Canice founded the monastic settlement here in the sixth century and by the 13th century the adjacent town had become an important base for Norman rule in Leinster. Parliaments were held here from the 13th to the 15th centuries. In 1366, the notorious Statute of Kilkenny was passed, forbidding English settlers from speaking Irish, wearing Irish clothes or marrying Irish women. The natives were excluded from the city and to this day the area around St Canice's, which lay beyond the city wall, is known as Irishtown. By the 17th century, however, the city had become a focal point of Catholic resistance. A confederate parliament was established in 1642, with money and arms from the Vatican. It dissolved acrimoniously in 1648, and by 1650 Cromwell arrived at the city gates with a considerable army. The siege lasted five days but was ended without the bloodletting that characterised his occupation of Wexford or Drogheda. Today, the city is best known for its beer – Smithwick's brewery occupies the site of the old Franciscan friary.

TAKE IN SOME HISTORY
Kilkenny Castle
kilkennycastle.ie
The Parade, Kilkenny | 056 770 4106 | Open daily Jun–Aug 9–5.30, Apr–May, Sep 9.30–5.30, Oct–Feb 9.30–4.30, Mar 9.30–5

The Anglo-Norman chief Richard de Clare (Strongbow) first built a wooden castle on the rocky bend above the river in 1172. His son-in-law, William Marshall, Earl of Pembroke, strengthened it with local stone and created the medieval stronghold that remains today. James Butler, third Earl of Ormond, bought the castle in 1391 and his family stayed until 1935, when the castle was acquired by the Irish state.

In the late 17th and early 18th centuries the Butler family's wealth grew and they improved their castle by adding a classical gateway and removing the war-damaged east wall. In the late 18th century came the gardens and stables (now Kilkenny Design Centre (see

Kilkenny

page 316). The 19th century saw the creation of the Long Gallery to house the family's considerable art collection, and the addition of the south curtain wall created extra bedrooms.

The castle you now see displays this Victorian elegance. As well as the impressive Long Gallery, with its portraits and hammer-beam roof, you see the Chinese Bedroom, reflecting the Victorians' Oriental obsession, the drawing room, library and ante room, all exquisitely furnished. The 50-acre parkland includes a formal rose garden as well as mature woodland. Off the servants' corridor, by the old kitchen (now a bookshop), is the Butler Gallery of Contemporary Art (free), with exhibitions by international artists and sculptors.

St Canice's Cathedral

stcanicescathedral.ie
The Close, Coach Road, Kilkenny
056 776 4971 | Open Jun–Aug
Mon–Sat 9–6, Sun 2–6, Apr–May,
Sep Mon–Sat 10–1, 2–5, Sun 2–5,
Oct–Mar Mon–Sat 10–1, 2–4,
Sun 2–4

The original site dates back to the sixth century and worship has taken place here for over 800 years. The present cathedral was built in the 13th century in the early English Gothic style, but suffered in 1332 when its tower collapsed under the weight of lead on its roof. This over-zealous application was a penance imposed on William Outlaw for consorting with Dame Alice Kyteler, who had been accused of witchcraft. The Kyteler family slab is the oldest memorial in the cathedral. The round tower, to the east of the building, has lost its cone but still commands impressive views of the town and countryside. It is 100 feet high and dates from AD 849, when the cathedral was at the core of a monastic settlement. You can see traces of this Romanesque structure in the arches of the choir's north wall and in the north transept door. Cromwell's troops stabled their horses inside, smashed all the windows and threw out the monuments. When they were put back no one could remember their original places, so they now stand in orderly lines. Just beyond the cathedral, on Kenny's Well Road, you will find a little well house containing St Canice's Holy Well, dating back to at least the sixth century.

VISIT THE MUSEUM
Rothe House
Parliament Street, Kilkenny, County Kilkenny | 056 772 2893 | Open Apr–Oct Mon–Sat 10.30–5, Sun 3–5, Nov–Mar Mon–Sat 10.30–4
Across the road from the courthouse, Rothe House was built in 1594 around a cobbled courtyard and is now home to a small museum.

GO SHOPPING
Kilkenny Design Centre
kilkennydesign.com
Castle Yard, Kilkenny, County Kilkenny | 056 772 2118
Drawing on the skills of more than 200 artisans from all over Ireland, this is a nationally recognised outlet for a wide range of crafts. The emphasis is

▼ Aerial view of Kilkenny

on natural fibres and materials, be they linen, silk, wool or cashmere for clothing, silver and gold for jewellery, locally made, hand-blown Jerpoint glassware, or traditional and contemporary gifts made from wood and porcelain. Upstairs is an excellent cafe and restaurant overlooking the courtyard, and a food hall where you can pick up tasty local specialities.

WALK AROUND TOWN

Kilkenny is a medieval gem. On many occasions, war and wild times have swept through the little town and, as well as its impressive castle and cathedral, a walk reveals so much more. Kilkenny's 16th-century tavern, Hole in the Wall, is in the oldest town house in Ireland, the 1582 Archer Inner House on 17 High Street. On Parliament Street, the courthouse has a 19th-century classical frontage on a fortified medieval house, built in 1210 and which once served as a prison. Ask at the tourist office, which is in the Tudor Shee Alms Houses, about the one-hour walking tours that give an amusing introduction to the town.

SAMPLE REAL ALES
The Smithwick's Experience
smithwicksexperience.com
Parliament Street, next to the courthouse, Kilkenny, County Kilkenny | 056 778 6377
Open daily 10–6
Take a tour to discover how this local ale was made into a world-class brew. The story begins in the 13th century and ends with a pint, of course.

CATCH A PERFORMANCE
Watergate Theatre
watergatetheatre.com
Parliament Street, Kilkenny, County Kilkenny | 056 776 1674
Enjoy professional and amateur drama, and contemporary and classical music at one of southeast Ireland's foremost arts complexes.

▼ Kilkenny Castle

PLAY A ROUND
Kilkenny Golf Club
kilkennygolfclub.com
Kilkenny, County Kilkenny
056 776 5400
One of Ireland's most pleasant inland courses, noted for its tricky finishing holes and its par threes. Features of the course are its long 11th and 13th holes and the challenge increases yearly as thousands of trees planted over the last 30 years or so are maturing. Sand-based greens make the course playable all year round.

EAT AND DRINK
Left Bank
leftbank.ie
The Parade, Kilkenny, County Kilkenny | 056 775 0016
Originally purpose-built for the Bank of Ireland in 1870, this is a splendid building now operating as a bar with a variety of venues over three storeys. Live music is a feature and food is served until 5pm.

Tynan's Bridge House
2 St John's Bridge, Kilkenny, County Kilkenny | 056 772 1291
A traditional and historic spot with lots of cosy corners, this classic old pub has a charming horseshoe bar. Don't miss the live music on Wednesdays and Sundays at 9pm.

▶ PLACES NEARBY
Speleologists will delight in the huge Dunmore Cave south of Kilkenny, while famous Jerpoint Abbey is further south on the River Nore.

Dunmore Cave
heritageireland.ie
Ballyfoyle, Castlecomer Road, Kilkenny | 056 776 7726 | Open mid-Jun to mid-Sep daily 9.30–6.30, mid-Mar to mid-Jun, mid-Sep to Oct daily 9.30–5, Nov to mid-Mar Wed–Sun 9.30–5
This impressive cave lies on a gentle rise in the limestone hills south of Kilkenny. An interpretative area guards the entrance, and visits to the fantastical arrays of stalactites and stalagmites below ground are by guided tour. A steep series of 706 steps leads into the cave, which has three main chambers and contains traces of occupation stretching back more than 3,500 years. The 23-foot-high 'Market Cross' is just one of the huge stalagmites in chasms known as the 'Cathedral' and the 'Town Hall'.

In the interpretative area you can see interactive displays of remains and treasures found in the cave. The most macabre remains are those of the 44 women and children who possibly suffocated during a Viking raid in AD 928. In 1999, Viking coins and silver jewellery were discovered here.

Jerpoint Abbey
heritageireland.ie
Thomastown, County Kilkenny
056 772 4623 | Open daily Jun to mid-Sep 10–6, Mar–May, mid-Sep to Oct 10–5, Nov–early Dec 10–4, Dec–Feb booked tours only
The highlights of the 12th-century Cistercian ruin of Jerpoint Abbey in the Nore

▲ Jerpoint Abbey

Valley are the Romanesque carved figures to be found in the chapels of the north and south transepts. Their surprisingly cartoon-like qualities give a warm, human feel to what would otherwise be another set of cold monastic ruins. There are smiling and weeping bishops, monks and knights, and a distinctive woman in a long pleated skirt. The Gothic tower, cloister and roofless nave date from the 14th and 15th centuries. The abbey was surrendered to King Henry VIII during the Dissolution of the Monasteries and was then acquired by James Butler, Earl of Ormond. A little visitor centre explains the significance of the carvings and traces the history of high crosses in the area.

Gowran Park Racecourse
gowranpark.ie
Mill Road, Gowran, County Kilkenny
056 772 6225
Gowran Park has made a name for itself as the place to see the up-and-coming young jump horses race in January and February. There are also some flat-race meetings.

Kendals Brasserie ◉
mountjuliet.ie
Mount Juliet Hotel, Thomastown, County Kilkenny | 056 777 3000
The kitchen concentrates on the style of French brasserie classics with some input from other cuisines.

The Lady Helen Restaurant ◉◉◉
mountjuliet.ie
Mount Juliet Hotel, Thomastown, County Kilkenny | 056 777 3000
If you want to play at being aristocracy, a stay at Mount Juliet should do the trick. The main attraction lies in the Lady Helen dining room. The tone of service is gently formal, but staff are friendly and keen, and have a good knowledge of what's on the menus. Suppliers and sources are credited in the preamble, from Wexford seafood to wild game.

▶ Killarney   MAP REF 376 C4

killarney.ie

Killarney has been a popular holiday spot since the Victorians came to admire the romantic scenery. These days it fills to bursting point in summer and a regular programme of festivals adds to its natural attractions. A poorly signed one-way system makes driving through the middle of town bewildering but, once you have parked your car, you'll find it quite compact. The stately Catholic cathedral, St Mary's, is on the western edge. The oldest public building is Killarney House, which dates back to the 1740s.

There are lots of ways to explore Killarney. Make the classic round trip from Kate Kearney's Cottage (see page 325) by horse-drawn jaunting car, on horseback or by bicycle, cross over the high pass called the Gap of Dunloe, and return to Killarney by cruise boat.

TAKE IN SOME HISTORY
St Mary's Cathedral
dioceseofkerry.ie
Cathedral Place, Killarney,
County Kerry | 064 663 1014
Open Mon–Fri 10–5.45.
See website for times of Mass
Killarney's Catholic cathedral was designed by English architect A W N Pugin and dates from 1842, but underwent restoration in the 1970s, and again in recent years.

CATCH A PERFORMANCE
INEC
inec.ie
Muckross Road, Killarney, County Kerry | 064 667 1555
Killarney's own national events centre includes a vast 3,000-seater auditorium that pulls in some major-league artists from a wide range of genres, and musical theatre is a favourite. The Waterboys, Kris Kristofferson and Irish accordion queen Sharon Shannon have all played here.

GO CYCLING
O'Sullivan Cycles
killarneyrentabike.com
064 663 1282
O'Sullivans offer three handy rental locations: opposite the official tourist office on Beech Road; opposite Murphy's Bar on College Street; and opposite Randles Court Hotel on Muckross Road.

RIDE IN A CARRIAGE
Tangney Tours
killarneyjauntingcars.ie
10B Muckross Close, Killarney,
County Kerry | 064 663 3358
The traditional way to see the scenery of the Killarney Lakes is by jaunting car, an open, one-horse carriage. The Tangney family have been in the business for over 200 years.

EAT AND DRINK
The Laurels
thelaurelspub.com
Main Street, Killarney, County Kerry
064 663 1149

This traditional family-run pub has a lovely open fire, great food – both in the pub and restaurant – and is something of a community hub.

▶ PLACES NEARBY

Scenic walks lead from the western end of New Street to Lough Leane and the lakeside tower of Ross Castle. On the peninsula of Ross Island is one of Europe's earliest Bronze Age copper mines. Nearby, you can rent a boat and row to Inisfallen Island, with its monastic remains.

Ross Castle

Killarney, County Kerry | 064 35851
Open mid-Mar to Oct daily
9.30–5.45

A square stone keep, surrounded by the remains of curtain walls, the castle dates from the late 15th century and was a residence of the O'Donoghues. It is famed as the last castle to stand out against Cromwell's English armies, falling at last in 1652, and guided tours show it furnished to reflect that period.

Ross Island

Ross Island is really a peninsula jutting into the lake. Copper was mined and processed here from as early as 2400 BC and items made using Ross Island copper have been found throughout Ireland and the west of Britain. Copper was also extracted during the 18th and 19th centuries, but the mines suffered from flooding and collapse and were closed. Archaeological investigation of the site began in the 1990s. There are information panels to explain the site, and visitors are asked to keep to the tracks, as the area should still be treated with caution.

Killarney Lake Tours

killarneylaketours.ie
Ross Castle, Killarney, County Kerry
064 663 2638

Cruise the lakes on MV *Pride of the Lakes* (cruises leave from Ross Castle). Trips in smaller boats can be arranged through Ross Castle Traditional Boat Tours (tel 085 174 2997). You can hire rowing boats at Ross Castle Pier (tel 064 663 2252).

Inisfallen Island

Hire a rowing boat at Ross Castle and explore the romantic island and ruins of the seventh-century monastery. The island has been an inspiration for poets since the 1800s.

▼ Ross Castle

▶ Killarney National Park

MAP REF 376 C5

For Ireland's first national park, we have to thank Californian William Bowers Bourn, who bought the Muckross estate in 1911 and, with his son-in-law Arthur Rose Vincent, presented it to the nation in 1932. The park encompasses three island-spotted lakes: Lough Leane, or Lower Lake, Muckross or Middle Lake, and Upper Lake. For a breathtaking overview, visit Ladies' View to the south. Macgillycuddy's Reeks, rising to 3,408 feet (1,039m), loom to the west.

The Gap of Dunloe is a deep cleft in the mountains to the west of the park, splitting Purple Mountain (2,729 feet/832m) from the long range of Macgillycuddy's Reeks. A rough road winds through the ravine and over the pass between the mountains, through the park's wildest scenery, and it's not hard to believe that the last wolf in Ireland was killed up here in 1700. You can drive only as far as Kate Kearney's Cottage (see page 325); after that, it's a walk of 7 miles to the other side, but in summer most people go by jaunting car or on the back of the somewhat jaded horses. On the way there are stone bridges dwarfed by sweeping mountains, dark pools (including the Black Lough, where St Patrick is said to have drowned the last Irish serpent), and magnificent views to the north and south. The road brings you to the shores of the Upper Lake and Lord Brandon's Cottage cafe, from where you can catch a boat (not during winter) through the lakes to Ross Castle (see page 321).

TAKE IN SOME HISTORY

Muckross Estate

muckross-house.ie

The National Park, Killarney, County Kerry | 064 667 0144 | House, gardens and craft centre open daily Jul–Aug 9–7, Sep–Jun 9–5.30. Farms: Jun–Aug 10–6, May 1–6, Mar–Apr, Sep–Oct Sat–Sun 1–6

The Muckross Estate, properly called Bourn-Vincent Memorial Park, lies within the national park, 4 miles south of Killarney. At its heart is the Victorian mansion of Muckross House, with its extensive gardens, a crafts centre and the Traditional Farms – three working farms, dating from the 1930s, complete with animals. The house was designed in 1843 by Edinburgh architect William Burns, and built for Henry Arthur Herbert, who was married to the watercolourist Mary Balfour. Its interior is comfortably and richly furnished. Highlights include the room where Queen Victoria stayed in 1861, items of Killarney inlaid furniture in the library, and watercolours of

◀ The Eagle's Nest, Killarney National Park

local views by Mary. The gardens include a Victorian walled garden noted for its azaleas and rhododendrons, and a water garden, and also has workshops, glasshouses, and a restaurant.

Horse-drawn jaunting cars are a great way to travel between Killarney town and Muckross, and the jarvies (drivers) have a fund of local knowledge and stories to entertain their customers.

Dinis Cottage

Killarney National Park, Killarney, County Kerry | 064 663 0085
Open summer daily 10–5.15
About 3 miles from Muckross House is Dinis Cottage, a former hunting lodge dating back to the 1700s, located near two of Killarney's beauty spots, The Meeting of the Waters and Old Weir Bridge. It is only open to the public during the summer months.

SADDLE UP
Killarney Riding Stables

killarney-riding-stables.com
Ballydowney, Killarney, County Kerry
064 663 1686
This large establishment, known locally as O'Sullivans, is run by a family and is located on the northwestern edge of town, on the N72 Killorglin road. It offers a wide range of trekking, hacking and trail riding, with excursions lasting from an hour to several days. The Killarney Reeks Trail operates from April to October and is a six-night trail with accommodation.

EAT AND DRINK
The Brehon ◉

thebrehon.com
Muckross Road, Killarney, County Kerry | 064 663 0700
The kitchen brings us fast-forwarding up to the present day with contemporary Irish cooking of ingenuity and impressive depth.

▼ Ladies' View, the Upper Lakes

Carrig House Country House and Restaurant ⦿

carrighouse.com
Caragh Lake, County Kerry
066 976 9100

The dining room in this Victorian manor house is the very image of 19th-century chic; all William Morris wallpapers, swagged curtains, polished floorboards and formally laid tables. The cooking, however, takes a more up-to-date approach, lining up superb local ingredients and sending them to finishing school.

The Lake Hotel ⦿⦿

lakehotelkillarney.com
On the shore, Muckross Road, Killarney, County Kerry
064 663 1035

The Castlelough Restaurant, built as part of the original house in 1820, has a kitchen that works around a slate of modern ideas based on classical traditions, using the area's tip-top ingredients.

Kate Kearney's Cottage

katekearneyscottage.com
Gap of Dunloe, Beaufort, Killarney, County Kerry | 064 664 4146

At the entrance to the Gap of Dunloe, Kate Kearney's has been welcoming visitors for over 150 years. There's a restaurant, bar and craft shops, and often live music in the evenings. Kate was a famous beauty, and she distilled wickedly strong potín here.

Lord Brandon's Cottage Cafe

Gearhameen, Beaufort, Killarney, County Kerry | 064 663 4730

Lord Brandon's Cottage was once a hunting lodge and it's a popular stop on the circular walk/ride/boat trip that takes in the Killarney Lakes and the Gap of Dunloe.

▶ PLACES NEARBY

A half-hour drive south takes you to pretty **Kenmare**. This is a gateway for the Ring of Kerry and the wild Ring of Bearra.

▶ Kilrush MAP REF 376 C3

There's an attractive Georgian air to Kilrush, a laid-back town near the mouth of the Shannon. Its name means 'Church of the Woods' but Kilrush looks seaward for its livelihood and entertainment: the marina contains 120 berths. Dolphin-watching trips run regularly from the town and there is a Dolphin Trail to help you understand their importance to the Shannon estuary. A fine monastic site here, with a 108-foot round tower and several ruined churches, belongs to the medieval monastery of St Senan. Other attractions here are the horse fairs and the Vandeleur Walled Garden.

GO DOLPHIN CRAZY
Shannon Dolphin and Wildlife Foundation
shannondolphins.ie
Merchants Quay, Kilrush, County Clare | 065 905 2326 | Open daily mid-May to mid-Sep 10–6
The Shannon dolphins are the only known resident population of bottlenose dolphins in Ireland. There are about 140 individuals, carefully monitored and studied by the researchers at the Shannon Dolphin and Wildlife Foundation. Take a tour with a marine biologist, and learn about the whale and dolphin species in Irish water.

GO ROUND THE GARDENS
Vandeleur Walled Garden
vandeleurwalledgarden.ie
Vandeleur Demesne, Killimer Road, Kilrush, County Clare | 065 905 1760 | Open Apr–Sep Mon–Fri 10–5, Sat, Sun 1–5, Oct–Mar Mon–Fri 10–5
This lovely walled garden, set in 420 acres of native woodland, has a horizontal maze, water features and a Victorian-style working glasshouse. You'll see unusual and tender plants in the area's microclimate.

▶ PLACES NEARBY
Offshore, Scattery Island has interesting historical buildings and the ocean itself offers sightings of marine wildlife.

Scattery Island
From Kilrush's marina you can take a 20-minute boat trip (Griffin Gerald Boat Hire, 065 905 1327) to Scattery Island. Its cathedral and monastery were an early Christian place of pilgrimage where St Senan founded a monastery in the Shannon estuary. Here are remains of his oratory and house, as well as seven small churches, a round tower and holy well. The informative visitor centre is by the pier.

Dolphin-watching trips
Dolphinwatch Information Centre, The Square, Carrigaholt, Loop Head Peninsula, County Clare | 065 905 8156 | Trips daily Apr–Oct. Advance booking recommended
Get out on the water and look for the dolphins yourself. There are guided trips of two to two-and-a-half hours, where you'll hopefully see the dolphins and probably other wildlife too.

▶ **Kinsale** MAP REF 377 E5

kinsale.ie

Kinsale has become known as the culinary capital of this part of Ireland, bolstered by the prestigious annual Gourmet Festival (see page 55). It has a mixture of interesting shops, art galleries and chic small hotels, including the famous Blue Haven on the site of the old fish market of 1784. Its brightly coloured buildings, set against the sea, make this an attractive place to walk round. The backstreets are stuffed with restaurants to suit all tastes and budgets.

Many streets are on land reclaimed from the sea during the 13th century. The modern harbour is popular for diving and fishing, including deep-sea angling and blue shark fishing. Wading birds occupy the mudflats, and swans complete the idyllic scene.

TAKE IN SOME HISTORY
Desmond Castle

Cork Street, Kinsale, County Cork
021 477 2263 | Open Easter–Oct
daily 10–6

The splendid castle (not to be confused with Desmond Castle in Adare, see page 159), built by the ninth Earl of Desmond, dates from 1500 and served as a prison in times of war. Since 1997 it has housed the International Museum of Wine.

Charles Fort

Summer Cove, Kinsale, County Cork
021 477 2263 | Open daily mid-Mar to Oct 10–6, Nov to mid-Mar 10–5
Charles Fort, a 17th-century fortress on the east side of the

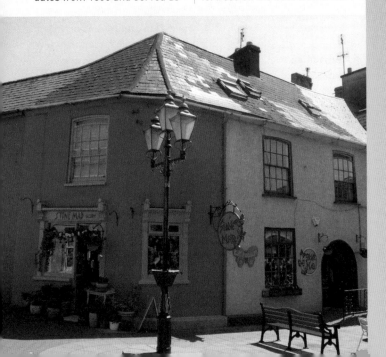

bay, is one of Ireland's largest military installations.

VISIT THE MUSEUM
Kinsale Regional Museum
Market Square, Kinsale, County Cork
021 477 7930 | Open Sat 10–5, Sun
2–5; reduced hours in winter
A huge, rusted iron buoy and anchors outside this small museum reflect the town's fishing and maritime heritage which is showcased inside.

HIT THE BEACH
Sandycove is a popular spot for experienced swimmers and there are other lovely beaches along the coast here, many of them suitable for swimming.

TAKE TO THE WATER
Sea Breeze Angling
seabreezeanglingkinsale.com
086 231 1672
Go fishing for pollack, ling, cod and conger among many others, or take a sightseeing trip instead.

Oceanaddicts
oceanaddicts.ie
087 790 3211 or 087 274 4992
Oceanaddicts operate from several locations in the southwest. You can stay aboard an ex-Royal Navy fleet tender at Kinsale and dive from a rib, experiencing the Wild Atlantic Way from beneath the waves.

TAKE A BOAT TRIP
Cruise of Kinsale Harbour
kinsaleharbourcruises.com
Summercove, Kinsale, County Cork
021 477 8946 and 086 250 5456

Enjoy a cruise of the harbour area aboard the *Spirit of Kinsale*, taking in some of the town's historic sights and stunning scenery along the way. The boat takes you to the outer harbour, and up the River Bandon, with full commentary. There's also music, a bar and snacks on board.

PLAY A ROUND
Kinsale Golf Club
kinsalegolf.ie
Farrangalway, County Cork
021 477 4722
Set in farmland surrounded by rolling countryside. It's a stiff yet fair challenge to be enjoyed by all standards of golfers.

EAT AND DRINK
The White House ⍟
whitehouse-kinsale.ie
Pearse Street, The Glen, Kinsale, County Cork | 021 477 2125
The White House has been in the hospitality game since the mid-19th century, and occupies a prime site in the centre of a town that holds a renowned Gourmet Festival every autumn. The kitchen here rises to the occasion with a resourceful repertoire of modern Irish dishes that draws inspiration from far and wide, but is also a dab hand at Irish stews, fish pies and the like.

▶ PLACES NEARBY

Less than a 19-mile drive north on the N71 is the county city of Cork (see page 229), with its interesting buildings and its lively atmosphere.

▶ Limerick   MAP REF 377 D3

Limerick was given a new lease of life when it was chosen as the country's first Irish City of Culture in 2014. A lively programme of arts, cultural and sporting events gave a new energy to the city which also has a newly renovated castle and attractive restaurants and cafes.

Limerick was founded by Vikings around AD 922 as a trading port and it prospered. In the 12th century, the settlement on King John's Island (between the Shannon and Abbey rivers) was fortified by a wall, and became known as English Town, with Irish Town on the opposite bank. In Georgian times it spread south, with the best developments around the People's Park, where you will find the art gallery. Today, the two areas are linked by ruler-straight O'Connell Street, parallel to the river and the main shopping street of the city.

TAKE IN SOME HISTORY

King John's Castle

shannonheritage.com
Nicholas Street, Limerick, County Limerick | 061 360 788 | Open daily 9.30–8

The great drum towers at King John's Castle, dating from 1200, loom above the river. Inside, the story of the castle is brought to life by animated and interactive exhibits. Adjacent is the restored palace that once housed the Protestant Bishops of Limerick, which is related to the English Palladian style with a classical facade. The house is currently occupied by Limerick Civic Trust, which looks after the fine architecture seen all around the city.

St Mary's Cathedral

cathedral.limerick.anglican.org
Bridge Street, Limerick, County Limerick | Open daily 8.30–5.30

Parts of the square-towered St Mary's Cathedral date back to 1168. It was founded by King Donal Mór O'Brien (also responsible for Cashel and Holy Cross), and restoration in the 1990s removed the interior plaster for greater authenticity. A new place has yet to be found for the oak misericords of 1480–1500, carved with griffins, swans, other beasts and angels, that lie in a side chapel. A limestone slab, more than 13 feet long, forms the altar, and the cannonballs date from 1691, when William of Orange's troops besieged the city.

VISIT THE MUSEUM AND GALLERY

The Hunt Museum

huntmuseum.com
Rutland Street, Limerick, County Limerick | 061 312 833 | Open Mon–Sat 10–5, Sun 2–5

The Hunt Museum, in a modest grey-fronted Georgian customs house of 1765, has an eclectic collection spanning 9,000 years, amassed by John and Gertrude Hunt. They include a virtually intact disk shield of c 750 BC, found in County Antrim; a

Roman pierced-bronze cooking strainer from the second century; a small bronze horse believed to be by Leonardo da Vinci; an emerald seal that belonged to Charles I; a delicate 17th-century German dish made of lapis lazuli; sketches by Henry Moore and paintings by Jack Butler Yeats; and a menu card by Picasso. Exhibits are beautifully displayed.

Limerick City Gallery of Art

gallery.limerick.ie

Carnegie Building, Pery Square, Limerick | 061 310 633

Open Mon–Wed, Fri, Sat 10–5.30, Thu 10–8, Sun 12–5.30

The gallery has an extensive collection of Irish art – from both Irish-born artists and those who have worked in Ireland – and runs a full range of temporary exhibitions concentrating on contemporary art from national and international artists.

▼ St Mary's Cathedral

CATCH A PERFORMANCE
University Concert Hall

uch.ie

University of Limerick Campus, Limerick, County Limerick

061 331 549

This 1,000-seat, purpose-built concert hall is home to the Irish Chamber Orchestra, while also providing a venue for American wrestling and performers such as Daniel O'Donnell. The sister venue is the smaller Millennium Theatre at Limerick Institute of Technology on the north side of the Shannon, which hosts drama, dance and music.

EAT AND DRINK
Limerick Strand Hotel ◉

strandlimerick.ie

Ennis Street, Sarsfield Bridge, Limerick, County Limerick

061 421 800

The restaurant in this hotel, set beside the river, sources ingredients from within the county and supplies a menu of populist brasserie dishes, with an Irish contemporary gloss on international ideas.

The Locke Bar

lockebar.com

3 George's Quay, Limerick, County Limerick | 061 413 733

This place is on the site of one of the city's oldest pubs that dates back to 1724. Beside the city's most historical landmarks and near the river, this is an award-winning, traditional Irish bar and restaurant with open fires and plenty of character. Enjoy live music in summer and seafood specialities.

Jody's

jodys.ie

The Potato Market, Merchants Quay, Limerick, County Limerick

083 452 3705

The 'best coffee in Limerick', great sandwiches and amazing patisserie to choose from.

▶ **PLACES NEARBY**

Ballyneety, south of Limerick, is home to possibly the largest stone circle in Ireland.

Lough Gur Stone Age Centre

loughgur.com

Ballyneety, County Limerick | 061 385 186 | Site open daily 24 hours. Visitor centre open May–Sep daily 10.30–5

Some 3,000 years ago, neolithic farmers chose crescent-shaped Lough Gur in County Limerick for their settlement. The site has been excavated, and its story is told in the replica roundhouse and longhouse above the lake. The ruined castle visible from the parking area dates from 1500, and is private. Nearby are a wedge tomb and the Grange stone circle. More antique sites can be seen from the lakeside.

Thomond Park Stadium

thomondpark.ie

Half a mile northwest of Limerick centre along High Street, County Limerick | 061 421 109

From 1995 until 2007, the Munster rugby team was undefeated at Thomond Park, which was rebuilt in 2008, the year they won the Heineken European Cup for the second time. Tours of the ground include its interactive, memorabilia-filled museum.

Castletroy Golf Club

castletroygolfclub.ie

Castletroy, County Limerick

061 335 753

Out of bounds left of the first two holes and well-maintained fairways demand accuracy off the tee. The long par five sixth hole is set into water. The par three 14th hole has a panoramic view from the tee with the green surrounded by water, while the picturesque 18th is a stern test to finish.

▶ **Lismore** MAP REF 378 B5

Dancer Fred Astaire was just one celebrity who succumbed to the charms of Lismore, as a blue plaque on Maddens Bar on Main Street testifies. He came to visit his sister Adèle, who lived in Lismore Castle, its square towers visible from the north bank of the River Blackwater. It had previously passed through the hands of Sir Walter Raleigh and Richard Boyle, father of the famous physicist Robert (1627–91), whose story is depicted at the heritage centre. The castle is now the Irish home of the Dukes of Devonshire and not open to the public, but visitors can explore the gardens (17 Mar–30 Sep daily 11–4.45). Edmund Spenser composed his poem *The Faerie Queene* (1590) here.

TAKE IN SOME HISTORY
Lismore Castle
lismorecastle.com

Lismore, County Waterford

058 54288

There's been a castle here since 1185, and the earliest part that remains dates to the 13th century. It's the Irish seat of the Duke of Devonshire and although you can't visit, if you're feeling flush you can hire the whole place for what would surely be the most splendid family gathering or party.

Lismore Cathedral
North Mall, Lismore, County Waterford | 058 54105 | Open daily Apr–Sep 9–6, Oct–Mar 9–4

North Mall leads to the cathedral, named in honour of St Carthagh, who founded a monastic school of international importance here in AD 633. The present building mostly dates from the 17th and 18th centuries. Highlights include a window in the south transept by English Pre-Raphaelite artist Edward Burne-Jones (1833–98), the splendidly carved 16th-century McGrath tomb, and the carved stones from earlier churches on the site, dating back to the ninth century. An unmarked spot in the northeast corner of the churchyard is the site of a famine grave.

VISIT THE HERITAGE CENTRE
Lismore Heritage Centre
discoverlismore.com

Lismore, County Waterford | 058 54975 | Open Mon–Fri 9–5 Sat, Sun 10–5

The heritage centre is the best place to start a visit to Lismore with its audiovisual journey through monastic, Viking, Norman and Medieval Lismore to the present day. The centre organises a number of themed days out, including those for foodies and garden-lovers. The centre also has a good shop where you can buy crafts, jewellery and souvenirs.

VISIT THE GALLERY
Lismore Castle Arts
lismorecastlearts.ie

Chapel Street, Lismore, County Waterford | 058 54061

Open Apr–Sep daily 10.30–5.30

In 2011, St Carthage Hall was opened as a second exhibition venue, for Lismore Castle Arts, behind the Lismore Heritage Centre. It is a modest gallery space with frequently changing exhibitions.

GET ON THE WATER
Blackwater Boating
blackwaterboating.ie

Cappoquin, County Waterford

058 54382 or 087 683 2872

Take a half- or full-day canoeing trip down the Blackwater admiring the beautiful scenery. Trips can be combined with camping or cycling.

GO WALKING
A 40-minute circular walk through the woods to the 19th-century folly towers of Ballysaggartmore is signposted from the road about a mile west of the town. Other walks

include a riverside walk where you can see herons, swans, mallards, water hens, snipe, tern, kingfisher and many more water birds. The River Blackwater is renowned for its salmon fishing.

▶ PLACES NEARBY
Leaving Lismore and tracking the Blackwater River by road south takes you to the coastal town of Youghal (see page 373). Just along the coast from here is Ardmore (see page 374).

▶ Loughcrew Cairns MAP REF 382 C6
loughcrew.com
Loughcrew, Oldcastle, County Meath | 049 854 1356 | Open Mar–Oct daily 12–6

Loughcrew is possibly the oldest cemetery in the world. In west County Meath, the Loughcrew Hills hold a remarkable series of 5,000-year-old passage graves. On these hilltops there are no interpretative displays or audiovisual tour. You may even have them to yourself. It's 440 yards or so from the road up to the eastern summit, where Cairn T is the most dramatic feature, 115 feet across, with 37 edging stones. Inside, a cross chamber is lined with inscribed stones. The western summit has more impressive cairns. The Patrickstown cairns are the most easterly group, virtually destroyed by 19th-century enthusiasts, but contain important neolithic artwork. You can get a key to Cairn T from the coffee shop at Loughcrew Historic Gardens about 2 miles away.

▶ PLACES NEARBY
Combine a trip to the cairns with a visit to Loughcrew Historic Gardens and interesting Oldcastle close by.

Loughcrew Historic Gardens
loughcrew.com
Loughcrew Gardens and Adventure Course, Loughcrew, Oldcastle, County Meath | 049 854 1356 Open mid-Mar to Oct Mon–Fri 9.30–5.30, Sat–Sun 11–5.30, Nov to mid-Mar Mon–Fri on request, Sat–Sun 11–4

These beautifully restored landscape and pleasure gardens date from the 17th and 19th centuries. The central area features extensive lawns and terraces, a lime avenue, physic border and herbaceous border. There's a medieval moote and you can take a longer walk around Lough Creeve.

Loughcrew Adventure Centre, including a zipline and assault course, is on the same site; see the website for details.

Oldcastle
This market town is the meeting point of Meath, Cavan and Westmeath, and is a good base for exploring the area. Lough Ramor, Lough Lene and the River Blackwater are all within 15 minutes of Oldcastle.

▶ **Monaghan** MAP REF 382 C4

monaghantourism.com

The 'little hills' from which the county town of Monaghan takes its name form a landscape of glacial drumlins, the low 'basket of eggs' topography caused by the passage of great ice sheets. Amid these countless ridges of boulder clay lie dozens of lakes, making this a popular county with anglers. The small county town has a neat shopping street, a good local museum and the nearby Market House, which is a surprisingly elegant Georgian affair from 1792. Grander in scale is the enormous Gothic-revival Roman Catholic Cathedral of St Macartan, standing high on the east side of town.

TAKE IN SOME HISTORY

The County Museum

monaghan.ie/museum

1–2 Hill Street, Monaghan, County Monaghan | 047 82928

Open Mon–Fri 11–5, Sat 12–5

Housed in a Victorian town house, the museum's 50,000 objects tell the story of the town and area from the Ice Age to the present day.

Cathedral of St Macartan

monaghan-rackwallace.ie

Dublin Road, County Monaghan

047 82300 | Check website for Mass times

Built from local limestone in the late 19th century, the cathedral is neo-Gothic in style. The exterior is elaborate, with a 240-foot spire and three large rose windows. Inside, the hammer-beam roof is quite stunning.

CATCH A PERFORMANCE

The Market House

themarkethouse.ie

Market Street, Monaghan, County Monaghan | 047 30500 | Open May–Sep Tue–Fri 10–5, Sat 1–5, Oct–Apr Tue–Fri 11–5, Sat 1–5

A mix of classical, traditional and contemporary music is offered in the 18th-century market building, now an arts venue. Performances include folk, jazz and poetry.

▶ PLACES NEARBY

The towns and villages of County Monaghan are largely the creation of 17th-century plantations, with perhaps Clones the most appealing.

Clones

Clones was the site of an early monastic settlement, and 12th-century abbey ruins, as well as a ninth-century round tower and high cross, can still be seen. You can also see the Norman motte and bailey. Clones was once famous as a centre of crochet lace-making and at one point 1,500 lace-makers were working here. There's an exhibition about Clones lace at the Ulster Canal Stores, which also houses the new Cultural and Tourist Centre (047 52125). You can take a historic walking tour of the town; book through the

Canal Stores, or George Knight on 047 51238.

Carrickmacross
This old market town prides itself on being 'the gourmet capital of the northeast', with award-winning restaurants and great local produce. There's plenty to see and do with various forest parks, loughs and activities for children.

▶ Mullet Peninsula (Leithinis an Mhuirthid)
MAP REF 380 B3

The Mullet Peninsula is an atmospheric area of unspoilt beauty stretching for 20 miles. It hangs like a ragged arm from the rounded shoulder of northwest County Mayo, one of the wildest and least-populated corners of Ireland. The low-lying, isolated Mullet, composed mostly of mountain and bog, is a Gaeltacht area, so you will hear only Irish spoken in the peninsula's sole village of Binghamstown (An Geata Mór). The eastern or landward side of the Mullet cradles Blacksod Bay (Cuan An Fhóid Dhuibh) and is sandy in parts, but also has mudflats.

Birding is sensational here, as it is by Termoncarragh Lake (Loch Tearmainn) at the head of the peninsula, where you might just spot the rare red-necked phalarope. The western or Atlantic coast of the peninsula has a succession of beautiful sandy (and seaweedy) strands. From the beaches of Belderra and Cross there are good views of the tiny island of Inishglora a mile out to sea, where – according to legend – the four children of Lir spent 300 years in exile in the shape of swans, thanks to the evil magic of their jealous stepmother.

HIT THE BEACH
Elly Bay beach is small, and Cross beach has views towards the islands. Termon beach is part of the Blacksod Bay Special Area of Conservation area and Mullagrhoe is a sheltered beach.

GO FISHING
Belmullet
Tackle Shop, American Street, Belmullet, County Mayo | 097 82093
Translated as the 'Mouth of the mullet', Belmullet is one of West Ireland's best centres for sea fishing.

▶ PLACES NEARBY
For a trip on the Atlantic ocean head west and visit small Inishglora Island or, to spend a day out walking in the nearby hills, drive south to the Nephin Beg Range.

Inishglora
Said to be the holiest of all the islands off the coast of Erris, there are various ecclesiastical ruins here, including three churches. According to Gerald of Wales, writing in the 12th century, corpses deposited here in the open air remained

uncorrupted, allowing people to see and recognise their distant ancestors.

The Nephin Beg Range

The waymarked Bangor Trail is an ancient trail once used by drovers herding their animals from the wilds of North Mayo to sell in Newport. The lonely long-distance path that runs for 30 miles from Bangor Erris south to Newport through the heart of the Nephin Beg Mountain Range, 15 miles of it through wild and deserted terrain, is a true challenge for strong and determined walkers.

The Great Western Greenway allows walkers and cyclists alike to drink in the beauty of the mountains' landscape as well as Clew Bay and Clare Island. Running for 26 miles, it is the longest off-road walking and cycling trail in Ireland.

▶ New Ross   MAP REF 378 C5

experiencenewross.com

New Ross, an old inland port on the Barrow River, is one of the oldest town's in Ireland, which felt the wealth of the euro boom, and its wharfside warehouses have been redeveloped. The narrow streets wind up the steep riverbank to the Three Bullet Gate, a remnant of a once-extensive town wall. Cromwellian destruction might have seen the end of the town were it not for the proximity of the Kennedys' ancestral home. Since the 1960s, this has ensured a steady stream of visitors. Lying on the banks of the River Barrow, summertime sees its waters come alive with pleasure cruisers.

VISIT THE MUSEUM
Dunbrody Famine Ship and Irish Emigrant Experience

dunbrody.com

South Quay, New Ross, County Wexford | 051 425 239 | Open daily Apr–Sep 9–6, Oct–Mar 9–5

The impressive *Dunbrody*, a full-scale reproduction of a New Ross emigrant vessel of the 19th century, has guides in period costume explaining the harsh conditions experienced by the passengers. There's a full database of those who made the journey to the US between 1820 and 1920. The 50-minute tour is preceded by a video about the construction of the ship.

GET ON THE WATER
The Galley

rivercruises.ie

The Quay, New Ross, County Wexford | 051 421 723

Cruise on the three rivers, Barrow, Nore or Suir, enjoy the scenery and take dinner or afternoon tea on the water.

▶ PLACES NEARBY

While you're in New Ross you can make a trip to the John F Kennedy Arboretum, 7 miles south of New Ross, off the

R733. Waterford (see page 359) lies to the southwest.

John F Kennedy Arboretum

heritageireland.ie
New Ross, County Wexford | 051 388 171 | Open daily May–Aug 10–8, Apr, Sep 10–6.30, Oct–Mar 10–5

The internationally recognised John F Kennedy Arboretum, with 4,500 types of trees and shrubs, opened in 1968. Visit this 622-acre arboretum in spring and autumn for the best experience, making sure not to miss the beautiful lake and nature trails.

Powerscourt MAP REF 379 E2

powerscourt.ie
Powerscourt Estate, Enniskerry, County Wicklow | 01 204 6000
Open daily 9.30–5.30 (gardens close at dusk in winter)

Powerscourt's gardens are among the most beautiful in the world. Drink in the view from the terrace, over a broad sweep of wooded garden to the graceful peak of the Great Sugar Loaf on the horizon. This superb vista is the set piece of a house and garden originally designed by Richard Cassels for the First

▼ Triton Lake in Powerscourt's gardens

Viscount Powerscourt in 1731. Subsequent additions included the Italian garden, which drops away from the terrace on a grand staircase lined by winged horses, leading to the circular Triton Lake and a 100-foot fountain. Looking back from here, your eye is carried up to the grey stone Palladian facade with its twin copper domes. This exquisite scene took more than 100 labourers 12 years to create in the middle of the 19th century. On the same level as the house, and dating back to the 1740s, lie the walled gardens. More formal than the rest of the estate but not as severe as some in the French style, they include vivid rose beds and fragrant borders. One entrance is through the Bamberg Gate, an intricate piece of wrought ironwork from Bavaria.

Take a walk through the 47 acres. Although you can pay for an audiovisual presentation to the house and gardens, pick up a free map that is provided for a self-guided tour of the estate. Highlights include the Dolphin Pond, the walled garden, the Japanese Gardens and Triton Lake. Take time to stop for tea or a snack at the restaurant and cafe and perhaps to browse at the estate shops. The eateries and retail outlets occupy the west wing.

The house itself was gutted by fire in 1974 and stood virtually derelict until 1996, when a clever regeneration was devised. The roof was restored, but most of the interior was left empty. An exhibition space was created and the ballroom carefully restored. Today, a visit to the house exhibition is a peculiar mix of building history and stately home, but the house is greatly overshadowed by the gardens.

The estate glasshouses now house the Powerscourt Garden Centre, and much of the land to the north front of the house is given over to golf courses.

EAT AND DRINK

Powerscourt Hotel ◉◉
powerscourthotel.com
Powerscourt Estate, Enniskerry, County Wicklow | 01 274 8888
With a sweeping Palladian mansion at its heart, the Powerscourt resort has a couple of golf courses, a luxurious spa and classy bedrooms. There's also an Irish pub called McGills, but the main event food-wise is the Sika Restaurant. There are glorious mountain views from its third-floor dining room, a chic space that has retained plenty of character. There's a chef's table, too.

▶ **PLACES NEARBY**

Also part of the estate, but three miles away, is the Powerscourt Waterfall, Ireland's highest at 398 feet. This is surrounded by specimen trees and is a popular location for wedding photographs.

▶ **Rock of Cashel** MAP REF 378 B4

cashel.ie
Cashel | 062 61437 | Open mid-Mar to mid-Jun 9.30–5.30, mid-Jun to mid-Sep 9–7, mid-Sep to mid-Oct 9–5.30, mid-Oct to mid-Mar 9–4.30
The Rock of Cashel rises triumphantly out of the rich farmland, visible for miles. This rural area may be scattered with ruined monastic sites, but this is the finest of them all. The rock was actually the seat of Munster kings from the fourth century, including Brian Boru, who later became king of the whole of Ireland. In 1101, King Muirchertach Ua Briain presented the site to the Church, and it remained in use until the mid-18th century, when its decaying buildings, costly to maintain, were abandoned in favour of St John's Church in the town below.

Taking the steep climb to the main door gives you a sense of the majesty and impregnability of the site, and will leave you breathless in all respects. Above is the outer wall of the Hall of the Vicar's Choral, constructed for the medieval choir and restored inside. Beyond the stairs of the gatehouse is a replica of the 12th-century St Patrick's Cross, then the first building you see is the mighty cathedral, a vast cruciform dating from 1230, and roofless since 1848. Look up at the gargoyles around the Gothic windows. The squat, brooding tower was added in the 15th century, when the archbishops were at the height of their power, and this end of the church was rebuilt as a fortified tower house.

In contrast, the older Cormac's Chapel, wedged uncomfortably between the choir and the south transept of the cathedral, seems positively light-hearted with its Romanesque arches and twin square towers. It was built by Bishop Cormac McCarthy in 1127, and traces of wall paintings in blue, red and gold can be seen in the chancel. The carving around the doorways is particularly good. The deeply carved tomb is probably Viking, and was moved here from the cathedral for shelter. The oldest building of the Rock is a round tower that is 92 feet high.

EXPLORE THE TOWN
Cashel Heritage Centre
Town Hall, Cashel, County Tipperary
062 61333 | Open Mar–Oct daily
9.30–5.30, Nov–Feb Mon–Fri
9.30–5.30
This centre portrays the history of the town and has a craft shop selling woollen items, ceramics and pottery, all handmade by local craftspeople.

The Folk Village
cashelfolkvillage.ie
Dominic Street, Cashel, County
Tipperary | 062 63601 | Open daily
May–Oct 9.30–7.30, Mar–Apr 10–6
This 'village', in a row of thatched cottages on Dominic Street, recreates 18th-century rural life and has displays on Republican history.

The Bolton Library
John Street, Cashel, County
Tipperary | 062 61944
Open Mon–Fri 10–4
The Bolton Library contains a fine collection of antiquarian books. Among the selection is a monk's encyclopaedia of 1168 and the smallest book in the world.

Brú Ború
bruboru.ie
Rock Lane, Cashel, County Tipperary
062 61122
A sculpted trio of dancing figures announces this cultural centre and performance venue, in the shadow of the Rock of Cashel. It serves as a base for Celtic and genealogical studies, and stages music, song, dance, storytelling and theatre. There's also a restaurant that holds evening banquets.

EAT AND DRINK
Palace Hotel
cashel-palace.ie
Main Street, Cashel, County
Tipperary | 062 62707
The handsome Cashel Palace Hotel was originally the archbishops' palace of 1732. Non-residents can have a half in the Guinness bar or an afternoon tea in the peaceful drawing room.

▶ PLACES NEARBY
While in the area, visit Athassel Priory, west of Cashel, and perhaps Beechmount Farm (052 613 1151, open Mon–Fri 9–5), in Fethard, where you can buy some of Ireland's famous farmhouse Cashel Blue cheese.

Athassel Priory
The broken remains of abbeys are scattered across this rich farmland, and Athassel Priory is a stony ghost of one of the biggest and best. Driving south from Golden, 4 miles west of Cashel, you will get a fine view over the riverside site, accessed over a stile. Founded in the late 12th century by William FitzAdelm de Burgo, and dedicated to St Edmund, this was one of the wealthiest and largest monasteries in Ireland until its destruction in 1447. A town had grown around it but was burned down and nothing remains of it. Today, the high walls of the ruined site form a tranquil, atmospheric spot.

▶ Sheep's Head Peninsula   MAP REF 376 B6

The fertile Sheep's Head Peninsula lies between Dunmanus and Bantry bays and its main town, Durrus, gives its name to a distinctive local raw milk cheese. Visitors can taste and buy the delicacy and even see it being made. Low rocky hills in the east give way to a rugged shoreline, and there are great views to the north and south from the Seefin Pass above Kilcrohane (1,136 feet).

Yachts moor in Ahakista Bay, and it feels like a prosperous, tranquil backwater. In summer, seal-spotting boat trips leave for the nearby islands. A memorial garden on the shore just east of the bay, however, shows that the area is also touched by tragedy: the garden honours the 329 people who were killed on 23 June 1985, when Air India Flight 182 from Montréal to Bombay exploded off the coast here.

EXPLORE THE PENINSULA

Durrus

Durrus is handy for some of West Cork's most stunning coastlines and great walking country. This planned village, laid out in the 1850s, is a popular staging point on the Wild Atlantic Way, and well known for good local produce, including Durrus Irish Farmhouse Cheese.

Durrus Farmhouse Cheese

durruscheese.com

Coomkeen Valley, Durrus, County Cork | 027 61100

Durrus cheese has been made on the Sheep's Head Peninsula since 1979. You can visit the dairy to buy cheese and watch the it being made. It's best to visit midweek, around 11 – but phone in advance, as open days vary each week.

GO WALKING

thesheepsheadway.ie

The Sheep's Head Way at the Sheep Head's Peninsula is a 125-mile walking and cycling trail that allows you to explore the landscape between Bantry Bay and Dunmanus Bay, enjoying local food and crafts and activities from horse-riding to sailing along the way.

EAT AND DRINK

Blairscove House and Restaurant ◉◉

blairscove.ie

Durrus, County Cork (R591 Durrus to Crookhaven) | 027 61127

Blairscove is a country hotel brimming with charm. The main house is Georgian, and the accommodation and restaurant face a lily pond. The dining room is full of character, not least from striking modern artworks, and so is the catering operation itself.

▶ PLACES NEARBY

Jutting out into the Atlantic either side of Sheep's Head Peninsula are Beara Peninsula (see page 175) and Mizen Peninsula (see page 173).

▶ The Skelligs MAP REF 376 A5

skelligsrock.com

Boats run Apr–Oct; weather permitting

The jagged islands off the end of the Iveragh Peninsula are Great Skellig, or Skellig Michael (An Sceilg Mhicil), and Little Skellig (An Sceilg Bheag), one of the largest gannetries in the world. Skellig Michael is the more distant of the pair, 8 miles offshore and up to 712 feet high, and has a lighthouse from 1820. Christian monks sought refuge here in the sixth century, surviving on trade with passing ships before abandoning it in the 11th century. Hundreds of precipitous steps lead up to their beehive huts.

Early Irish monks built a monastery here in the most challenging location they knew, as a demonstration of their devotion. For them, the islands, literally on the edge of their world, were inhabited by devils and dragons and would have been even more terrifying than they are today. Take some time to feel the history of the place. Step inside the beehive hut that served as the church, pointed out by the guides, and close your eyes and meditate for a moment on the monks who did this day in and day out before you.

Visitors arrive from Portmagee at the landing at Skellig Michael, weather permitting, to climb the precipitous original sixth-century steps to one of the best-preserved monasteries in Europe. Great care is needed; the climb is not for those suffering from vertigo or for the faint hearted and there are only a few yards of handrails. Book ahead online or direct with one of the boatmen. Places are limited and landings are often not possible due to bad weather. If you do persevere you will be rewarded with an experience that will

▼ Skellig Michael

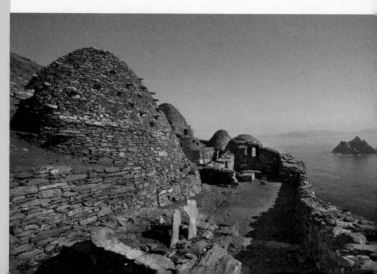

possibly stay with you forever, and it is worth bearing in mind that, if rumour is right, it won't be long before archaeologists prevent anyone from visiting the site.

Star Wars: The Force Awakens, released in 2015, was filmed on Great Skellig and it is easy to see why location scouts picked this spot. Rising like a massive Machu Picchu out of the sea, it is truly spectacular.

GET ON THE WATER
Casey's Skellig Michael Tours
skelligislands.com
066 9472437
Boat trips depart daily at 10am from Portmagee, weather permitting, and you need to book well in advance. The trip takes about 45 minutes and you get two to two-and-a-half hours on the island. The boat stops for a while at Little Skellig so you can see the bird colony and the seals.

▶ PLACES NEARBY
Around 10 miles northwest of the Skellig Islands is Valentia Island, one of Ireland's most westerly points, reached by ferry (April to October) from Renard Point, Cahersiveen or by a road bridge which spans the Portmagee Channel.

Valentia Island
valentiaisland.ie and
skelligexperience.com
Visitor centre: 066 947 6306
Open Jun–Aug daily 10–7, Apr–May, Sep–Oct Mon–Fri 10–5
Valentia, just off the tip of the Iveragh Peninsula, is 7 miles long and boasts its own signposted ring drive and a coastal walk. Once on the island, shortly after the bridge crossing from Portmagee, look for the clifftop memorial marking the spot where the first transatlantic telegraph message was sent in 1866.

The slate slabs used in the walls of some of the field boundaries came from the old quarry, signposted north of Knightstown, which has a grotto to Our Lady and St Bernadette. On the eastern end of the island is the Georgian village of Knightstown. Glanleam Subtropical Gardens, west of here, were created in the mid-19th century.

The visitor centre near the causeway that links Valentia to the mainland tells the story of the Skelligs and its significant bird population with an audiovisual display and models.

A trackway consisting of fossilised tetrapod dinosaur footprints from the Devonian period has been discovered on the island and is considered to be one of the four most significant trackways of its kind in the world.

Portmagee
This small fishing village serves as the departure point for visitors to Skellig Michael and is also where you'll find the road bridge which crosses to Valentia Island.

▶ Slane Castle   MAP REF 383 D6

slanecastle.ie

Slane, County Meath | 041 982 0643 | Open mid-May to mid-Aug
Sun–Thu 12–5

Slane Castle is best known for the huge rock concerts that take place in its grounds, attracting big names such as Queen, David Bowie and U2, along with crowds approaching 100,000. The ancestral home of the Conynghams offers guided tours: don't miss the neo-Gothic ballroom ceiling and the Capability Brown-designed courtyard. In 2015, it was announced that a new Irish whiskey distillery is to be built on the estate grounds, and is due to open in 2017.

EAT AND DRINK

Conyngham Arms Hotel ◉

conynghamarms.ie

Main Street, Slane, County Meath
041 988 4444

This 18th-century coaching inn is still a refuge for weary travellers, and it can put on a rather good wedding these days too. It's also home to a smart brasserie-style restaurant offering straightforward, unfussy food from breakfast through to dinner.

Tankardstown ◉◉

tankardstown.ie

Rathkenny, Slane, County Meath
041 982 4621

Tankardstown is a much-extended Georgian manor house that is geared up for weddings and business gatherings, and it does not lack country charm. In this idyllic spot, there is also an excellent dining proposition in the shape of the Brabazon restaurant. Situated in the one-time cow shed, expect a smart rustic finish with lots of exposed stonework, a central fireplace and pretty terrace.

▶ PLACES NEARBY

Just outside Slane is Slane Hill, a place steeped in Irish myth.

Slane Hill

Slane Hill features fine sweeping views, and the ruins of a friary church and college established in 1512. Slane is a tidy estate village, with four identical Georgian houses that face each other over the crossroads. Take the winding lane off the N2 in the north of the town, up to the Hill of Slane. From here, St Patrick is said to have lit a Paschal (Easter) fire in AD 433, in defiance of the pagan King of Tara, to announce the arrival of Christianity in Ireland.

◀ Slane Castle

▶ **Sligo** MAP REF 381 E3

sligotourism.ie

Sligo is the heart of Yeats Country and a good starting point for exploring the delightful countryside that surrounds it. This is where Ireland's national poet William B Yeats and his painter brother Jack are commemorated and celebrated. Victorian shopfronts line the narrow streets, yet it has all the amenities of a modern town. It is extremely walkable, with a tight grid of central streets containing most of the attractions. The Garravogue River bisecting the town is spanned by Hyde Bridge and New Bridge and one block to the south, running parallel to the river, is the main shopping thoroughfare of Castle Street.

On the main route between the ancient provinces of Ulster and Connacht, Sligo was always an important town. Georgian and Victorian houses, churches and commercial premises survive in large numbers, giving it an appealingly settled and old-fashioned air. It's the Yeats connection, however, that fixes Sligo on the tourist map. The long holidays that William and Jack spent here with their Pollexfen cousins in the 1870s and 1880s installed Sligo deep in the affections of both brothers, and Yeats aficionados come from all over the world to see the place that inspired so many memorable poems and paintings.

DISCOVER THE YEATS CONNECTION

Yeats Memorial Building

yeatssociety.com

Hyde Bridge, Sligo, County Sligo

071 9142693 | Open Mon–Fri 10–5, Sat 10–2

One of the English language's greatest poets is honoured in the handsome red-brick building at the west end of Hyde Bridge. The headquarters of the Yeats Society is dedicated to promoting the work and reputation of Ireland's national poet, William Butler Yeats (1865–1939) and the Society hosts an annual Yeats summer School in the first two weeks of August, with talks, readings and excursions to Yeats sites, attracting thousands. Whatever your question about W B Yeats, you'll find your answer here. The Hyde Bridge Gallery within the building showcases artistic endeavours from the environs as well as further afield. There's also a cafe overlooking the Garravogue River.

Yeats Statue

Stephen Street, Sligo, County Sligo

Rowan Gillespie's bronze sculpture of W B Yeats was erected on Stephen Street, at the east end of Hyde Bridge, by the people of Sligo in 1989 to commemorate the 50th anniversary of the poet's death. Yeats is shown in archetypal poetic stance, luxuriant locks streaming, one hand artistically poised. His billowing cloak is overprinted with a jumble of lines from his poems.

TAKE IN SOME HISTORY
Sligo Abbey
Abbey Street, Sligo, County Sligo
071 914 6406 | Open Apr to
mid-Oct 10–6
The 13th-century Dominican
friary, under an arched tower,
is in a remarkably good state of
preservation, considering its
history of fires and vandalism. It
has a beautiful medieval rood
screen, elaborate carving on
the high altar and the tomb of
Cormac O'Crean (d 1506), and
a graceful east window. It also
retains cloister arches and a
chapter house.

St John's Cathedral
John Street, Sligo, County Sligo
071 915 7993 | Visitors welcome for
Sunday Services or Jul–Aug Wed, Thu
and Sat 2–5
The Cathedral of St John the
Baptist owes its design to the
star of Dublin architecture
Richard Cassel, who laid out its
central crossing in 1730. Sadly,
to truly appreciate Cassel's
work you have to see past the
'improvements' made in the
19th century. The churchyard
contains the grave of Catherine
Stoker (née Thornley), mother
of novelist Bram Stoker.

VISIT THE MUSEUM
Sligo County Museum
sligoarts.ie
City Hall, Quay Street, Sligo, County
Sligo | 071 911 1679 | Open May–
Sep Tue–Sat 9.30–12.30, 2–4.50,
Oct–Apr Tue–Sat 9.30–12.30
A former presbytery is home to
Sligo County Museum, which
gives an enjoyable run-through
of local history via photographs
and objects, including a fiddle
that belonged to Michael
Coleman, one of the brightest
stars in Ireland's traditional
music firmament. The Yeats
Room contains formal and
informal photographs (including
images of his funeral), as well
as letters and his 1923 Nobel
Prize for literature.

VISIT THE ARTS CENTRE
The Model
themodel.ie
The Mall, Sligo, County Sligo | 071
914 1405 | Open Tue–Sat 10–5.30,
Thu 10–8, Sun 12–5
One of Ireland's foremost arts
centres, The Model puts on
concerts of jazz, contemporary
and classical music, and runs
literary and music festivals. It is

◀ Statue of W B Yeats

home of the Niland Collection, based on a collection started by Sligo's late county librarian Nora Niland, and has a dazzling range of art, with Irish artists predominating. Pride of the gallery is its definitive collection of paintings, watercolours and drawings by Jack B Yeats (1871–1957), brother of poet William. Yeats's elliptical Sligo landscapes-with-figures, such as *The Sea and The Lighthouse*, and especially the haunting late work *Leaving The Far Point*, are wonderful to linger over. Among the other works are landscapes by Paul Henry and Séan Keating, and the subtle portraits of Estella Solomons.

CATCH A PERFORMANCE
Hawk's Well Theatre
hawkswell.com

Temple Street, Sligo, County Sligo

071 916 1518

The Hawk's Well is a good quality provincial theatre that stages a variety of events. These include classical concerts and gigs by well-known Irish bands, musicals, plays, dance, singers and traditional musicians, comic plays and stand-up comedians.

EAT AND DRINK
The Belfry
belfrypub.com

John F Kennedy Parade, Thomas Street, Sligo, County Sligo

071 916 1250

Award-winning bar food is on the menu all day and with four bars over three levels and two outdoor heated garden areas, the Belfry always has a fantastic atmosphere. Customers can enjoy a game of American pool or snooker on the championship size tables.

Thomas Connolly
Holborn Street, Sligo, County Sligo

071 916 7377

In a town that has more than its fair share of traditional pubs, this one stands out. There is a lovely cosy, traditional interior featuring huge glass mirrors and old timber and on the menu are fine wines and local ales.

▶ PLACES NEARBY
Sligo is positioned at the epicentre of an area rich in ancient burial grounds, such as at Carrowmore, and historic church cemeteries at Drumcliff and Skreen. Also nearby are scenic Lough Gill and interesting Parke's Castle.

Carrowmore Megalithic Cemetery
heritageireland.ie

Carrowmore, County Sligo | 071 916 1534 | Open Apr to mid-Oct 10–6

This is not only the oldest but also the largest prehistoric burial site in Ireland. Out in low-lying country west of Sligo town, off the Strandhill road (look for brown 'heritage' road signs), are these scattered burial sites collectively known as the Carrowmore Megalithic Cemetery. The oldest tombs may date back more than 7,000 years to early Stone Age times.

Over centuries many of the tombs have been robbed of

their stone; others were dug into out of curiosity or in hope of unearthing valuable buried treasure, but around 30 are still easily identifiable. Some tombs are not much more than a pile of stones but others retain their doorways and side walling. The dates of burial items recovered from the graves span some 3,000 years and include the remains of human bones that had been cremated.

A little way to the north is Creevykeel court tomb, signposted off the N15 at Cliffony, some 14 miles north of Sligo. In contrast to the older and cruder Carrowmore tombs, this structure, dating from 3000–2000 BC, is a sophisticated mound with several chambers.

Drumcliff

It was near Drumcliff in AD 561 that St Columba's kinsmen killed around 3,000 followers of St Finian in the Battle of the Book. The grey stone Protestant church of Drumcliff is dedicated to St Columba, who founded a monastery here. The main attraction at Drumcliff, though, is the grave of poet W B Yeats in the churchyard, marked by a plain limestone headstone bearing his self-penned epitaph: 'Cast a cold Eye / On Life, on Death. / Horseman, pass by!'

Lough Gill

One of the area's most attractive lakes, surrounded by hazel woodlands, Lough Gill straddles the Sligo–Leitrim border. There are plenty of sites around the western or Sligo end of this beautiful body of water, which both the Yeats brothers – poet William and painter Jack – knew and loved from early boyhood. The R286, 287 and 288 roads form a circuit of Lough Gill, a lovely half-day excursion. On the southern shore, the R287 leads past the signposted Dooney Rock beauty spot, a clifftop viewpoint over the lake, and Slish Wood where young William once camped alone overnight.

Parke's Castle

heritageireland.ie
Fivemile Bourne | 071 64149
Open Mar–Oct daily 10–6

On the north shore, the R286 makes a delightful lakeside run east over the Leitrim border to Parke's Castle, a strikingly impressive and complete-looking fortified manor house with a turreted *bawn* or enclosed courtyard. It was built on the site of a stronghold of the O'Rourke family in 1609 by Captain Robert Parke, and after centuries of dereliction has been restored with Irish oak roofs pegged in traditional style. From the shore there's a good view of tiny, thickly wooded Innisfree, subject of Yeats's best-known poem, 'The Lake Isle of Innisfree'. You can rent a boat at the jetty and row out to where he dreamed of living: 'I will arise and go now, and go to Innisfree, / And a small cabin build there, of clay and wattles made.'

Skreen Churchyard

On the N59 Sligo–Ballina road, between Dromard and Templeboy

Take your time here and you'll discover some fine pieces of stone carving among the undergrowth. Many of the stone grave slabs and tomb chests are heavily carved with cherubim, seraphim, skulls, crossbones and other *mementi mori*. Most are the work of the Diamond family, a dynasty of stonemasons that has been living and working locally for more than 200 years. The most notable was 'Old Frank' Diamond, whose final work may have been the tomb of Mark Dowdican.

Sligo Folk Park

sligofolkpark.com

Millview House, Riverstown, County Sligo | 071 916 5001 | Open mid-Apr to Sep Mon–Sat 10–5.30, Sun 12.30–6, Oct to mid-Apr Mon–Fri 10–5

Incorporating a craft centre and shop, this folk park portrays life in rural Sligo in the late 19th century. A village street is recreated in the main exhibition hall and there are displays about farming, spinning, blacksmithing and milling.

VOYA Seaweed Baths

voyaseaweedbaths.com

Strandhill, County Sligo | 071 916 8686 | Open daily 10–8

Strandhill is nestled at the foot of Knocknarae mountain in 'the land of heart's desire' (W B Yeats). Visit Voya and relax into a luxurious steaming bath of fresh seawater and wild, organic seaweed. At the beginning of the 20th century there were an estimated 300 seaweed bath houses in Ireland, many of them clustered around the small town of Strandhill alone. Today Voya products are revered by beauty experts around the world.

Wilderness Ireland

wildernessireland.com

Unit 3, Sligo Airport Business Park, Strandhill, Sligo | 091 457 898

Wilderness Ireland offers hiking, sea kayaking, cycling, family and tailor-made trips, both locally and throughout Ireland. The dedicated and highly knowledgeable team know Ireland's wilderness well and may be the best in the country. Expect innovative trips, stand-out customer service and a highly responsible approach to tourism.

▼ High cross at Drumcliff

County Sligo Golf Club

countysligogolfclub.ie

Rosses Point, County Sligo

071 917 7134

Located a short 5-mile drive from the city centre and considered to be one of the top links courses in Ireland, County Sligo Golf Club is host to a number of international competitions. Set in an elevated position on cliffs overlooking three large beaches, the prevailing winds provide an additional challenge. Tom Watson described it as 'a magnificent links, particularly the stretch of holes from the 14th to the 17th'.

Waterfront House ◉

waterfronthouse.ie

Sea Front, Cliff Road, Enniscrone, County Sligo | 096 37120

The white-fronted hotel with red-framed windows is situated on the Wild Atlantic Way that is the Sligo coast, where spectacular sunsets are the norm. Customers dine in a light-filled, wooden-floored room with views over the miles of beach, its homely ambience offset with napkins and staff neckties in daring lime-green. Seafood is very much to the fore, with tasting banquets on the first Friday of the month, and not everything is necessarily traditional.

Radisson Blu Hotel and Spa Sligo ◉

radissonblu.ie/sligo

Rosses Point Road, Ballincar, County Sligo | 071 914 0008 and 919 2400

Sligo is W B Yeats country, and the Radisson Blu is ideally placed to cater for the annual pilgrimage of devotees who come to see the places the poet loved. It's a classy modern hotel, designed in boutique manner with plenty of vivid colour, notably reds and purples in the Classiebawn dining room. Here, the bill of fare is the finest contemporary Irish cooking of notable technical ambition.

▸ Strokestown Park   MAP REF 381 E5

strokestownpark.ie

Signposted in Strokestown, County Roscommon, on the N5 between Scramoge and Tulsk, 14 miles west of Longford | 071 963 3013 | Open mid-Mar to Oct daily 10.30–5.30, Nov to mid-Mar 10.30–4

Strokestown Park is a fine, predominantly 18th-century Palladian building that includes the Famine Museum. The story of the Mahons is similar to that of many other Anglo-Irish families: a huge 17th-century grant of land by the English Crown, the laying out and working of a vast estate, the building and improvement of the fine mansion, three centuries of ease and prosperity as bastions of the Ascendancy followed by a gradual decline during the 20th century and the eventual sale of house and lands. The difference here is that the family's

▲ Strokestown Park

attitudes to its tenants are explored with insight and honesty in the remarkable museum dedicated to the Great Famine.

What distinguishes Strokestown Park from most of the other mansions open to the public is the very strong image of successive generations of its owners that visitors receive. This highly personal atmosphere springs from the fact that everything you see was chosen and used by the owners over their three centuries of incumbency, right up until the sale of the property in 1979 by Olive Pakenham-Mahon, the last of the family to live here, in a poignant genteel poverty.

A conducted tour starts in the entrance hall and continues by way of the drawing room and library. On the upper floor you view the Lady's and Gentleman's bedrooms, the schoolroom and nursery. The Schoolroom (1930s copybooks – 'Please rule your margins all the same width' – neatly laid out on tiny desks) and playroom show the privileged yet highly regulated life of an Ascendancy child. The tour then descends to the dining room where you discover the world of the family's servants in the kitchen.

The Famine Museum that occupies the old stable block is arranged in a series of rooms. Room 1 sets the Ascendancy scene, Room 2 shows the growth of destitution among the Irish poor. Room 3 examines the role of the potato in 19th-century Ireland and the beginning of the catastrophic potato blight, while rooms 4 and 5 look at the relief efforts that were employed during the Great Famine. There's also a display on eviction and emigration, and some images and discussion of famines across the world today. The walled garden provides a quiet place to process the stark, terrible images of famine.

As with the house, the impact of the Famine Museum comes from the interplay between the intimate details of the Mahon family's attitudes and behaviour during the Great Famine, and the wider picture in Ireland and in mainland Britain.

The exhibition describes how incoming 17th-century Anglo-Protestants took over most of Ireland. In the 1620s Irish Catholics owned two-thirds of the land, but after the Cromwellian suppressions of the 1650s, only 30 years later, they held less than one-tenth. In those decades, one in three of the Catholic population died of famine, disease or massacre, a far higher proportion than died during the Great Famine, and the system of land tenure kept the poor in abject poverty. British political cartoons depicted the Irish tenants as 'indolent, idle, inclined to do evil, and beyond the pale of civilisation', and the Anglo-Irish landlords as feckless drunkards. Such contemptuous attitudes contributed to the disaster of the Great Famine of 1845–49, when the *Phytophthora infestans* fungus wiped out the potato crops on which the people were utterly dependent. The British government fumbled its relief efforts with clumsiness and callousness; mass evictions and emigration added to the misery.

Against this background moves the story of the Mahons on their estate, which stretched for 5,930 acres, and of the evictions carried out by Major Denis Mahon during the famine. Family papers exhibited include a letter of 7 November 1847 from Mahon's agent proposing the eviction and enforced emigration to America of two-thirds of the local population, and a letter to the Major from his tenants which asks, 'What must we do? – our families really and truly suffering at present, and we cannot much longer withstand their cries for food'. The letter makes veiled threats of action unless relief is forthcoming; and such action did follow, later that year, when the Major was shot dead. The picture of seigneurial hard-heartedness is balanced by a thoughtful coda by the Major's great-great-grandson, pointing out that landlords like Denis Mahon had insufficient resources and no government grants to help their tenants, and that paying for them to emigrate was preferable to letting them starve.

In 1997, the refurbished walled gardens were opened to the public after years of neglect. You can enjoy roses, wild flowers and the longest herbaceous border in the British Isles, as well as the neat green swards of the lawn tennis court and the croquet lawn, a magnificent lily pond and some shady walkways under the trees.

> ### ▷ PLACES NEARBY

Another of the great houses of County Roscommon can be reached by driving west to Clonalis House (see page 210) just outside Castlerea. Full of historical documents and artefacts, the house is well worth the 40-minute drive from Strokestown.

▶ Tory Island (Toraigh) MAP REF 382 A1

The crossing to Tory Island can be a corkscrew affair. The rough waters of Tory Sound can make the ferry crossing impossible even in summer. All the more pleasant, then, to be welcomed with a handshake or a kiss by the King of Tory, a post first created by St Columba in the sixth century AD, and still filled by a resident Tory islander. The 'walls' of Tory are formidable cliffs, topped by a flat, treeless and windswept plateau. Around 150 Irish-speaking people live on Tory Island, and they are often cut off for weeks at a time in winter; they are correspondingly hospitable and pleased to see visitors.

If the weather allows, birdwatching and walking are superb here, and there is a tremendous atmosphere in the pubs when musicians are on the island, especially during the Tory Island Festival in July.

VISIT THE GALLERY
Dixon Gallery
toryislandpaintings.com
086 262 0154

This interesting little gallery began in the 1950s when the late Derek Hill used to come to the island to paint. Islander

▼ The Anvil on Tory Island

James Dixon joked he could do better himself and they became good friends. The Tory School of painting developed from here, and the style of the various artists is generally considered 'primitive' or 'naïve'. Sadly, the gallery is in a state of bad repair and the artists are currently fundraising.

GET ON THE WATER
Turasmara Ferry
toryislandferry.com
074 953 1320/ 953 1340 | Sailings daily all year, subject to weather
Donegal Coastal Cruises operate the foot passenger cruiser from Bunbeg and Magheroarty.

EAT AND DRINK
Harbour View Hotel
hoteltory.com
074 913 5920
This hotel offers traditional Tory Island hospitality, with food, accommodation and often live music from locals.

▶ PLACES NEARBY
The ferry to Tory Island can be caught from Bunbeg, a small coastal village, or Magheroarty, another small fishing village with a lovely beach of pinkish sands and views of the islands. It's popular with surfers, windsurfers and kayakers. There's a famous Gaelic summer school here, too.

▶ Tralee   MAP REF 376 B4
tralee.ie

Tralee is the county town of Kerry, the northeast gateway to the Dingle Peninsula and known for its Rose of Tralee International Festival (see page 54) – a week-long party and beauty pageant that brings more than 200,000 visitors into town in August. The town sprawls on the flatlands east of Tralee Bay and has plenty of accommodation and sandy beaches nearby at Banna and Derrymore. The town was founded in the 13th century by the Earls of Desmond.

VISIT THE MUSEUM
Kerry County Museum
kerrymuseum.ie
Ashe Memorial Hall, Denny Street, Tralee, County Kerry | 066 712 7777
Open Jun–Oct daily 9.30–5.30, Nov–May Tue–Sat 9.30–5
The town's chequered history is told in time-journey style at the Kerry County Museum, located in the Ashe Memorial Hall. There is also an exhibit on Irish Antarctic explorer Tom Crean.

CATCH A PERFORMANCE
Siamsa Tíre Theatre
siamsatire.com
Townpark, Tralee, County Kerry
066 712 3055
This striking modern building is home to the National Folk Theatre of Ireland, with nightly performances in summer. The company was set up in 1974, and maintains an accessible, entertaining schedule of drama, mime, dance and music.

▲ Banna Beach

GO SWIMMING
Aqua Dome
aquadome.ie
Dingle Road, Tralee, County Kerry
066 712 9150 | Open Mon–Fri
10–10, Sat, Sun 10–8
You can enjoy water-based fun in all weathers here. There's a wave pool, water slides, rapids and geysers, a health suite for adults and even an 18-hole aqua golf course. Outside there's a miniature golf course and remote-controlled toys.

GO SHOPPING
A lovely, local farmers' market takes place every Saturday (10–2.30) at the Brandon car park, Tralee. Shop for locally made crafts, gifts, food and other produce at this lively weekly spot.

▶ PLACES NEARBY
From Tralee you can explore the beautiful coastline and beaches of Tralee Bay or head inland and north to haunting Ardfert Cathedral. Further north brings you to Listowel town on the River Feale. Head south from here to Crag Cave and its amazing mineral deposits.

Ardfert Cathedral
heritageireland.ie
Ardfert, County Kerry
066 713 4711
The main structure of this ecclesiastical site, just north of the village of Ardfert, is the roofless Ardfert Cathedral, which dates from the 13th to 17th centuries. Look out for the Romanesque sawtooth carvings around arched doorways, and the blind staircase. In the low-lying coastal landscape north of Tralee, locally born St Brendan 'The Navigator' (AD 484–577) founded a monastery in the sixth century. Nothing remains but the importance of this site can be gauged by the three medieval churches here, and the 13th-century friary to the east. There are also remains of two other churches, one a fine example of late Romanesque, the other much plainer.

Crag Cave

cragcave.com

Crag, Castleisland, County Kerry
066 714 1244 | Open Apr–Dec daily
10–6, Jan–Mar Fri–Sun 10–6

In the summer, tours run every half hour at Crag Cave, which is thought to be a million years old. Guides show visitors the stalagmites and stalactites accompanied by a dramatic sound-and-lighting backdrop.

Crazy Cave Indoor and Outdoor Adventure Centre

cragcave.com

Crag, Castleisland, County Kerry
066 714 1244 | Open Apr–Dec daily
10–6, Jan–Mar Fri–Sun 10–6

For families with children up to 12 years, the Crazy Cave Indoor and Outdoor Adventure Centre adjoins Crag Cave, with all manner of activities and fun.

The Seanchaí Centre: Kerry Writers' Museum

kerrywritersmuseum.com

The Square, Listowel, County Kerry
068 22212 | Open Jun–Sep daily
9.30–5, Oct–May Mon–Fri 10–4

Listowel has two main claims to its place on the visitors' map: an antique monorail and an imaginative literary museum. Seanchaí (pronounced 'Shanakey'), meaning 'storyteller', is in a fine Georgian house on the town square. The museum celebrates the works of John B Keane, Bryan MacMahon, Brendan Kennelly, Maurice Walsh and others.

▶ Tralee Golf Club

Listowel Monorail

lartiguemonorail.com

John B Keane Road, Listowel, County
Kerry | 068 24393 | Check the
website for the timetable

From 1888 to 1924 the steam-powered monorail took freight, passengers and livestock the 9 miles between Listowel and Ballybunion. It's the only monorail of its type to run successfully on a commercial basis. You can take a short demonstration trip on a full-scale diesel-powered replica. There's a museum, too.

Tralee Bay Wetlands Centre and Nature Reserve

traleebaywetlands.org

Ballyard, Tralee, County Kerry
066 712 6700 | Open daily Jul,
Aug 10–7, Mar–Jun, Sep, Oct 10–5,
Nov–Feb 11–4

Visitors have been flocking to enjoy the beautiful and varied reserve since it opened in 2012. Don't miss the chance to scale the 66-foot viewing tower and take a safari boat tour. There's a cafe, hides for birders and water sports for the energetic.

Blennerville Windmill

Blennerville, Tralee, County Kerry
066 712 1064 | Open daily Apr–Oct
10–5

Climb to the top of this white-painted windmill with red sails to enjoy sweeping views of Tralee Bay. This dominant landmark was built in 1780 by Roland Blennerhasset, after whom the village is named, and has been restored to working order. Its audiovisual room tells of Blennerville's role as an emigration port in the 19th century and children can grind their own wheat into flour. The windmill is a mile from Tralee, beside the N86, and a fun way to get there is by vintage steam train from the town.

Banna Beach

This beautiful sweep of golden sand, with dunes rising up to 40 feet high, is popular with Tralee residents in the summer. There's a memorial to Roger Casement, who in 1916 came ashore here from a German U-Boat, in an attempt to land arms for Irish Republicans.

Derrymore Beach

Another fantastic sandy beach, perfect for walking. Derrymore Island, to the eastern end of the strand, is a nature reserve.

Tralee Golf Club

traleegolfclub.com
West Barrow, Ardfert, 9 miles from
Tralee | 066 713 6379

The first Arnold Palmer-designed course in Europe, this magnificent 18-hole links is set in spectacular scenery on the Barrow Peninsula, surrounded on three sides by the sea. The most memorable hole is the par four 17th, which plays from a high tee, across a deep gorge to the green. The back nine is challenging and is not suitable for beginners.

Ballyseede Castle

ballyseedecastle.com
Ballyseede, County Kerry
066 712 5799

The O'Connell Restaurant looks like something you would find happily placed in a stately home. An impression of 'Resplendent grandeur' heads

the menu, but the cooking is far more down-to-earth than the aesthetics might suggest – the kitchen clearly taking a more contemporary view on all matters culinary. Woodland and well-tended grounds surround the crenellated and turreted castle, which dates from the late 16th century.

▶ Trim   MAP REF 379 D1

meathtourism.ie

The small, quiet town of Trim on the banks of the River Boyne is home to the largest Anglo-Norman castle in Ireland.

Across the river, the Sheep's Gate and the Yellow Steeple, the belfry tower of an Augustinian abbey, rise from a meadow, left undeveloped on their medieval sites when the town's focus shifted towards the opposite bank in the 18th century.

Downstream of the castle, on the edge of new housing developments, the ruins of the 13th-century cathedral of saints Peter and Paul is connected to the Hospital of St John the Baptist by an ancient bridge, on the north side of which is one of Ireland's oldest pubs. In the visitor centre near the castle, 'The Power and the Glory', a multimedia presentation, documents the impact of the arrival of the Normans.

TAKE IN SOME HISTORY
Trim Castle

heritageireland.ie

Castle Street, Trim, County Meath
046 943 8619 | Open Easter–Sep daily 10–6, Oct daily 9.30–5.30, Nov–Jan Sat–Sun 9–5, Feb–Easter Sat–Sun 9.30–5.30

Its curtain wall is more than a quarter of a mile long and encloses a site of 3 acres. The central keep is 70 feet high and the walls are 11 feet thick. Together with the 10 D-shaped towers in the surrounding walls, the keep has barely been altered since the 13th century, though it does bear the scars you would expect from a fortification so close to the edge of the English Pale (the area under English influence). Many of the castle scenes in the film *Braveheart* (1995) were filmed here at this castle. Access to the keep is by 45-minute guided tour only.

EAT AND DRINK
The James Griffin

jamesgriffinpub.ie

High Street, Trim, County Meath
046 943 1295

The James Griffin has been providing the people of Trim with friendly hospitality since it opened in 1904. Full of cosy nooks and corners, it's a welcoming, traditional place.

▶ PLACES NEARBY

Bective Abbey (see page 178) lies to the northeast of Trim beside the River Boyne. Further east from these abbey ruins is the Hill of Tara (see page 304).

▶ **Waterford** MAP REF 378 C5

discoverwaterfordcity.ie

Ireland's oldest city, Waterford has the largest collection of medieval walls and towers still standing in Ireland. It dates back to 7000 BC, when Stone Age hunter-gatherers congregated on the banks of the River Suir. By 2000 BC settlers were mining copper all along this coast. Viking raids in AD 795 turned to settlement after 914, with a fort called Dundory built on the triangle of high ground between two rivers, and the establishment of a town they called Vadrafjordr. The Anglo-Normans gained power here in the 12th century, and largely held on to it until the upheavals of the mid-17th century, when the city walls failed to repel Cromwell's army.

The city is attractively spread along the south bank of the River Suir. Broad Merchant's Quay runs beside the river, with a variety of shops, hotels and other buildings facing the water.

The main shopping area lies in the warren of small streets behind Merchant's Quay, by the Port of Waterford Company building at the top of Gladstone Street. Architect John Roberts' Catholic Cathedral of the Most Holy Trinity of 1793, lit inside by 10 chandeliers, is equally elegant.

TAKE IN SOME HISTORY

Cathedral of the Most Holy Trinity

waterford-cathedral.com

Barronstrand Street, Waterford, County Waterford | 051 875 166

Ireland's oldest Catholic cathedral, dating from 1793, was designed by John Roberts.

Christ Church Cathedral

christchurchwaterford.com

Cathedral Square, Waterford, County Waterford | 051 858 958

Open Mon–Sat 10–5

Also designed by John Roberts, Christ Church Cathedral makes Waterford the only city in Europe with Protestant and Catholic cathedrals conceived by the same person. There's been a cathedral on the site since 1096, and the current building, Ireland's only neoclassical Georgian cathedral, is one of the finest 18th-century ecclesiastical buildings in the country.

VISIT THE MUSEUMS

Waterford Treasures

waterfordtreasures.com

The Mall, Waterford, County Waterford | 051 304 500 | Open Jun–Aug Mon–Fri 9.15–6, Sat 9.30–6, Sun 11–6, Sep–May Mon–Fri 9.15–5, Sat 10–6, Sun 11–5

Waterford Treasures is three museums, in the Viking Triangle: the Bishop's Palace, Reginald's Tower and Medieval Museum. Learn the story of the city's development in the context of the history of the rest of Ireland as a whole. Many of the artefacts were discovered during the extensive archaeological excavations in the city centre between 1986 and 1992. A glass lift rises to the third floor for a tour of the Viking, Anglo-Norman and medieval city, then you proceed to the 18th century on the second floor, where a 12-minute audiovisual show takes you to the 19th century and beyond.

Look for a curved Viking flute (c 1150), made from a swan or goose bone; a gold kite-shaped brooch of the same

▼ The Bishops Palace

era; the medieval Great Charter Roll, depicting all the lord mayors of Waterford; and a red velvet hat given to the mayor in 1536 by Henry VIII. There's also the tale of local boy Thomas Francis Meagher, convicted of treason after the Young Ireland Rebellion of 1848. He escaped being sent to Australia and fled to New York, where he became a Civil War hero and founded the *Irish News*; he is also credited with introducing the Irish flag. Other famous sons of Waterford featured include Shakespearean actor Charles Kean (1811–68) and opera composer William Vincent Wallace (1812–65).

Waterford Crystal
waterfordvisitorcentre.com
The Mall, Waterford, County Waterford | 051 317 000 | Open Apr–Oct Mon–Sat 9–4.15, Sun 9.30–4.15, Nov–Mar Mon–Fri 9.30–3.15

It is easy to take for granted the sparkling chandeliers made of hand-cut crystal that adorn the public and private buildings of Waterford Crystal and, indeed, the rest of the world. But visit a factory where some of that crystal is made and you realise how much skill and time goes into every piece of glass.

Glassmaking became an industry here in 1783 and thrived until 1851, when heavy taxation and a lack of funds stopped production. Waterford Crystal was revived in 1947, and now dominates the top end of the market in much of Europe and America. But the industry became a high-profile victim of the recession in 2009, when its flagship factory, covering a vast 40-acre site on the edge of town, was closed.

Production continues in Germany and the Czech Republic, and on a very much smaller scale in the newly built

▼ Waterford crystal

visitor experience – the House of Waterford Crystal on The Mall in the city centre. Combining an artisan craft manufacturing area, design centre and shop, it's a pale shadow of the brand's former presence in Waterford, but is nonetheless interesting.

CATCH A PERFORMANCE
Theatre Royal
theatreroyal.ie
The Mall, Waterford, County Waterford | 051 874 402
The most prestigious of Waterford's three theatres, in the City Hall behind a modern glass front, hosts Irish and international opera and drama productions. A permanent display of local art can be found in the public areas.

SADDLE UP
Stonehaven Equestrian Centre
stonehavenec.com
Gracedieu, Waterford, County Waterford | 051 873 816
Explore the natural beauty of the riverbank and nearby mountains on horseback, on day or longer trips.

GO WALKING
Waterford Walking Tours
jackswalkingtours.com
Waterford Tourist Services, Jenkin's Lane, Waterford, County Waterford
051 873 711 | Open daily Mar–Oct 11.45, 1.45
There are many fascinating facts to discover about Waterford. It's all revealed on a one-hour guided walking tour; there's no need to book.

PLAY A ROUND
Waterford Castle Hotel and Golf Resort
waterfordcastle.com
The Island, Ballinakill, Waterford, County Waterford | 051 871 633
This is a unique island course beside the River Suir that is accessed by private ferry; the only true island course in Ireland. It meanders through mature woodland, and water features dominate the second, third, fourth and 16th holes; Swilken Bridge is on the third hole. Two of the more challenging holes are the par fours at the ninth and 12th; the ninth being a 414-yard uphill, dog-leg right. The 456-yard 12th is a fine test of accuracy and distance. The views from the course are superb.

EAT AND DRINK
Bistro at the Tower ❂
towerhotelwaterford.com
The Mall, Waterford, County Waterford | 051 862 300
With so many fishing villages hereabouts, it comes as no surprise to find that fish and seafood are strong suits at the Bistro. The decor is inspired by the marina.

Geoff's
9 John Street, Waterford, County Waterford | 051 874 787
A landmark bar in the centre of town near Apple Market offering filling, unfussy pub grub with vegetarian options. There's usually a friendly welcome from bar staff and locals alike.

Henry Downes

Thomas Street, Waterford, County
Waterford | 051 874 118

This pub was founded way back
in 1759 and still tops the list of
best pubs in town. They bottle
their own whiskey and don't
dare to disobey their sign telling
you to turn off your mobile
phones. This place is legendary.

▶ PLACES NEARBY

Head north out of Waterford to
visit the Ahenny High Crosses
which are signed off the R697
Kilmaganny road, north of
Carrick-on-Suir. From any
other direction, signposting is
poor. East of Waterford is
12th-century Dunbrody Abbey.

Ahenny High Crosses

There is a dignity and
remoteness about this pair of
wheel crosses standing 8 feet
high in a graveyard on a hillside.
The pinkish sandstone of these
monuments was carved by
unknown hands in the eighth
century. Moss and lichen
mellow the effect of the
intricately carved Celtic motifs,
spirals and geometric designs;
human figures can be seen on
the bases.

Dunbrody Abbey

dunbrodyabbey.com
Campile, New Ross, County Wexford
086 275 9149 | Open mid-May to
mid-Sep daily 11–6

Dunbrody Abbey, dating from
1182, lies in open meadows by a
tributary of the Barrow River.
There's a visitor centre, in the
courtyard of a ruined castle, a
tea room and a craft shop.

Faithlegg House Hotel and Golf Resort ❀❀

faithlegg.com
Faithlegg, County Waterford
051 382 000

The original mansion, built in
the 1780s, opened as a
country-house hotel in 1998
after immaculate restoration. It
has its own 18-hole golf course
and leisure centre, while the
high-ceilinged restaurant looks
over the garden. The cooking
makes an impact, based as it is
on native produce and a range
of neat ideas.

▶ Westport   MAP REF 380 C5

destinationwestport.com

Westport is a pleasant town. Before good roads were built into
western Mayo during the 19th century, it was an isolated place,
and still retains that sense of self-sufficiency. Westport was
laid out for the Marquess of Sligo in the 1780s by James Wyatt,
one of the supreme architects of the Georgian era. His grid
pattern, with the parallel thoroughfares of Bridge Street and
James Street running uphill from The Mall beside the
Carrowbeg River, still survives, and gives the town an orderly,
manageable air. At the top of Bridge Street there's a tall clock
tower; on the Octagon, at the top of James Street, a column

supports a statue of St Patrick, whose holy mountain of Croagh Patrick is visible from the outskirts of town.

The Westport Arts Festival takes place in late September or early October and brings music, plays, painting, poetry, street theatre and other events to the town. Westport is also one of the best towns in Ireland for traditional music session pubs. The best known of these is the bar on Bridge Street that's named after its owner, Matt Molloy (see below and right). Other venues include Hoban's at the Octagon, and McHale's on Lower Peter Street.

TAKE IN SOME HISTORY
Westport House
westporthouse.ie

Westport, County Mayo | 098 27766

Open daily May–Aug 10–6, Mar, Apr, Sep–Nov 10–4

Westport House was completed in 1779 by James Wyatt, and contains beautiful furniture, silver, glass and pictures that reflects the taste of the Browne family, marquesses of Sligo. The grounds are great for children; the Pirate Adventure Park takes its theme from the notorious local pirate queen Grace O'Malley.

VISIT THE MUSEUM
Clew Bay Heritage Centre
westportheritage.com

The Quay, Westport, County Mayo 098 26852 | Open Apr, May, Oct Mon–Fri 10–2, Jun–Sep Mon–Fri 10–5, Jul, Aug Mon–Fri 10–5, Sun 3–5

Westport Quay is lined with restored stone warehouses converted into restaurants, a hotel and shops. Here you'll find the Clew Bay Heritage Centre, with a small museum that gives an introduction to the Bay, which opens from Westport Bay to the west.

EXPLORE BY BIKE
Clew Bay Bike Hire
clewbayoutdoors.ie

Distillery Road, Westport, County Mayo | 098 24818

Taking advantage of the dedicated cycle routes in this part of Ireland, Clew Bay Bikes will kit you out with everything you need for a day's pedalling. Perhaps the most exciting route is the 48-mile Great Western Greenway from Newport to Mulrany, which follows the line of a disused railway. Clew Bay Bike Hire operates a pick-up and drop-off service too, making trips to Achill and Clare islands possible, as well as around Westport and Clew Bay. Family deals, tagalongs and trailers are also available. Highly recommended sailing, sea kayaking and longer trips can also be organised here.

LISTEN TO LIVE MUSIC
Hoban's
The Octagon, Westport, County Mayo 098 27249

This friendly and welcoming traditional pub, dating back to the late 1790s, offers live music, good beer and an excellent atmosphere.

▲ Matt Molloy

Matt Molloy's
Bridge Street, Westport, County Mayo | 098 26655
Matt Molloy plays flute with Ireland's best-known traditional band, The Chieftains. When he's at home he's usually found joining in the session in the bar of his own pub. Soak up the atmosphere in one of Ireland's most delightful pubs.

McCarthy's Bar
Quay Street, Westport, County Mayo
098 27050
McCarthy's is a central, family-run pub with a warm and friendly atmosphere. Visit on a Friday night when you can enjoy live music with your drink.

SADDLE UP
Equestrian Holidays Ireland
gotrekking.ie and westportwoodshotel.com

Westport Woods Hotel, Quay Road, Westport, County Mayo
087 260 5672
Gallop along beaches and canter through mountains with this riding company, which operates out of Westport Woods Hotel. It's part of Equestrian Holidays, the recommended nationwide riding company.

PLAY A ROUND
Westport Golf Club
westportgolfclub.com
Carrowholly, Westport | 098 28262
This is a beautiful course with wonderful views of Clew Bay and the holy mountain Croagh Patrick. It's a challenging course and has many memorable holes. Perhaps the most exciting is the par five 15th, 580 yards long with a long carry from the tee over an inlet of Clew Bay.

EAT AND DRINK

Knockranny House Hotel @@

knockrannyhousehotel.ie
Castlebar Road, Westport, County
Mayo | 098 28600

The Noonans' tranquil spa hotel
has stunning views over Clew
Bay. Inside you will find all the
accoutrements of an upmarket
hotel, including a full-dress
dining room, La Fougère, which
eschews modern minimalism in
favour of immaculate table
linen and glassware.

▶ PLACES NEARBY

As well as seaside Clew Bay,
Westport is close to the
wonderful National Museum of
Ireland at Turlough and the
historic Foxford Woollen Mills.

Clew Bay

There may not really be 365
islands in Clew Bay, as locals
claim, but there are certainly
a lot of them. Clew Bay is a
beautiful wide bay, some 8
miles wide and 13 miles long,
lined with sandy beaches at
Mulrany on the north and
between Louisburgh and
Murrisk on the south. The
tourist information office has
details of sporting activities.

National Museum of Ireland – Country Life

museum.ie
Turlough Park, Turlough, Castlebar,
County Mayo | 094 903 1755
Open Tue–Sat 10–5, Sun 2–5

Housing the national collection
of objects representing
traditional Irish life from 1850
onwards, the National Museum
of Ireland – Country Life is the
country cousin to the Dublin-
based National Museum of
Ireland (see page 260). It offers
a fascinating glimpse into this
important time in Irish history.
It is set over four floors in a
purpose-built building in the
Turlough Park estate, and
the exhibits will take you
through the myths and the often
grim realities of life in rural
Ireland. The context is set
through displays on the natural
environment and national
events, while individual exhibits
reveal the day-to-day lives of
country folk – their crafts, trade
and farming traditions. Rare
archive film and photography
show that this was not a time of
romance but of real poverty,
though many of the activities
and traditions depicted are
familiar to us today in our
stereotyped view of Irish life.
Temporary exhibits have

included the story of migrant women and the gold Cross of Cong and other items which reflect the wealth of the national collection, and there is a full calendar of events and activities.

Turlough Park House replaced its Georgian predecessor in 1865 as the home of the FitzGerald family, who owned 8,150 acres hereabouts, mostly farmed by local tenants. The estate retains its 18th-century parkland, including a lake and the remains of the former house.

Foxford Woollen Mills
foxfordwoollenmills.com
Foxford, County Mayo
094 925 6104
Open Mon–Sat 10–6, Sun 12–6
A multimedia tour takes visitors on a journey exploring the history of Foxford Woollen Mills, dating from the 1800s, which still operates as a working mill, one of the last of its kind in Ireland. Here you can shop for fabrics, as well as fine homeware and giftware, from its master craftsmen in the Mill Shop.

Mulranny Park Hotel ◉◉
mulrannyparkhotel.ie
Mulrany, County Mayo
098 36000
A sumptuous country-house operation, this former railway station hotel offers sweeping views over the Atlantic from the Nephin dining room, where swagged drapes and linen tables set the tone, with more informal eating in the Waterfront Bar. Modern Irish cooking is the stock-in-trade, using local ingredients.

▼ Westport town

▶ **Wexford** MAP REF 379 D5

discoverireland.ie

The long, narrow main street of Wexford runs parallel with the quay, which is only lightly used today. There are some interesting pockets of history around the town and it is a good base for exploring attractions in the surrounding area. Little remains of the old town, the Westgate tower being the sole survivor of the 14th-century walls.

The Vikings established Wexford as a port and shipbuilding town in the eighth century. In the Middle Ages it was an important English garrison town, but when Oliver Cromwell and his army arrived in 1649 the rebellious spirit of the townspeople cost them dearly and several hundred were executed on the Bullring. Rebelliousness continued, however, and in 1798 a republic was declared here. A statue of a pikeman on the Bullring is a memorial to the town's role in the 1798 rebellion. Nearby are the ruins of Selskar Abbey.

TAKE IN SOME HISTORY
Selskar Abbey
visitwexford.ie
Selskar, Wexford, County Wexford
086 107 9497 | Ruins: open access
Selskar Abbey, now a ruin, was built by Henry II in penitence for the murder of Thomas Becket. The opera festival held here every October attracts performers and devotees from all over the world.

▲ Wexford at night, Selskar Abbey, The Pikemen sculpture

GET OUTDOORS
Wexford Wildfowl Reserve
wexfordwildfowlreserve.ie
North Slobs, Wexford, County
Wexford | 053 912 3129
Open daily 9–5

Wexford Wildfowl Reserve lies behind the sea wall on the north side of Wexford Harbour where the North Slobs are 10 feet below high tide level. This wetland area was drained from marshland in the 19th century for farmland, but its meadows and drainage channels also provided an ideal habitat for bird life. In winter you might see 29 different species of duck and 42 types of wader. The 10,000 or so Greenland white-fronted geese form as much as one-third of the world's total population, and the pale-bellied Brents also arrive on a globally significant scale.

The reserve's 247 acres include a series of accessible hides from which visitors can observe the birds. One is next to the Victorian pumping station – its chimney is a landmark, though its steam pump has long since been replaced by an electric version.

GO BACK IN TIME
Irish National Heritage Park
inhp.com
Ferrycarrig, Wexford, County
Wexford | 053 912 0733
Open daily May–Aug 9.30–6.30,
Sep–Apr 9.30–5.30

On the edge of Wexford, just off the northern bypass, the Irish

National Heritage Park is a good place to stop if you have just entered the country from the Rosslare ferry. In 5 acres of reclaimed marsh and swamp, 9,000 years of Irish history have been recreated through a series of full-scale models.

There's a Mesolithic site with its dolmen and camp, a Bronze Age area showing how a cist burial would have looked, and a ring fort, a common feature of the Irish landscape. You can see a re-creation of a monastic settlement, with its high cross, oratory and watermill, visit a *crannóg*, reconstructed on an island in the marsh, and appreciate the craft of the Viking shipbuilders who settled this area.

Against the criticism that this is 'theme park Ireland' (in summer actors in costume roam around the site), the reconstructions can prove invaluable when you are trying to interpret many of the sites you will see in the rest of the country, putting the early Christian era in perspective and helping you to understand other remains such as those at the Hill of Tara or Kells.

PLAY A ROUND
Wexford Golf Club
wexfordgolfclub.ie
Mulgannon, Wexford, County Wexford | 053 42238
Parkland with panoramic views of the Wexford coastline and mountains. There has been extensive redevelopment in recent years.

EAT AND DRINK
Bugler Doyles Bar
buglerdoyles.ie
83 South Main Street, Wexford, County Wexford | 053 912 2261
This no-nonsense pub in the centre of town is right on the main street. It has been in existence since the 1850s and is now run by brothers Andy and Pat Doyles, who also offer accommodation upstairs.

▶ **PLACES NEARBY**
A short hop south from Wexford is Johnstown Castle with its agricultural and famine museums. Go to the National 1798 Centre at Enniscorthy for an explanation of the politics of that time, or head for coastal Kilmore Quay to take a boat trip for fishing or to explore the Saltee Islands.

Johnstown Castle
irishagrimuseum.ie
Johnstown Castle Estate, 4 miles from Wexford, County Wexford
053 918 4671 | Gardens: daily Jun–Aug 9–7, Mar–May, Sep, Oct 9–5.30, Nov–Feb 9–4.30; Museum: Jun–Aug Mon–Fri 9–6.30, Sat, Sun 11–6.30, Mar–May, Sep, Oct Mon–Fri 9–5, Sat, Sun 11–5, Nov–Feb Mon–Fri 9–4, Sat, Sun 11–4
Close to the route from the Rosslare ferry port, Johnstown Castle is well signposted off the N25, just south of the Duncannon intersection. The site is a little confusing, being also the home of an agricultural college and an array of government departments relating to countryside matters,

but at its heart lies the fabulously Gothicised castle, and the agricultural and famine museums. The foyer is as far inside the castle as visitors can get, but you can wander in its 50 acres of gardens, seeing the peacocks, walled garden and ornamental lakes. The agricultural museum recreates country trades and scenes from the last 200 years. Displays explain transport and farming and show a large collection of furniture and implements. The famine exhibition, within the museum, attempts to put this national tragedy of the 1840s in perspective, explaining the role of the potato and the changes that followed in the wake of the disastrous blight. A series of farmhouse kitchens in the agricultural museum compares the domestic lifestyles of 1800, 1900 and 1950.

National 1798 Centre

1798centre.ie

Mill Park Road, Enniscorthy, County Wexford | 054 37596 | Open Mon–Fri 9.30–5, Sat–Sun 1–5

If you are a bit unsure of the details of the 1798 rebellion in the south of Ireland, the superb visitor attraction of National 1798 Centre in Enniscorthy, built to mark the rising's bicentenary, puts the whole period in perspective. Using a mix of audiovisuals and informative displays, it takes you through the economic and political conditions that led up to the conflict. The culmination is a reconstruction of the

eventual showdown on Vinegar Hill, where the Crown's forces under General Lake stormed the rebels' headquarters, defended by 20,000 pikemen. In the confusion, the rebel army was able to slip away with barely 500 dead.

The hill rises up on the far side of the Slaney River, while the town itself climbs up the western bank of the river; there is a more traditional museum in the Norman castle near the pedestrianised centre of town.

Saltee Islands

salteeislands.com

Great and Little Saltee sit in St George's Channel off the coast of County Wexford. Great Saltee is probably the best known bird sanctuary in Ireland and is a very popular destination for birdwatchers and other visitors. The privately owned islands are a haven for gannets, puffins, Manx shearwaters and gulls, and lie

10 beautiful beaches

▲ The Saltee Islands

on an important migratory path. Great Saltee also has a population of grey seals.

Autumn Dream

kilmoreangling.com
Kilmore Quay, County Wexford
053 912 9723

Kilmore Quay is home to one of Ireland's largest and most modern charter boat fleets, and an enormous variety of fish in a wide range of habitats can be found within a 15-mile radius. Wreck, reef, bass and deep-sea fishing can be arranged, as well as evening trips and sight-seeing.

Beaches Restaurant at Kelly's Resort Hotel ◉◉

kellys.ie
Rosslare, County Wexford
053 913 2114

The Beaches restaurant is aptly named, as it sits on five miles of golden sands in Rosslare. The Kelly family have run their resort hotel since 1895. Local produce is as good as it gets, and the kitchen has the experience and confidence to treat it all simply and let the sheer quality do the talking in simple contemporary dishes.

La Marine Bistro ◉

Kelly's Resort Hotel and Spa,
Rosslare, County Wexford
053 913 2114

The more casual stand-alone restaurant of Kelly's Resort Hotel is an easy-going venue with views of the chefs at work in the open kitchen. The shipshape French bistro theme suits the beachside setting to a T, as does its menu of classic Gallic bistro fare, which is all built on the eminently solid foundations of spankingly fresh local produce.

▶ **Youghal** MAP REF 378 B6

youghal.ie

Youghal (pronounced 'Yawl') is a lovely walled seaport and one of the best-preserved 13th-century market towns in Europe. A self-guided walking tour of the key sights can be downloaded from the website, from where tours can also be booked.

At the mouth of the Blackwater River on a broad, sandy bay, in the 16th century Youghal was plagued by pirates, and the rebel Earl of Desmond landed here in 1579. For helping to suppress the Desmond rebellion, English adventurer Sir Walter Raleigh was rewarded with lands in the area. Legend has it this is where he first smoked tobacco from the New World and planted the first potato in Irish soil. One of the most notable buildings in town is the Clock Gate of 1777, straddling the narrow Main Street.

VISIT THE MUSEUM
Fox's Lane Folk Museum
North Cross Lane, Youghal, County Cork | 024 91145 | Open Apr–Oct Tue–Sat 10–1, 2–6
The low-key Fox's Lane Folk Museum is dedicated to the development of domestic gadgets spanning a century, beginning with household equipment used in the 1800s. There are also displays of early gramaphones and much more.

SEE ONE OF IRELAND'S NATIONAL MONUMENTS
Collegiate Church of St Mary
youghal.cloyne.anglican.org
North Emmet Place, Youghal, County Cork | 024 91014 | Open Mon–Sat 10.30–4 (to 4.30 in summer), Sun 12.30–4
Protected by medieval walls, this church is the oldest site of Christian worship in Ireland and has National Monument of Ireland status. The building has undergone several changes over the centuries and the work of several master stonemasons is evident among the detailed carvings of its walls. Notable figures associated with the church are Richard Boyle (architect of gas 'Boyles Law') who died in Youghal in 1643 and has a chapel named after him; explorer Sir Walter Raleigh who had a house next to the church; and Oliver Cromwell, who is thought to have briefed his army here. Sunday morning worship still takes place at the church each week.

▼ Collegiate Church of St Mary

PLAY A ROUND

Youghal Golf Club

youghalgolfclub.ie

Youghal, County Cork | 024 92787

This course offers a good test of golf and is well maintained for year-round play. There are panoramic views of Youghal Bay and the Blackwater estuary.

EAT AND DRINK

Clancy's Bar

clancysyoughal.com

Front Strand, Youghal, County Cork

024 25444

This may be a modern offering to the local scene, but it still provides something authentic and highly enjoyable. Visit for a drink, dinner and to soak in some local atmosphere.

▶ PLACES NEARBY

Along the coast to the east and west of Youghal are lovely seaside villages such as Ardmore, Shanagarry and Ballycotton, all with cliffside walks and stunning sea views.

Ardmore

Golden sands and a stone pencil-tower, 95 feet tall, mark the coastal village of Ardmore, Ireland's oldest Christian settlement. It stands at the western end of the scenic South Coast Drive, and the start of St Declan's Way, stretching for 59 miles to Cashel on an old pilgrimage route. St Declan chose Ardmore for a church in the fifth or sixth century, and is believed to have been buried in the small oratory in the churchyard. The lofty round stone tower is a fine example of its kind, built as a retreat to safety for the monks and their treasures in a time of Viking raids. The most extensive remains are those of the 12th-century cathedral.

Ballycotton

This small fishing village edged with golden sandy beaches overlooks Ballycotton Bay. However, the area suffers from serious erosion and the current village is, in fact, a resettlement of an older village which was completely lost to the waves. Ballycotton is now the site of international research into coastal erosion. The views from the Ballycotton Cliff Walk are breathtaking.

Ballymaloe House ◉◉

ballymaloe.com

Shanagarry, County Cork

021 465 2531

Ivan and Myrtle Allen were way ahead of the curve some 50 years ago when they opened a restaurant in their farmhouse when no one had heard the term 'farm to fork'. Now there's a world-class cookery school here run by Darina Allen, author and promoter of the slow food movement in Ireland. The restaurant and cookery school are supplied from Ballymaloe House's kitchen and herb garden. The idea of fresh produce brought to the table in double-quick time and served simply now just seems normal You can also stay in the beautiful hotel accommodation.

ATLAS

- ★ A-Z places listed
- • Places Nearby

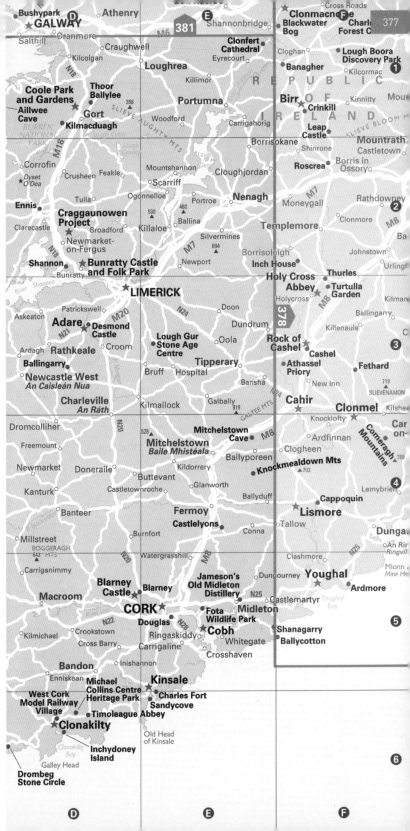

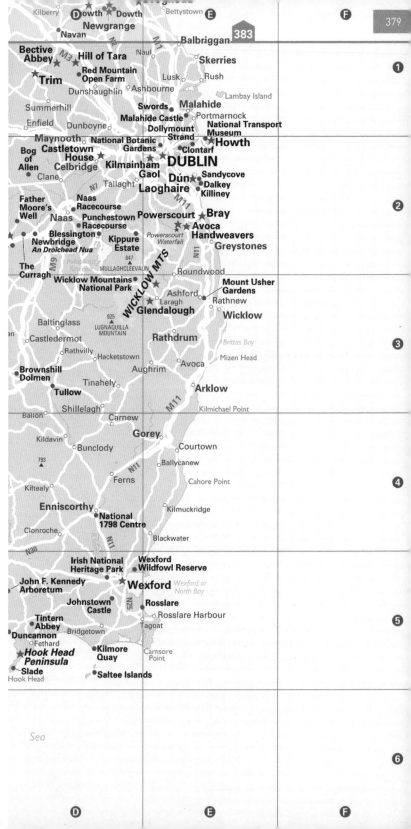

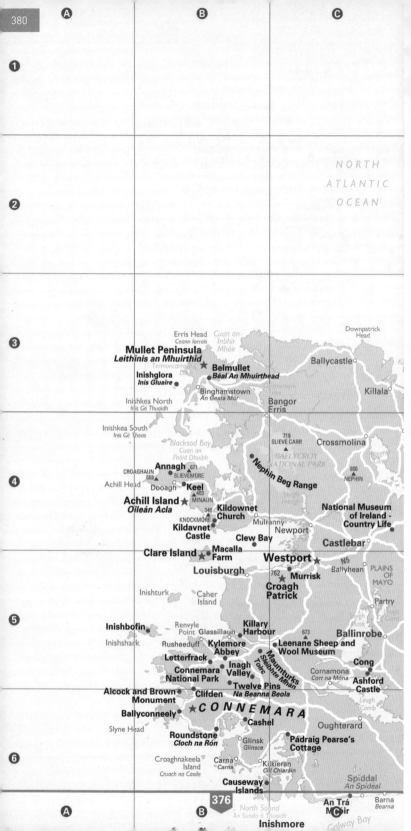

A   B   C

1

2

NORTH
ATLANTIC
OCEAN

3

Erris Head
Ceann Iorrais

Downpatrick
Head

Mullet Peninsula
Leithinis an Mhuirthid

Cuan an
Inbhir
Mhóir

Ballycastle

Termoncarra...
...

Belmullet
Béal An Mhuirthead

Killala

Inishglora
Inis Gluaire

Binghamstown
An Geata Mór

Bangor
Erris

Inishkea North
Iris Gé Thuaidh

Inishkea South
Inis Gé Theas

Blacksod Bay
*Cuan an
Fhóid Dhuibh*

719
SLIEVE CARR

Crossmolina

lough
Con...

**BALLYCROY
NATIONAL PARK**

Annagh
671
SLIEVEMORE

806
NEPHIN

4

CROAGHAUN
668

Achill Head

Dooagh

Keel
403
MINAUN

Nephin Beg Range

Achill Island
Oileán Acla

340
KNOCKMORE

**Kildownet
Church**

**National Museum
of Ireland -
Country Life**

**Kildavnet
Castle**

Mulranny

Newport

Castlebar

Clare Island

**Macalla
Farm**

Clew Bay

Westport

Louisburgh

762
Murrisk

Ballyheen

PLAINS
OF
MAYO

N5

Inishturk

Caher
Island

**Croagh
Patrick**

Partry

5

Inishbofin

Renvyle
Point

Glassillaun

**Killary
Harbour**

673

**Leenane Sheep and
Wool Museum**

lough
Mask

Ballinrobe

Inishshark

Rusheeduff

**Kylemore
Abbey**

Letterfrack

**Connemara
National Park**

**Inagh
Valley**

Maumturks
*Sléibhte Mhan
Toirc*

Cornamona
Corr na Móna

Cong

**Ashford
Castle**

**Alcock and Brown
Monument**

Clifden

Twelve Pins
Na Beanna Beola

C O N N E M A R A

Lough
Corrib

Ballyconneely

Slyne Head

Roundstone
Cloch na Rón

Cashel

Glinsk
Glinsce

**Pádraig Pearse's
Cottage**

Oughterard

6

Croaghnakeela
Island
Cruach na Caoile

Carna
Carna

Kilkieran
Cill Chiaráin

Spiddal
An Spidéal

**Causeway
Islands**

North Sound
An Sundo ó Thuaidh

**An Trá
Móir**

Barna
Bearna

376

A   B   C

Inishmore

Galway Bay

D **E** **F**

Creeslough
Millford Rath

①

Arranmore
Árainn Mhór
(Aran Island) ★
Leabgarrow
An Leadhb Gharbh

Bunbeg
An Bun Beag **Errigal**
An Earagail ▲752 **Glenveagh**
● **Castle** Kilmacrenan Rathmelton

Crolly
Croithli **GLENVEAGH**
Burtonport **NATIONAL PARK**
Ailt An Chorráin **Letterkenny** ●

Dunglow (Dungloe)
An Clochán Liath

Carrigans

Gweebarra Bay
Béal an Bheara

N13 N14

Portnoo ○

Lifford

Glenties Stranorlar

②

Ballybofey ○ N15 Clady

Ardara

Blue Stack Mountains N15

Glencolumbkille
Gleann Cholm Cille ★

Castled
Castle

Lough
Eske ★

Malin More
Málainn Mhóir Carrick
An Charraig

Killybegs ★ **Donegal**

Drumquin

Bunglass
Kilcar
Cill Charthaigh Dunkineely

Ballintra

St John's
Point Rossnowlagh ○ Pettigo

③

Castle
Caldwell
Forest **Castle**
Archdale
Forest Dromore

Ballyshannon
Bundoran N15

Mullaghmore ○ Kinlough
Cliffony ○ **Belleek**
Pottery ★ **Tully**
Castle ● ★ **Killadeas**

Inishmurray ○ Grange ○ Garrison **Lough**
Navar
Forest Derrygonnelly Ballinan

647
▲
TRUSKMORE **Drumcliff** ● Blacklion **Marble**
Arch
Caves **Florence**
Court

Rosses Point ● **Lough**
Gill **Manorhamilton** **Enniskillen** ★ Castle (
Lisb

Easky ● **Ballincar** ● **Sligo** ★ **Parke's**
Castle N16 Cavan

Sligo Bay **Strandhill** ● Dromahair Blacklion Burren
Park

Ilala
Bay **Skreen** ● **Carrowmore**
Megalithic
Cemetery Dowra ○ Swanlinbar Derrylin

Enniscrone ● Colloney ○ Drumkeeran ○

④

Slieve Gamph or The Ox Mountains **Sligo**
Folk Park ● IRON MTS Ballyconnell ○

Ballina **Ballymote** Ballinamore

Tobercurry **Ballyfarnon** ● Drumshanbo ○ Killashandra ○

Foxford
Woollen Mills Curry ○ **Drumanone**
Dolmen ● **Lough Key**
Forest Park Fenagh ○ Carrigallen ○

Foxford ● **Charlestown** **Boyle** ★ **Battlebridge** ● **Carrick-on-**
Shannon ★

N5 Mohill ○ Arvagh ○

Swinford N5

Kiltamagh ○ **Ballaghaderreen** ○ Frenchpark Roosky ○

⑤

Knock ● **Clonalis**
House ★ **Castlerea** **Strokestown**
Park ★ Granard ○

Loughglinn ○ N5 Strokestown ★

Ballyhaunis ○ Ballinlough ○ Tulsk ○ N5 **Longford**
N4 Tu
Cas

Claremorris Ballymoe ○ ○ Ballintober Edgeworthstown ○ G

Ballindine ○ Lanesborough Rathowen ○

N17 **Roscommon** ○ Keenagh

Dunmore ○ ○ Fuerty Inchcleraun

⑥

Glennamaddy ○ Athleague ○ **Lough**
Ree Ballymahon ○ Mu

Shrule ○ **Tuam** Ballygar ○ Inchbofin ○ **Irish Farm**
Safari Park ●

Headford ○ Mountbellew
Bridge ○ Dysart Kiltoom ○ **Hodson**
Bay Hare Island **Lillipu**
House

Caltra ○ Ballykeeran ○

Ahascragh ○ **Athlone** ★ M6 **Kilbeggan**
Race Course ●

Monivea ○ **Glendeer** ●
Open Farm

Bushypark ● **Athenry** **Ballinasloe** Doon
Cross Roads K

★ **GALWAY** Shannonbridge ○ **Clonmacnoise** ★ Cla
Blackwater **Charleville**
Salthill Oranmore **Bog** **Forest Castle**

Dcolgan ○ Craughwell M6 **Clonfert**
Cathedral Cloghan ○ **Pough Boora**
Discovery Park

Loughrea Eyrecourt ○ **Banagher** ●

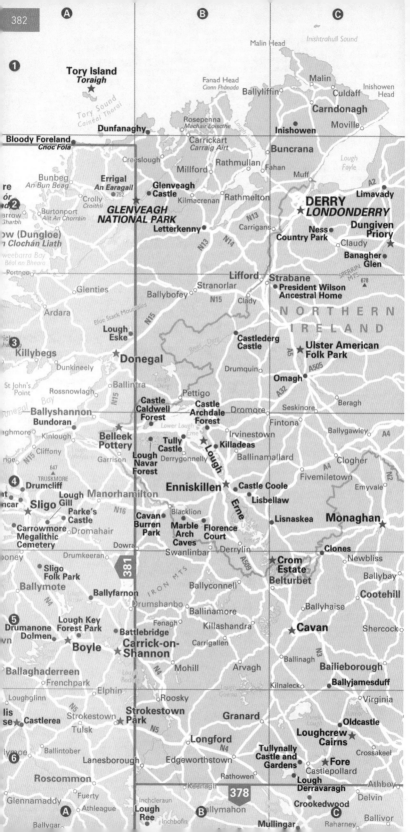

D **E** **F**

1

Kebble Cliffs
National Nature Reserve
Rathlin Island
Carrick-a-Rede Rope Bridge
Kinbane Castle
Murlough Bay
Giant's Causeway
Dunluce Castle
Bushmills Distillery
Bonamargy Friary
Ballycastle
Portrush
Portstewart
Coleraine
Armoy
Ballycastle Forest
Ballypatrick Forest
Glens of Antrim
Cushendun
Downhill Demesne and Hezlett House
Breen Forest
Slieveanorra National Nature Reserve
Ossian's Grave
Cushendall
Garron Point

2

Ballymoney
508
551 TROSTAN
Ardclinis Church
Aghadowey
Dunloy
Glenariff Forest Park
Carnlough
Garvagh
Kilrea
Rasharkin
436 ▲ CARNCORMICK
Glenarm
Swatragh
Portglenone
Galgorm
Broughshane
438 SLEMISH
Carnfunnock Country Park
Maghera
A6
Ahoghill
Ballymena
A36
Larne
Islandmagee

3

Draperstown
Crosskeys Inn
Kells
Ballyboley Forest
Gobbins Path
Whitehead
Randalstown
Ballyclare
Magherafelt
Springhill
M22
Antrim
M2
Carrickfergus Castle
Carrickfergus
Crawfordsburn
Groomsport
Wellbrook Beetling Mill
Newtownabbey
Zoological Gardens
Cave Hill
Holywood
BANGOR
Cookstown
Ardboe Old Cross
Crumlin
BELFAST
Stormont Castle
Somme Heritage Centre
Donaghadee
Lough Neagh
Glenavy
Dunmurry
Scrabo Tower
Newtownards
Mount Stewart
Ballywalter
Coalisland
Comber
Strangford Lough
Grey Abbey
Dungannon
Lisburn
Carryduff
Castle Espie
ARDS PENINSULA

4

Peatlands Park
Magheralin
Saintfield
Killinchy
Portavogie
The Argory
Lurgan
Craigavon
Dromore
Dorn
Ardress House
Portadown
Ballynahinch
Saul Church
Exploris
Benburb
Gilford
Banbridge
Quoile Pondage
Portaferry
Armagh
SLIEVE CROOB 532
Lecale Peninsula
Castle Ward
N12
Tandragee
Gosford Forest Park
Inch Abbey
Struell Wells
Killclief
Markethill
Downpatrick
Killough
Keady
Castlewellan Forest Park
Dundrum
St John's Point
Middletown
Castlewellan
Ardglass
Newtownhamilton
Bryansford
Dundrum Bay
Newry
Hilltown
Newcastle

5

N2
Slieve Gullion Forest Park
MTS OF MOURNE
850 SLIEVE DONARD ▲
Castleblayney
Rostrevor
Annalong
Crossmaglen
Warrenpoint
Kilbroney Park
Kilkeel
Carlingford
Dundalk
Carlingford Lough
Greenore
Carrickmacross
Dundalk Bay
IRISH SEA
Kingscourt
Castlebellingham
Ardee
Dunany Point

6

Dunleer
Nobber
Moynalty
Brú na Bóinne
Monasterboice
Termonfeckin
Kells
Mellifont Abbey
Slane Castle
Drogheda
Kilberry
Knowth
Dowth
Bettystown
Newgrange
Navan
Bective Abbey
Hill of Tara
Naul
Balbriggan

379

D Red Mountain Open Farm
E Rush
Trim
Lusk
Skerries

D **E** **F**

Index, themed

Page numbers in **bold** refer to main entries; page numbers in *italics* refer to town plans

Index, places

Page numbers in **bold** refer to main entries; page numbers in *italics* refer to town plans

The Automobile Association wishes to thank the following photographers and organisations for their assistance in the preparation of this book.

Abbreviations for the picture credits are as follows – (t) top; (m) middle; (b) bottom; (l) left; (r) right; (c) centre; (AA) AA World Travel Library.

4tl AA/C Coe; 4b AA/C Hill; 4–5t AA/K Blackwell; 5tr AA/S Hill; 5bl AA/Stockbyte; 5br AA/C Jones; 8–9 AA/C Hill; 11 AA/K Blackwell; 12t AA/C Hill; 12b Tourism Ireland/Rob Durston; 13t Tourism Ireland; 13c, 13b Tourism Ireland/Chris Hill; 14t Fáilte Ireland/Lukasz Warzecha; 14c Tourism Ireland/Chris Hill; 14b AA/C Jones; 15t Tourism Ireland/Brian Morrison; 15b Tourism Ireland/macmillan media; 16t NITB Photographic Library/Brian Morrison; 16c AA/K Blackwell; 16b Tourism Ireland/Chris Hill; 17t NITB Photographic Library/Brian Morrison; 17b Tourism Ireland/Brian Morrison; 18 AA/K Blackwell; 20 Tourism Ireland/Chris Hill; 21 AA/D Forss; 22 Tourism Ireland/Brian Morrison; 24 Classic Image/Alamy; 25 Tourism Ireland/Tony Pleavin; 27 NITB Photographic Library; 28–9 Tourism Ireland/Chris Hill; 29r Fáilte Ireland/Martin Fleming; 30 NITB Photographic Library; 32 Tourism Ireland/Chris Hill; 34 Tourism Ireland/Gardiner Mitchell; 36 Tourism Ireland/Brian Morrison; 37, 39 Tourism Ireland/Chris Hill; 40 NITB Photographic Library/Brian Morrison; 40–1 NITB Photographic Library; 42–3 Tourism Ireland/Jonathan Hession; 43 Tourism Ireland; 45 NITB Photographic Library/David Cordner; 46 AA/S McBride; 48 AA/J Tims; 50 Tourism Ireland/Adrian Sadlier; 51 GL Archive/Alamy; 53 Fáilte Ireland; 56 AA/J Tims; 58 NITB Photographic Library/David Cordner; 60–1 AA/C Hill; 62–3 Tourism Ireland/Matthew Woodhouse; 63r AA/C Hill; 64 NITB Photographic Library/Brian Morrison; 65 NITB Photographic Library; 67 AA/C Hill; 68 nigel pye/Alamy; 69 NITB Photographic Library/Brian Morrison; 71 NITB Photographic Library/Tony Pleavin; 72 NITB Photographic Library; 73 AA/C Hill; 75, 77, 79 NITB Photographic Library/Brian Morrison; 80 David

Nixon/Alamy; 83 NITB Photographic Library/David Cordner; 84 AA/I Dawson; 87 NITB Photographic Library; 89 Tourism Ireland/Chris Hill; 90 NITB Photographic Library/Tony Pleavin; 91 Fáilte Ireland; 92 AA/I Dawson; 93, 94, 95 NITB Photographic Library/Brian Morrison; 96–7 Andrew Paton/Alamy; 97 NITB Photographic Library/David Cordner; 101 Tourism Ireland/Arthur Ward; 102 NITB Photographic Library/Tony Pleavin; 103, 105 NITB Photographic Library; 107 NITB Photographic Library/David Cordner; 108 NITB Photographic Library/Tony Pleavin; 110, 112 NITB Photographic Library/Brian Morrison; 114 NITB Photographic Library/Courtesy of Tyrone and Sperrins destination; 116 NITB Photographic Library/Chris Heaney; 117 NITB Photographic Library; 120 NITB Photographic Library/Brian Morrison; 122 NITB Photographic Library/Courtesy of Fermanagh District Council; 123 Tourism Ireland/Arthur Ward; 125 NITB Photographic Library/David Cordner; 127 Tourism Ireland/Matthew Woodhouse; 129 NITB Photographic Library/Brian Morrison; 130 Tourism Ireland/Chris Hill; 132–3 NITB Photographic Library; 135, 137 NITB Photographic Library/Brian Morrison; 138 Tourism Ireland/Gardiner Mitchell; 140 scenicireland.com/Christopher Hill Photographic/Alamy; 142–3 NITB Photographic Library/Brian Morrison; 144 Tourism Ireland/Chris Hill; 144–5 NITB Photographic Library/Tony Pleavin; 147 NITB Photographic Library; 150 NITB Photographic Library/Courtesy of Tyrone and Sperrins destination; 151 NITB Photographic Library; 152–3 Fáilte Ireland; 155 George Munday/Alamy; 156 Fáilte Ireland; 158 AA/P Zollier; 160 scenicireland.com/Christopher Hill Photographic/Alamy; 161, 162 Fáilte Ireland; 162–3 Tourism Ireland/Chris Hill; 164 Fáilte Ireland; 169 Fáilte Ireland/Raymond Fogarty; 170 Fáilte Ireland/Padraig Whooley; 171 Design Pics Inc/Alamy; 172 Tourism Ireland; 174, 175 Tourism Ireland/Arthur Ward; 177 Tourism Ireland/Chris Hill; 179, 181 Tourism Ireland; 183 Tourism Ireland/Chris Hill; 184 Design Pics Inc/Alamy; 187 Tourism Ireland/Tony Pleavin; 188, 188–9 Fáilte Ireland; 190 Tourism Ireland/Tony Pleavin; 191, 192 Fáilte Ireland; 194t, 194b, 194–5, 198 Tourism Ireland/Chris Hill; 203 Gareth McCormack/Alamy; 204 Design Pics Inc/Alamy; 207 Fáilte Ireland/Kevin Gilmor; 208, 211, 212 Tourism Ireland/Chris Hill; 218 Jon Arnold Images Ltd/Alamy; 220 Tourism Ireland/Brian Morrison; 221, 222–3 Tourism Ireland/Chris Hill; 227 Fáilte Ireland/Kevin Gilmor; 229 Michael Walsh/Alamy; 232, 237 Fáilte Ireland; 239 Gareth McCormack/Alamy; 243 Fáilte Ireland; 244 brianireland/Alamy; 245 Norman Barrett/Alamy; 248–9 Tourism Ireland/Brian Morrison; 252 Fáilte Ireland/Andrew Bradley; 253 Fáilte Ireland/DUBLIN REGIONAL TOURISM AUTHORITY; 255 Fáilte Ireland; 256–7 Tourism Ireland/Chris Hill; 258 AA/K Blackwell; 260 Fáilte Ireland; 261 Fáilte Ireland/Rob Durston; 264 Werner Dieterich/Alamy; 267, 269 Fáilte Ireland/Rob Durston; 271 Tourism Ireland/Brian Morrison; 273 AA/K Blackwell; 277 Fáilte Ireland/Rob Durston; 282, 286–7 Fáilte Ireland; 289 scenicireland.com/Christopher Hill Photographic/Alamy; 290, 297 Tourism Ireland/Brian Morrison; 298–9 Tourism Ireland/Chris Hill; 301, 302–3 Tourism Ireland/Gardiner Mitchell; 304 Tourism Ireland/Macmillan media; 305 Fáilte Ireland/Liam Murphy; 306 Fáilte Ireland/Hook Tourism; 307 Tourism Ireland; 308, 309 Tourism Ireland/Brian Morrison; 316 Fáilte Ireland; 317, 319 Tourism Ireland/Chris Hill; 321 Fáilte Ireland; 322, 324–5 Tourism Ireland/Chris Hill; 328 Fáilte Ireland/Cathy Donovan; 330 Tourism Ireland/Brian Morrison; 337 Tourism Ireland; 339 Tourism Ireland/Brian Morrison; 342 Fáilte Ireland/Valerie O'Sullivan; 344 Fáilte Ireland; 346 Tourism Ireland/Chris Hill; 349 Fáilte Ireland/Noel Kennedy; 351 Fáilte Ireland/Derek Cullen; 353 Stephen Emerson/Alamy; 355 Fáilte Ireland/Raymond Fogarty; 356–7 Fáilte Ireland; 359 Design Pics Inc/Alamy; 360–1, 361 Fáilte Ireland; 365 Tourism Ireland/Chris Hill; 366–7 Fáilte Ireland/Derek Cullen; 368–9 Fáilte Ireland/Derek Cullen; 369t Fáilte Ireland/Luke Myers; 369b Maurice Savage/Alamy; 372 Tourism Ireland; 373 Tourism Ireland/Chris Hill; 400 AA

Every effort has been made to trace the copyright holders, and we apologise in advance for any unintentional omissions or errors. We would be pleased to apply any corrections in any following edition of this publication.

Series editor: Rebecca Needes
Project editors: Sheila McCarthy & Karen Kemp
Author: Jane Egginton
Copy editor: Julia Sandford-Cooke

Proofreader: Kathryn Glendenning
Indexer: Marie Lorimer
Designers: Liz Baldin & Kat Mead
Digital imaging & repro: Ian Little
Art director: James Tims

Additional writing by other AA contributors. *Lore of the Land* feature by Ruth Binney. Some content may appear in other AA books and publications.

Has something changed? Email us at travelguides@theaa.com.

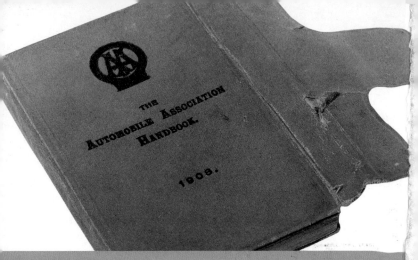

YOUR TRUSTED GUIDE

The AA was founded in 1905 as a body initially intended to help motorists avoid police speed traps. As motoring became more popular, so did we, and our activities have continued to expand into a great variety of areas.

The first edition of the AA Members' Handbook appeared in 1908. Due to the difficulty many motorists were having finding reasonable meals and accommodation while on the road, the AA introduced a new scheme to include listings for 'about one thousand of the leading hotels' in the second edition in 1909. As a result the AA has been recommending and assessing establishments for over a century, and each year our professional inspectors anonymously visit and rate thousands of hotels, restaurants, guest accommodations and campsites. We are relied upon for our trustworthy and objective star, Rosette and Pennant ratings systems, which you will see used in this guide to denote AA-inspected restaurants and campsites.

In 1912 we published our first handwritten routes and our atlas of town plans, and in 1925 our classic touring guide, *The AA Road Book of England and Wales* appeared. Together, our accurate mapping and in-depth knowledge of places to visit were to set the benchmark for British travel publishing.

Since the 1990s we have dramatically expanded our publishing activities, producing high quality atlases, maps, walking and travel guides for the UK and the rest of the world. In this new series of travel guides we are drawing on over a hundred years of experience to bring you the very best of that Ireland has to offer.